Extracting Accountability from Non-State Actors in International Law

The human rights of communities in many resource-rich, weak governance States are adversely affected, not only by the acts of States and their agents, but also by powerful non-State actors. Contemporary phenomena such as globalisation, privatisation and the proliferation of internal armed conflict have all contributed to the increasing public influence of these entities and the correlative decline in State power.

This book responds to the persistent challenges stemming from non-State actors linked to extractive industries. In light of the intersecting roles of multinational enterprises and non-State armed groups in this context, these actors are adopted as the primary analytical vehicles. The operations of these entities highlight the practical flaws of existing accountability regimes and permit an exploration of the theoretical challenges that preclude their direct legal regulation at the international level. Drawing insights from discursive democracy, compliance theories and the Pure Theory of Law, the book establishes a conceptual foundation for the creation of binding international obligations addressing non-State actors. Responding to the recent calls for a binding business and human rights treaty at the UN Human Rights Council, and the growing influence of armed non-State actors, the book makes a timely contribution to debates surrounding the direction of future developments in the field of international human rights law.

Lee McConnell is a lecturer at Northumbria University, UK.

Human Rights and International Law
Series Editor: Professor Surya P. Subedi, O.B.E.

This series will explore human rights law's place within the international legal order, offering much-needed interdisciplinary and global perspectives on human rights' increasingly central role in the development and implementation of international law and policy.

Human Rights and International Law is committed to providing critical and contextual accounts of human rights' relationship with international law theory and practice. To achieve this, volumes in the series will take a thematic approach that focuses on major debates in the field, looking at how human rights impacts on areas as diverse and divisive as security, terrorism, climate change, refugee law, migration, bioethics, natural resources and international trade.

Exploring the interaction, interrelationship and potential conflicts between human rights and other branches of international law, books in the series will address both historical development and contemporary contexts, before outlining the most urgent questions facing scholars and policy makers today.

Available titles:

Human Rights and Charity Law
International Perspectives
Kerry O'Halloran

Human Rights and Development in International Law
Tahmina Karimova

The Emerging Law of Forced Displacement in Africa
Development and Implementation of the Kampala Convention on Internal Displacement
Allehone M. Abebe

Business and Human Rights
History, Law and Policy – Bridging the Accountability Gap
Nadia Bernaz

Socio-Economic Human Rights in Essential Public Services Provision
Marlies Hesselman, Antenor Hallo de Wolf and Brigit Toebes

Forthcoming titles:

Adoption Law and Human Rights
International Perspectives
Kerry O'Halloran

The Right to Truth in International Law
Victims' Rights in Human Rights and International Criminal Law
Melanie Klinkner and Howard Davis

Tax Havens and International Human Rights
Paul Beckett

About the Series Editor

Professor Surya P. Subedi, O.B.E., is Professor of International Law, University of Leeds, member of the Institut de Droit International and former UN Special Rapporteur for human rights in Cambodia.

Extracting Accountability from Non-State Actors in International Law

Assessing the Scope for Direct Regulation

Lee McConnell

Routledge
Taylor & Francis Group

LONDON AND NEW YORK

First published 2017
by Routledge
2 Park Square, Milton Park, Abingdon, Oxon OX14 4RN

and by Routledge
711 Third Avenue, New York, NY 10017

*Routledge is an imprint of the Taylor & Francis Group,
an informa business*

British Library Cataloguing in Publication Data
A catalogue record for this book is available from the British Library

Library of Congress Cataloging in Publication Data
Names: McConnell, Lee, author.
Title: Extracting accountability from non-state actors in international
law: assessing the scope for direct regulation / Lee McConnell.
Description: New York: Routledge, 2016. | Series: Human rights and
international law | Includes bibliographical references and index.
Identifiers: LCCN 2016022513| ISBN 9781138656901 (hbk) |
ISBN 9781315621647 (ebk)
Subjects: LCSH: International law and human rights. | Non-state
actors (International relations) | Liability (Law) | Human rights.
Classification: LCC KZ1266.M33 2016 | DDC 341.4/8–dc23
LC record available at https://lccn.loc.gov/2016022513

ISBN: 978-1-138-65690-1 (hbk)
ISBN: 978-1-315-62164-7 (ebk)

Typeset in Galliard
by Florence Production Ltd, Stoodleigh, Devon, UK

Contents

Table of cases		vii
Table of legislation		xv
Acknowledgements		xix
1	Introduction	1
2	The State as the basis of legal validity	15
3	The practical failings of State-centric accountability regimes	72
4	The theoretical scope for direct non-State actor regulation	131
5	Abandoning the State: towards an alternative theoretical framing	185
6	Conclusion	238
	Selected bibliography	243
	Index	268

Table of cases

Domestic cases

Australia

Barrow and Heys v Colonial Sugar Refinery (CSR) Ltd [1988] Unreported,
  Library No 7231 (Supreme Court of Western Australia) 110
CSR Ltd v Wren [1997] 44 NSWLR 463; [1998] Aust Tort Rep
  81–461 111
CSR Ltd v Young [1998] Aust. Tort Rep 81–468 111
Dagi v Broken Hill Proprietary Company Limited (No 2) [1997]
  1 VR 428 111

Canada

Angelica Choc et al v Hudbay Minerals Inc et al (2013) ONSC 1414
  (Ontario Superior Court) 109
Anvil Mining Ltd v Association Canadienne Contre l'Impunité (2012)
  QCCA 117 (Québec Court of Appeal) 109
Piedra v Copper Mesa Mining Corp (2011) ONCA 191 (Ontario
  Superior Court) 109
The Queen v Van Bergen (2000) 261 AR 387 (Alberta Court of
  Appeal) 217

Democratic Republic of the Congo

*Public Prosecutor v Adémar Ilunga, Sadiaka Sampanda, Anvil Mining
  Company Congo and Others*, Military Court of Katanga, Congo,
  RP No 010/2006 92

Ecuador

Aguinda v Chevron-Texaco, Case No 11–1150 (3 January 2012) (Appellate
  Panel, Ecuador) 226

England and Wales

British South Africa Co v Companhia de Moçambique [1893] AC 602 111
Calgar and Others v Billingham (Inspector of Taxes) [1996] STC 150 55
Chandler v Cape [2012] EWCA Civ 525 108–11
Connelly v RTZ [1998] AC 854 110
Duke of Brunswick v King of Hanover (1848) 2 HL Cas. 1 113
Lubbe v Cape Plc [2000] UKHL 41 111
Ngcobo v Thor Chemical Holdings Ltd [1995] TLR 597 (10 November
   1995) 110
Sithole v Thor Chemical Holdings Ltd [1999] EWCA Civ 706 110
Spiliada Maritime v Cansulex Ltd [1987] AC 460 106

The Netherlands

Akpan & anor v Royal Dutch Shell plc & anor (2013) (Final Judgment)
   LJN BY9854 (District Court of The Hague) 104–7
Dooh v Royal Dutch Shell plc & anor (2013) (Final Judgment) LJN
   BY9854 (District Court of The Hague) 105
Efanga & Oguru v Royal Dutch Shell plc & anor (2013) (Final Judgment)
   LJN BY9850 (District Court of The Hague) 105

Nigeria

Allar Irou v Shell BP, Unreported Suit No W/89/71 (High Court
   of Warri, Nigeria) 94
*Attorney General of Ondo State v Attorney General of the Federation
   & 35 Others* (7 June 2002) No SC.200/2001 (Supreme Court
   of Nigeria) 94
Gbemre v SPDC (2005) FHC/B/CS/53/05 (Federal High Court of
   Nigeria) 97–8
*Ikechukwu Opara & Others v Shell Petroleum Development Company
   Nigeria Ltd & 5 Others* (2005) FHC/PH/CS/518/2005
   (Federal High Court of Nigeria) 98
Mobil Producing (Nig) United v Monokpo (2003) 18 NWLR 852 95
*Shell Petroleum Development Company (SPDC) of Nigeria v Dr Pere
   Ajuwa and Honourable Ingo Mac-Etteli* (27 May 2007) No
   CA/A/209/06 (Court of Appeal, Abuja Division, Nigeria) 95
Shell v Enoch (1992) 8 NWLR 335 94

United States of America

Balintulo v Daimler AG, 727 F.3d 174 (2d Cir 2013) 113
Doe v Unocal Corp, 395 F.3d 932 (9th Cir 2002) 9, 80, 112
Filártiga v Peña-Irala, 630 F.2d 876 (2d Cir 1980) 112
Gulf Oil v Gilbert, 330 US 501 (Supreme Court 1947) 106

Heller v US, 776 F.2d 92 (3rd Cir 1985) 40

Kadic v Karadic, 70 F.3d 232 (2nd Cir 1995) 112

Kiobel v Royal Dutch Petroleum (Slip Opinion) 569 US
    (Supreme Court 2013) 113

Kiobel v Royal Dutch Petroleum Co, 621 F 3d 148
    (2nd Cir App 2010) 78, 113

Morrison v National Australia Bank, 561 US 247
    (Supreme Court 2010) 113

*National Association of Manufacturers v Securities and Exchange
    Commission*, No 13–5252 (D.C. Cir, 14 April 2014) 227

Piper Aircraft v Reyno, 454 US 235 (Supreme Court 1981) 106

Presbyterian Church of Sudan v Talisman Energy, 582 F.3d 244
    (2nd Cir 2009) 109

Re Union Carbide Corporation Gas Plant Disaster at Bhopal, India,
    809 F.2d 195 (2nd Cir 1987) 97

Sanchez-Llamas v Oregon, 548 US 331 (Supreme Court 2006) 217

Tel-Oren v Libyan Arab Republic, 726 F.2d 774 (D.C. Cir 1984) 155

Trial of Henry Wirz, US 40th Congress, 2d Session (House Executive
    Document No 23, 7 December 1867) 147

Wiwa v Royal Dutch Petroleum Co, 226 F.3d 88 (2nd Cir 2000) .. 106, 112

Regional courts and commissions

African Commission on Human and People's Rights

*Constitutional Rights Project, Civil Liberties Organisation and Media
    Rights Agenda v Nigeria*, African Commission on Human and
    Peoples' Rights, Comm Nos 140/94, 141/94, 145/95 (1999) 41

*Social and Economic Rights Action Centre (SERAC) and Another v
    Nigeria*, African Commission on Human and Peoples' Rights,
    Comm Nos 155/96 (2001) 74

European Court of Human Rights

Abuyeva and Others v Russia App No 27065/05 (ECtHR, Judgment
    of 2 December 2010) 149

Al-Jedda v United Kingdom App No 27021/08 (ECtHR 2011) 230

Al-Saadoon & Mufdhi v United Kingdom App No 61498/08
    (ECtHR, 2009) 229

Al-Skeini and Others v United Kingdom App No 55721/07
    (ECtHR, 2011) 229–30

Andreou v Turkey App No 45653/99 (ECtHR 2008) 230

Costello-Roberts v United Kingdom App No 13134/87
    (ECtHR, 1993) 78

Ilaşcu and Others v Moldova and Russia App No 48787/99
    (ECtHR 2004) 78

Isayeva, Yusupova and Bazayeva v Russia App Nos 57947/000,
    57948/00 and 57949/00 (ECtHR, Judgment of 24 February
    2005) 149
Isayeva v Russia App No 57950/00 (ECtHR, Judgment of
    24 February 2005) 149
Loizidou v Turkey App No 15318/89 (ECtHR, 1995) 79
Medvedyev and Others v France App No 3394/03 (ECtHR, 2010) 229

European Court of Justice

Case T-512/12 *Frente Polisario v Council* [2015] (not yet published) 51
Case 281/02 *Owusu v Jackson* [2005] ECR 1383 107
Case 26/62 *Van Gend en Loos v Netherlands Inland Revenue
    Administration* [1963] ECR 1 35

Inter-American Commission on Human Rights

Riofrío Massacre (6 April 2001) IACommHR No 62/01 232

Inter-American Court on Human Rights

Mapiripán Massacre (Colombia) (15 September 2005) IACtHR
    (ser. C) No 134 232
Right to Information on Consular Assistance in the Framework
    of Guarantees of the Due Process Law (1 October 1999)
    OC-16/99 IACtHR, (ser. A) No 16 217
Velasquez Rodriguez (29 July 1988) 28/96 IACtHR, (ser. C) No 4 74

International cases

International Criminal Court

Prosecutor v Germain Katanga, ICC-01/04-0/07 (7 March 2014) 9
Prosecutor v Jean-Pierre Bemba Gombo, ICC-01/05-01/08
    (21 March 2016) 9
Prosecutor v Thomas Lubanga Dyilo, ICC-01/04-01/06
    (14 March 2012) 9, 87, 118

International criminal tribunals

Prosecutor v Akayesu (Trial Chamber Judgment) ICTR-96-4-T
    (2 September 1998) 83
Prosecutor v Babić (Appeals Judgment) IT-03-72 (18 July 2005) 87
Prosecutor v Brima, Kamara and Kanu (the AFRC Accused)
    SCSL-04-16-T (20 June 2007) 87

Prosecutor v Issa Hassan Sesay, Morris Kallon and Augustine Gbao
(the RUF accused) (Appeal judgment) SCSL-04-15-A
(26 October 2009) 87
Prosecutor v Jelisic (Judgment) IT-95-10-T (14 December 1999) 118
Prosecutor v Kordić & Čerkez (Order for the Production of Documents
by the European Community Monitoring Mission and its Member
States) IT-95-14/2-T (4 August 2000) 178
Prosecutor v Kunarac (Judgment) IT-96-23/1-A (June 5 2001) 118
Prosecutor v Limaj, Bala and Musliu (Trial Judgment) IT-03-66-T
(30 November 2005) 157
Prosecutor v Martić IT-95-11-R61 (8 March 1996) 87, 156, 215
Prosecutor v Milutinović and Others (Decision on Request of the
North Atlantic Treaty Organisation for Review, Appeals Chamber)
IT-05-87AR108bis1 (15 May 2006) 178
Prosecutor v Musema (Trial Chamber) ICTR-96-13-A (27 January
2000) 86, 117
Prosecutor v Sam Hinga Norman (Decision on Preliminary Motion
Based on Lack of Jurisdiction) SCSL-2004-14-AR72(E)
(31 May 2004) 134, 151
Prosecutor v Sesay, Kallon and Gbao (Appeals Chamber, Decision
on Challenge to Jurisdiction: Lome Accord Amnesty)
SCSL-04-15-PT-060-II (13 March 2004) 87, 153
Prosecutor v Šešelj (Initial Indictment) IT-03-67 (15 January 2003) 87
Prosecutor v Simic and Others (Decision on the Prosecution Motion
under Rule 73) IT-95-9 (27 July 1999) 214
Prosecutor v Strugar (Trial Judgment) IT-01-42-T
(31 January 2005) 133, 157
Prosecutor v Tadić (Decision on the Defence Motion for
Interlocutory Appeal on Jurisdiction) IT-93-1-AR72
(2 October 1995) 84, 152, 156, 176
Prosecutor v Tadić (Appeals Chamber) IT-94-1-A
(15 July 1999), ... 79, 139

International military tribunals

International Military Tribunal at Nuremberg, Judgment and
Sentences (1 October 1946) reproduced in (1947)
41 AJIL 221 114
Re Flick and Others (1947) 14 AD 267 115
Re Krauch and Others (IG Farben Trial) (1948) 15 AD 678 115
Re Krupp and Others (1948) 15 AD 627 115
Zyklon B Case, Trial of Bruno Tesch and Two Others, British
Military Court, Hamburg, (1–8 March 1946) in UN War
Crimes Commission, 'Law Reports of Trials of War Criminals'
Vol 1 (1947) 115

International Court of Justice

Application of the Convention on the Prevention and Punishment of
the Crime of Genocide (Bosnia and Herzegovina v Serbia and
Montenegro) (Merits) [2007] ICJ Rep 43 231
Arrest Warrant Case (Democratic Republic of the Congo v Belgium)
ICJ Reports [2002] 103–4
Barcelona Traction, Light and Power Company (Belgium v Spain)
(Second Phase) ICJ Reports [1970] 99, 100, 103
Case Concerning Avena and Other Mexican Nationals (Mexico v
United States) ICJ Reports [2004] 137, 217
Certain Expenses of the United Nations (Advisory Opinion)
ICJ Reports [1962] 55
Competence of the General Assembly for the Admission of a State to
the United Nations (Advisory Opinion) ICJ Reports [1950] 271
Corfu Channel (Advisory Opinion) ICJ Reports [1949] 156
International Status of South West Africa (Advisory Opinion,
Pleadings) ICJ Reports [1949] 178
Interpretation of the Agreement of March 25 1951 between the WHO
and Egypt (Advisory Opinion) ICJ Reports [1980] 67
LaGrand Case (Germany v United States of America) ICJ Reports
[2001] 137, 216–18
Legal Consequences of the Construction of a Wall in the Occupied
Palestinian Territory (Advisory Opinion) ICJ Reports [2004] 178
Legality of the Use by a State of Nuclear Weapons in Armed Conflict
(Advisory Opinion) ICJ Reports [1996] 61, 64, 101
Military and Paramilitary Activities (Nicaragua v United States
of America) (Advisory Opinion) ICJ Reports [1986] 79, 156
North Sea Continental Shelf (Advisory Opinion) ICJ Reports [1969] 49
Reparation for Injuries Suffered in the Service of the United
Nations (Advisory Opinion) ICJ Reports [1949] 39, 60–4, 66–7,
71, 153, 199
Territorial Dispute (Libyan Arab Jamahiriya/Chad)
(Advisory Opinion) ICJ Reports [1994] 217
Western Sahara (Advisory Opinion) ICJ Reports [1975] 50

Permanent Court of International Justice

Acquisition of Polish Nationality (1923) PCIJ (ser. B) No 7 217
Jurisdiction of the Courts of Danzig (1928) PCIJ (ser. B)
No 15 .... 33–4, 137, 216
Mavrommatis Palestine Concessions (Greece v UK) (1924) PCIJ
(ser. A) No 2 .... 34, 216
The Case of the SS 'Lotus' (France v Turkey) (1927) PCIJ (ser. A)
No 10 .... 35, 102
Wimbledon (1923) PCIJ (ser. A) No 1 42

Mixed arbitral tribunals

Deutsche Continental Gas-Gesellschaft v Polish State (1929) 5
    Annual Digest of Public International Law, 11, 15 49

International arbitration

Amco Asia Corporation and Others v The Republic of Indonesia
    (Resubmitted Case: Award on the Merits, 1990), 1 ICSID
    Reports 569 219
*Chevron Corporation and Texaco Petroleum Corporation v Republic
    of Ecuador*, UNCITRAL, PCA Case No 2009–23 (Order of
    the US District Court in the *Republic of Ecuador v Stratus
    Consulting Inc*, 29 May 2013) 226
*Chevron Corporation and Texaco Petroleum Corporation v Republic
    of Ecuador*, UNCITRAL, PCA Case No 2009–23 (First
    Interim Award, 25 January 2012) 226
Mondev International Ltd v United States (2002) 42 ILM 85 218
Revere Copper (1978) 17 ILM 1321 218
Société Générale de Surveillance (SGS) v Republic of the Philippines
    (Decision on Objections to Jurisdiction, 2004), 8 ICSID
    Reports 518 218
Texaco v Libya (1978) 17 ILM 1 218

League of Nations Official Journal

Aaland Islands Question (1920) League of Nations Official Journal
    Spec Supp 3 54
Aaland Islands Question (On the Merits) (1921) Report by the
    Commission of Rapporteurs, League of Nations Council
    Document B7 21/68/106, 22 54
Commission on the Responsibility of the Authors of the War and on
    Enforcement of Penalties, 'Report Presented to the Preliminary
    Peace Conference, Annex II' (1920) 14 Am J Int'l L, 95, 129 40

International law reports

Eichmann (1968) 36 ILR 103

UN treaty monitoring bodies

Chief Bernard Ominayak and the Lubicon Lake Band v Canada,
    Communication 167/1984, UN Doc CCPR/C/38/D/167/
    1984 (1990) 74
Hopu and Bessert v France, Communication 549/1993,
    UN Doc CCPR/C/60/D/549/1993/Rev. 1 (1997) 74

Ilmari Länsman et al v Finland, Communication 511/1992,
UN Doc CCPR/C/52/D/511/1992 (1994) 74
Love et al v Australia, Communication 983/2001, UN Doc
CCPR/C/77/983/2001 (2003) 74
Sadiq Shek Elmi v Australia, Communication 120/1998,
UN Doc CAT/C/22/D/120/1998 (1999) 150

Table of legislation

Domestic legislation

England and Wales

Modern Slavery Act (2015) 109

Ghana

State Lands Act (1962) 93

The Netherlands

Wetboek van Burgerlijke Rechtsvordering (Dutch Civil Procedure
    Code) (2010) 107

Nigeria

Companies and Allied Matters Act, Laws of the Federation of Nigeria
    (1968) 95
Companies and Allied Matters Act, Laws of the Federation of Nigeria
    (1990) 95
Constitution of the Federal Republic of Nigeria, Laws of the Federation
    of Nigeria (1999) 97–8
Land Use Act, Laws of the Federation of Nigeria (1990) 93

United States of America

Alien Tort Claims Act (1789) 9, 97, 111–13
American Law Institute, The Restatement (Third) of Foreign
    Relations Law (1986) 57, 99
Foreign Sovereign Immunities Act (1976) 113
Instructions for the Government of Armies of the United States in
    the Field (Lieber Code) General Order 100 (24 April 1863) 126

Regional legislation and legal instruments

European Union documentation

Convention on Jurisdiction and the Recognition and Enforcement of
Judgments in Civil and Commercial Matters (Lugano Convention)
[2007] OJ L 339/3 107
Council Regulation (EC) No 44/2001 on Jurisdiction and the
Recognition and Enforcement of Judgments in Civil and
Commercial Matters (Brussels Regulation) OJ L012 107

Organisation of the African Union documentation

African Charter on Human and Peoples' Rights (27 June 1981)
CAB/LEG/67/3 rev. 5, 21 ILM 58 .... 41, 97
Charter of the African Union (25 May 1963) 41

Inter-American Commission on Human Rights documentation

Inter-American Commission on Human Rights, 'Annual Report
of the Inter-American Commission on Human Rights 1990–1991'
(22 February 1991) OEA/Ser.L/V/II.79.rev. 1 76
Inter-American Commission on Human Rights, 'Third Report on
the Human Rights Situation in Colombia' (26 February 1999)
OEA/Ser.L/V/II.102 76

International treaties and conventions

Agreement for the Prosecution of Major War Criminals of the European
Axis (8 August 1945) 82 UNTS 279 115
Charter of the United Nations (26 June 1945) 1 UNTS
XVI 25, 37–8, 60–1, 84, 87
Convention on Biological Diversity (5 June 1992) 1760 UNTS 79 101
Convention on International Liability for Damage Caused by
Space Objects (29 March 1972) 961 UNTS 187 232–3
Convention on the Elimination of All Forms of Discrimination
Against Women (18 December 1979) 1249 UNTS 13 73
Convention on the Law of the Sea (10 December 1982) 1833
UNTS 2 .... 219, 232
Convention on the Prohibition of the Development, Production,
Stockpiling and Use of Chemical Weapons and on their
Destruction (13 January 1993) 1974 UNTS 45 156
Convention on the Prohibition of the Use, Stockpiling, Production
and Transfer of Anti-Personnel Mines and on their Destruction
(Ottawa Convention) (18 September 1997) 2056 UNTS 211 127

Convention on the Protection of the Rights of All Migrant Workers
and Members of their Families (18 December 1990)
A/RES/45/158 73

Convention on the Rights of Persons with Disabilities
(24 January 2007) A/RES/61/106 73

Convention on the Settlement of Investment Disputes Between
States and Nationals of Other States (18 March 1965) 575
UNTS 159 219

Geneva Convention for the Amelioration of the Condition of the
Wounded and Sick in Armed Forces in the Field (First Geneva
Convention) (12 August 1949) 75 UNTS 31 .... 81, 131

Geneva Convention for the Amelioration of the Condition of
Wounded, Sick and Shipwrecked Members of Armed Forces
at Sea (Second Geneva Convention) (12 August 1949)
75 UNTS 85 .... 81, 131

Geneva Convention Relative to the Protection of Civilian Persons
in Time of War (Fourth Geneva Convention) (12 August 1949)
75 UNTS 287 .... 81, 131

Geneva Convention Relative to the Treatment of Prisoners of
War (Third Geneva Convention) (12 August 1949)
75 UNTS 135 .... 81, 131

Hague Convention (II) with Respect to the Laws and Customs of
War on Land and its annex: Regulations concerning the Laws
and Customs of War on Land (29 July 1899) 82

Hague Convention (IV) Respecting the Laws and Customs of War
on Land and Its Annex: Regulations Concerning the Laws and
Customs of War on Land (18 October 1907) 82

Hague Convention for the Protection of Cultural Property in the
Event of Armed Conflict (14 May 1954), ... 82

ILO, Indigenous and Tribal Peoples Convention No 169
(27 June 1989) 173

International Covenant on Civil and Political Rights (16 December
1966) 999 UNTS 171 74

International Covenant on Economic, Social and Cultural Rights
(16 December 1966) 993 UNTS 3 100

Montevideo Convention on the Rights and Duties of States
(26 December 1933) 165 LNTS 17 .... 16, 31, 48, 51, 54, 71, 198

Optional Protocol to the Convention on the Rights of the Child
on the Involvement of Children in Armed Conflict (25 May 2000)
A/RES/54/263 .... 73, 146

Protocol Additional to the Geneva Conventions of 12 August 1949,
and relating to the Protection of Victims of Non-International
Armed Conflicts (8 June 1977) 1125 UNTS 609 .... 81, 87,
131–3, 135–6, 139, 144–5,
148, 150, 152, 155–7

Protocol Additional to the Geneva Conventions of 12 August 1949,
    and relating to the Protection of Victims of International Armed
    Conflicts (8 June 1977) 1125 UNTS 3 .... 127, 133
Statute of the International Court of Justice, as annexed to Charter
    of the United Nations (26 June 1945) 1 UNTS XVI 122, 176
Statute of the International Criminal Tribunal for Rwanda
    (8 November 1994) 86, 115
Statute of the International Criminal Tribunal for the Former
    Yugoslavia (25 May 1993) 115
The Lateran Treaty (11 February 1929) 130 British and Foreign
    State Papers 791 203
Treaty Establishing the European Economic Community
    (25 March 1957) 298 UNTS 11 35
Treaty of Versailles (28 June 1919) British and Foreign State Papers
    (1919) Vol CXIII (HM Stationery Office, 1922) 33, 203
United Nations Convention Against Corruption (31 October 2003)
    UN Doc A/58/422 228
Vienna Convention on Consular Relations (24 April 1963) 500
    UNTS 95 .... 137, 216, 217
Vienna Convention on the Law of Treaties (23 May 1969)
    1155 UNTS 331 .... 48, 73, 143, 144,
                                                              146–7, 155
Vienna Convention on the Law of Treaties between States and
    International Organisations or Between International
    Organisations (21 March 1986) 25 ILM 331 (not yet in force) 55

Other international instruments

ILO, Tripartite Declaration of Principles Concerning Multinational
    Enterprises and Social Policy (4th edn, Geneva, 2006) 119
OECD Guidelines for Multinational Enterprises, 2011 edn 119, 122
UN Commission on Transnational Corporations, 'Draft United
    Nations Code of Conduct on Transnational Corporations'
    (7–18 March & 9–21 May 1983) UN Doc E/1983/17/
    Rev. 1 .... 90, 99
UN Draft Norms on the Responsibilities of Transnational
    Corporations and Other Business Enterprises with Regard to
    Human Rights (2003) UN Doc E/CN.4/Sub.2/2003/12/
    Rev. 2 .... 75, 119, 177
UN Guiding Principles on Business and Human Rights 2011,
    HR/PUB/11/04 .... 75, 119, 121, 229

Acknowledgements

Sincere gratitude is owed to the following individuals who have greatly aided me in the completion of this monograph. Thanks first and foremost to Rhona Smith for all of her personal and professional support over the years. This book would have been impossible without her dedicated guidance and mentoring, and for them I am enormously thankful.

Huge thanks are also owed to Sorcha MacLeod, whose constructive feedback spurred me on to reach new standards, and whose comments on early drafts of this work helped me to draw out a once rather buried argument.

Thanks to Conall Mallory, Rebecca Moosavian, David McGrogan, James Grey, Sue Farran and Hakeem Yusuf for their encouragement and detailed reflections on earlier drafts of this work. Thanks to Katie Bales for putting up with my rants in a dimly lit room in Ellison Terrace for the best part of 3 years. Thanks to my office-mates at Northumbria, Richard Glancey, Charlotte Emmett and Siobhan McConnell. Thanks to Michael Stockdale, Debbie Rook, Sarah Mercer and Eileen Fry for their sage advice. Thanks to the PGR community at Northumbria, in particular Brian Brewis, Dominic O'Brien, Adam Ramshaw and Lauren Clayton-Helm.

Thanks to my parents, John Brian McConnell and Janet McConnell, for their encouragement, patience, and support.

Thanks to the series editor, Professor Surya P. Subedi, for the opportunity to include this work in the Human Rights and International Law series, and to the team at Routledge for all of their support, particularly Katie Carpenter and Olivia Manley.

1 Introduction

The populations of resource-rich States are often vulnerable to severe human rights abuses. The adversities experienced by these communities do not solely emanate from the operations of States and their agents, but increasingly stem from the activities of so-called 'non-State actors'. Two of the most notable are perhaps multinational enterprises (MNEs) and non-State armed groups.[1] The pattern of negative consequences arising from the intersection of these entities is replicated across the developing world, evidenced by instances of protracted internal armed conflict, torture and threats to physical security, pervasive sexual violence, as well as the recruitment of child soldiers.[2] In addition, these actors have contributed to rising levels of poverty, environmental degradation and poor labour standards, often leading to widespread ill health.[3] Despite the diversity in the motives and goals of these entities, as well as the clear disparity in their

---

1 Naomi Gal-Or, Cedric Ryngaert and Math Noortmann (eds), *Responsibilities of the Non-State Actor in Armed Conflict and the Market Place: Theoretical and Empirical Findings* (Leiden, Netherlands, Brill, 2015).

2 Aderoju Oyefusi, 'Oil and the Probability of Rebel Participation Among Youths in the Niger Delta of Nigeria' (2008) 45 *J Peace Res* 539; Paul Collier and Anke Hoeffler, 'On Economic Causes of Civil War' (1998) 50 *Oxf Econ Pap* 563; Ian Smillie, 'Blood Diamonds and Non-State Actors' (2013) 46 *Vand J Transnat'l L* 1003, 1005; Jill Marshall, 'Torture Committed by Non-State Actors: The Developing Jurisprudence from the ad hoc Tribunals' (2005) 5 *Non-State Actors & Int'l L* 171; Anna Maedl, 'Rape as Weapon of War in the Eastern DRC? The Victims' Perspective' (2011) 33 *Hum Rts Q* 128; Claude Rakistis, 'Child Soldiers in the East of the Democratic Republic of the Congo' (2008) 27 *Refugee Survey Q* 108.

3 Michael L Ross, *The Oil Curse: How Petroleum Wealth Shapes the Development of Nations* (Princeton, NJ, Princeton University Press, 2012); Paul Orogun, 'Resource Control, Revenue Allocation and Petroleum Politics in Nigeria: The Niger Delta Question' (2010) 75 *GeoJournal* 459; Stuart Kirsch, 'Mining and Environmental Human Rights in Papua New Guinea' in Scott Pegg and Jedrzej George Frynas (eds), *Transnational Corporations and Human Rights* (Basingstoke, UK, Palgrave Macmillan, 2003) 118–22; Jonathan Drimmer, 'Human Rights and the Extractive Industries: Litigation and Compliance Trends' (2010) 3 *JWEL & B* 121, 123–5; Loong Wong, 'Revisiting Rights and Responsibility: The Case of Bhopal' (2008) 4 *Soc Resp J* 143, 144.

economic power and political legitimacy, dominant scholarship continues to reflect their broad terminological classification as 'non-State actors'. This binary categorisation makes the simple distinction between those entities that are sovereign States – the traditional addressees of international legal obligations – and those that are not.[4]

The interplay between the various subsets of public international law and the extent to which they offer effective protection from the threats highlighted above remains contentious. Given the traditional primacy accorded to States in the international legal system, the onus has typically fallen on these actors alone to effectively safeguard their populations from private entities operating within their jurisdictions. In light of the proliferation of non-State actors, and the correlative decline in State power,[5] the practical efficacy of this position is now being called into question by scholars, States and non-governmental organisations (NGOs) alike.[6] This monograph aims to respond to this scenario. It seeks to expose the practical challenges to the extant State-centric model of international law and will examine whether this theoretical framing can conceivably accommodate the direct application of international law to non-State actors. In addition, the study provides a critical appraisal of an alternative theoretical foundation and indicates areas for future normative development in international human rights law.

This introductory chapter establishes the field of research in which the present monograph is situated, defining the aims of the study and explaining the methodological approaches adopted. In doing so, it contextualises: (a) the State-centric focus of mainstream international legal scholarship; (b) the

---

4   Hersch Lauterpacht, 'The Subjects of International Law' in Andrea Bianchi (ed), *Non-State Actors and International Law – The Library of Essays in International Law* (Aldershot, UK, Ashgate, 2009) 3; Anne Peters, Lucy Koechlin and Gretta Fenner Zinkernagel, 'Non-State Actors as Standard Setters: Framing the Issue in an Interdisciplinary Fashion' in Anne Peters, Lucy Koechlin, Till Förster and Gretta Fenner Zinkernagel (eds), *Non-State Actors as Standard Setters* (Cambridge, UK, CUP, 2009) 14.

5   Rafael Domingo, 'The Crisis of International Law' (2009) 42 *Vand J Transnat'l L* 1543, 1551; Guido Acquaviva, 'Subjects of International Law: A Power-based Analysis' (2008) 38 *Vand J Transnat'l L* 345; Martin van Creveld, *The Rise and Decline of the State* (Cambridge, UK, CUP, 1999) 336–414.

6   Eric De Brabandere, 'Human Rights Obligations and Transnational Corporations: The Limits of Direct Corporate Responsibility' (2010) 4 *Hum Rts & Int'l Legal Discourse* 66; Zakaria Daboné, 'International Law: Armed Groups in a State-Centric System' (2011) 93 *Int'l Rev Red Cross* 395; Cristina Lafont, 'Accountability and Global Governance: Challenging the State-Centric Conception of Human Rights' (2010) 3 *Ethics & Global Politics* 193; Human Rights Council, 'Republic of Ecuador: Statement on behalf of a Group of Countries at the 24th session of the Human Rights Council, Transnational Corporations and Human Rights' (Geneva, September 2013) http://business-humanrights.org/media/documents/statement-unhrc-legally-binding.pdf, accessed 19 April 2016; Stop Corporate Impunity, 'Statement to the Human Rights Council in Support of the Initiative of a Group of States for a Legally Binding Instrument on Transnational Corporations' (13 September 2013) www.stopcorporateimpunity.org/?p=3830, accessed 19 April 2016.

phenomena that have contributed to the significant political and economic influence wielded by non-State actors; and (c) the consequences that this scenario produces vis-à-vis the human rights of vulnerable civilian populations. Accordingly, the chapter begins with a brief contextualisation of the complex nature of non-State actor dynamics, followed by an exposition on the scenario that served as the initial stimulus for this research. It then defines the specific non-State actors adopted as analytical tools throughout the monograph and indicates the trajectory of the research by sketching the focus of the forthcoming chapters.

1.1 Non-State actor dynamics and contemporary challenges

The term 'non-State actor' notoriously evades precise definition. Josselin and Wallace suggest that the term includes entities that are:

> i) largely or entirely autonomous from central government funding and control: emanating from civil society, or from the market economy, or from political impulses beyond State control and direction; ii) operating as or participating in networks which extend across the boundaries of two or more States – thus engaging in 'transnational relations', linking political systems, economies, societies; iii) acting in ways which affect political outcomes, either within one or more States or within international institutions – either purposefully or semi-purposefully, either as their primary objective or as one aspect of their activities.[7]

Although the utility of this detailed approach is acknowledged, McCorquodale suggests that it is both too restrictive, in that it fails to include individuals and inter-State organisations, and too broad, in that violations of international human rights law do not necessarily need to produce transnational effects.[8] In line with this reading, the present monograph adopts a broader general definition that, it is suggested, is truer to the literal meaning of the term and better reflects the binary approach adopted in classical State-centric scholarship. Thus, for the purpose of this study, the term 'non-State actor' may refer to all individuals, groups and organisations that do not constitute sovereign States.[9]

---

7 Daphné Josselin and William Wallace, 'Non-State Actors in World Politics: A Framework' in Daphné Josselin and William Wallace (eds), *Non-State Actors in World Politics* (Basingstoke, UK, Palgrave Macmillan, 2001) 3–4.

8 Robert McCorquodale, 'Non-State Actors and International Human Rights Law' in Sarah Joseph and Adam McBeth (eds), *Research Handbook on International Human Rights Law* (Cheltenham, UK, Edward Elgar, 2010) 98.

9 Mary Ellen O'Connell, 'Enhancing the Status of Non-State Actors through a Global War on Terror?' (2005) 43 *Colum J Transnat'l L* 435, 437.

One of the most fundamental challenges presented by this field of study is its expansive scope. It has long been acknowledged that the polar distinction between entities that are 'States' and those that are 'not States' is excessively reductive.[10] A plurality of actors fall within the latter category, which may include any 'non-State' entity, from central institutions within the international legal system, to wholly private, corporate entities, and even armed factions operating on the fringes of weak governance States. In spite of the intensely varied economic influence and political legitimacy exhibited by these actors, their treatment and legal status in dominant scholarship remain essentially synonymous: non-State actors are merely *objects*, as opposed to direct addressees of international law.[11] It will be argued throughout this study that, although undeniably problematic, it is the theoretical foundations of this division that underpin the binding quality of international law in State-centric scholarship. This is a factor that cannot be ignored, for, as Green suggests, 'an incoherent approach to non-State actors would have undesirable consequences not only for non-State actors, but for the international legal system as a whole'.[12]

Irrespective of the uniform categorisation of non-State actors, catch-all regulatory initiatives would likely prove highly undesirable. Such schemes would fail to account for the diversity in the willingness and capacity of these entities to comply with legal obligations, and would be unable to cater to the specific demands of each scenario. For instance, the form and content of the legal mechanisms required to ensure the effective regulation of an NGO will be entirely different to those for a multinational oil company or a terrorist cell. Thus, the formulation of effective international legal provisions addressing non-State actors is an extremely complex task.[13] The numerous bodies of law relevant to the regulation of these entities, at both the domestic and international level, are vast, from domestic human rights initiatives, criminal, tort and company law, to the international human rights, humanitarian and criminal law regimes. Clearly, it is beyond the scope of this monograph to provide a detailed practical and theoretical analysis in relation to each and every non-State actor operational today. Rather, this study focuses on two specific categories of actor: MNEs and non-State armed groups. These entities have

10 Philip Alston, 'The "Not-a-Cat" Syndrome: Can the International Human Rights Regime Accommodate Non-State Actors?' in Philip Alston (ed), *Non State Actors and Human Rights* (Oxford, UK, OUP, 2005) 15–20.
11 Andrew Clapham, *Human Rights Obligations of Non-State Actors* (Oxford, UK, OUP, 2006) 59–84; Rosalyn Higgins, *Problems and Process: International Law and How We Use It* (Oxford, UK, Clarendon Press, 1994) 49.
12 Fergus Green, 'Fragmentation in Two Dimensions: The ICJ's Flawed Approach to Non-State Actors and International Legal Personality' (2008) 9 *Melb J Int'l L* 47, 76.
13 Janne E Nijman, 'Non-State Actors and the International Rule of Law: Revisiting the Realist Theory of International Legal Personality' in Cedric Ryngaert and Math Noortmann (eds), *Non-State Actor Dynamics in International Law: From Law-Takers to Law-Makers* (Aldershot, UK, Ashgate, 2010) 92.

been selected owing to the power and influence they exert in international affairs, their intersecting roles and their utility as vehicles for complex practical and theoretical analysis. The foregoing caveat notwithstanding, the adoption of these particular actors will permit the elucidation of a number of key theoretical findings that are generalizable to the field as a whole.

A second general challenge presented by non-State actors relates to the expanding roles they perform in society and the undeniable rise in their political and economic influence over the course of the twentieth century.[14] A number of contemporary phenomena have proven conducive to this proliferation.[15] First, the globalisation of the world economy has led to a scenario in which MNEs boast greater gross domestic product (GDP) than many States and control vast resources.[16] This process has encouraged deference to 'certain economic models which aim almost exclusively to provide the conditions for "free markets" and foreign direct investment with little regard for the immediate effect of these policies on the marginalised or the poor'.[17] Although this power shift has not rendered the territorial State completely redundant in international affairs, it has substantially affected the willingness and capacity of States to constrain the behaviour of private actors, particularly those upon which they are economically dependent. Second, the privatisation of traditional State functions has significantly increased the role of non-State actors at the domestic level, and 'insufficient attention has been given to the implications for international law of the changing internal role of the State'.[18] The privatisation of law enforcement, prisons, healthcare, education, telecommunications and broadcasting, tied to the Western neo-liberal project of free-market capitalism, is exacerbated by the State-centric focus of international human rights accountability mechanisms, which are unable to respond effectively to the rising influence of private actors.[19]

A third factor relates to the nature of warfare. Since the conclusion of the Second World War, armed conflict has become increasingly fragmented and is now dominated by catastrophic internal strife.[20] Non-State armed groups – a catch-all term adopted throughout this study to represent opposition groups, rebels, militias and insurgent movements – feature heavily in what the International Committee of the Red Cross (ICRC) has termed 'anarchic'

---

14 Ibid. 93; Alston, 'Not-a-Cat' (n 10) 6.
15 Clapham (n 11) 3.
16 Gare Smith, 'An Introduction to Corporate Social Responsibility in the Extractive Industries' (2008) 11 *Yale Hum Rts & Dev LJ* 1, 3.
17 Clapham (n 11) 4.
18 Philip Alston, 'The Myopia of the Handmaidens: International Lawyers and Globalisation' (1997) 8 *EJIL* 442.
19 Clapham (n 11) 8–9.
20 Sandesh Sivakumaran, *The Law of Non-International Armed Conflict* (Oxford, UK, OUP, 2012) 1.

conflicts.[21] In situations in which a State's governmental or judicial infrastructure is weak or collapsing, it would be naïve to suggest that it possesses the capacity to protect its population from serious human rights abuses.[22] Moreover, 'the extreme individualisation of the factions has made contacts and negotiations very uncertain. Every soldier – adult or child – virtually becomes a spokesperson, or in any case someone with whom to negotiate.'[23] The loose structure of these factions makes it 'difficult, if not impossible to distinguish between combatants and civilians'.[24] This study recognises the importance of effectively responding to these international developments. The particular actors comprising the focus of this monograph in many ways epitomise the phenomena described above, and their utility will contribute to a robust, practical, theoretical analysis that accounts for, and responds to, the adverse consequences they engender.

The preceding discussion notwithstanding, the influence of non-State actors in public life is no longer a particularly novel concept. Scholarship produced throughout the 1990s was then described as 'adventuresome and timely'.[25] It is recognised that, some 20 years later, such remarks are essentially platitudes. Although these phenomena remain relevant and highlight the fundamental societal changes that have taken place in recent decades, legal responses to date have proven inadequate. The threats that non-State actors pose to human rights are persistent and are now more critical than ever. In the words of De Brabandere, 'the role that non-state actors play and should play in implementing human rights is . . . still largely under-theorised, while nevertheless being at the forefront of current legal, political and ethical debates'.[26] The present monograph aims to respond to this challenge. It critically examines the malleability of the dominant, State-centric approach to non-State actor regulation, revealing its core concepts and practical flaws. It demonstrates that the exposure of theoretical weaknesses can help to explain practical failings and may contribute to the advancement of effective responses. The desirability and efficacy of potential developments will be evaluated and weighed against alternatives. This broader, more conceptual analysis will be explored in relation to non-State armed groups and MNEs and, it is hoped, will positively contribute

---

21 ICRC, 'Preparatory Document for the First Periodical Meeting on International Humanitarian Law: Armed Conflicts Linked to the Disintegration of State Structures' (Geneva, 19–23 January 1998) www.icrc.org/eng/resources/documents/misc/57jplq.htm, accessed 19 April 2016.

22 Anthony Vinci, 'Anarchy, Failed States and Armed Groups: Reconsidering Conventional Analysis' (2008) 52 *Int'l Stud Q* 295; David McDonough, 'From Guerrillas to Government: Post-Conflict Stability in Liberia, Uganda and Rwanda' (2008) 29 *Third World Q* 357.

23 ICRC, 'Preparatory Document' (n 21).

24 Ibid.

25 Henry Steiner, 'Book Review: Human Rights in the Private Sphere by Andrew Clapham' (1995) 89 *AJIL* 844.

26 Eric De Brabandere, 'Non-State Actors, State-Centrism and Human Rights Obligations' (2009) 22 *LJIL* 191, 192.

to the establishment of a more coherent accountability regime for non-State actors generally.

1.2 Resource extraction in weak governance States

Much of the analysis in the present study is situated in the context of extractive industries operating in what are termed 'weak governance' States. The Organisation for Economic Co-operation and Development (OECD) has adopted similar descriptors, defining 'weak governance zones' as:

> investment environments in which public sector actors are unable or unwilling to assume their roles and responsibilities in protecting rights ... providing basic public services ... and ensuring that public sector management is efficient and effective. These 'governance failures' lead to broader failures in political, economic and civic institutions.[27]

The adoption of any terminology of this kind is inherently problematic, owing to the negative political connotations such terms often come to represent. Indeed, the Special Representative of the Secretary-General, John Ruggie, has expressed such concerns in relation to the term 'weak governance zones'.[28] Although it is vital that scholars remain cognisant of such sensitivities, some degree of pragmatism must prevail, and there is clear utility in the adoption of terms enjoying common usage among relevant international institutions. For Simons and Macklin, 'what matters is that the definition be available to scrutiny, reasonably capable of neutral application, and explicitly attend to the human rights and humanitarian dimensions of weak governance/conflict.'[29] In line with this recent scholarship, the term has been adopted throughout this work.

The circumstances in many weak governance States magnify the challenges posed by non-State actors. Although mainstream scholarship has proven largely reluctant to move beyond State-based regulatory initiatives,[30] many such States lack the necessary governmental and judicial infrastructure to effectively safeguard their populations.[31] At the same time, corruption and economic

---

27 OECD, 'Investments in Weak Governance Zones, Summary of Consultations' (September 2005) 2, www.oecd.org/corporate/mne/35397593.pdf, accessed 19 April 2016.

28 OHCHR, 'Workshop on Attributing Corporate Responsibility for Human Rights Under International Law' (17 November 2006) 5, http://business-humanrights.org/sites/default/files/media/bhr/files/Workshop-Corp-Responsibility-under-Intl-Law-17-Nov-2006.pdf, accessed 19 April 2016.

29 Penelope Simons and Audrey Macklin, *The Governance Gap: Extractive Industries, Human Rights and the Home State Advantage* (Oxford, UK, Routledge, 2014) 294.

30 Robert McCorquodale, 'Overlegalising Silences: Human Rights and Non-State Actors' (2002) 96 *ASIL Proc* 384, 384–5.

31 Daniel Thürer, 'The Failed State and International Law' (1999) 81 *Int'l Rev Red Cross* 731, 741–2; Walter Kälin, 'Late Modernity: Human Rights Under Pressure?' (2013) 15 *Punishment & Society* 397, 402.

dependence on foreign direct investment (FDI) directly affect the willingness of these States to provide regulation and redress.[32] It is estimated that around 15 per cent of States are located within weak governance zones, with a particularly high concentration in sub-Saharan Africa.[33] The situation in the Democratic Republic of the Congo (DRC) is illustrative of the extremes experienced across the African continent, with conflict in the region having led to the deaths of more than six million people.[34] A defining characteristic of recent African armed conflict is that it is funded almost exclusively by natural resources.

> All commentaries on [the DRC] are unanimous that the real reason for the protracted armed conflict that has been going on in the country since 1993 is the exploitation of the country's mineral resources . . . rather than security concerns.[35]

Extractive companies have been implicated in the deliberate financing of rebellions in anticipation of new market opportunities or more favourable concession rights, contributing to the displacement of civilian populations.[36] In early 2007, several thousand people in the DRC's Kasai Oriental province fled their villages following a conflict over a local diamond mine.[37] Similarly,

32 Daniel Leader, 'Business and Human Rights – Time to Hold Companies to Account' (2008) 8 *Int'l CLR* 447, 452; De Brabandere, 'Human Rights Obligations and Transnational Corporations' (n 6) 77.
33 OECD, 'Risk Awareness Tool for Multinational Enterprises in Weak Governance Zones' (OECD, June 2006) 9, www.oecd.org/daf/inv/corporateresponsibility/36885821.pdf, accessed 19 April 2016.
34 Stephen Kirchner, *Wartime Rape: Sexual Terrorism in the Eastern Provinces of the DRC* (GRIN Verlag, 2008) 21; Jeffrey Herbst and Greg Mills, 'The Invisible State – It's Time We Admit the Democratic Republic of Congo Does Not Exist' (2013) 201 *Foreign Policy* 78–80; Theodore Trefon, *Reinventing Order in the Congo: How People Respond to State Failure in Kinshasa* (London, Zed Books, 2004) 1–2.
35 Phoebe Okowa, 'Natural Resources in Situations of Armed Conflict: Is there a Coherent Framework for Protection?' (2007) 9 *Int'l CL Rev* 237, 239; UNSC, 'Final Report of the Panel of Experts on the Illegal Exploitation of Natural Resources and Other Forms of Wealth of the Democratic Republic of the Congo' (16 October 2002) UN Doc S/2002/1146, Annex III.
36 Olga Martin-Ortega, 'Human Rights Due Diligence for Corporations: From Voluntary Standards to Hard Law at Last?' (2014) 32 *Neth Q Hum Rts* 44, 46–9; Sara Greenen and Klara Claessens, 'Disputed Access to the Gold Sites in Luhwindja, Eastern Democratic Republic of the Congo' (2013) 51 *JMAS* 85; Adam McBeth, 'Crushed by an Anvil: A Case Study on Responsibility for Human Rights in the Extractive Industry' (2008) 11 *Yale Hum Rts & Dev LJ* 127; Global Witness, 'Oil and Mining in Violent Places: Why Voluntary Codes for Companies Don't Guarantee Human Rights' *Global Witness* (London, 2007) www.globalwitness.org/documents/17491/oil_and_mining_in_violent_places.pdf, accessed 19 April 2016.
37 Greta Zeender and Jacob Rothing, 'Displacement Trends in DRC' (2010) 36 *Forced Migration Review* 10.

in North Kivu, a Hutu militia forced the civilian population to act as slave porters for their mining operations, and competition between communities over access to fishing ponds in Équateur developed into an insurgency that displaced 200,000 civilians.[38] There is also evidence to suggest that many extractive companies based in North America have entered into direct mineral exploitation deals with rebel groups.[39] Indeed, as a rebel leader, Laurent Kabila took the view that he was entitled to grant exploitation rights to multinational extractive companies in areas of territory under his control.[40] Additionally, the recent jurisprudence of the International Criminal Court (ICC) concerning Jean-Pierre Bemba Gombo, Germain Katanga and Thomas Lubanga Dyilo further emphasises the timely analysis of issues regarding non-State actors in this region.[41] Yet, although the DRC's recent history encapsulates the complex issues arising from the operations of non-State actors, in order to demonstrate the full extent of these challenges, it will not serve as the sole geographical focus of this monograph. Instead, the study will draw from a wide pool of relevant scenarios across the globe, while focusing heavily on human rights abuses stemming from resource extraction.

The significant exploration costs demanded by mining, oil and gas ventures often impede the exploitation of natural resources without the involvement of MNEs.[42] The litigation initiated under the United States' (US) Alien Torts regime, particularly in *Unocal*[43] and *Talisman*,[44] demonstrates the willingness of companies to engage in joint ventures in resource extraction with State partners with an identifiable history of human rights violations and war crimes.[45]

38 Ibid.
39 Ross (n 3) 174–8; John F Clark, *African Stakes of the Congo War* (Basingstoke, UK, Palgrave Macmillan, 2004); OECD, 'Conducting Business with Integrity in Weak Governance: Issues for Discussion and a Case Study of the Democratic Republic of the Congo' (OECD, 7–8 March 2005) www.oecd.org/investment/mne/34304653.pdf, accessed 19 April 2016; Global Witness, 'Congo's Mineral Trade in the Balance: Opportunities and Obstacles to Demilitarisation' *Global Witness* (London, May 2011) www.globalwitness.org/en-gb/archive/opportunity-change-eastern-congos-mines-must-be-seized-now/, accessed 19 April 2016.
40 Okowa (n 35) 239; Jim Freedman, 'Tackling the Tin Wars in DR Congo' (2011) 24 *Mineral Economics* 45.
41 *Prosecutor v Jean-Pierre Bemba Gombo*, ICC-01/05–01/08 (21 March 2016); *Prosecutor v Germain Katanga*, ICC-01/04–0/07 (7 March 2014); *Prosecutor v Thomas Lubanga Dyilo*, ICC-01/04–01/06, (14 March 2012).
42 Olubayo Oluduro, *Oil Exploitation and Human Rights Violations in Nigeria's Oil Producing Communities* (Cambridge, UK, Intersentia, 2014) 30.
43 *Doe v Unocal Corp*, 395 F.3d 932 (9th Cir 2002).
44 *Presbyterian Church of Sudan v Talisman Energy*, 582 F.3d 244 (2nd Cir 2009); Simons and Macklin (n 29) 22–78.
45 Karen Ballentine, 'DESA Expert Group Meeting on Conflict Prevention, Peace-building and Development, Natural Resources, Governance, Development and Conflict' (UN Department of Economic and Social Affairs, 15 November 2004) 3, www.un.org/esa/peacebuilding/Action/DesaTaskForce/papers_egm20041115/Natural_Resources_KBallentine.pdf, accessed 19 April 2016.

Non-State armed groups often seek to appropriate large areas of territory from the *de jure* State in anticipation of future economic benefits from MNEs.[46] These business actors often supply the economic resources that provide the motives and means to perpetuate armed conflicts, including payments of bribes or remittances to local armed groups in exchange for the protection of their facilities.[47] For instance, South Africa's AngloGold Ashanti (a subsidiary of Anglo American) provided logistical and financial support to Nationalist and Integrationist Front (FNI) leaders, 'even as FNI combatants were carrying out witch hunts, executions, arbitrary detentions, torture and forced labour'.[48] Other actors, sometimes described as 'violence entrepreneurs', do not necessarily represent political movements, but 'use violence to control resources, trading networks or make money from protection or ransom'.[49] The activity of these non-State entities in the extractive process has led to claims detailing the utilisation of torture, rape and other sexual violence,[50] the recruitment of child soldiers[51] and environmental destruction violating the health and physical integrity of civilians, to name but a few issues.[52]

As is now all too apparent, MNEs operating in weak governance States frequently provide:

46 UN Office for the Coordination of Humanitarian Affairs (OCHA), 'Monthly Humanitarian Bulletin: Colombia' (March 2013) http://reliefweb.int/sites/reliefweb.int/files/resources/Monthly_Humanitarian_Bulletin_March2013.pdf, accessed 19 April 2016.

47 Paul Kapelus, Ralf Hamann and Edward O'Keefe, 'Doing Business with Integrity: The Experience of AngloGold Ashanti in the Democratic Republic of the Congo' (2005) 57 *Int'l Social Science J* 119; M Cherif Bassiouni, 'Criminal Law: The New Wars and the Crisis of Compliance with the Law of Armed Conflict by Non-State Actors' (2008) 98 *J Crim L & Criminology* 711, 776–8; Achim Wennmann, 'Economic Dimensions of Armed Groups: Profiling the Financing, Costs, and Agendas and their Implications for Mediated Engagements' (2011) 93 *Int'l Rev Red Cross* 333, 337.

48 International Network for Economic, Social and Cultural Rights, 'Corporate Accountability Working Group, Consultation on Human Rights and the Extractive Industry' (Geneva, 10–11 November 2005) 15, www.escr-net.org/sites/default/files/ESCR-Net_on_HR_and_Extractive_Industry.pdf, accessed 19 April 2016; Human Rights Watch, 'The Curse of Gold' *Human Rights Watch* (New York, 2005) 58–77, www.hrw.org/sites/default/files/reports/drc0505_0.pdf, accessed 19 April 2016.

49 Dieter Neubert, 'Local and Regional Non-State Actors on the Margins of Public Policy in Africa' in Peters, Koechlin and Förster (n 4) 40.

50 Susan Bartels, Jennifer Scott, Jennifer Leaning, Denis Mukwege, Robert Lipton and Michael VanRooyen, 'Surviving Sexual Violence in Eastern Democratic Republic of the Congo' (2010) 11 *J Int'l Women's Stud* 37; Katie Richey, 'Several Steps Sideways: International Legal Developments Concerning War Rape and the Human Rights of Women' (2007) 17 *Tex J Women & L* 109.

51 Mary Fox, 'Child Soldiers and International Law: Patchwork Gains and Conceptual Debates' (2005) 7 *Hum Rts Rev* 27; Janet McKnight, 'Child Soldiers in Africa: A Global Approach to Human Rights Protection, Enforcement and Post-Conflict Reintegration' (2010) 18 *Afr J Int'l L* 113.

52 Hakeem Yusuf, 'Oil on Troubled Waters: Multinational Corporations and Realising Human Rights in the Developing World with Specific Reference to Nigeria' (2008) 8 *AHRLJ* 79.

the chief *raison d'être* for the armed groups. The war and 'criminality' in the Congo are examples of real existing capitalism itself, transformed by the erosion of national States and by the growth of private capital and also contributing actively to that process.[53]

Thus, not only are the distinct practical challenges presented by these actors at their most extreme in resource-rich regions, but these fragile States also often act as a point of convergence.[54] The variety of entities categorised as non-State actors and their interplay highlight the need to account for this plurality in the development of effective legal strategies to address the adverse human rights impacts to which they give rise. Today, international actors cannot be taken to operate in a vacuum. This much is underscored by recent scholarship, not only relating to the confluence of actors dependent on extractive industries,[55] but also in diverse and developing fields relating to global public–private partnerships.[56] By utilising non-State armed groups and MNEs as specific examples, this study will account for this diversity. Despite sharing a clear factual connection in many resource-rich States, these entities remain entirely distinct in terms of their economic power and political legitimacy. As such, these specific actors serve an important critical purpose in relation to the evaluation of the practical and theoretical consequences of extant State-centric scholarship and any alternative conceptions proposed.

Faced with the inherent practical failings of purely State-based approaches to the regulation of these actors, some members of the international community have begun to contemplate the enactment of directly enforceable international obligations for non-State actors. Most recently, a submission was made by the State representative for Ecuador during the 24th session of the Human Rights Council in September 2013, primarily motivated by the State's turbulent litigation against Texaco/Chevron in pursuit of financial redress for alleged environmental and human rights abuses stemming from oil extraction.[57] Although the success of such initiatives remains highly dubious, the present monograph aims to assess the practical failings of existing regulatory regimes and the capacity to square direct non-State actor regulation with established

---

53 David Renton, David Seddon and Leo Zellig, *The Congo: Plunder and Resistance* (London, Zed Books, 2007) 211.

54 Georgette Gagnon and John Ryle, 'Report of an Investigation into Oil Development, Conflict and Displacement in Western Upper Nile, Sudan' (London and Toronto, 15 October 2001) 48, www.globaloilwatch.com/reports/oil-development-sudan-report-gagnon-103001.pdf, accessed 19 April 2016.

55 Simons and Macklin (n 29); Gal-Or, Ryngaert and Noortmann (n 1); Neubert (n 49) 52.

56 Lisa Clarke, *Public–Private Partnerships and Responsibility Under International Law: A Global Health Perspective* (Oxford, UK, Routledge, 2014); Davinia Aziz, 'Global Public–Private Partnerships in International Law' (2012) 2 *Asian JIL* 339.

57 Christopher Whytock, 'Chevron–Ecuador Case: Three Dimensions of Complexity in Transnational Dispute Resolution' (2012) 106 *ASIL Proc* 425.

State-centric doctrine. It will critically explore the feasibility of developing an alternative approach that is theoretically sound and practically workable and has desirable consequences for the future development of international law. The work is given focus and specificity through the utilisation of practical illustrations drawn from weak governance states and by its focus on the intersection of MNEs and non-State armed groups. The suitability of each of these actors as vehicles for analysis will be further demonstrated below in the context of the argumentative structure of this work.

1.3 The structure of this monograph

Having contextualised the aims of this monograph, this final section describes the approach taken in each of the substantive chapters. Following directly from the general field of research established in this introduction, Chapter 2 aims to provide detailed context on the central position accorded to States in the international legal system, a concept that is critical to the dominant positivist approach. It explores how this conception developed and has been justified historically and defines its theoretical framing. Although the chapter is primarily expository, it simultaneously serves an important critical purpose. It aims to expose the weakness of the historical justifications and theoretical concepts upon which classical State-centric scholarship is built. The chapter will demonstrate the relatively recent domination of the territorial State, which has given rise to a system founded on a number of opaque legal constructs that are unable to respond effectively to the adverse effects produced by non-State actors. The context provided is vital to the analytical approach taken in subsequent chapters and is drawn upon extensively both during practical and theoretical evaluations of State-based regulatory approaches and in conceiving alternative models that may prove more receptive to direct non-State actor regulation.

Advancing this analysis, Chapters 3 and 4 demonstrate the failings of the State-centric approach in the context of non-State armed groups and MNEs. Although parallels are drawn between both actors where possible, Chapter 3 primarily focuses on the latter. MNEs are particularly illustrative of the *practical* challenges to State responsibility and existing paths to domestic redress. This is owing to the almost exclusively State-based approach to their regulation, which is seemingly at odds with the transnational reach of their corporate structures. In practice, this scenario has led to complex legal questions relating to the jurisdictional competence of forums in both 'host' countries and the Western States in which the parent company is often domiciled. Similarly, the selection and application of a particular State's law, and the utilisation of procedural challenges by corporate defendants, may impede the avenues to redress available to vulnerable victims. In addition, Chapter 3 demonstrates that direct regulation via soft law standards and other *ad hoc* measures remains largely ineffective, and the international criminal law regime is ill suited both to the prosecution of corporate defendants and in terms of the prevention and management of humanitarian atrocities.

With the practical failings of State-centric accountability mechanisms having been detailed, Chapter 4 addresses the *theoretical* impediments to the establishment of direct international obligations for non-State actors. Here, the primary focus shifts to non-State armed groups. The analytical utility of these actors partly stems from the contentious political factors surrounding their status, but also results from the clear attempts made under the international humanitarian law regime to impose direct duties on to actors that are unable to consent formally to multilateral treaties or to participate in the formation of conventional and customary international legal rules. This chapter examines various scholarly justifications for the direct application of international humanitarian law to non-State armed groups. In doing so, it demonstrates that the doctrinal weaknesses of these approaches are directly connected to the framework underlying the State-based conception of international law. Given the unwillingness/inability of weak governance States to effectively regulate human rights abuses arising from the operations of non-state actors within their territory, the question arises as to why States, as the primary actors in the international legal system, cannot simply elect to impose direct obligations on non-State actors via conventional and customary law. There are a number of reasons that explain the unwillingness of States to confer rights and obligations on to non-State actors, particularly those that threaten the territorial integrity of the State directly.

These *political* legitimacy concerns aside, there are deeper, theoretical issues at play that are equally applicable to armed groups and MNEs and may even be generalised to other non-State actors. Chapter 4 also critically discusses the *legal* legitimacy of ascribing direct international obligations to non-State armed groups under State-centric doctrine. Drawing on scholarship from the field of discursive democracy, the chapter devises a potential vision of direct non-State actor regulation, legitimated by multi-stakeholder law-making. It will be argued that this participation in the law-making process is necessitated by consequence of the State-centric school's theoretical groundwork, in particular, its reliance on consent – on validation by the actors that are the addressees of the legal norms in question. It is argued that States cannot have their cake and eat it; the justifications for the view that non-State armed groups are subject to direct obligations under the State-based conception are weak. Most non-State actors are regarded as 'objects' of the international legal system and are unable to formally consent to treaty obligations or participate in the formulation of conventional and customary law. Any attempt to reconcile this view under the State-centric approach undermines the strength and authority of the international legal system as it is traditionally conceived. In addition, the chapter will evaluate the political and practical implications arising from non-State actor participation in law-making processes, as well as concerns that presently accepted international standards would be subject to severe erosion.

In light of the potentially undesirable consequences stemming from dominant scholarship, Chapter 5 advances and evaluates an alternative theoretical approach to direct non-State actor regulation. Contrary to the State-centric approach, which treats the State as a supreme validating entity – as the primary subject/ addressee from which all international legal rules emerge – this chapter adopts a very different conception of the international legal system. Drawing on the Pure Theory of Law,[58] the chapter demonstrates that, by detaching international law from the State, thereby undermining its deified position as the primary subject, law-maker and component of legal validity, and instead finding that international legal norms both define the State and prescribe which actors those norms address, it is theoretically possible to establish directly binding international obligations for non-State actors. In turn, it will be argued that this approach may produce a far more robust theoretical framework for direct non-State actor regulation. Whereas other approaches still emphasise the importance of law-making capacity for addressees as a means of bolstering compliance and promoting global democratisation,[59] the theory adopted bypasses this requirement entirely, including any potentially negative consequences that follow. In line with the approach taken in the preceding chapters, the desirability of this model will be assessed. In particular, it will be questioned whether, in the absence of an effective accountability mechanism, the decentralised nature of the international legal system would continue to result in widespread impunity, in spite of firmer theoretical foundations.

In sum, the present study takes as its theoretical point of departure the dominant positivist conception of international law, which has traditionally emphasised the primacy of the State as the principal addressee and validating organ of the international legal system. It situates its analysis in the context of the extractive industry in weak governance States, in order to magnify the practical and theoretical failings of this approach in light of contemporary phenomena, and utilises as the primary vehicle for analysis two particular categories of actor. The roles of non-State armed groups and MNEs coalesce in this practical context, demonstrating the definitional challenges that pervade State-centric scholarship, the diversity of international actors whose behaviour may cumulatively affect vulnerable populations, and the impediments to the design of an effective catch-all system of legal regulation. These specific actors hold significant analytical utility. They expose the flaws of wholly State-based regulatory initiatives as they are currently conceived and highlight the theoretical challenges that preclude the effective regulation of non-State entities. In addition, this study responds to the theoretical consequences produced by State-centric scholarship and explores appropriate alternatives. In assessing the feasibility and desirability of each potential model, it consistently draws on the practical scenario adopted as an evaluative tool, thus enabling it to weigh more conceptual findings against established international practice. It is hoped that this approach will go some way towards remedying the pervasive doctrinal and practical concerns relating to non-State actor regulation, which have remained unaddressed for so long.

58 Hans Kelsen, *The Pure Theory of Law* (Max Knight trans, 2nd edn, Berkeley, CA, University of California Press, 1970).
59 Thomas Franck, *The Power of Legitimacy among Nations* (Oxford, UK, OUP, 1990) 24; Cedric Ryngaert, 'Imposing International Duties on Non-State Actors and the Legitimacy of International Law' in Ryngaert and Noortmann (n 13) 69.

2 The State as the basis of legal validity

International law is usually perceived as a system governing inter-State relations, whereby States are regarded as the primary actors operating on the international plane. As the principal addressees of international rights and obligations, States perform central roles in the creation and application of international law. This view, widely accepted as an attribute of positivist international legal scholarship, has produced lasting practical and doctrinal effects.[1] It has severely limited the scope for the direct regulation of non-State actors that significantly affect the enjoyment of fundamental human rights. Instead, States are tasked with the primary responsibility to regulate potential threats occurring within their jurisdiction. The practical failings of this approach will be explored in greater depth later; the aim of the present chapter is twofold. First, it seeks to contextualise the historical emergence, development and theoretical under-pinnings of the State-centric conception of international law. Second, the chapter serves an underlying critical purpose, in that it aims to expose the weaknesses of the core theoretical concepts upon which State-centric scholarship is built. It will demonstrate that the dominance of the territorial State system is a relatively recent,[2] Western phenomenon,[3] built on uncertain, ill-defined constructs that, in today's globalised world, fail to reflect diminished State power and are unable to respond effectively to the threats posed by non-State entities.

This chapter begins by contextualising the role accorded to States by the prevailing positivist perspective. In doing so, it reflects on the historical development of international law and its connection to the emergence and solidification of the territorial State system. By engaging this scholarship on its

---

1 Anthony Anghie, *Imperialism, Sovereignty and the Making of International Law* (Cambridge, UK, CUP, 2007) 33; Christopher Harding, 'Statist Assumptions, Normative Individualism, and New Forms of Personality: Evolving a Philosophy of International Law for the Twenty First Century' (2001) 1 *Non-State Actors & Int'l L* 107, 108.
2 Christopher W Morris, *An Essay on the Modern State* (Cambridge, UK, CUP, 2002) 1; Joseph Strayer, *On the Medieval Origins of the Modern State* (Princeton, NJ, Princeton University Press, 1972) 3.
3 Anghie (n 1) 5.

own terms, this section demonstrates that, contrary to the dominant view, the modern State was not necessarily always a central concern in the creation and application of international law. Indeed, international law may have preceded the dominance of modern territorial States in some form. Second, the chapter discusses the highly influential nineteenth and early-twentieth century conception of the State. It seeks to demonstrate the lasting influence of the scholarship of this period, which conceived of the State as a 'social fact': an empirical basis for the validity or binding quality of international law.[4] Third, the chapter highlights the doctrinal effects of State-centrism, which, it is argued, give rise to many of the peculiarities of the international legal system, including its decentralised structure, its binding character over apparently sovereign entities, and the emphasis placed on consent in the law-making process. Fourth, the chapter demonstrates the inherent fluidity in legal conceptions of the modern State, highlighting the challenges that non-State actors pose to current conceptual understandings. It is argued that, even if the social/historical significance of the State is presumed, the pervasive definitional challenges related to this foundational concept are significant and are exacerbated by the rise of non-State entities. The final section examines the unhelpful circularity presented by the doctrine of 'international legal personality', a concept that purports to distinguish between entities that can and cannot be direct addressees of international rights and obligations. In doing so, the chapter provides a detailed, critical analysis of State-centric scholarship that will be consistently drawn upon in later chapters, in further demonstration of its failings and in order to inform potential solutions.

2.1 The territorial State and the origins of international law

Contemporary scholarship generally identifies four empirically observable features of States: (1) a fixed territory, (2) a permanent population, (3) an effective government and (4) the capacity to enter into international relations with other States.[5] These criteria are extremely reductive. They offer very little in terms of the requisite features, competences and capacities necessary for actors to operate within an international legal order, and the rise of powerful non-State actors has undoubtedly contributed to this obfuscation. From a historical perspective, even the most sophisticated systems of social ordering that were pervasive prior to the seventeenth century would likely fall outside these basic criteria. The centralised structures that gradually emerged between 1100 and 1300 AD likely lacked the fundamental features of modern States,[6] in particular:

---

4 Tom Ginsburg and Gregory Shaffer, 'How does International Law work?' in Peter Cane and Herbert Kritzer (eds), *The Oxford Handbook of Empirical Legal Research* (Oxford, UK, OUP, 2010) 760–1.

5 Montevideo Convention on the Rights and Duties of States (26 December 1933) 165 LNTS 17, Article 1 (hereafter, Montevideo Convention).

6 Antonio Cassese, *International Law* (2nd edn, Oxford, UK, OUP, 2004) 23.

the appearance of political units persisting in time and fixed in space, the development of permanent, impersonal institutions, agreement on the need for an authority which can give final judgements, and acceptance of the idea that this authority should receive the basic loyalty of its subjects.[7]

Even sixteenth century social orders were absent the 'distinctively modern idea of a State as a form of public power separate from both the ruler and the ruled, constituting the supreme political authority within a certain defined territory'.[8] Thus, the emergence of States as they are conceived today was very gradual, from boundaries to borders, to territorial jurisdiction and the growth of centralised governmental organs.[9] Even in the context of early-modern Europe, 'these changes were not easily discernible. By the nineteenth century they were. Today, they are taken for granted and treated as unremarkable'.[10]

The relationship between international law and the territorial State is highly definition dependent. At one extreme, the term 'international law' may reflect the development of devices merely intended to foster the predictability of basic international relations. From this perspective, its 'origin may be placed virtually as far back as recorded history itself'.[11] For instance, 'maximalist' scholars have found it appropriate to speak of 'a structurally unchanged European law of nations spanning two and a half millennia'.[12] The philosophical contemplation of terms familiar to today's legal lexicon, such as *jus gentium*, is arguably demonstrable in ancient societies,[13] and the evolution of a body of law regulating the conduct of hostilities is visible prior to the solidification of the

---

7 Strayer (n 2) 10.
8 Quentin Skinner, *The Foundations of Modern Political Thought* (Cambridge, UK, CUP, 1978) 353.
9 Christopher W Morris, 'The State' in George Klosko (ed), *The Oxford Handbook of the History of Political Philosophy* (Oxford, UK, OUP, 2011) 548.
10 Ibid.
11 Stephen C Neff, 'A Short History of International Law' in Malcolm Evans (ed), *International Law* (2nd edn, Oxford, UK, OUP, 2006) 4; Carlo Gocarelli, 'The Early Doctrine of International Law as a Bridge from Antiquity to Modernity and Diplomatic Inviolability in 16th and 17th Century European Practice' in Randall Lesaffer (ed), *The Twelve Years Truce (1609): Peace, War and Law in the Low Countries at the Turn of the 17th Century* (The Hague, Netherlands, Martinus Nijhoff, 2014) 210–32.
12 Wilhelm Georg Grewe, *The Epochs of International Law* (revised edn, Berlin, De Gruyter, 2000) 8; Laurens Winkel, 'The Peace Treaties of Westphalia as an Instance of the Reception of Roman Law' in Randall Lesaffer (ed), *Peace Treaties and International Law in European History* (Cambridge, UK, CUP, 2004) 222–3; Heiner Steiger, 'From the International Law of Christianity to the International law of the World Citizen – Reflections on the Formation of the Epochs of the History of International Law' (2001) 3 *J Hist Int'l L* 180, 181.
13 Nicholas Onuf, 'Civitas Maxima: Wolff, Vattel and the Fate of Republicanism' in Nicholas Onuf, *International Legal Theory: Essays and Engagements 1966–2006* (Oxford, UK, Routledge, 2008) 318–44. For a critical view rejecting meaningful continuity between these terms: David Bederman, *International Law in Antiquity* (Cambridge, UK, CUP, 2001) 1–15; Randall Lesaffer, 'Argument from Roman Law in Current International Law: Occupation and Acquisitive Prescription' (2005) 16 *EJIL* 25.

modern State system.[14] Instances of silent trading, documented by Herodotus,[15] between Carthaginians and North African tribes in the sixth century BC could be said to constitute the foundations of rudimentary international relations,[16] but, compared with the elaborate global interactions demonstrable today, both at inter-State level and between non-State actors, such transactions appear extremely primitive.[17] Indeed, despite the willingness of some scholars to recognise concepts and normative rules governing the relations between political communities existing prior to the modern State system, the continuity in the scope and application of early doctrines is rightly debated.[18]

At the other extreme, if international law is defined as the establishment of a single international community operating under the rule of law, 'then the nineteenth century would be the earliest date (perhaps a trifle optimistically)'.[19] Dominant positivist scholarship has come to imbue the territorial State with the status of primary addressee and law-maker, and international law is presented as a natural by-product of consensual and customary State practice.[20] Viewed from this perspective, international law is conceived as an incredibly recent phenomenon.[21] In the words of Lesaffer:

> historiography has suffered under the modern identification – again stemming from the 19th century – of the law of nations with the sovereign State . . . the scope of the field has been greatly reduced. The law of nations, so it is traditionally held, only emerged after the sovereign State came into being. Therefore its history cannot go back beyond the beginnings of the sovereign State.[22]

The role of nineteenth century scholarship in bolstering this view will be dealt with in subsequent sections of this chapter. In line with Lesaffer, it is argued

14 Frederick H Russell, *The Just War in the Middle Ages* (Cambridge, UK, CUP, 1977) 214, 259–63; Cassese, *International Law* (n 6) 23.

15 Herodotus, *Histories* (440 BC, Aubrey de Sélincourt trans, London, Penguin, 1954) 336.

16 Paulo Fernando de Moraes Farias, 'Silent Trade: Myth and Historical Evidence' (1974) 1 *History in Africa* 9; Stephen C Neff, *Justice Among Nations: A History of International Law* (Cambridge, MA, Harvard University Press, 2014) 36.

17 Martin van Creveld, *The Rise and Decline of the State* (Cambridge, UK, CUP, 1999) 1–58.

18 Steiger (n 12); Martti Koskenniemi, 'International Law and *raison d'état*: Rethinking the Prehistory of International Law' in Benedict Kingsbury and Benjamin Straumann (eds), *The Roman Foundations of the Law of Nations* (Oxford, UK, OUP, 2010) 1–18; Winkel (n 12).

19 Neff, 'A Short History' (n 11) 30.

20 David Kennedy, 'International Law and the Nineteenth Century: History of an Illusion' (1997) 17 *QLR* 99, 113–14.

21 Andrew Clapham, *Brierly's Law of Nations: An Introduction to the Role of International Law in International Relations* (7th edn, Oxford, UK, OUP, 2012) 1.

22 Randall Lesaffer, 'International Law and its History: The Story of an Unrequited Love' in Matthew Craven, Malgosia Fitzmaurice and Maria Vogiatzi (eds), *Time, History and International Law* (The Hague, Netherlands, Martinus Nijhoff, 2007) 30–1.

that the modern territorial State does not necessarily determine the scope of the field of international legal history.[23] Rather, it is in light of the recent dominance of positivist scholarship, coupled with the adoption of a genealogical statist origin story, that the field of enquiry has been limited retrospectively.[24] Indeed, by subjecting the factual basis of the dominant school's claims regarding the relationship between the State and international law to critical examination, the validity of its historiographical/sociological line of argumentation may be called into question, along with the centrality, certainty and historical prestige with which the State is traditionally regarded.

This study argues that the strict State-centrism that emerged during the late nineteenth century sought to exaggerate the deep historical and social significance of the State as justification for its method.[25] Today's mainstream scholarship itself continues to utilise a linear narrative of the development of international law, constantly 'reiterat[ing] its own history so as to present the field as a narrative of inevitable progress and modernisation'.[26] As with many historiographical justifications for the origins of contemporary legal phenomena, the dominant approach 'leads to anachronistic interpretations of historical phenomena, clouds historical realities that bear no fruit in our own times, and gives no information about this phenomenon one claims to recognise'.[27] The aim of such approaches is not to understand in context what occurred in a particular period of history, but to selectively highlight the lineage of contemporary ideas in the distant past in order to instil greater certainty. The following sub-sections provide the necessary contextual groundwork for the arguments developed in later chapters of this study and, at the same time, highlight the subjective reading of historical events that are regularly ascribed significance in mainstream scholarship. In doing so, they reveal that the certainty with which the dominant positivist tradition has situated itself in social and scholarly history is not beyond dispute. Rather, it is submitted that it is vital for scholars to remain both cognisant of competing histories outside dominant historical narratives and cautious of overreliance on subjective historical interpretations as the justification for their contemporary methodological claims.

2.1.1 The significance of Grotian scholarship

Contrary to the statist narrative, international legal principles rooted in naturalism are visible prior to the firm establishment of the modern territorial

23 Ibid.
24 Randall Lesaffer, 'The Classical Law of Nations (1500–1800)' in Alexander Orakhelashvili (ed), *Research Handbook on the Theory and History of International law* (Cheltenham, UK, Edward Elgar, 2011) 409.
25 Randall Lesaffer, 'The Grotian Tradition Revisited: Change and Continuity in the History of International Law' (2002) 73 *Brit YB Int'l L* 103, 109.
26 Deborah Cass, 'Navigating the Newstream: Recent Critical Scholarship in International Law' (1996) 65 *Nord J Int'l L* 341, 354; Kennedy, 'History of an Illusion' (n 20) 101.
27 Lesaffer, 'International Law and its History' (n 22).

State system.[28] Neff emphasises the overarching cultural and religious commonalities that enabled standardised practices to emerge across areas of ancient Eurasia and served as a basis for nascent forms of international law.[29] As major religions spread and became more universal, broad-based systems of ordering became possible, and principles of universal justice began to emerge. These natural rules, advanced by scholars such as Aristotle[30] and Cicero, 'spread through the whole human community, unchanging and eternal'.[31] With the gradual permeation and eventual demise of the Roman Empire and Christian Church,[32] natural law concepts took hold in medieval Europe.[33] A long-standing distinction in natural law was made by scholars of this period between *jus naturale* and *jus gentium*.[34] The former was regarded as a body of law that was truly universal in the natural world, whereas the latter was considered a sub-category of law comprised of 'universal customs of purely human creation . . . a sort of supplement to natural law properly speaking'.[35] Thus, *jus gentium* was a universal law of the human world. Despite the contemporary usage of this term to reflect a *positive* law of nations,[36] its definition has varied widely throughout history.[37] In the Roman period, *jus gentium* 'was more in the nature of an ethical system of universal or trans-cultural scope, setting out general norms of conduct, as opposed to a legal code listing prohibitions.'[38]

It is often claimed that the publication of Grotius's *De jure belli ac pacis libri tres* (1625) signalled the beginnings of international law proper.[39] Grotius is

28 Frederick Pollock, *Essays in the Law* (Macmillan, 1922) 63; Stephen Hall, 'The Persistent Spectre: Natural Law, International Order and the Limits of Legal Positivism' (2001) 12 *EJIL* 269, 269–70.
29 Neff, 'A Short History' (n 11) 31.
30 Aristotle, *Rhetoric* (W Rhys Roberts trans, Oxford, UK, Clarendon Press, 1924) Bk I, Ch 13, 1373b.
31 Cicero, *The Republic* (54 BC) Bk II, 33.
32 Neff, *Justice Among Nations* (n 16) 45.
33 Neff, 'A Short History' (n 11) 31.
34 Kaius Tuori, 'The Reception of Ancient Legal Thought in Early Modern International Law' in Bardo Fassbender and Anne Peters (eds), *The Oxford Handbook of the History of International Law* (Oxford, UK, OUP, 2012) 1018–20; Neff, *Justice Among Nations* (n 16) 63.
35 Neff, 'A Short History' (n 11) 32–3.
36 Gordon Sherman, '*Jus Gentium* and International Law' (1918) 12 *AJIL* 56.
37 Hersch Lauterpacht, 'Private Law Sources and Analogies of International Law' in Elihu Lauterpacht (ed), *International Law: Collected Papers of Hersch Lauterpacht* Vol 2 (Cambridge, UK, CUP, 1975) 189; William Conklin, 'The Myth of Primordialism in Cicero's Theory of Jus Gentium' (2010) 23 *LJIL* 479, 504.
38 Neff, 'A Short History' (n 11) 33.
39 Lassa Oppenheim, *International Law: A Treatise* Vol I (Ronald Roxburgh ed, 3rd edn, London, Longmans, Green, 1920) 101. For a critical view: Giorgio Del Vecchio, 'Grotius and the Foundation of International Law' (1962) 37 *NYU L Rev* 260; Andreas Osiander, 'Sovereignty, International Relations and the Westphalian Myth' (2001) 55 *Int'l Organisation* 251, 261.

credited with the transformation of the concept of *jus gentium* from the mere 'human element' of a broader field of natural law to a distinct, positive 'law of nations'.[40] For Grotius, international law governing the interaction between States comprised two components: 'natural law and the positive law of which the majority or all States have expressly or implicitly established by contract'.[41] As the broad category of natural law applied universally to both States and individuals, Grotius reserved *jus gentium* 'for law established by treaties between States. Thus the term *jus gentium* acquired the new, clearly delimited meaning of positive international law'.[42] This characterisation of *jus gentium* as a positive law of nations arising voluntarily from the will and custom of States is cited as evidence of a shifting theoretical position on the source of international law during a period of increasing European secularisation.[43] The content and validity of the law of nations were not prescribed through divine revelation, as held by the voluntarist natural law tradition, nor was it a logical emanation from nature discoverable by human reason, as held by rationalists.[44] Rather, the law was created by the activity of States and 'received its obligatory force from the will of all nations, or of many nations'.[45] Grotius's affirmation of the application of natural law, even absent the existence or intervention of God in human affairs, is often credited as a precursor to the widespread secularisation of legal thought.[46] However, it has been suggested that, in reality, this merely signalled Grotius's Catholic 'adherence to the rationalist (or intellectualist) tradition of natural law . . . as distinct from voluntarist philosophy, which had been the dominant view of Protestantism'.[47] Indeed, Grotius's naturalism is evident in his reliance on Stoic and Christian traditions synonymous with the period, including the conception of binding norms of justice and morality that were equally valid for all of mankind.[48]

Moreover, the extent to which the Grotian conceptualisation of *jus gentium* can be said to underscore the development of contemporary international law

40 Peter Haggenmacher, 'Hugo Grotius' in Fassbender and Peters (n 34) 1098; James Crawford, *Brownlie's Principles of Public International Law* (8th edn, Oxford, UK, OUP, 2012) 7–8; Cassese, *International Law* (n 6) 22–4.

41 Hendrik van Eikema Hommes, 'Grotius on Natural and International Law' (1983) 30 *NILR* 61, 62.

42 Ibid.

43 Mark Somos, *Secularisation and the Leiden Circle* (Leiden, Netherlands, Brill, 2011) 390–1.

44 Jerome Schneewind, *The Invention of Autonomy: A History of Modern Moral Philosophy* (Cambridge, UK, CUP, 1997) 9–10.

45 Hugo Grotius, *De jure belli ac pacis libri tres* Vol 2 (first published 1625, Francis W Kelsey trans, Oxford, UK, Clarendon Press, 1925) Bk I, 44; Vladimir Ðuro Degan, *Developments in International Law: Sources of International Law* (The Hague, Netherlands, Martinus Nijhoff, 1997) 27–8.

46 Hommes (n 41) 9.

47 Neff, 'A Short History' (n 11) 34.

48 Thomas Mautner, 'Grotius and the Sceptics' (2005) 66 *J Hist Ideas* 577, 578.

is disputed.[49] It has been suggested that the 'voluntary' creation of laws by States that Grotius espoused was not identical to the fully-fledged positivist tradition that would later achieve dominance in the nineteenth century. Rather, the term had been applied 'hesitantly, almost apologetically, in cases in which, for various reasons, the natural law could not readily be applied'.[50] Indeed, it has been argued that Grotius's scholarship rests entirely on deductions from natural law.[51] Crawford has suggested that, for Grotius, 'the State, like the men who compose it, was automatically bound by the law of nations which was practically identical to the law of nature'.[52] Similarly, for Knight, *jus gentium* is 'rarely to be found . . . apart or even distinguishable from natural law, and is, apparently, nothing but natural law itself in one of its aspects'.[53] Although such views arguably oversimplify the Grotian conception, it is clear that his scholarship and much of what preceded it was strongly underscored by a methodological dualism, diminishing the landmark significance with which it is often treated in dominant positivist discourse.

The reduction of the origins of positive international law to the Grotian characterisation of *jus gentium* also ignores expressions of a nascent appreciation of customary law in scholarship that preceded,[54] including Vitoria[55] and Suarez.[56] Yet, even for Gentili, taken to have made 'the first step towards making international law what it is, namely, almost exclusively positivist, international law still appears to be based on natural reason and derived from a law of nature superior to nations'.[57] In line with the above critique of the perceived continuity of international legal doctrine from antiquity through to the modern age, Koskenniemi is highly critical of any such assertions prior to 1870.[58] Indeed, Koskenniemi cites Gentili's scholarship as one of many 'mythical

49 Kinji Akashi, *Cornelius Van Bynkershoek: His Role in the History of International Law* (The Hague, Netherlands, Martinus Nijhoff, 1998) 139–45; Peter Haggenmacher (n 40) 1099.

50 Neff, 'A Short History' (n 11) 39.

51 CG Roelofsen, 'Some Remarks on the "Sources" of the Grotian System of International Law' (1983) 30 *NILR* 73, 76.

52 James Crawford, *The Creation of States in International Law* (Oxford, UK, OUP, 2007) 6; Oppenheim, *International Law* (n 39); Thomas Hobbes, *De Cive* (first published 1642, Richard Tuck and Michael Silverthorne eds, Cambridge, UK, CUP, 1998) 32–3; Samuel Pufenforf, *De Jure Nature et Gentium Libri Octo* (1729) Bk II, Ch 3, 150.

53 William Stanley McBean Knight, *The Life and Works of Hugo Grotius* (No 4, Grotius Society, London, Sweet & Maxwell, 1925) 213.

54 James Brown Scott, *The Catholic Conception of International Law* (first published 1934, Clark, NJ, The Lawbook Exchange, 2007) 483.

55 Fransisco De Vitoria, *De Potesate Civili* (1528); Anghie (n 1) 13.

56 Francisco Suarez, *De Legibus, ac Deo Legislatore* (GL Williams trans, Oxford, UK, Clarendon Press, 1944) 348–9.

57 Leo Gross, 'The Peace of Westphalia 1648–1948' (1948) 42 *AJIL* 20, 34; Jeremy Waldron, 'Jus Gentium: A Defence of Gentili's Equation of the Law of Nations and the Law of Nature' in Kingsbury and Straumann (n 18) 283–97.

58 Martti Koskenniemi, 'International Law and *raison d'état*' (n 18) 297–8.

origins of modern international law'.[59] Additionally, on the evolving definition of *jus gentium*, he suggests that, '[w]hat began with Grotius . . . not only did *not* amount to anything resembling a legal system between nations, it was part of a late-humanist attack on the idea that such a system was embedded and discoverable in Roman Law.'[60] Similarly for Kennedy, it is tendentious to speak of the scholarship of Vitoria, Suarez, Gentili and Grotius as precursors:[61]

> The tone, method and doctrinal argument of these texts suggest that early scholars addressed international legal problems similar to those treated by later scholars, but in a fashion so dissimilar from later work that historians who focus on the role as 'founders' of modern international law distort their texts' opposition to modernity.[62]

Though it may constitute a 'strong tonic for disciplinary doubts',[63] this form of historical interpretation and emphasis is essentially subjective.[64] Although indisputably influential, the scholarship of Grotius and his contemporaries was not strictly limited to the establishment of positive international legal rules by territorial States and does not signal such clear-cut doctrinal shifts.

2.1.2 The peace of Westphalia and territoriality

It is often claimed that the conclusion of the Westphalian Peace Treaties in 1648 was largely a consequence of European secularisation and was fundamental in shaping the positivist vision of a State-centric international legal system.[65] The event marked the end of the Thirty Years' War, 'settling a system of territorial authority over religious questions . . . [and] came to be remembered as the legal inauguration of the "State system", and the beginning

---

59 Ibid. 297.
60 Ibid. 324.
61 David Kennedy, 'A New Stream of International Law Scholarship' (1988) 7 *Wis Int'l LJ* 1, 13–14.
62 Ibid. 16.
63 Ibid. 15.
64 Outi Korhonen, *International Law Situated: An Analysis of the Lawyer's Stance towards Culture, History and Community* (London, Kluwer Law International, 2000) 129–30; Olga Butkevych, 'History of Ancient International Law: Challenges and Prospects' (2003) 5 *J Hist Int'l L*, 189; Jean d'Aspremont, *Formalism and the Sources of International Law: A Theory of the Ascertainment of Legal Rules* (Oxford, UK, OUP, 2012) 39.
65 Henry Wagner Halleck, *Halleck's International Law* Vol 1 (G Sherston Baker ed, 2nd edn, London, Kegan Paul, 1878) 12–14; Oppenheim, *International Law* (n 39) 65; James Leslie Brierly, *The Law of Nations* (first published 1928, 6th edn, Oxford, UK, Clarendon Press, 1963) 5–6; Antonio Cassese, 'States: Rise and Fall of the Primary Subjects of the International Community' in Fassbender and Peters (n 34) 50; Christoph Stumpf, *The Grotian Theology of International Law: Hugo Grotius and the Moral Foundations of International Relations* (Berlin, De Gruyter, 2006) 2.

of international law'.[66] In addition, it led to the international recognition of the Protestant religion by establishing equality between Protestant and Catholic States[67] and legitimised the existence of States based on Calvinist or Lutheran faith.[68] It also conferred an increased status on a plurality of newly independent territories, formerly subsumed within the Holy Roman Empire, largely eliminating the superior authority once held by the Church.[69]

However, the significance of the Peace of Westphalia in the dominant historiographical narrative of international law has been disputed.[70] Contrary to the view that 1648 constituted the birth of the European order of modern States, it has been suggested that:

> the struggle for sovereignty had not yet been resolved, the dualism between the Emperor and Princes continued to dominate imperial (and thus European) politics during the decades that followed. The interpretation of the Peace of Westphalia as guaranteeing the Empire's fall may well be coloured with hindsight.[71]

In essence, the Treaties laid down a new constitutional basis for the Holy Roman Empire[72] and dealt largely with internal imperial disputes between the Emperor and estates, and between the estates themselves.[73] Although the Treaty of Osnabrück granted international capacity or sovereignty for the estates, it stipulated that any resulting alliances must be:

> neither against the Emperor nor the Empire, nor the public Peace, nor against this Transaction especially; and that they be made without prejudice in every respect to the Oath whereby every one of them is bound to the Emperor and Empire.[74]

---

66 Kennedy, 'History of an Illusion' (n 20) 112.
67 Gross (n 57) 22.
68 Malcolm Evans, *Religious Liberty and International Law in Europe* (Cambridge, UK, CUP, 2008) 42.
69 Cassese, *International Law* (n 6) 23.
70 Stephen Krasner, 'Westphalia and All That' in Judith Goldstein and Robert Keohane (eds), *Ideas and Beliefs, Institutions, and Political Change* (Ithaca, NY, Cornell University Press, 1993) 235; Stéphhane Beaulac, 'The Westphalian Model in Defining International Law: Challenging the Myth' (2004) 8 *Aust J Leg Hist* 181; Osiander (n 39) 260–87; Marc G Pufong, 'State Obligation, Sovereignty and Theories of International Law' (2001) 29 *Politics & Policy* 478.
71 Janne E Nijman, *The Concept of International Legal Personality: An Inquiry into the History and Theory of International Law* (The Hague, Netherlands, TMC Asser Press, 2004) 34.
72 Randall Lesaffer, 'The Grotian Tradition' (n 25) 129.
73 Nijman (n 71).
74 Peace Treaty between the Emperor and Sweden/Osnabrück, Article VIII(1) in Wilhelm Georg Grewe (ed), *Fontes Historiae Iuris Gentium: Sources Relating to the History of the Law of Nations* Vol 2 (Berlin, De Gruyter, 1988) 194.

Clearly, the transition to territorial autonomy was far less clear-cut.

However, the significance of the Westphalian Peace Treaties continued to be emphasised throughout the twentieth century.[75] An explicit example is the suggestion that the principle of religious equality established by the Treaties created a far-reaching precedent apparent even in the preamble of the United Nations (UN) Charter.[76] The same has been said of the guarantee of peace.[77] These considerations led Gross to conclude that:

> it can hardly be denied that the Peace of Westphalia marked an epoch in the evolution of international law. It undoubtedly promoted the laicisation of international law by divorcing it from any particular religious background and the extension of its scope to include, on a footing of equality, republican and monarchical States.[78]

In an overtly critical article, Osiander suggests that the prevalence of the Westphalian myth derives from the emphasis it received in the nineteenth and twentieth centuries and 'has been further distorted through the probable intermediation of Leo Gross . . . his commentary on the settlement . . . [having] gained near-canonical acceptance'.[79] Kennedy's critical account of the narrative strategy adopted in early-twentieth century historical accounts of international law echoes this sentiment:

> In their more generous moods, historians find analogies in pre-1648 works for contemporary doctrines or theoretical positions . . . We find pre-1700 anticipations of the League of Nations, of the debate between naturalism and positivism . . . Each of these readings reaffirms the centrality, even the inevitability of the project and method of later international legal scholarship.[80]

In line with this critical view, it is submitted that the emphasis placed on the Peace of Westphalia constitutes the continued restatement of a persistent myth.[81] The empirically observable, historical emergence of the modern State

---

75 Richard A Falk, *Law in an Emerging Global Village: A Post-Westphalian Perspective* (New York, Transnational, 1998) 4; Cassese, *International Law* (n 6) 22–24; James Crawford, *Brownlie's Principles* (n 40).

76 Gross (n 57) 24; cf Charter of the United Nations (26 June 1945) 1 UNTS XVI, Article 1(2) (hereafter, UN Charter).

77 Ibid. 25.

78 Ibid. 26.

79 Osiander (n 39) 268; Peter Stirk, 'The Westphalian Model and Sovereign Equality' (2012) 38 *Rev Int'l Stud* 641.

80 Kennedy, 'A New Stream' (n 61) 14–15.

81 Beaulac, 'The Westphalian Model' (n 70) 185–6; Lesaffer, 'International Law and its History' (n 22) 40.

parallel to the establishment of the international legal order is thereby disputed, and the strength of dominant positivist scholarship's reliance on historiographical justifications is doubted. Moreover, the inability of the statist conception of the international legal order to which the Westphalian myth gives rise to respond to the proliferation of non-State actors is of major concern.[82]

2.1.3 The domination of Vattelian legal positivism

A third element cited as underpinning the State-centric conception of international law is the dominance achieved by the positivist school during the eighteenth century. This factor pervades in the enlightenment narrative adopted by jurists of the late nineteenth and early twentieth centuries.[83] Particular significance is often placed on the scholarship of the Swiss philosopher and diplomat Emmerich de Vattel,[84] and, as such, his scholarship must be contextualised. Whereas Vattel's precursors emphasised the complex, dualistic quality of international law, his recourse to natural law principles, although still evident, was distinct and far less frequent.[85] Vattel's widely circulated[86] treatise *The Law of Nations* (1758)[87] explicitly defined international law as 'the science which teaches the rights subsisting between nations or States, and the obligations correspondent to those rights'.[88] He defined nations/States as:[89]

> societies of men unified together for the purpose of promoting mutual safety and advantage by joint efforts of their combined strength. Such a society has her affairs and her interests; she deliberates and takes resolutions in common; thus becoming a moral person who professes an understanding and will particular to herself, and is susceptible of obligations and rights.[90]

---

82 A Claire Cutler, 'Critical Reflections on the Westphalian Assumptions of International Law and Organisation: A Crisis of Legitimacy' (2001) 27 *Rev Int'l Stud* 133.

83 Kennedy, 'A New Stream' (n 61) 19–26.

84 Matthew Craven, 'Statehood, Self-Determination and Recognition' in Malcolm Evans (ed), *International Law* (3rd edn, Oxford, UK, OUP, 2010) 211; Crawford, *Brownlie's Principles* (n 40) 12; Alexander Orakhelashvili, 'The Origins of Consensual Positivism – Pufendorf, Wolff, and Vattel' in Orakhelashvili (n 24) 93–4; Rafael Domingo, 'Gaius, Vattel, and the New Global Law Paradigm' (2011) 22 *EJIL* 627; Roland Portmann, *Legal Personality in International Law* (Cambridge, UK, CUP, 2010) 31.

85 Stéphane Beaulac, 'Emer de Vattel and the Externalisation of Sovereignty' (2003) 5 *J Hist Int'l L* 237, 268–9.

86 Arthur Nussbaum, *A Concise History of the Law of Nations* (Macmillan, 1954) 161.

87 Emmerich de Vattel, *The Law of Nations: Or, Principles of the Law of Nature Applied to the Conduct and Affairs of Nations and Sovereigns* (1758).

88 Ibid. §3.

89 Vattel used these terms interchangeably: ibid §1; Philip Allott, *Health of Nations: Society and Law Beyond the State* (Cambridge, UK, CUP, 2002) 58.

90 Vattel, *The Law of Nations* (n 87) §§1–2.

Thus, for Vattel, the State was a voluntary, contractual relationship between individuals, giving rise to a sovereign entity with a distinctive personality and separate will.[91]

Although Vattel did make recourse to natural law principles, he excised Christian morality and utopian ideals, refusing to generalise the application of natural law and confining the role of natural law to ensuring the freedom of States to 'do anything that dovetails with their self-interests'.[92] For Vattel, there are three forms of human-made international law.[93] Two such types, conventional and customary international law, are familiar to most. However, the third exhibits Vattel's limited recourse to natural law. For Vattel, *voluntary law*:

> was presumed to reflect the will of States in order to preserve basic principles of the international community . . . [Vattel] proclaimed a hierarchy of norms in international law, according to which State-made law could not contradict voluntary law or the proper natural law of principles.[94]

Positive law remained constrained to the principles fundamental to the international community. Koskenniemi denies the value of the narrative emphasising the linear progression from Vattel to contemporary international legal scholarship, suggesting that it 'reduces the field . . . and fails to account for the external pressures to which the doctrines of those men sought to provide responses'.[95] Yet, Philip Allott insists that the central failings of contemporary international law stem directly from Vattelian scholarship,[96] suggesting that Vattel's reworking of Christian von Wolff's *Jus Gentium Methodo Scientifica Pertractum* (1749)[97] determined the course of history over the next 250 years.[98] For Allott, it was Vattel:

> who made the myth of the state of nature into the metaphysics of a law of nations . . . And the reified abstractions inhabiting the international state of nature are not fictions. They are persons . . . These pseudo-persons have what Vattelians call 'international relations', pseudo-psychic conditions of amity and enmity, as petulant and whimsical as the personal relations of medieval monarchs or oriental potentates.[99]

---

91 Ibid. §27; Beaulac, 'Vattel and the Externalisation of Sovereignty' (n 85) 266–9; Portmann (n 84) 36.
92 D'Aspremont, *Formalism* (n 64) 63–4.
93 Vattel, *The Law of Nations* (n 87) §27.
94 Portmann (n 84) 38.
95 Martti Koskenniemi, *The Gentle Civiliser of Nations: The Rise and Fall of International Law 1870–1960* (Cambridge, UK, CUP, 2002) 8.
96 Allott (n 89) 406.
97 Christian von Wolff, *Jus Gentium Methodo Scientifica Pertractum* (1749).
98 Allott (n 89) 406–16.
99 Ibid. 58.

Similar criticisms against the dominant positivist school that adopted Vattel as its precursor have been advanced by the Austrian jurist Hans Kelsen, as will be explored in subsequent chapters.[100] Despite Allott's emphasis on Vattel's influence, he recognises that it was the scholarship of the nineteenth century that finally gave effect to a wholly positivist, State-centric international law.[101] This scholarship consolidated the subsisting genealogical narrative of international law, emphasising the social and historical significance of the State and its primacy in the creation and application of international law. In light of the above discussion, it is suggested that such an approach provides rather weak foundations. The method is almost tautological, in that it justifies the view that States are the principal addressees and creators of international law by limiting the field of enquiry to the positive law of modern States. Its analysis is skewed by subjectivity, seeking only 'to give current ideas or practices roots in the distant past. This kind of historiography sins against the most basic rules of historical methodology, and the results are deplorable'.[102] Yet it is this method that underlies the view that came to achieve prevalence in the nineteenth century, remains prevalent in contemporary scholarship, and must today be subjected to scrutiny in light of its incapacity to respond to the rise of non-State actors. These criticisms notwithstanding, it will later be demonstrated that even the assumption of a socially and historically derived grounding does not preclude the approach from significant practical and theoretical criticism.

2.2 The State as an empirical basis of validity

Thus far, this chapter has examined the historical evolution of the State and its varying role within international legal theory. Rather than pertaining to a consistent, linear pattern of development, punctuated by doctrinal shifts underscored by landmark social and political events, it has been argued that the relationship between the origins of international law and the modern State is far from clear-cut. Advancing the above, this section argues that the subsisting contemporary treatment of the State as a historically rooted, empirical entity – as opposed to an abstract juridical construction – was strongly influenced by far more recent scholarship. It contextualises the emergence of this view and its conceptual groundwork, before evaluating its impact on current perceptions of the international legal system. In many respects, this section lays the foundation for an examination of the feasibility of the ascription of direct international obligations to non-State entities in Chapters 4 and 5. This context is frequently overlooked in recent literature examining non-State actor

---

100 Hans Kelsen, *General Theory of Law and State* (first published 1945, Andres Wedberg trans, Cambridge, MA, Harvard University Press, 1949) 197–8.
101 Allott (n 89) 416.
102 Lesaffer, 'International Law and its History' (n 22) 34.

regulation, and it is submitted that this analysis is vital to the formulation of a robust response to the challenges presented by such entities.

Contemporary scholarship has come to treat the State with certainty, perhaps as a result of the socially and historically significant role it is perceived to have played in the emergence of the discipline. The State is considered an empirically observable fact of social life, fundamentally tied to the creation and application of law. The basis of this view, and perhaps the most vehement exposition on State centrality, is apparent in the work of German and Italian legal scholars during the late-nineteenth and early-twentieth centuries. It was in the wake of the protracted unification process between the diverse principalities and sovereign territories that preceded the solidification of the German and Italian States[103] that such conceptions are thought to have found their footing.[104] Though it is not suggested that international legal scholarship has completely failed to progress beyond such absolutist views, scholarly perceptions of international law have clearly retained certain defining characteristics, including an overall predisposition to the treatment of the State as a factual entity, rather than a juridical construct.[105] Such an approach has had significant impact on extant explanations of the nature of the international legal system.

The legacy of late-nineteenth century scholarship is apparent in the domination of State-centric legal positivism,[106] the resulting theoretical deification of the State,[107] and the elaboration of the law of nations from a strictly European, Christian union, to a universal community of 'civilised' nations.[108] During this period, scholars came to regard the State as being 'firmly connected to a *real* personality of the State or at least a pre-legal, factual *existence* of a State entity'.[109] The emphasis placed on the strong social and historical basis of the State is no more apparent than in the influential work of Hegel. Describing the State as 'the ethical whole, the actualisation of freedom',[110] Hegel emphasised that the true freedom and moral standing of the individual can only be fully realised when subsumed within the State.[111] He charted the historical

---

103 John Breuilly, *The Formation of the First German Nation-State: 1800–1871* (Macmillan, 1996); Lucy Riall, *The Italian Risorgimento – State, Society and National Unification* (Oxford, UK, Routledge, 1999).
104 Portmann (n 84) 52.
105 Kelsen, *General Theory of Law and State* (n 100) 189.
106 Allott (n 89) 415–16.
107 Georg Wilhelm Friedrich Hegel, *Philosophy of Right* (1821) §258.
108 Nijman (n 71) 114.
109 Reut Yael Paz, *A Gateway Between a Distant God and a Cruel World: The Contribution of Jewish German-Speaking Scholars to International Law* (The Hague, Netherlands, Martinus Nijhoff, 2012) 144–5; Janne E Nijmann, 'Non-State Actors and the International Rule of Law: Revisiting the Realist Theory of International Legal Personality' in Cedric Ryngaert and Math Noortmann (eds), *Non-State Actor Dynamics in International Law: From Law-Takers to Law-Makers* (Aldershot, UK, Ashgate, 2010) 110.
110 Hegel (n 107).
111 Ibid. §328.

evolution of the State from its origins as clan and family connections to 'the realisation of the Idea in the form of the nation'.[112] For Hegel, the individual may only find true existence as part of the State. Thus, the State precedes the individual. He dismissed the view that the Holy Roman Empire constituted a State-like federation.[113] Although he recognised that, 'there may be confederations of States, like the Holy Alliance for example . . . these are always relative only and restricted'.[114] Hegel's understanding of the State was 'more factual and historic . . . [he] did not regard a formal contract or constitution as a basis for statehood'.[115]

Hegel's influence is evident in the work of nineteenth century scholars such as Otto von Gierke and Georg Jellinek. These theorists took different approaches to the notion of 'State will', the former framing it in organic terms, as originating from the collective consciousness of individuals,[116] and the latter inorganic, emphasising the will of State organs.[117] Yet both conceptions stress the State's factual, socially and historically grounded existence. In fairly conspicuous Hegelian terms, Gierke's organic view 'regards the State and other associations as social organisms, it posits the existence of composite organisms . . . as above individual organisms'.[118] Thus, Gierke emphasised the 'real and peculiar nature'[119] of the State; he 'considered the State as a real entity with a life and will of its own. He reified the social and legal personality of the State'.[120]

Jellinek wrote in terms of the 'metaphysic of history', finding that the State's power to dominate its population came into existence 'in a factual, historical context . . . separated from other powers only by the fact that it is a particularly well organised and differentiated social union'.[121] Although famous for his synthesis of a two-sided theory of the State (*Zwei-Seiten-Theorie*), which recognised both sociological and juristic (empirical and normative) aspects of the State,[122] he nevertheless felt that:

---

112 Ibid. §349.
113 Heinz HF Eulau, 'Theories of Federalism under the Holy Roman Empire' (1941) 35 *APSR* 643; Peter H Wilson, 'Still a Monstrosity? Some Reflections on Early Modern German Statehood' (2006) 49 *Hist J* 565.
114 Hegel (n 107) §259.
115 Portmann (n 84) 55.
116 Ewart Lewis, 'Organic Tendencies in Medieval Political Thought' (1938) 32 *APSR* 849.
117 Eric Voegelin, *Published Essays 1922–1928* (Columbia, MO, University of Missouri Press, 2003) 71–5.
118 Otto von Gierke, *Das Wesen der Menschlichen Verbände* (1902) 12, cited and translated in Fritz Berolzheimer, *The World's Legal Philosophies* (Clark, NJ, The Lawbook Exchange, 1929) 371.
119 Ibid.
120 Nijman (n 71) 113.
121 Michael Stolleis, *Public Law in Germany 1800–1914* (New York, Berghahn Books, 2001) 442.
122 Koskenniemi, *The Gentle Civiliser of Nations* (n 95) 441–2.

the theoretical basis for the juristic conception of the State is the indisputable natural, historical phenomenon of a people settled within the boundaries of their territories and governed by a ruling class which characterises all communities of mankind that are termed States in learned discourse.[123]

Thus, although he recognised a duality in his scientific description of State theory, these perspectives did 'not determine the object of observation, but rather presumed its (the State's) existence'.[124] The *a priori* presumption of the State's empirical existence was a necessary component of his theoretical approach: 'Jellinek never sought to undermine the traditional presupposition of the German historical view of the State, the historical view not only remains the basis of his approach, he also deepens and strengthens the essentiality of the State'.[125] Indeed, Jellinek emphasised the indicative, pre-legal criteria of power, population and territory (later enshrined by the Montevideo Convention) in which the State was empirically grounded[126] and which carried the capacity to enter into international relations with other States: 'Without the State, one cannot conceive social and/or legal relationships, which only reduces the chances of civilisations' progress'.[127]

Jellinek's theory served as a synthesis of many characteristics of both his contemporaries and influential predecessors.[128] For instance, his recognition of the two-sided nature of States is closely related to the work of Paul Laband, whose technique 'turns out to be a cross between a logical and . . . historical formation of concepts'.[129] Laband's influential treatise on *The State Law of the German Empire*[130] propagated the view that statehood resulted from a historical process, evident in the eventual formation of the German State in 1871.[131] Indeed, the establishment of the Second German Reich prompted an increased emphasis on legal positivism for German law students and led to the promotion of the combination of the positivist method with the historical view of the State as a social fact.[132] Similarly, for Laband's mentor Carl Friedrich von Gerber,

---

123 Georg Jellinek, *Allemeine Staatslehre* (Berlin, Häring, 1905) 21, cited and translated in Jo Eric Kushal Murkens, *From Empire to Union: Conceptions of German Constitutional Law Since 1871* (Oxford, UK, OUP, 2013) 19.
124 Portmann (n 84) 57.
125 Paz (n 109) 148; Jochen von Bernstorff, *The Public International Law Theory of Hans Kelsen* (Cambridge, UK, CUP, 2010) 37.
126 Murkens (n 123) 19.
127 Paz (n 109) 148.
128 Ibid. 147–51.
129 Voegelin (n 117) 71.
130 Paul Laband, *Das Staatsrecht des Deutschen Reiches* (first published 1880, 5th edn, Aalen, Germany, Scientia, 1964).
131 Portmann (n 84) 56.
132 Paz (n 109) 145.

the State constituted a 'moral organism existing as a social fact'.[133] In Gerber's words, the State is not:

> an artificial and mechanical combination of many individual wills, but the ethical total of the self-conscious people. Its existence and nature is not based on an arbitrary determination and premeditated creation, but its natural power . . . The juristic expression of State-power is domination.[134]

The formulation of what is termed the *Gerber–Laband Gesetzespositivismus*, a legal doctrine that combined positivism with the factual, State-centric conception of the international legal system, led to the promotion of the view that law emanated purely from expressions of State will.[135] The *a priori* concepts of 'State', 'State power' and 'State will' were said to precede positive legislation and constitute the possibility of its existence.[136] Thus, the State preceded the law and served as its creator and validator.

This strict positivist method was further developed by Carl Bergbohm, who also recognised that the creation of international law was wholly dependent on the explicit or implicit will of States.[137] Such a view goes some way to explaining the purported role of State will in the formulation of both conventional international law (explicit State will in the form of multilateral treaties) and customary international law (implicit State will arising from widespread State practice and *opinio juris*).[138] As the sole creators and contracting parties in international agreements via treaties, States were regarded as the sole addressees of the international rights and obligations conferred therein. Individuals were seen as entirely subsumed within the State. The role of consent, a recurring theme that is critical to extant explanations for the binding quality of international law, will be explored in further detail below. It will be argued in later chapters that the conception of the State as a factual entity preceding international legal norms has produced lasting consequences, precluding the direct extension of international obligations to non-State actors.[139]

133 Portmann (n 84) 56.
134 Carl Friedrich von Gerber, *Grundüge des Deutschen Staatsrechts* (1880) 19–22, cited and translated in David Lidenfeld, *The Practical Imagination: The German Sciences of State in the Nineteenth Century* (Chicago, IL, University of Chicago Press, 2008) 204.
135 Peter Caldwell, *Popular Sovereignty and the Crisis of German Constitutional Law: The Theory & Practice of Weimar Constitutionalism* (Duke University Press, 1997) 36; Koskenniemi, *The Gentle Civiliser of Nations* (n 95) 186–7.
136 Kaarlo Tuori, *Ratio and Voluntas: The Tension Between Reason and Will in Law* (Aldershot, UK, Ashgate, 2011) 136; Caldwell (n 135).
137 Carl Bergbohm, *Staatsverträge und Gesetze als Quellen des Völkerrechts* (1877) 89; Bernstorff (n 125) 23; Portmann (n 84) 61.
138 Lauri Mälksoo, 'The Science of International Law and the Concept of Politics: The Arguments and Lives of the International Law Professors at the University of Dorpat/The Iur'ev/Tartu 1855–1985' (2005) 75 *Brit YB Int'l L* 383, 425–30.
139 See Chapter 4 at 4.2.

Thus far, the influence of late-nineteenth century German scholarship has been charted. Rather than considering in detail the Italian scholarship of the same period, which reflects broadly similar themes, it is perhaps more illuminating to demonstrate the currency with which such views were reflected in practice throughout the twentieth century.[140] It is submitted that the factual conception of the State remains heavily embedded in relatively recent international practice, not least in the views of the Italian jurist Dionisio Anzilotti. The approach of the Permanent Court of International Justice (PCIJ) in its *Jurisdiction of the Courts of Danzig* Advisory Opinion has been subject to contrasting interpretations.[141] Commentators such as Humphrey Waldock and Hersch Lauterpacht were keen to interpret the opinion as recognising the direct imposition of international rights and obligations on individuals via treaty law.[142] Yet Anzilotti, then President of the PCIJ and one of the drafters of the opinion, expressly regarded it as State-centric in its approach.[143] The case concerned the status of the Free City of Danzig, which, under the Treaty of Versailles, had been ceded by Germany in order to permit Poland access by sea.[144] It was also agreed that the operation of the railways in the Free City were to be administered by Poland.[145] An agreement (*Beamtenabkommen*) was adopted to regulate the entry of Danzig workers into Polish employment.[146] Following the initiation of a number of employment-related disputes with the Polish Railway Administration by former Danzig railway officials, the PCIJ was asked to consider whether the *Beamtenabkommen* applied directly to individual railway officials, as it was only then that the agreement would permit individual actions before the Danzig courts.[147] It was submitted by the Polish government that international treaties created rights and obligations only for State parties and not individuals, in line with the State-centric view discussed above.

Depending on one's perspective, the PCIJ concurred: 'according to a well-established principle of international law, the *Beamtenabkommen*, being an international agreement, cannot, as such, create direct rights and obligations

---

140 Portmann (n 84) 49–50.

141 *Jurisdiction of the Courts of Danzig* (1928) PCIJ (ser. B) No 15 (hereafter *Danzig*).

142 Humphrey Waldock, 'Third Report on the Law of Treaties' (1964) Yearbook of the International Law Commission Vol II, UN Doc A/CN.4/167 and Add.1–3, 46; Hersch Lauterpacht, *The Development of International Law by the Permanent Court of International Justice* (London, Longmans, Green, 1934) 50–3; Hersch Lauterpacht, *The Development of International Law by the International Court* (Cambridge, UK, CUP, 1982) 173.

143 Dionisio Anzilotti, *Cours de droit international* (Paris, Librarie de Recueil Sirey, 1929) 407–8; Kate Parlett, *The Individual in the International Legal System: Continuity and Change in International Law* (Cambridge, UK, CUP, 2011) 18.

144 Treaty of Versailles (28 June 1919) British and Foreign State Papers (1919) Vol CXIII (HM Stationery Office, 1922) Article 102.

145 Ibid. Article 104(3).

146 The *Beamtenabkommen*, reproduced in *Danzig* (n 141) Annex 2, 37–43.

147 Ole Spiermann, *International Legal Argument in the Permanent Court of International Justice* (Cambridge, UK, CUP, 2005) 170.

for private individuals'.[148] However, the Court did not stop there. It proceeded to acknowledge that it could not be disputed that the object of the treaty, according to the intention of the parties, implied the adoption of 'some definite rules creating individual rights and obligations and enforceable by the national courts'.[149] The views of Lauterpacht and others, keen to emphasise the capacity of individuals to bear international rights and duties, have been mentioned above.[150] However, it has been suggested that the more convincing view is that put forward by Anzilotti.[151] Anzilotti's approach is essentially dualist:[152] States bear the international obligations under treaty law, and the individual comes to possess rights and duties at the national level, as the State may be required to give effect to the treaty's provisions domestically.[153] Equally, it has been suggested that this perspective exhibits a 'wilful blindness', as the treaty had not, in fact, been incorporated into domestic law.[154] A similar view by Anzilotti is also apparent in the *Mavrommatis Palestine Concessions* opinion, which held that the exercise of diplomatic protection invokes the exercise of rights *held by a State*, rather than a State's *enforcement* of a right held directly by an individual.[155]

Today, the direct enforcement of certain international obligations against individuals such as those established under the international criminal law regime is no longer contentious. It is not suggested that contemporary international law has entirely failed to move beyond the statist view espoused by Jellinek, Laband and Gerber. Rather, it is the overall conception of the State as a social and historical fact – as an empirical entity that precedes the law and operates as primary addressee and law-maker – that has remained and continues to preclude the direct regulation of non-State entities.

> When Triepel, Anzilotti and Oppenheim postulate . . . that the international community consists only of States and that there is no entity above the State level, this can be understood as viewing the State as a historical fact, being the highest social institution . . . Statehood was conceived as a social fact from which legal analysis departed; it was not a legal question whether a State existed or not.[156]

---

148 *Danzig* (n 141) 17.
149 Ibid. 17–18.
150 Markos Karavias, *Corporate Obligations under International Law* (Oxford, UK, OUP, 2013) 10.
151 Portmann (n 84) 70.
152 Giorgio Gaja, 'Positivism and Dualism in Dionisio Anzilotti' (1992) 3 *EJIL* 123; Karavias (n 150) 10.
153 Parlett (n 143) 23.
154 Ibid. 24–9.
155 *Mavrommatis Palestine Concessions (Greece v UK)* (1924) PCIJ (ser. A) No 2, 12.
156 Portmann (n 84) 59.

Keen to promote a strictly State-centric approach, Anzilotti viewed the State as the principal subject of international law, an entity that precedes and participates in its creation,[157] as famously reflected in the *Lotus* opinion of the PCIJ in which he participated: 'the rules of law binding upon States therefore emanate from their own free will as expressed in conventions or by usages generally accepted as expressing principles of law'.[158]

Recourse to this view is also demonstrable more recently. Erich Kaufmann, a legal advisor to the Federal Republic of Germany in the 1950s and member of the *Institute de droit international*, considered the view that international law was superior to the State[159] to be 'unhistorical moral nihilism . . . [He] expounded a theory of the total State as Europe's historical and spiritual reality'.[160] The State-centric approach is also evident in the practice of the European Court of Justice (ECJ). The manner in which the principle was restated is somewhat paradoxical. In *Van Gend en Loos* (1963),[161] the ECJ declared that Article 12 of the Treaty Establishing the European Economic Community (EEC),[162] which prohibits 'any discrimination on the grounds of nationality', *applied directly* to individuals.[163] The Court held that:

> the Community constitutes a new legal order of international law for the benefit of which States have limited their sovereign rights, albeit within limited fields, and the subjects of which comprise not only Member States but also their nationals.[164]

Thus, whereas regular international treaties 'merely create rights and obligations as between the Contracting Parties', the EEC Treaty represented a constitutional charter directly applicable to individuals within the *separate* legal system of the European Community.[165] As such, the Court had indirectly restated the State-centric view of international law, by choosing to regard the European Community as a legal order distinct from the international sphere.[166]

---

157 Dionisio Anzilotti, *Teoria generate delta responsabilita dello Stato nel diritto internazionale* (1902); Gaja (n 152) 127.

158 *The Case of the SS 'Lotus' (France v Turkey)* (1927) PCIJ (ser. A) No 10, 18.

159 On this view, see Chapter 5 at 5.1.2.2.

160 Erich Kauffmann, *Das Wesen Volkerrechts und die Clausula rebus sie stantibus* (Tübingen, Germany, Mohr, 1911) 146; Koskenniemi, *The Gentle Civiliser of Nations* (n 95) 179.

161 Case 26/62 *Van Gend en Loos v Netherlands Inland Revenue Administration* [1963] ECR 1.

162 Treaty Establishing the European Economic Community (25 March 1957) 298 UNTS 11.

163 *Van Gend en Loos* (n 161) 12.

164 Ibid.

165 Ibid.

166 Portmann (n 84) 70.

Recent academic discourse also reflects the extent to which this view remains embedded. It has been suggested that even the title of James Crawford's influential work *The Creation of States in International Law* attributes to international law 'an excessively grandiose role. States are surely not "created" by international law . . . rather they typically emerge through the spontaneous or organised political action on the part of a community who articulate their common destiny in terms of political independence'.[167] According to this view, the role of international law in the 'creation' of States is 'almost entirely *ex post facto*'.[168] Rather, the factual existence of a State is necessary if it is to satisfy the empirical requirements generally accepted in international law. For Craven, to attribute the creation of States to international law would be analogous to 'the idea of the status of "criminality" being generated through the institutions and structures of criminal law, or of "insanity" through the discipline of psychiatry'.[169] Scholars of this view affirm the *a priori* conception of the State discussed above. It is not international law that *creates* States; rather, it *recognises* them and subsequently confers a legal status.[170]

The foregoing discussion demonstrates the relatively recent dominance of the conception of States as socially and historically constituted entities, the wills of which coalesce to form international rights and obligations binding upon States. This influential approach has produced lasting implications for contemporary conceptions of international law. As Portmann cogently summarises:

> [by] conceiving of the State as a social fact that existed independently of legal provisions, law was regarded as solely emanating from this pre-existing State will. Because the State was viewed as the highest social institution, there was no source of law other than the will of the State. The State preceded law.[171]

It is not disputed that international law has expanded its purview over the course of the last century, to include not only individuals in certain exceptional circumstances, but also international organisations demonstrating proximity to States. These examples will be explored below. Yet the pre-legal manner in which the State is conceived has largely persisted.[172] This factual approach is in stark contrast to the conceptions advanced by Kelsen[173] and Hart,[174] in

---

167 Craven, 'Statehood, Self-Determination and Recognition' (n 84) 218.
168 Ibid.
169 Ibid.
170 Cf Kelsen, *Principles of International Law* (New York, Rinehart, 1952) 206–7.
171 Portmann (n 84) 61.
172 See Section 2.3; Ian Brownlie, *Principles of Public International Law* (7th edn, Oxford, UK, OUP, 2008) 89–90.
173 Kelsen, *General Theory of Law and State* (n 100) 197–8.
174 HLA Hart, *The Concept of Law* (first published 1961, 2nd edn, Oxford, UK, Clarendon Press, 1997) 116–17; d'Aspremont, *Formalism* (n 64) 54.

which 'the legal system precedes the law-making authority ... [L]aw is inevitably the result of a law-making process defined by the law itself'.[175] The utility of such approaches in terms of the direct regulation of non-State entities will be examined in subsequent chapters.[176] Before proceeding to this analysis, it is necessary to contextualise the theoretical effects of the empirical approach on the nature of the international legal system, including the manner in which theorists have come to justify the binding quality of international law in the absence of a central executive body, and its implications for the concept of State sovereignty.

2.3 The effects of State-centric scholarship

In the post-Westphalian era, international law has come to represent a legal order without a centralised authority or executive.[177] Rather, the purpose of international law is to regulate the interactions between equal sovereign entities.[178] States, under the late-nineteenth century characterisation as distinct empirical entities, determine the content of international legal rules of which they themselves are the addressees. This section reviews some of the primary effects of this view on the framing of the international legal system. It begins by examining the notion of sovereignty and the confusion to which it continues to give rise. Attention then turns to the manner in which the dominant school has sought to reconcile the binding quality of international law with this decentralised statist legal order. As will be demonstrated, these preliminary matters, regularly neglected in recent scholarship contemplating non-State actors, are key to fully understanding the practical and theoretical challenges to their direct legal regulation.

The perception of the international legal order as a decentralised system, the rules of which are dictated by its sovereign addressees, has produced manifold effects. It has led to a 'lack of strong universal commitments among States ... [and] to their failure to feel obligated or to consider themselves bound by rules of international law'.[179] As Bodin famously remarked:

> it is the distinguishing mark of the sovereign that he cannot in any way be subject to the commands of another, for it is he who makes law for the subject, abrogates law already made, and amends obsolete law.[180]

---

175 D'Aspremont, *Formalism* (n 64) 53.
176 See Chapter 5.
177 Pufong (n 70) 492; Cassese, *International Law* (n 6) 5–6; Gérard Kreijen, *State Failure, Sovereignty and Effectiveness* (The Hague, Netherlands, Martinus Nijhoff, 2004) 9–11.
178 UN Charter (n 76) Article 2(1); James Crawford, *Brownlie's Principles* (n 40) 447–50.
179 Pufong (n 70) 492.
180 Jean Bodin, *Six Books of the Commonwealth* (first published 1576, MJ Tooley trans, New York, Barnes & Noble, 1967) 28.

As sovereign States are perceived to possess the attributes of autonomy and ultimate supremacy over their territory, attempts to establish a binding system of overarching regulation, detached from Papal supremacy or universal natural law, are problematic.[181] Given the persistence of the doctrine of sovereignty in international legal thought, and its key role in the dominant school's justification for the binding quality of international law, some further contemplation of the term is worthwhile.

The concept of 'sovereignty' has had a troubled and varied history and continues to evade precise definition or consensus.[182] The term derives from the work of Bodin and Hobbes on ideology, which constituted an attempt to justify political acts by reference to abstract, metaphysical ideals.[183] Bodin viewed sovereignty as 'that absolute and perpetual power vested in a commonwealth'.[184] Hobbes's approach varied slightly, in that he related the concept to the earthly supremacy of the head of State and the divine power of God.[185] On this view, it may be suggested that modern political evolution reflected the sacralisation of the State, rather than the secularisation of the sovereign.[186] The approaches of both scholars depart from pre-Westphalian notions of church sovereignty, favouring any reliable State government, whether tyrannical, constitutional or imposed.[187] During the nineteenth century, the emphasis began to shift from the absolute sovereign autonomy of States, as they began to 'forego self-sufficiency and to cooperate internationally to maintain domestic sustainability'.[188] Later still, the drafting of the UN Charter attempted to foster interdependency in the modern international human rights regime, which sought 'to provide a legal basis for objecting to the acts of national sovereigns'.[189] Yet the balancing

---

181 Arnold Brecht, 'Sovereignty' in Hans Speier and Alffed Kahler, *War in Our Time* (London, WW Norton, 1939) 64.

182 Crawford, *The Creation of States* (n 52) 33; Gregory Fox, Georg Nolte, Brad R Roth and Helen Stacy, 'Sovereignty: Essential, Variegated, or Irrelevant' (2005) 99 *ASIL Proc* 387; Stephen D Krassner, 'The Hole in the Whole Sovereignty, Shared Sovereignty and International Law' (2004) 25 *Mich J Int'l L* 1075, 1077.

183 John R Worth, 'Globalisation and the Myth of Absolute National Sovereignty: Reconsidering the "Un-signing" of the Rome Statute and the Legacy of Senator Bricker' (2004) 79 *Ind L Rev*, 245, 258; Jean Bethke Elshtain, 'Sovereign God, Sovereign State, Sovereign Self' (1991) 66 *Notre Dame L Rev* 1355, 1363.

184 Bodin (n 180).

185 Thomas Hobbes, *Leviathan* (first published 1651, Richard Tuck ed, Cambridge, UK, CUP, 1996) 120–1.

186 Paul Kahn, 'The Question of Sovereignty' (2004) 40 *Stan J Int'l L* 259, 268–9; Carl Schmitt, *Political Theology: Four Chapters on the Theory of Sovereignty* (George Schwab trans, Cambridge, MA, MIT Press, 1985) 36–52.

187 Sophie Clavier, 'Contrasting Franco-American Perspectives on Sovereignty' (2008) 14 *Ann Surv Int'l & Comp L* 1, 8.

188 Worth (n 183) 260.

189 Bruce P Frohnen, 'A Problem of Power: The Impact of Modern Sovereignty on the Rule of Law in Comparative and Historical Perspective' (2012) 20 *Transnat'l L & Contemp Probs* 599, 604.

of international obligations with claims relating to national sovereignty and autonomy remains controversial.[190]

Given the increased economic and political interaction between States throughout the twentieth century, scholars have cautioned against the confusion of the concept of sovereignty in international law[191] with the constitutional lawyer's question of supreme domestic competence, the exercise of sovereign rights (which may today be allocated to international organisations) and the *actual* equality of all rights and competences.[192] Indeed, it has been suggested that there are, in fact, three aspects of sovereignty that are neither empirically nor logically related:[193] (1) *international legal sovereignty*, emphasising the territorial independence of a State and permitting a State to enter into any agreement it chooses; (2) *Westphalian* or *Vattelian sovereignty*, emphasising non-interference in the domestic affairs of other States and the right to independently determine systems of government;[194] and (3) *domestic sovereignty*, referring to effective internal governance by a particular State's institutions.[195]

In light of this confusion, Crawford suggests that the approach of the International Court of Justice (ICJ) in its *Reparations* Advisory Opinion reflects the term's most common usage,[196] namely the possession by States of the 'totality of international rights and duties recognised by international law'.[197] Yet, sovereignty is not a right or precondition of statehood; rather, it is an attribute of all States:[198]

> As a legal term, 'sovereignty' refers not to omnipotent authority . . . but to the totality of powers that States may have under international law. By contrast, as a political term its connotations are those of untrammelled authority and power and it is in such discourse that the term can be problematic.[199]

It has been suggested that the concern that the acceptance of international obligations degrades State sovereignty is purely political and has no theoretical

190 Ibid.
191 Crawford, *The Creation of States* (n 52) 34.
192 Milena Sterio, 'A Grotian Moment, Changes in the Legal Theory of Statehood' (2011) 39 *Denv J Int'l L & Pol'y* 209, 220.
193 Krassner (n 182) 1078.
194 Milena Sterio, 'On the Right to External Self-Determination: Selfistans, Secession and the Great Powers Rule' (2010) 19 *Minn J Int'l L*, 137, 153–4.
195 Krassner (n 182) 1077.
196 Crawford, *The Creation of States* (n 52) 33.
197 *Reparation for Injuries Suffered in the Service of the United Nations* (Advisory Opinion) ICJ Reports [1949] 180.
198 Crawford, *The Creation of States* (n 52) 33.
199 Ibid. 34.

legal foundation.[200] The *Heller* judgment corroborates this view. Here, a US court found that the argument favouring absolute sovereignty:

> ignores the distinction between sovereignty, or the legal personhood of the nation, and jurisdiction, or rights and powers of the nation over its inhabitants. It is incontrovertible that nations, even though they are recognised as full members of the international community, must modify their internal affairs as a result of their participation in the international community.[201]

However, the remnants of the historically espoused absolutist view remain visible in the recent conduct of this very State. Despite its general support for the *ad hoc* tribunals in Rwanda and the former Yugoslavia,[202] as well as the Nuremberg and Tokyo tribunals in the aftermath of the Second World War, in May 2002, the US controversially withdrew as a signatory to the Rome Statute of the ICC.[203] This reticence has led some scholars to conclude that, '[t]he movement for global justice has been a struggle against sovereignty'.[204] It has been suggested that the US continues to restate a classical Westphalian approach,[205] in direct contrast to European attitudes in the wake of the establishment of the European Union (EU)[206] and the notion of collective or pooled sovereignty.[207]

Absolute sovereignty has also received greater emphasis in former African colonies comparatively recently,[208] such notions having been built into the

200 Josef L Kunz, *On the Theoretical Basis of the Law of Nations* (Sweet and Maxwell, 1919) 129–30.
201 *Heller v US*, 776 F 2d 92 (3rd Cir 1985) 96–7.
202 Worth (n 183) 257.
203 William Schabas, 'United States Hostility to the International Criminal Court: It's All About the Security Council' (2004) 15 *EJIL* 701, 705; cf Commission on the Responsibility of the Authors of the War and on Enforcement of Penalties, 'Report Presented to the Preliminary Peace Conference, Annex II' (1920) 14 *AJIL* 95, 129.
204 Geoffrey Robertson, *Crimes against Humanity: The Struggle for Global Justice* (London, Penguin, 2006) xxx; Lyn Sellers Bickley, 'US Resistance to the International Criminal Court: Is the Sword Mightier than the Law?' (2000) 14 *Emory Int'l L Rev* 213, 216.
205 Clavier (n 187) 16.
206 Paul Craig, 'The United Kingdom, the European Union, and Sovereignty' in Richard Rawlings, Peter Leyland and Alison Young, *Sovereignty and the Law: Domestic, European and International Perspectives* (Oxford, UK, OUP, 2013) 165–86.
207 Robert O Keohane, 'Ironies of Sovereignty: The European Union and the United States' in Iain Begg, John Peterson and Joseph HH Weiler (eds), *Integration in an Expanding European Union: Reassessing the Fundamentals* (London, Blackwell, 2003) 312; Clavier (n 187) 16.
208 Nii Lante Wallace-Bruce, 'African and International Law – the Emergence of Statehood' (1985) 23 *JMAS* 575; OC Okafor, 'After Martyrdom: International Law, Sub-State Groups, and the Construction of Legitimate Statehood in Africa' (2000) 41 *Harv Int'l LJ* 503.

Charter of the African Union.[209] It is suggested that this is a result of *quasi* or *weak* States having 'few other cards to play'.[210] Frohnen supports this view, noting that sovereignty in Africa is considered a 'sacred notion . . . used to prop up regimes that do not functionally exist (as in Somalia) or that exist only through the repression of minorities'.[211] The political emphasis placed on sovereignty and statehood in the wake of decolonisation has led to various negative consequences visible across the African continent. 'Important international human rights agreements themselves undermine human rights through clawback provisions allowing sovereign States to set their limits.'[212] Such provisions permit, 'in normal circumstances, breach of an obligation for a specified number of public reasons'.[213] This is true of the African Charter on Human and People's Rights, which provides in Article 10(1) that, 'every individual shall have the right to free association provided that he abides by the law'.[214] Thus, some of the rights contained within the Charter are subject to the operation of domestic laws, and, as such, their application may vary between African States. Frohnen continues, '[e]ven nations specifically adopting international charters guaranteeing specific rights may subject such charters to local law, as happens, for example, with regard to women's property rights in Zimbabwe'.[215] The same is true of many Muslim States, which often enter broad reservations subjecting the operation of human rights provisions to the constraints of Sharia law.[216]

The persistent political and legal confusion surrounding the doctrine of sovereignty having been established, discussion now turns to the manner in which international obligations are reconciled. Long-standing questions remain as to the validity or binding quality of international law absent a centralised executive and enforcement mechanism with the capacity to issue punitive sanctions comparable to the domestic setting.[217] Deprived of natural law rules

---

209 Charter of the African Union (25 May 1963) Article 3; Christopher Clapham, 'Degrees of Statehood' (1998) 24 *Rev Int'l Stud* 143, 145.

210 Ibid.

211 Frohnen (n 189) 624.

212 Ibid. 625–6.

213 Rosalyn Higgins, 'Derogations under Human Rights Treaties' in Rosalyn Higgins, *Themes and Theories, Selected Essays, Speeches and Writings in International Law* Vol 1 (Oxford, UK, OUP, 2009) 457–8.

214 African Charter on Human and Peoples' Rights (27 June 1981) CAB/LEG/67/3 rev. 5, 21 ILM 58, Article 10(1); cf Articles 8, 9(2), 12(1) and 13(1).

215 Frohnen (n 189) 625–6; cf *Constitutional Rights Project, Civil Liberties Organisation and Media Rights Agenda v Nigeria*, African Commission on Human and Peoples' Rights, Comm Nos 140/94, 141/94, 145/95 (1999) paras 66–7.

216 Nisrine Abiad, *Sharia, Muslim States and International Human Rights Treaty Obligations: A Comparative Study* (British Institute of International and Comparative Law, 2008) 67–85.

217 John Austin, *The Province of Jurisprudence Determined* (2nd edn, London, John Murray, 1832) 177.

that receive their binding force from the divine, the positivist tradition has addressed this deficit by concluding that:

> obedience to the law is based on the material realm of self-interest or utility . . . if a State consents to a law explicitly through treaties or implicitly through customary practice, then the particular rule is binding on the State . . . Positivists view consent as the basis of international law because in their view, it represents the willingness of States to obey the law as well as the awareness that their interests could be maximised through obedience.[218]

The validity of the law is thus derived from the creators and addressees of those obligations, in a largely contractarian fashion.[219] There are some clear problems with the consent-based position taken by many positivists, including the necessary existence of some prior principle to explain the status that the doctrine of consent has attained.[220] Yet, the influential theorists of the late nineteenth century were keen to emphasise the consensual underpinnings of the international legal order, the importance of State will and the capacity for auto-limitation.[221] Such theoretical devices, although not the exclusive explanations of binding quality, remain frequently cited today.[222]

If States are truly sovereign and autonomous, and thus able to operate without external influence, what is there to prevent States from operating in breach of international law? A related question is whether, through their express or tacit consent to obligations, States forfeit or diminish their sovereignty by submitting to some higher authority, albeit decentralised.[223] These concerns have been rebutted by the jurisprudence of the PCIJ in its *Wimbledon* decision.

> The Court declines to see, in the conclusion of any treaty by which a State undertakes to perform or refrain from performing a particular act, an abandonment of its sovereignty . . . the right of entering into international engagements is an attribute of sovereignty.[224]

Yet, this remains a matter of political concern to many States. Interestingly, despite Henkin's insistence that there is 'no satisfying jurisprudential explanation

---

218 Pufong (n 70) 495; Neff, *Justice among Nations* (n 16) 247–9.
219 Thomas Franck, *Fairness in International Law and Institutions* (Oxford, UK, OUP, 1998) 28.
220 David Armstrong, Theo Farrell and Helene Lambert, *International law and International Relations* (2nd edn, Cambridge, UK, CUP, 2012) 14; Kelsen, *General Theory of Law and State* (n 100) 354.
221 Portmann (n 84) 62.
222 Duncan B Hollis, 'Why State Consent Still Matters – Non-State Actors, Treaties and the Changing Sources of International Law' (2005) 23 *Berkeley J Int'l L* 137.
223 Frohnen (n 189) 602.
224 *Wimbledon* (1923) PCIJ (ser. A) No 1, 25.

as to why a nation cannot totally reject international law',[225] he acknowledges that no State explicitly does so.[226]

Realist critics of the quality of international law have stressed the deficit in the enforceability of its obligations:

> States exist in an overall context of international anarchy that impels them towards ceaseless competition in pursuit of separate interests . . . neither moral nor legal principles will significantly constrain States and cooperation among them will always be limited and short term.[227]

Such scholars argue that the political conditions necessary to make international law effective are entirely absent from society as a result of this competitive self-interest of States and the lack of a coercive authority to enforce State obligations.[228] Hobbes's *Leviathan* famously proclaims that, '[c]ovenants without the sword, are but words, and of no strength to secure a man at all'.[229] Similarly, John Austin classically denied that international law constituted law 'properly so-called', conceiving of laws as commands issued by a sovereign, backed by the 'power to affect others with evil or pain and of forcing them, through fear of that evil, to fashion their conduct to one's wishes'.[230] For Austin, international law did not adhere to this formulation and was enforced purely by moral sanctions.[231]

Rather than seeking evidence of comparable manifestations of 'command and sanction' at the international level in the vein of Hans Kelsen,[232] other scholars have entirely disputed this Austinian framing.[233] For instance, it has been suggested that, '[t]he fact that international rules are invariably treated in practice as being legal in character necessarily becomes the consideration of most importance in determining their true place'.[234] H.L.A. Hart, another eminent positivist, expressly disputes the significance of coercion in all legal norms, suggesting instead that social rules exist without coercion, emanating from the general practice or convergence of group behaviour.[235] Any

225 Louis Henkin, *How Nations Behave: Law and Foreign Policy* (2nd edn, Cambridge, UK, CUP, 1979) 89.
226 Pufong (n 70) 501; ibid 49–68.
227 Armstrong, Farrell and Lambert (n 220) 9.
228 Henkin (n 225) 23–4; Hans Morgenthau, *Politics Among Nations* (New York, McGraw-Hill, 1948) 266.
229 Hobbes (n 185) 117.
230 Austin (n 217) 17–18.
231 Ibid. 146–7.
232 Kelsen, *General Theory of Law and State* (n 100) 328–9; see Chapter 5 at Section 5.1.2.4.
233 Kunz (n 200) 128.
234 William E Hall, *A Treatise on International Law* (A Pearce Higgins ed, 7th edn, Oxford, UK, Clarendon Press, 1917) 16.
235 Hart (n 174) 56–7.

deviations are regarded as faults open to criticism and peer pressure.[236] Thus, obligations:

> may be wholly customary in origin: there may be no centrally organised system of punishments for breach of the rules; the social pressure may take only the form of a general diffused hostile or critical reaction … Conversely, when physical sanctions are prominent or usual among the forms of pressure, even though these are neither closely defined nor administered by officials but are left to the community at large, we shall be inclined to classify the rules as a primitive or rudimentary form of law.[237]

For Hart, the simplistic, reductive definition of law as commands enforced by sanction ignores the guiding and evaluative functions of law.[238]

In his earlier career, Joseph Raz appeared to side with Austin in his categorisation of law as 'normative, institutionalised and … coercive in that obedience to it, and its application, are internally guaranteed, ultimately, by the use of force. Naturally, every theory of legal system must be compatible with an explanation of these features'.[239] In his subsequent work, Raz has moved from this position to emphasise instead the institutionalised, normative character of legal systems. He acknowledges: '[i]t is doubtless controversial to claim that resort to sanctions, though universal and likely to remain so … is not a feature which forms part of our concept of law'.[240] Raz suggests that, although it is logically possible for a legal system to exist without coercive sanctions, it is humanly impossible, in that human nature requires coercive enforcement, where necessary, to prevent societal breakdown. Yet, he posits that it is possible to imagine beings that acknowledge reasons to obey law regardless of sanction.[241] For Raz, even a 'society of angels' would require a legal system to co-ordinate conflicting interests, and courts would still be required to adjudicate 'factual disagreements and disputes about the interpretation of legal transactions and their legal effects'.[242] This ideal society, however, would not require coercive sanction or the use of force: 'despite the undoubted importance of sanctions and the use of force to enforce them in all human legal systems, the sanction-directed attempt to explain the normativity of the law leads to a dead end'.[243] In essence, Raz is suggesting that, although human societies may

236 Ibid.
237 Ibid. 86.
238 Ibid. 40.
239 Joseph Raz, *The Concept of a Legal System – An Introduction to the Theory of Legal System* (2nd edn, Oxford, UK, Clarendon Press, 1980) 3; cf 185–6.
240 Ibid. 158–9.
241 Ibid. 160.
242 Ibid.
243 Ibid. 160–1.

require elements of coercive sanction in order to enforce laws, this component does not form part of law's fundament. Legal systems could still operate effectively in idealised societies without coercive sanction – a more philosophical approach than Hart, perhaps, but nevertheless an attempt to sever coercive sanctions from nature of legal systems, rebutting Austin's critique. Yet clearly, the practical utility of Raz's thought experiment is questionable.

Henkin takes a similar view to Hart and Raz, though he places greater emphasis on the role of the complexity of politics and international relations in shaping how States behave. He suggests that, although much is made of the decentralised structure of the international legal system, factors other than the threat of punitive sanction may induce nations to observe law.[244] Thomas Franck has highlighted the compliance-pull exerted by procedural factors undertaken by States in the process of international law creation.[245] Others have argued that, 'derivative benefits from interdependence and cooperation in the current global economy outweigh the risk of being denied access or being isolated in an assumed state of self-sufficiency or independence'.[246] Thus, many theorists now take the view that coercion alone cannot guarantee compliance. Indeed, factors such as established norms and procedures of international institutions, taken in hand with phenomena such as globalisation and an increased emphasis on international cooperation, appear to play a significant role in encouraging States to comply with international legal obligations, irrespective of their sovereignty concerns.[247]

In a sense, the indeterminacy and confusion that have resulted from the strictly statist conception of international law are best summarised by Koskenniemi, who has highlighted the argumentative, often binary nature of international legal theory. International law is punctuated by polar concepts – sovereignty/obligation, community/society, naturalism/positivism, idealism/realism, rules/processes.[248] The quality of international law is not disputed here. Such a debate is beyond the scope of this work. Rather, the aim of this section is to highlight the consequences of the statist approach, and the fundamental challenges they present. Absent a centralised executive, the process of international law creation and enforcement lies primarily with States. Their sense of obligation and mutual compliance in such a system has been explained in several ways, variously emphasising the role of command and sanction, social/political pressure, the maintenance of diplomatic and trade relations,[249] the doctrine of

244 Henkin (n 225) 49.
245 Franck (n 219) 26; see Chapter 4 at Section 4.2.1.1.
246 Pufong (n 70) 487.
247 Lassa Oppenheim, *The Future of International Law* (Oxford, UK, OUP, 1921) 11; Nijman (n 71) 116–18.
248 Martti Koskenniemi, *From Apology to Utopia: The Structure of International Legal Argument* (Cambridge, UK, CUP, 2006) 59.
249 Jennifer A Zerk, *Multinationals and Corporate Social Responsibility: Limitations and Opportunities in International Law* (Cambridge, UK, CUP, 2006) 65.

pacta sunt servanda,[250] or a combination of these approaches. Yet, for the dominant, State-centric perspective, international law results from the coalescence of the wills of sovereign States, and thus it is primarily State consent that establishes the validity of international rights and obligations. This process is further legitimised by the participation of States, the primary addressees of international rules, in the formation of the conventional and customary laws that purport to bind them.[251] What consequences this view engenders regarding the ascription of direct rights and duties to non-State actors that lack the capacity to formally consent to international obligations and have not participated directly in the formation of international legal rules, will be explored in subsequent chapters.[252] At present, it suffices to highlight the conceptual implications of the influential framing of States as factual entities existing *a priori* to international law, which continues to be restated in contemporary scholarship.

2.4 The fluidity of modern States

In spite of the primacy with which States are often treated, the ascription of a legal definition serving as a complete enumeration of the features of which all States comprise has proven highly problematic.[253] This section examines the characteristics that have commonly served as empirically observable marks of statehood: the distinguishing features that set State entities apart from other societal actors and purportedly justify their centrality in international legal discourse. The standards by which statehood is measured have a clear relationship with the criteria that are indicative of international legal personality (ILP). The impact of this proximity on the recognition of other entities operating internationally will be examined in further detail in the final substantive section of this chapter. The present section demonstrates the fluidity of the concept of 'statehood', which has led to an illogical polarity. At one extreme, failed States exhibiting few features of which modern States are said to comprise continue to be recognised as subjects of international law and as capable of regulating the abuses of powerful non-State entities. At the other, non-State armed groups possessing widespread territorial control and operating as *de facto* governments evade direct regulation. Thus, it will demonstrate that, even if the historical justifications for the State-centric conception of international law are presumed correct, such an approach is incapable of responding to the realities of contemporary international affairs. At a more fundamental level, the challenges

---

250 Hans Wehberg, 'Pacta Sunt Servanda' (1959) 53 *AJIL* 775.
251 Cedric Ryngaert, 'Imposing International Duties on Non-State Actors and the Legitimacy of International Law' in Ryngaert and Noortmann (n 109) 69–89; See Chapter 4 at Section 4.2.
252 See Chapters 4 and 5.
253 Crawford, *The Creation of States* (n 52) 37.

presented by non-State actors serve to highlight the pervasive indeterminacy of even the most basic concepts upon which international law is said to operate, further undermining the practical relevance of the State-centric paradigm.

2.4.1 Defining the State – a brief historical sketch

There are few authoritative sources that offer a workable definition of statehood.[254] Although the concept has been contemplated by Classical and Hellenistic Greek philosophers such as Plato,[255] Aristotle[256] and Polybius,[257] Cicero's formal definition is thought to be the first of its kind.[258] Cicero's conception is relatively abstract: a State consists of 'a union of a large number of men in agreement in respect to what is right and just and associated in the common interest'.[259] On this reading, the State is the property of a 'people' consisting of 'all male adult citizens regardless of property, rank, class, or status . . . Any State consistently violating the principles of natural justice ceases to be a State by definition . . . Every State possesses a government to conduct its day to day affairs'.[260] Many of the criteria that are today identified in positive law as indicative of statehood are outlined in Cicero's definition and are similarly visible in the work of Vitoria.[261] Clear emphasis is placed on independence and governmental infrastructure, and such traits are also apparent in Vattel's classical definition of the State, outlined above.[262] Although the jurist Henry Wheaton generally endorsed this approach, he expressly excluded 'corporations, public or private, created by the State itself, under whose authority they may exist, whatever may be the purposes for which individuals composing such bodies politic may be associated'.[263] He also sought to distinguish the State from 'voluntary associations of robbers or pirates, the outlaws of society', and from an 'unsettled horde of wandering savages', emphasising the importance of the size and habitual obedience of the population, as well as a 'definite territory in order to

---

254 Thomas D Grant, 'Defining Statehood: The Montevideo Convention and its Discontents' (1999) 37 *Colum J Transnat'l L* 413.

255 Plato, *The Republic* (380 BC, Benjamin Jowett trans, New York, Dover, 2000); Raphael Demos, 'Paradoxes in Plato's Doctrine of the Ideal State' (1957) 7 *Classical Q* 164.

256 Aristotle, *Politics* (350 BC, Benjamin Jowett trans, New York, Dover, 2000); Fred Miller Jr, 'The State and the Community in Aristotle's Politics' (1974) 1 *Reason Papers* 61–9.

257 Polybius, *The Histories* (Robin Waterfield trans, Carolyn Dewald ed, Oxford, UK, Oxford World Classics, 2008); Neal Wood, *Cicero's Social and Political Thought* (Berkeley, CA, University of California Press, 1988) 26.

258 Ibid. 126.

259 Cicero (n 31) Bk I, 39.

260 Wood (n 257) 126–8.

261 Fransisco De Vitoria, *De Indis et De Jure Belli Reflectiones* (first published 1532, John Pawley Bate trans, Ernest Nys ed, New York, Oceana, 1963).

262 Vattel, *The Law of Nations* (n 87) §§1–2.

263 Henry Wheaton, *Elements of International Law* (Coleman Phillipson ed, 5th edn, London, Stephens, 1916) 33.

enjoy sovereignty and international personality'.[264] These limitations are particularly interesting in light of the MNEs and non-State armed groups that comprise the focus of this monograph.

More recent attempts to define the State have focused on the practice of the UN.[265] Given the increasing institutionalisation of the international legal system in the aftermath of the Second World War, O'Connell noted that, in contrast to its perceived primacy, 'the State of today, and more certainly the future, is tending to become more subordinate to a new type of legal entity, the international organisation'.[266] Although an intention to codify international law and definitively establish the terms under which legal personality and statehood would arise was expressed by both the League of Nations and the UN, neither was accomplished.[267] The closest they came was a Draft Declaration produced by the International Law Commission (ILC) on the Rights and Duties of States.[268] Though the governments of the United Kingdom (UK) and India suggested that a definition was a prerequisite for the Draft Declaration, it was ultimately decided 'that no useful purpose would be served by an effort to define the term "State" . . . In the Commission's draft, the term "State" is used in the sense commonly accepted in international practice'.[269] The same issue arose during the drafting of the Vienna Convention on the Law of Treaties (VCLT) 1969. An early draft of Article 6 by Special Rapporteur Gerald Fitzmaurice,[270] which had previously included fairly non-contentious criteria for the identification of statehood, was simply reduced to '[e]very State possesses the capacity to conclude treaties'.[271]

Today, the most regularly cited source of the elements of which States comprise remains the aforementioned Montevideo Convention on Rights and Duties of States.[272] The criteria listed in Article 1 include '(a) permanent population; (b) defined territory; (c) government; and (d) capacity to enter into relations with other States'.[273] These factors are usually utilised by adherents to the declaratory theory of statehood, which recognises entities as States on the basis of factual criteria, rather than political recognition by other States, as

264 Ibid. 34.
265 Grant (n 254) 412.
266 Daniel Patrick O'Connell, *International Law* Vol 1 (London, Stevens, 1965) 304.
267 Craven, 'Statehood, Self-Determination and Recognition' (n 84) 219.
268 UNGA Res 375(VI) Draft Declaration on Rights and Duties of States (6 December 1949) Annex, http://legal.un.org/ilc/texts/instruments/english/commentaries/2_1_1949.pdf, accessed 20 April 2016.
269 ILC, 'Report of the International Law Commission on the Work of its First Session' (12 April–9 June 1949) UN Doc A/CN.4/13.
270 Gerald Fitzmaurice, 'Report on the Law of Treaties' (1956) Extract from the Yearbook of the International Law Commission Vol II, UN Doc A/CN.4/101, 107–8.
271 Vienna Convention on the Law of Treaties (23 May 1969) 1155 UNTS 331, Article 6.
272 Grant (n 254) 414; Crawford, *The Creation of States* (n 52) 45.
273 Montevideo Convention (n 5) Article 1.

favoured by constitutive theory.[274] However, these criteria should serve as a basis for further investigation, rather than a complete enumeration of features.[275] Indeed, the 'threshold' of each of these criteria appears to strongly depend on practical circumstances. Craven suggests that the Montevideo terms are:

> either too abstract or too strict. They are too abstract in the sense that to say an entity claiming to be a State needs to be able to declare itself as having people, territory and a form of government is really to say very little . . . it may exclude Wheaton's Private Corporation or his nomadic society, but one may ask what else? And to what end?[276]

The extent to which the indeterminacy of the Montevideo criteria has been bolstered by the proliferation of non-State actors and political sensitivities is the subject of examination in the sub-section below.

2.4.2 *The flexibility of the Montevideo criteria*

The Montevideo criteria are frequently the subject of varying interpretations. Turning first to the 'defined territory' condition, it seems that a reasonably stable political community that is in control of an area is all that is required to meet this threshold.[277] The issue was considered by the ICJ in its *North Sea Continental Shelf* Advisory Opinion:

> The appurtenance of a given area, considered as an entity, in no way governs the precise delimitation of its boundaries, any more than uncertainty as to its boundaries can affect territorial right. There is for instance no rule that the land frontiers of a State must be fully delimited and defined, and often in various places and for long periods they are not.[278]

This point is illustrated in relation to Albania, which received formal recognition as an independent State in May 1913, despite an absence of settled frontiers.[279] Israel was admitted to the UN in 1949, despite continuing conflict over its

---

274 Brownlie (n 172).
275 Ibid. 70.
276 Craven, 'Statehood, Self-Determination and Recognition' (n 84) 220.
277 Stephen Ratner, 'Foreign Occupation and International Territorial Administration: The Challenges of Convergence' (2005) 16 *EJIL* 695.
278 *North Sea Continental Shelf* (Advisory Opinion) ICJ Reports (1969) 31, para 42; *Deutsche Continental Gas-Gesellschaft v Polish State* (1929) 5 Annual Digest of Public International Law, 11, 15.
279 Miranda Vickers, *The Albanians: A Modern History* (London, IB Tauris, 2006) 71. On the delimitation of Albania on the basis of language and other ethnographic criteria: Nicola C Guy, 'Fixing the Frontiers? Ethnography, Power Politics, and the Delimitation of Albania 1912–1914' (2005) 5 *Studies in Ethnicity and Nationalism* 27.

borders,[280] and, more recently, the UN General Assembly has voted in favour of increased status for Palestine, which has been upgraded to a non-member observer State.[281] The case of Palestine offers an example of a situation in which a non-State armed group, as the Palestinian Liberation Organisation was once regarded, may eventually attain greater recognition on the basis of its alignment with the Montevideo criteria.[282]

In North Africa, the frontier between Morocco and the disputed territory of Western Sahara remains unsettled. Prior to the colonisation of the territories by Spain and France, the indigenous communities that populated the region were traditionally nomadic, wandering between Mauritania and Morocco without concern over defined frontiers.[283] Indeed, it is suggested that these indigenous communities present a:

> fascinating platform for questioning the primacy of the principle of territoriality in statist discourse. [The Bilad Shinguitti] did not have a defined territory or fixed population at the time of the Sahara's colonisation . . . It could not even be identified as having a single authority that tribes swore allegiance to or contested taxes against.[284]

During decolonisation, Morocco and Mauritania each asserted a claim to the territory of the Western Sahara, believing that it would not be possible to form a third State fronted by the Popular Front for the Liberation of Saguia el-Hamra and Río de Oro (Polisario) to the satisfaction of the international community.[285] An Advisory Opinion from the ICJ in 1975 devastated these claims.[286] A visiting mission observed overwhelming support for independence and the Polisario Front.[287] The ICJ upheld Western Sahara's right to a referendum and dismissed Moroccan and Mauritanian historical claims to the territory. Following a lengthy conflict, a ceasefire was achieved in 1991 under the promise of implemention of a referendum, though this never took place, and the dispute between Morocco and the Polisario Front continues.[288] It is

---

280 UNSC Official Records (2 December 1948) UN Doc S/PV.383 11.
281 UNGA Res 67/19 'Status of Palestine in the United Nations' (4 December 2012) UN Doc A/RES/67/19.
282 Nicholas Laham, *Crossing the Rubicon: Ronald Reagan and US Policy in the Middle East* (Aldershot, UK, Ashgate, 2004) 84–6.
283 Joshua Castellino, 'Territory and Identity in International Law: The Struggle for Self-Determination in the Western Sahara' (1999) 28 *Millennium J Int'l Stud* 523, 537.
284 Ibid. 534.
285 Castellino (n 283) 537.
286 *Western Sahara* (Advisory Opinion) ICJ Reports [1975].
287 Jacob Mundy, 'The Morocco–Polisario War for Western Sahara, 1975–1991' in Barry Rubin (ed), *Conflict and Insurgency in the Contemporary Middle East* (Oxford, UK, Routledge, 2009) 213.
288 Castellino (n 283) 539–46.

interesting to note the General Court of the European Union's recent affirmation of the standing of the Polisario Front on the basis of its 'moral personality', despite its failure to pronounce on the group's legal personality in international law.[289]

The 'permanent population' criterion may also be illuminated by the situation in Western Sahara. The historical inhabitants of this area were predominantly nomadic, and these populations were more concerned with the acquisition and maintenance of natural resources than adherence to territorial boundaries. As Wallace-Bruce summarises in the African context:

> [o]bviously there must be a people identifying themselves with the territory if it is to be regarded as a State. But it appears not to matter if they, on occasions, transcend territorial frontiers, provided they are socially and politically organised.[290]

Indeed, Brownlie suggests that the population criterion is intended to be used in association with that of defined territory.[291] The apparent co-dependence of these criteria has already been alluded to in the above description of a defined territory as a 'stable political community'. The Vatican City boasts fewer than a thousand non-permanent residents, suggesting that there is no prescribed minimum number of inhabitants.[292] Though the Vatican is quite exceptional, in that it fulfils very few of the criteria referenced in the Montevideo Convention, Crawford suggests that, '[t]he chief peculiarity of the international status of the Vatican City is not its size or population – or the lack of them – but the unique and complex relation between the City itself and its government, the Holy See'.[293]

Further to this point, the 'effective government' criterion is particularly interesting in light of the political influence wielded by non-State armed groups, which may possess greater territorial control than a recognised State government.[294] Areas in which territorial control is particularly fractious may even be termed 'failed States', which feature:

> the collapse of State institutions, especially the police and judiciary, with resulting paralysis of governance, a breakdown of law and order, and

289 Case T-512/12 *Frente Polisario v Council* [2015] (not yet published); Geraldo Vidigal, 'The General Court Judgment in Frente Polisaro v Council and the Protection of Fundamental Rights Abroad', www.ejiltalk.org/13901–2/, accessed 20 April 2016.
290 Wallace-Bruce (n 208) 590.
291 Brownlie (n 172) 71.
292 Crawford, *The Creation of States* (n 52) 223.
293 Ibid.; Guido Acquaviva, 'Subjects of International Law: A Power-based Analysis' (2008) 38 *Vand J Transnat'l L* 345, 353–7.
294 Dawn Steinhoff, 'Talking to the Enemy: State Legitimacy Concerns with Engaging Non-State Armed Groups' (2010) 45 *Tex Int'l LJ* 297, 304; Scott Pegg, *International Society and the de facto State* (Aldershot, UK, Ashgate, 1989) 26.

general banditry and chaos. Not only are the functions of the government suspended, but its assets are destroyed or looted and experienced officials are killed or flee the country.[295]

The collapse of internal infrastructure often results in civil war, rendering the government incapable of representing the State in international affairs. Thus, despite retention by the State of *de jure* authority, it:

> has, for all practical purposes lost the ability to exercise it. A key element in this respect is the fact that there is no body which can commit the State in an effective and legally binding way, for example, by concluding an agreement.[296]

It is already apparent that all of the Montevideo criteria are somewhat interdependent. Without an effective government, the capacity of a State to conclude treaties and other international agreements is significantly compromised, and the breakdown of political, judicial and administrative bodies can result in fragmented internal conflict and territorial disputes. As with the other criteria outlined above, the precise qualities of an 'effective government' are open to debate,[297] particularly in light of globalisation,[298] and there is clear evidence of State recognition before governmental stability has been fully achieved. The States of Rwanda and Burundi resulted from two indigenous African kingdoms, formerly colonised under German East Africa, but later separated in the aftermath of the First World War. The verdict of a UN-supervised referendum favoured a return to the pre-colonial independence of the entities. Though it was initially asserted that the entities should exist as a unified State[299] and did not fulfil the criterion of effective government, opposition eventually prevailed, and independence was granted.[300] As such, the entities were admitted to membership of the UN,[301] even though 'the new

---

295 UNGA, 'Supplement to an Agenda for Peace' (25 January 1995) UN Docs A/50/60 & S/1995/1, 12–13.

296 Daniel Thürer, 'The Failed State and International Law' (1999) 81 *Int'l Rev Red Cross* 731, 733–4.

297 Sterio, 'A Grotian Moment' (n 192) 235; cf DJ Devine, 'Requirements of Statehood Re-examined' (1971) 34 *MLR* 410, 411–412.

298 Sterio, 'A Grotian Moment' (n 192) 230–1.

299 UNGA Res 1605(XV) 'Question of the future of Ruanda–Urundi' (21 April 1961) UN Doc A/RES/1605.

300 UNGA Res 1746(XVI) 'The Future of Ruanda–Urundi (27 June 1962) UN Doc A/RES/1746.

301 UNGA Res 1748(XVN) 'Admission of the Republic of Rwanda to Membership of the United Nations' (18 September 1962) UN Doc A/RES/1748; UNGA Res 1749(XVN) 'Admission of the Kingdom of Burundi to Membership of the United Nations' (18 September 1962) UN Doc A/RES/1749.

governments clearly lacked effective control'.[302] Thus, today, there is some flexibility with regard to the possession of an effective government, particularly as a strict application could conflict with the UN endorsement of the principle of self-determination.[303]

States may also continue in the event of governmental collapse.[304] Once the existence of a State has been established, events such as 'extensive civil strife or breakdown of order through foreign invasion or natural disasters are not considered to affect personality'.[305] Following the independence of the Belgian Congo in 1960, which resulted in fierce political tension between State officials, a financial crisis and separatist movements, Zaire's statehood was not questioned, despite its authority structures being completely ineffective for years.[306] The preferred view appears to differentiate between the *actual exercise* of authority and the *right or title* to do so.[307] In the context of the Congo, prior to 1960:

> Belgium had that right, which it later resigned in favour of the new entity . . . It is to be presumed that a new State granted full formal independence by a former sovereign has the international right to govern its territory – hence the United Nations action in support of that right.[308]

The independence of Finland from the Russian Empire via revolutionary action in 1917 exemplifies the potential for the adoption of a stricter threshold. The issue was raised as to whether the Aaland Islands, a former Swedish territory[309] later resigned to Russian control along with Finland, could exercise self-determination, or whether they now existed within the newly independent territory of Finland.[310] Whether Finland fulfilled the requirements of statehood post-independence needed to be determined. In light of an unstable political infrastructure in Finland, the Commission of Jurists appointed by the League of Nations remarked that it was:

302 Rosalyn Higgins, *Problems and Process: International Law and How We Use It* (Oxford, UK, Clarendon Press, 1994) 40.
303 Wallace-Bruce (n 208) 592; Craven, 'Statehood, Self-Determination and Recognition' (n 84) 226.
304 Chiara Giorgetti, *A Principled Approach to State Failure: International Community Actions in Emergency Situations* (Leiden, Netherlands, Brill, 2010) 61.
305 Brownlie (n 172) 71; Robert Jennings and Arthur Watts (eds), *Oppenheim's International Law* (9th edn, 1992) 122.
306 Wallace-Bruce (n 208) 591.
307 Crawford, *The Creation of States* (n 52) 57–8.
308 Ibid.
309 Birgit Sawyer and Peter Hayes Sawyer, *Medieval Scandinavia: From Conversion to Reformation, Circa 800–1500* (Minneapolis, MN, University of Minnesota Press, 1993) 67–8.
310 Suzanne Lalonde, *Determining Boundaries in a Conflicted World: The Role of Uti Possidetis* (London, McGill-Queen's University Press 2002) 66–78.

difficult to say what exact date the Finnish Republic . . . actually became a definitely constituted sovereign State. This certainly did not take place until the public authorities had become strong enough to assert themselves throughout the territories of the State without the assistance of foreign troops.[311]

Crawford suggests that this strict application of the test 'reflects the requirement of government in a secessionary situation'.[312] In this case, the Commission of Rapporteurs felt that more emphasis should be placed on the Soviet recognition of the Finnish State, and its continued personality.[313] They ultimately held that Finland constituted a State from the moment of its independence, and that the Aaland Islands 'were indubitably included'.[314] A similar finding was made in relation to the Congo.[315] Thus, in cases where recognition is not so apparent, or in the presence of outright opposition to secessionary claims, it appears the test will be more strictly applied.[316] These differing circumstances illuminate the balance that needs to be struck in weighing the generally accepted criteria of statehood with self-determination,[317] a right that is not qualified by the requirement of effective government.[318]

The final element articulated in the Montevideo Convention is that of the capacity to enter into international relations. This criterion is somewhat problematic, in that some scholars have suggested that this capacity is, 'in effect, a consequence rather than a condition of statehood'[319] and 'is not constant but depends on the status and situation of particular States'.[320] Indeed, it may be argued that the requirement essentially constitutes an articulation of the constitutive theory of State recognition,[321] 'a condition of the establishment of formal, optional, and bilateral relations, including diplomatic relations and the conclusion of treaties'.[322] Though *capacity* may exist in the absence of recognition by other States, in order to form such relations in practice, an entity

---

311   *Aaland Islands Question* (1920) League of Nations Official Journal Spec Supp 3, 8–9.
312   Crawford, *The Creation of States* (n 52) 58.
313   *Aaland Islands Question* (On the Merits) (1921) Commission of Rapporteurs, League of Nations Council Document B7 21/68/106, 22.
314   Ibid. 23.
315   Ralph Wilde, *International Territorial Administration: How Trusteeship and the Civilising Mission Never Went Away* (Oxford, UK, OUP, 2010) 130.
316   Crawford, *The Creation of States* (n 52) 60.
317   Brownlie (n 172) 71.
318   Malcolm Shaw, *Title to Territory in Africa: International Legal Issues* (Oxford, UK, OUP, 1986) 157.
319   Ingrid Detter DeLupis, *The International Legal Order* (Aldershot, UK, Ashgate, 1994) 43.
320   Crawford, *The Creation of States* (n 52) 61.
321   Oppenheim, *International Law* (n 39) 135.
322   Brownlie (n 172) 89.

will require recognition from other States.[323] In the case of *Calgar and Others*, it was held that the non-recognition of the Turkish Republic of Northern Cyprus by the international community resulted in the absence of functional independence, and, thus, it could not fulfil the criterion.[324] It is suggested that such reasoning has led to a 'vicious circle because it confuses a condition for statehood with (most likely) a consequence of statehood. It must, therefore, be rejected'.[325]

Grant is also critical of the capacity requirement, noting that, 'the proliferation of "capacity" to entities other than States casts doubt on its inclusion in the definition of statehood'.[326] For example, the capacity to conclude treaties and enter into international relations is also held by international organisations, most notably the UN,[327] and sub-State entities within federations such as the US also possess the ability to enter into agreements.[328] Some national liberation movements (NLMs) have received recognition from the General Assembly and regional international organisations throughout the process of decolonisation[329] and 'are accorded the capacity to conclude binding international agreements with other international legal persons . . . [Their] legal capacity is reflected in the right to participate in the proceedings of the United Nations as observers'.[330] Other groups were considered for inclusion by Special Rapporteur Gerald Fitzmaurice in his report to the ILC on treaty-making status. This early draft of the Articles on the Law of Treaties included 'para-Statal entities recognised as possessing a definite if limited form of international personality, for example,

323 Sterio, 'A Grotian Moment' (n 192) 234; Michael J Kelly, 'Pulling at the Threads of Westphalia: "Involuntary Sovereignty Waiver" – Revolutionary International Legal Theory or Return to Rule by the Great Powers?' (2005) 10 *UCLA J Int'l L & Foreign Aff* 361, 365.

324 *Calgar and Others v Billingham (Inspector of Taxes)* [1996] STC 150 para 182.

325 David Raič, *Statehood and the Law of Self-Determination* (The Hague, Netherlands, Martinus Nijhoff, 2002) 73.

326 Grant (n 254) 435.

327 Vienna Convention on the Law of Treaties between States and International Organisations or Between International Organisations States (21 March 1986) 25 ILM 331, Preamble (not yet in force); *Certain Expenses of the United Nations* (Advisory Opinion) ICJ Reports [1962] 168.

328 Herch Lauterpacht, 'Report on the Law of Treaties' (1953) Extract from the Yearbook of the International Law Commission, Vol II, UN Doc A/CN.4/63, 139; Duncan B Hollis, *The Oxford Guide to Treaties* (Oxford, UK, OUP, 2012) 127–8; Hollis, 'Why State Consent Still Matters' (n 222) 145–55.

329 UNGA Res 3236 (XXIX) 'Question of Palestine' (November 22 1974) UN Doc A/RES/3236; UNGA Res 2918 (XXVII) 'Question of Territories under Portuguese Administration' (14 November 1972) UN Doc A/8889; Official Records of the Diplomatic Conference on the Reaffirmation and Development of International Humanitarian Law Applicable in Armed Conflicts (Geneva 1974–1977), (Library of Congress, 1979) Vol II, 15; Alan Boyle and Christine Chinkin, *The Making of International Law* (Oxford, UK, OUP, 2007) 48–9.

330 Brownlie (n 172) 62.

insurgent communities recognised as having belligerent status – *de facto* authorities in control of specific territories'.[331] These 'other subjects of international law' were ultimately omitted from the version adopted by the ILC in 1969, which favoured instead treaties concluded between States, but the intention to cover insurgents in the drafting process is clear.[332]

It has been suggested that the practice of belligerent and insurgent communities evidences their capacity to enter into legal relations and conclude valid agreements with other international actors.[333] For instance, the preamble to the San José Agreement on Human Rights between El Salvador and the Frente Farabundo Martí para la Liberacíon Nacional (FMLN) explicitly states that, 'the [FMLN] has the capacity and the will and assumes the commitment to respect the inherent attributes of the human person'.[334] This agreement was also signed by the Representative of the Secretary-General, Alvaro de Soto, which, alongside acceptance of UN monitoring initiatives, 'suggests that this would constitute an agreement governed by international law between entities recognised as having the requisite international status to assume rights and obligations under international law'.[335] Similarly, the Lusaka Protocol, which was signed by the President of the Republic of Angola and UNITA, was countersigned by the Special Representative of the Secretary-General in the presence of the representatives of the US, Russia and Portugal.[336] As such, it has been suggested that, 'insurrectionist movements who are parties to an internationalised peace-agreement or have committed themselves in such an agreement have legal obligations under international law'.[337] These matters will be considered in further detail below in the context of ILP, and in subsequent chapters detailing the international regulation of non-State armed groups specifically.[338] For now, it suffices to note the wide range of entities operating internationally that exhibit some capacity to conclude international agreements and enter into international relations.[339] The proliferation of such actors casts further doubt on the usefulness of this criterion as a determinant of statehood.

---

331 Gerald Fitzmaurice, 'Third Report on the Law of Treaties' (1958) Extract from the Yearbook of the International Law Commission Vol II, UN Doc A/CN.4/115, 24.

332 Brownlie (n 172) 63.

333 Andrew Clapham, 'Human Rights Obligations of Non-State Actors in Conflict Situations' (2006) 88 *Int'l Rev Red Cross* 491, 493.

334 UNGA, 'The Situation in Central America' (16 August 1990) UN Doc A/44/971 & S/21541, Annex, 2.

335 Clapham, 'Non-State Actors in Conflict Situations' (n 333).

336 Pieter Kooijmans, 'The Security Council and Non-State Entities as Parties to Conflicts' in Karel Wellens (ed), *International Law: Theory and Practice* (The Hague, Netherlands, Martinus Nijhoff, 1998) 338.

337 Ibid.

338 See Chapter 4 at Section 4.1.

339 Emmanuel Roucounas, 'Non-State Actors: Areas of International Responsibility in Need of Further Exploration' in Maurizio Ragazzi (ed), *International Responsibility Today: Essays in Memory of Oscar Schachter* (Leiden, Netherlands, Brill, 2005) 391–404.

It is evident from the above discussion that the extent to which each of these criteria must be fulfilled in order to indicate statehood varies according to the practical circumstances and the interplay between the individual criteria. The usefulness of each as an empirical determinant of statehood is also disputed. Such criticism is clearly reflected by the American Law Association's Comment to the *(Third) Restatement of Foreign Relations Law*, which recognises that, 'each of these elements may present significant problems in unusual situations'.[340] Yet, surely it is the situations in which statehood is contentious that the Montevideo criteria should most usefully be employed. It seems the exact opposite is true: the criteria merely serve to confirm or deny statehood in the most obvious instances.[341] It is argued here that the Montevideo criteria, the most widely accepted standards against which statehood is judged, are antithetical to their purpose. In spite of the social and historical certainty with which dominant international legal scholarship continues to treat the State, even the definition of this core concept is extremely fluid. There exist no clearly defined, politically neutral, empirical criteria by which a State's factual existence may be measured. This is particularly apparent in light of the rise of non-State actors. Thus, even if the historical prestige of the State and its principal role in the development of international law are presumed, the centrality with which it continues to be treated fails to reflect the realities of international life.

2.5 The restrictive doctrine of ILP

Thus far, discussion has pertained to the primacy accorded to States by dominant positivist scholarship, the manner in which they are purported to have attained this status historically and the effects that such conceptions have had on the way in which international law is applied today. Advancing this analysis, this section demonstrates the mutually dependent nature of statehood and 'subjectivity' in mainstream scholarship. It considers the problematic notion of ILP, which, it is argued, severely restricts the recognition of non-State entities as subjects of international law. This analysis will be supplemented by reference to the peculiarities of the international legal system highlighted above and the potentially legitimising effects of law-making capacity that arise from these novel features. This examination exposes the fragility of the central components of the international legal system and thus questions whether the edifice of State-centrism has been irredeemably eroded, given its failure to serve the contemporary needs of the international community.

It was argued above that the very notion of the 'State' remains ill-defined. Various entities that can barely be said to fulfil the requisite characteristics of statehood are accorded recognition by the UN and other sovereign States,

340 American Law Institute, Restatement (Third) of Foreign Relations Law (1986) §201.
341 Acquaviva (n 293) 349.

whereas insurgent and belligerent communities boasting widespread territorial and governmental control are denied the ascription of such status. This position emphasises that, although the Montevideo criteria are prerequisites, they are not guarantors of statehood. The *subjects doctrine* in international law is fraught with similar problems, many of which clearly stem from the interrelated nature of the two concepts. As Craven suggests, the definition of States has become:

> a vehicle not merely for the purposes of description (providing an analytical framework for understanding the character of international society for the purposes of law) but also for distinguishing between those political communities that might properly be regarded as subjects of international law.[342]

Thus, despite the difficulties encountered in the articulation of the exact features of which States comprise, statehood continues to serve as the litmus test for those entities that are capable of bearing international duties.

The categorisation of different entities as 'subjects' and 'objects' is an attempt to distinguish between social actors that are relevant to international law and those that are excluded from its purview.[343] Lauterpacht has suggested that legal subjects are 'the persons, national and judicial, upon whom the law confers rights and imposes duties ... According to what may be described as the traditional view in the matter, States only and exclusively are the subjects of international law'.[344] Thus, on the traditional view at least, the problematic criteria of statehood also serve as the determinants for those entities that may be described as subjects of international law. Entities other than States are regarded as:

> objects of this system either in the same sense as territory or rivers are objects of the system because there are (State created) legal rules about them, or in the sense that they are beneficiaries under the system, so that treaties ... are seen as only indirectly benefiting individuals.[345]

An early dissatisfaction with this view is visible in the 1895 work of Thomas Joseph Lawrence, who complained that:

> while sovereign States are by far the most important class among the units to which our science applies, there are other communities which come

---

342 Craven, 'Statehood, Self-Determination and Recognition' (n 84) 217.

343 Portmann (n 84) 1.

344 Hersch Lauterpacht, 'The Subjects of International Law' in Andrea Bianchi (ed), *Non-State Actors and International Law – The Library of Essays in International Law* (Aldershot, UK, Ashgate, 2009) 3.

345 Robert McCorquodale, 'Beyond State Sovereignty: The International Legal System and Non-State Participants' (2006) 8 *Int'l L Rev Colomb* 103, 122.

under its rules to a greater or less extent and in some cases, corporations and individuals are subject to it.[346]

Clearly, the situation, even then, was far more complex than the subject/object dichotomy suggests, and the proliferation of expansion of non-State entities operating internationally today has exacerbated the issue.

The traditional view detailed by Lauterpacht is largely evident in Oppenheim's 1920 treatise, though this approach does stretch the strict, State-centric conception slightly, by recognising States *and* the League of Nations as the exclusive subjects of international law. The formation of this view is based on Oppenheim's interpretation of the Law of Nations as 'a law for the intercourse of States with one another, not for individuals'.[347] Thus, he suggests that:

> [s]ince now the Family of Nations has become an organised community under the name of the League of Nations with distinctive international rights and duties of its own, the League of Nations is an international person *sui generis* . . . But apart from the League of Nations, sovereign States exclusively are international persons.[348]

Clapham has described this approach as:

> self-consciously subjective . . . Everything turns on the conception one has of the Law of Nations . . . later editions of the treatise have been amended to take into consideration the role of the United Nations and of individuals. But such amendments beg the question: why do we stop here?[349]

As will later be demonstrated, one's theoretical conception of the purpose and operation of the international legal system will significantly affect one's inclination to accept the inclusion of non-State entities as international legal subjects.[350] As a preliminary point, it is suggested that the *subjects doctrine*, much like the notion of statehood examined above, is steeped in relativity.

'Legal subjects' and 'international legal personality' are terms that are often confusingly entangled.[351] The relationship between these terms is therefore worthy of further consideration. Although many academics appear to treat the terms as essentially synonymous, Klabbers believes that, despite their frequent

---

346 Thomas Lawrence, *The Principles of International Law* (New York, Heath, 1895) 55.
347 Oppenheim, *International Law* (n 39) 2.
348 Ibid. 125.
349 Andrew Clapham, *Human Rights Obligations of Non-State Actors* (Oxford, UK, OUP, 2006) 61.
350 Jean d'Aspremont, 'International Law-Making by Non-State Actors: Changing the Model or Putting the Phenomenon into Perspective' in Ryngaert and Noortmann (n 109) 172.
351 Clapham, *Human Rights Obligations of Non-State Actors* (n 349) 59.

conflation, they are nevertheless distinct.[352] He suggests that, whereas 'subject' is a status bestowed by the academic community in recognition of an entity that falls within the parameters of international legal study, 'international legal personality' is a status conferred by the legal system.[353] It would therefore appear that 'subjectivity' may be a notion dependent upon particular conceptions of the international legal system. It is also evident that the term 'subject' may be favoured in a broader relational context with the term 'object', as hinted at in Lauterpacht's discussion of the term. ILP, on the other hand, suggests the legal recognition of an entity's existence and separate or independent identity under international law: 'ILP is the shield or mask which the law addresses and, behind which an inner life takes place'.[354] Yet, despite his academic distinction between the two terms, Klabbers concedes that there is 'nothing particularly wrong with treating them as [one and the same] in pragmatic fashion'[355] and proceeds to examine essentially identical criteria in relation to both terms.[356] Given that their conflation appears to have little practical effect, both terms will be used interchangeably throughout the remainder of this study.

2.5.1 *The ICJ's approach to the ILP*

At this juncture, it is necessary to consider in detail the indicators of subjectivity that were articulated in the ICJ's *Reparation for Injuries* Advisory Opinion. Although generally considered the most authoritative judicial statement on the issue, the *subjects doctrine* remains elusive. Though the ICJ was able to provide some guidance as to the essential elements of ILP, the Court's rationale in arriving at these criteria is unclear, and the open-ended nature of its judgment breeds significant uncertainty. The Court in *Reparation* sought to determine whether the UN, an international organisation, had been endowed with the requisite characteristics to possess ILP. The case concerned the fallout from the establishment of the State of Israel. The region had subsequently experienced significant political unrest that prompted the UN to send, as a chief negotiator, Count Folke Bernadotte. The Count and his associates were killed during the mission, which in turn raised the question as to whether the UN was entitled to make a claim for reparations against the responsible entity for the damage incurred by the UN and its agents.[357] The ICJ decided to consider the nature of the organisation and the wording of its constituent instrument (the UN Charter) in order to establish whether the institution

---

352 Portmann (n 84) 1; Nijman (n 71) 4.
353 Jan Klabbers, *An Introduction to International Institutional Law* (2nd edn, Cambridge, UK, CUP, 2009) 43–4.
354 Nijman (n 71) 3–4.
355 Klabbers (n 353) 43.
356 Ibid. 45–57.
357 *Reparation* (n 197) 175.

possessed the capacity to bring international claims, or, in other words, possessed ILP.[358] The Court accepted that:

> [t]his is no doubt a doctrinal expression, which has sometimes given rise to controversy. But it will be used here to mean that if the Organisation is recognised as having that personality, it is an entity capable of availing itself of obligations incumbent upon its Members.[359]

Though the UN Charter was silent on the issue, the Court held that the organisation was of a character independent of its members (despite the necessity of their assistance in any action it undertakes) and was politically charged with 'tasks of an important character, and covering a wide field, namely, the maintenance of international peace and security'.[360] As such, the Court opined that the UN:

> was intended . . . and is in fact exercising and enjoying, functions and rights which can only be explained on the basis of the possession of a large measure of international personality and the capacity to operate upon an international plane.[361]

Thus, the ICJ confirmed that it is possible for entities other than States to possess ILP. The UN was considered a direct addressee of international law. The Court's reasoning is relatively open-ended. It clearly permitted the expansion of the *subjects doctrine* on the basis of the requirements of international life,[362] which, it was argued, had already 'given rise to instances upon the international plane by certain entities which are not States'.[363] The Court therefore explicitly holds open the door for reconsideration as international legal norms progress and the needs of the international community develop.[364]

Unfortunately, the Court's justification for this view has proven quite impenetrable. At its most basic level, a subject of international law constitutes 'an entity capable of possessing international rights and duties and having the capacity to maintain its rights by bringing international claims'.[365] This definition is circular and vaguely tautological.[366] It essentially provides that,

---

358 *Reparation* (n 197) 178.
359 Ibid.
360 Ibid. 179.
361 Ibid.
362 Ibid. 178–80; *Legality of the Use by a State of Nuclear Weapons in Armed Conflict* (Advisory Opinion) ICJ Reports [1996] 79 para 25 (hereafter, *Nuclear Weapons*).
363 *Reparation* (n 197) 179.
364 Ibid. 178.
365 Ibid. 179.
366 Brownlie (n 172) 57; Clapham, *Human Rights Obligations of Non-State Actors* (n 349) 64.

'[i]nternational law recognises the capacity to act at an international level of an entity that is already capable of acting at the international level'.[367] It is not clear whether these features are preconditions or consequences of legal personality.[368] In what is likely an attempt to offer a relatively neutral verdict, while at the same time justifying the personality of the UN, all the Court is able to offer as evidence is 'a large measure of international legal personality and the capacity to operate on the international plane'.[369] International personality and capacity to act internationally are presented as preconditions that give rise to the exercise of rights and duties, '[b]ut the Court also said that when it spoke of "international personality", it meant the capacity to have rights and to exercise them!'[370] Thus, these core concepts prove frustratingly nebulous and have resulted in numerous different readings of the judgment.

It is least problematic to demonstrate these approaches in relation to international organisations, which the *Reparation* opinion explicitly addressed. The practice of the ICJ demonstrates that, absent an express provision in the organisation's constituent document detailing its legal personality, other factors will need to be considered.[371] These include factors surrounding the creation of the organisation, and subsequent international practice.[372] Two distinct theories have been utilised to explain the approach in *Reparation*. Amerasinghe notes that the ICJ 'did not hesitate to refer to the intention of the founders of the UN'.[373] This can be said to constitute the first and most popular theory of the legal personality of international organisations. It is an inductive approach: the powers, capacities, rights and duties of an international organisation are implied through the intentions of its founding members.[374] This approach is similarly described by Klabbers as 'will theory', which places emphasis on the will of the organisation's founders and thus conforms to the positivist, consent-based conception of international law.[375]

It is suggested by Amerasinghe that, 'the Court was not referring to some subjective intention in the minds of the founders, but to an objective that was to be found in the circumstances of creation and constitution'.[376] Clearly, this theory proves problematic when the constituent document of the organisation

---

367 Clapham, *Human Rights Obligations of Non-State Actors* (n 349) 48.
368 Fergus Green, 'Fragmentation in Two Dimensions: The ICJ's Flawed Approach to Non-State Actors and International Legal Personality' (2008) 9 *Melb J Int'l L* 47, 55.
369 *Reparation* (n 197) 179.
370 Clapham, *Human Rights Obligations of Non-State Actors* (n 349) 66.
371 Dapo Akande, 'International Organisations' in Evans, *International Law* (n 84) 256.
372 Chittharanjan F Amerasinghe, *Principles of the Institutional Law of International Organisations* (2nd edn, Cambridge, UK, CUP, 2005) 81.
373 Ibid.
374 Manuel Rama-Montaldo, 'International Legal Personality and Implied Powers of International Organisations' (1970) *Brit YB Int'l L* 111, 112.
375 Klabbers (n 353) 53.
376 Amerasinghe (n 372) 81–2.

lacks explicit reference to legal personality, as was the case in *Reparation*. Further, the intentions of the members of the organisation matter very little if no other capable entity is willing to engage with the organisation or provide it recognition.[377] Thus, when the inductive approach or will theory is examined in a practical context, it is evident that there are more factors at play than pure intention. That said, the very fact that international organisations are composed of two or more sovereign States suggests that their members, at the very least, would be willing to engage in international relations with these entities and provide some measure of international recognition. Nevertheless, it has been suggested that the issue of recognition reiterates the conceptual proximity between subjectivity and statehood:

> The 'subject'/'object' dichotomy privileges and reifies the voices of States alone because all potential participants are compared to States and States alone decide the outcome. It is an exclusionary fiction, which silences alternative voices . . . recognition is essentially a group-identification relationship process.[378]

Thus, the central position accorded to States by the dominant conception of international law has left 'subjectivity' to be determined by States alone.[379]

These criticisms lead us to the second view. It is suggested by Seyersted that ILP may be established by the fulfilment of objective factors, comparable to the way in which statehood is determined via the Montevideo criteria.[380] Though Seyersted was the first to articulate these indicators of the legal personality of international organisations,[381] Brownlie's more contemporary version is far easier to follow:

> (1) a permanent association of States with lawful objects, equipped as organs; (2) a distinction, in terms of legal powers and purposes, between the organisation and its member States; (3) the existence of legal powers exercisable on the international plane and not solely within the national systems of one or more States.[382]

Though this approach provides empirical features by which ILP may be determined, it suggests that an organisation could be deemed an international

---

377 Klabbers (n 353) 54.
378 McCorquodale (n 345) 123.
379 Ibid. 122; Hilary Charlesworth and Christine Chinkin, *The Boundaries of International Law: A Feminist Analysis* (Manchester, UK, Manchester University Press, 2000) 142.
380 Finn Seyersted, 'Objective International Personality of Intergovernmental Organisations: Do their Capacities Really Depend on the Conventions Establishing Them?' (1964) 34 *Nordisk Tidsskrift Int'l Ret* 46, 47.
381 Ibid. 48.
382 Brownlie (n 172) 677.

legal person irrespective of the intentions of its founding members. Thus, for Klabbers, the approach 'elevates itself to *jus cogens* status' by overruling the intentions of the founders on the basis of a general principle of law.[383] Instead, a presumptive approach is favoured: when an international organisation acts in such a way as to suggest that it possesses legal personality, it will be presumed to possess this characteristic. This is a line of reasoning clearly evident in the *Reparation* decision,[384] the only drawback being that, 'it tends to make a mockery of the few instances where founders have actually made a provision granting their creation international legal personality'.[385]

Determining which of these approaches the ICJ actually favoured in *Reparation* is challenging. Although the Court, on a number of occasions, emphasised the importance of the parties' intentions in conferring ILP, it did not necessarily favour the inductive or 'will' approach. For Akande, the Court seemed to be saying that, 'the members had ascribed characteristics to the organisation which satisfied the criteria required for conferring ILP. While the key factor is the possession of those characteristics, they necessarily arise out of the will of the members'.[386] On this reading, the line is blurred. It may be argued that the operation of the two theories is not radically different,[387] and a merger or third way may also be possible.[388] A re-reading focusing on the principle of effectiveness has also been proposed.[389] Clapham suggests that legal personality may arise, 'not because the capacity to bring a claim exists, but in order to ensure that the intention of States to confer rights and duties is effective'.[390] But again, it is questionable as to whether this approach is particularly helpful, as it predominantly hinges on the intention of States. Although it is reasonable to expect States to confer separate ILP upon certain international organisations of which they themselves are members in order to ensure effective international relations are maintained, can the same be said for other non-State actors? It would seem unlikely, particularly in light of the economic and political power exercised by the entities upon which later chapters of this monograph focus.

2.5.2 *Extrapolating the ICJ's approach to other non-State actors*

Although the *Reparation* decision went some way towards clarifying the manner in which international organisations may attain ILP, attempts to ascertain how these criteria might be applied to other non-State entities have proven more

---

383   Klabbers (n 353) 55.
384   *Reparation* (n 197) 179.
385   Klabbers (n 353) 56.
386   Akande (n 371) 253.
387   Ibid.
388   Amerasinghe (n 372) 81–91.
389   This approach echoes that taken in *Nuclear Weapons* (n 362) 66 para 19.
390   Clapham, *Human Rights Obligations of Non-State Actors* (n 349) 65.

problematic. It may be argued that the very fact that the membership of international organisations is composed entirely of sovereign States, and that their wills and intentions are reflected in constituent documents or subsequent practice, lends significant legitimacy to the legal personality of these entities.[391] International organisations are, in a sense, only one step removed from States:[392] they are simply organised collectives of States operating with a distinct and independent personality.[393] For powerful economic actors, such as MNEs, and non-State armed groups, which may directly threaten State sovereignty, the ascription and recognition of international personality will be far more contentious.[394]

Though the characteristics of domestic legal personality are variable from State to State and, as such, retain elements of fluidity, there are particular features of the international legal system that make the concept more problematic.[395] Indeed, these peculiarities go some way to explaining the central position accorded to States and the hesitancy in breaking away from the statist conception. First, the very fact that international law lacks a central legislative authority, akin to municipal systems, that can definitively determine the exact features of ILP has led to substantial uncertainty as to even the most central concepts of international law.[396] This position has been considered in detail above and arises from the very nature of international law as a body of law *between*, rather than *above*, sovereign States. The second issue is concomitant and strikes at the heart of the debate surrounding the legal regulation of non-State entities in international law. Not only does ILP denote the capacity of entities to possess rights and obligations, but it is often perceived to carry with it, as a consequence, the competence to create international law.[397]

McCorquodale traces the ties between States, subjectivity and law-making capacity to the dominant positivist tradition, which permitted States alone to determine the subjects of international law and 'led to the interpretation that only a subject of law could be involved in international law-making . . . hence that only States could make international law'.[398] But this is, perhaps, an

---

391 Johan Karlsson Schaffer, 'Legitimacy, Governance and Human Rights' in Andreas Føllesdal, Birgit Peters *et al* (eds), *The Legitimacy of International Human Rights Regimes: Legal, Political and Philosophical Perspectives* (Cambridge, UK, CUP, 2013) 219–20; Allen Buchanan and Robert O Keohane, 'The Legitimacy of Global Governance Institutions' in Rüdiger Wolfrum and Volker Roben (eds), *Legitimacy in International Law* (The Hague, Netherlands, Springer, 2008) 35–40.
392 Cassese, *International Law* (n 6) 135.
393 David J Bederman, 'The Souls of International Organisations: Legal Personality and the Lighthouse at Cape Spartel' (1996) 36 *Va J Int'l L* 275, 324–36.
394 Green (n 368).
395 Klabbers (n 353) 49.
396 Portmann (n 84) 9.
397 Brownlie (n 172) 58–63; ibid 8–9.
398 McCorquodale (n 345).

oversimplification of the issue. As has already been established, it is a more fundamental question of how international law receives its binding quality in a decentralised legal system. The position is justified by the central role performed by consent. International law is considered binding upon States as a result of their express consent to treaty obligations or tacit consent expressed as emanations of State practice and *opinio juris*. In order to be subject to international obligations, that is, in order to be *bound* by international duties, an entity must be able to consent, and perhaps even participate in the formulation of those duties. This is the basis of international obligation, according to the State-centric view established above. As Portmann highlights, although the position occupied by States is not contentious, '[w]hat is disputed is whether this is a necessary attribute of an international person more generally or whether there also can be international persons lacking the competence to create law'.[399] The legitimacy of imposing direct obligations on non-State entities without the ability to formally consent or participate in the international law-making process will be discussed at length in subsequent chapters. It is sufficient at this point to highlight the challenge posed by bringing 'new' international legal persons into the sphere of international regulation, while at the same time according influence, via law-making capacity, to powerful actors potentially operating outside the public interest.

Clearly, the UN possesses several unique characteristics, which the ICJ utilised to further substantiate its opinion. Aside from the special character of its duties,[400] significant emphasis was placed on the 'supreme' nature of the institution.[401] Its connection to the 'vast majority of the members of the international community' was also used to bolster the UN's status as an entity with separate, objective personality.[402] The prominence it accorded to these novel features in making its determination suggests that the Court's approach may be of little help in ascertaining the personality of other international organisations, let alone wholly distinct non-State actors.[403] There are, perhaps, a few generalizable features that can be extrapolated and applied to other entities. Brownlie categorises three main contexts in which the personality of an entity is most frequently considered to have arisen: first, in respect of the capacity to make claims in response to breaches of international law; second, in respect of the capacity to make treaties and agreements valid on the international plane; and finally, in respect of the enjoyment of privileges and immunities from national jurisdictions.[404] Though similar criteria are cited by

399   Portmann (n 84) 9.
400   *Reparation* (n 197) 179.
401   Ibid.
402   Ibid. 185; Crawford, *The Creation of States* (n 52) 30.
403   Green (n 368) 57.
404   Brownlie (n 172) 57.

several scholars,[405] Klabbers finds that the latter condition of privileges and immunities places the yardstick too far in the sphere of statehood,[406] reiterating the long-standing criticism that, although 'any entity can aspire to international personality . . . it will need to look an awful lot like a traditional State in order to meet the requirements'.[407] But, outside these core characteristics, there is simply no further authoritative guidance on the issue.

Moreover, the Court, in *Reparation*, explicitly stated that the rights and obligations ascribed to 'other' subjects of international law will not simply mirror those of States[408] and may vary from subject to subject: '[t]he subjects of law in any legal system are not necessarily identical in their nature or in the extent of their rights, and their nature depends on the needs of the community'.[409] Thus, even if one is able to establish that a non-State actor fits the vague criteria indicative of legal personality, the question remains as to the exact extent of the rights and duties conferred on it.[410] This is an explicit rejection of a one-size-fits-all approach to legal personality. Although this position may, on one level, appear to solve the problematic conferral of parallel law-making capacities on more politically dubious non-State entities, it will later be argued that this position raises insurmountable issues in establishing the binding quality of international obligations for actors that are unable to formally consent to these obligations and have played no part in their formation.[411]

Though there has been some indication as to the rights and obligations of international organisations, they remain ambiguous and further emphasise the proximity of such entities to States. In *Interpretation of the Agreement of March 25 1951 between the WHO and Egypt*,[412] the ICJ opined:

> International organisations are subjects of international law and, as such, are bound by any obligations incumbent upon them under general rules of international law, under their constitutions or under international agreements to which they are parties.[413]

---

405 Ibid.; Cassese, *International Law* (n 6) 138–9; Akande (n 371) 258; Higgins, *Problems and Process* (n 302) 91; August Reinisch, *International Organisations before National Courts* (Cambridge, UK, CUP, 2000) 246–8.
406 Klabbers (n 353) 44 fn 9.
407 Philip Alston, 'The "Not-a-Cat" Syndrome: Can the International Human Rights Regime Accommodate Non-State Actors?' in Philip Alston (ed), *Non-State Actors and Human Rights* (Oxford, UK, OUP, 2005) 20.
408 *Reparation* (n 197) 179.
409 Ibid. 178.
410 Klabbers (n 353) 44.
411 See Chapter 4 at Section 4.2.
412 *Interpretation of the Agreement of March 25 1951 between the WHO and Egypt* (Advisory Opinion) ICJ Reports [1980] 73.
413 Ibid. 89–90.

As such, the Court suggests that, additional to the express powers conferred by treaty and the implied powers that are necessary for the organisation's effective operation, international organisations may also possess rights and duties stemming from established international custom and the general principles of international law.[414] But will this be true of all non-State entities, or only of (certain) international organisations? Green laments that, 'even under the relatively well settled law concerning international organisations, the scope of such customary rights and obligations is far from clear'.[415] In general, academic attention has focused on the capacity of potential subjects to *make claims* rather than to *fulfil obligations*.[416] It has been suggested that the positive obligations placed on international organisations could draw from 'the law governing relations between States'[417] and 'principles of immutability applied in the customary law of State responsibility, particularly for injuries to aliens'.[418] Even the manner in which *jus cogens* norms are justified as being applicable to international organisations is framed in statist terms. In the words of the ILC:

> [d]espite a personality which is in some respects different from that of the States Parties to such treaties, [international organisations] are none-theless the creation of those States. And it can hardly be maintained that States can avoid compliance with peremptory norms by creating an organisation.[419]

But do these suggestions not go against the explicit articulation of the ICJ when it distinguished the obligations of 'other subjects' from those of States? Clapham too remains cynical, noting that, '[i]t remains to be seen how exactly such analogies will be drawn'.[420] These approaches entirely fail to elucidate the rights and obligations of non-State actors other than international organisations.

In light of the above, it is obvious why scholars are critical of the significance placed on the recognition of other entities as 'subjects' of international law possessing 'international legal personality'.[421] These are descriptive but normatively empty concepts, which give no indication of the rights and duties conferred on each particular non-State entity.[422] A catch-all standard or even

---

414 Green (n 368) 57; Clapham, *Human Rights Obligations of Non-State Actors* (n 349) 66.
415 Green (n 368) 58.
416 Clapham, *Human Rights Obligations of Non-State Actors* (n 349) 65.
417 Amerasinghe (n 372) 400.
418 Ibid. 401.
419 ILC, 'Report of the International Law Commission on the Work of its Thirty-Fourth Session' (3 May–23 July 1982) UN Doc A/37/10, 56.
420 Clapham, *Human Rights Obligations of Non-State Actors* (n 349) 66; Amerasinghe (n 372) 401.
421 Clapham, *Human Rights Obligations of Non-State Actors* (n 349) 62–3; Higgins, *Problems and Process* (n 302) 49.
422 Klabbers (n 353) 57.

a generalisation between broad categories of actors cannot be made. So far, it is generally accepted that States possess the full spectrum of rights and duties necessary to operate on the international plane, and that certain international organisations may also possess some limited capabilities. But, despite the rising influence of powerful non-State entities capable of producing adverse human rights impacts in the wake of contemporary phenomena, we are yet to move far beyond Oppenheim's 1920 treatise, which exclusively recognised States and the League of Nations as legal persons.[423] The international criminal responsibility of individuals is one notable exception and will be examined in greater detail in subsequent chapters.[424] The recognition of other subjects remains tied to the criteria of statehood. International organisations demonstrate a clear proximity, operating as collective groups of States and acting in their mutual interests, but, beyond these actors, little can be said with any certainty. Although the fluid nature of 'statehood' could theoretically permit the inclusion of some non-State armed groups exhibiting widespread territorial control and operating as *de facto* governments, the ascription of such status is impeded by political considerations such as threats to State sovereignty.[425] What authoritative information we have on the concept of ILP provides little more than a circular enumeration of features that confer variegated rights and duties and are fundamentally limited by the dominant conception of international law. As such, the field of non-State actor regulation exposes the fragility of the State-centric view of the international legal system, where even the most fundamental concepts upon which it relies are plagued with inconsistency.

2.6 Concluding remarks

The foregoing analysis serves as the groundwork for the argument presented in this study. The chapter contextualised five preliminary issues that are central to understanding the practical and theoretical hurdles that inhibit the ascription of direct international obligations to non-State actors. First, attention was drawn to the definitional indeterminacy of international law in light of potential manifestations of nascent international legal principles prior to the emergence of the modern territorial State. Parallel to this analysis, the chapter prescribed caution in the treatment of popular genealogical interpretations of the development of international law. Rather than asserting that contemporary international law is the inevitable consequence of a continuous evolutionary process, it was argued that various forms of international law have existed throughout world history. It is the former flawed historiographical approach to which State-centric scholars frequently fall victim in their continuous

423 Eric C Ip, 'Globalisation and the Future of the Law of Sovereign State' (2010) 8 *ICON* 636; Clapham, *Human Rights Obligations of Non-State Actors* (n 349) 3.
424 Mark Janis, 'Individuals as Subjects of International Law' (1984) 17 *Cornell Int'l LJ* 61.
425 Steinhoff (n 294) 316.

restatement of the significance of Grotian scholarship, the dominance of Vattelian legal positivism and the solidification of the territorial State system in the wake of the Westphalian Peace Treaties. Although undeniably important, in all three of these examples, the State was far from the exclusive concern. Rather, it was suggested that a far more recent trend in international legal scholarship has selectively fashioned the narrative of these events in retrospect to lend credence to the dominant framing of international law. As such, the social and historical prestige with which the modern territorial State is often treated was called into question.

In its second section, this chapter demonstrated the lasting influence of German and Italian scholarship throughout the late nineteenth and early twentieth centuries. This period engendered the deification of the sovereign State and the adoption of a strict positivist methodology and resulted in the complete eschewal of natural law justifications for the content and binding quality of international law. This scholarship came to regard the State as a socially and historically rooted entity that existed *a priori* to international law. The State was even considered to precede the individual, in that it was only through State membership that an individual could know true freedom and existence. The State came to be regarded as an empirical fact from which all law emanated, rather than a mere juridical construction. The consequences of this 'social fact' approach were contextualised in the third section of this chapter. It was demonstrated that international law is conceived as emanating solely from the will of purportedly equal sovereign States. The notion of sovereignty in international law was briefly explored in order to demonstrate the effects of the decentralised nature of the international legal system. States are conceived of both as possessing absolute power and influence over their territory and yet also as subject to the international obligations to which they have consented. Although the notion of absolute sovereignty has been significantly eroded in today's globalised world, the absence of a central authoritative, executive or enforcement body system has raised persistent questions relating to the binding quality of international law. Despite the purported lack of coercive sanctions, other justifications have emerged to supplement the obligatory character of international law. Although the overall quality of international law was not explicitly disputed, the section stressed the importance of State consent and participation in law creation in the validation of international obligations. In the absence of recourse to the divine, States are treated as empirical sources of validity for international legal rules. The consequences of the State-centric school's conflation between law-maker and addressee for the direct regulation of non-State actors will be explored at greater length in subsequent chapters.

The final two sections established the indeterminacy exhibited by two of the most fundamental features of dominant scholarship: the modern State and the doctrine of ILP. Despite the factual certainty and theoretical centrality with which the State is regarded, international law is still absent an authoritative definition detailing the empirical criteria by which its existence may be determined. The qualities enshrined by the Montevideo Convention are extremely fluid, and the recognition of States remains fundamentally tied to political concerns. The international legal system is willing to recognise the continuing existence of failed or weak governance States that fulfil very few of the opaque criteria enumerated in the Convention, yet fails to recognise politically contentious non-State actors that may possess extensive territorial control and operate as *de facto* governments. Thus, even if the historical significance accorded to the State is accepted, its contemporary relevance as the principal subject of international law is highly contentious. Moreover, it was demonstrated that the determination of those entities capable of possessing international rights and duties and of operating on the international plane remains largely tied to the concept of statehood. The circular logic of the ICJ in *Reparation* remains the only authoritative judicial guidance on the subject. Although it is accepted that the purview of international law has been subject to some limited expansion to include other addressees of international rights and obligations, with the exception of natural persons, it is only on those entities that are proximate to, and formally recognised by, States that this greater status is conferred. As such, these final sections highlight the increasing redundancy of the enduring State-centric conception, which is unable to respond to the rise of powerful non-State actors. The practical failings of this approach will be further elaborated throughout the next chapter.

3 The practical failings of State-centric accountability regimes

The foundations of the State-centric approach to international law having been contextualised, it is now necessary to critically examine the practical operation of the accountability mechanisms underpinned by this theoretical framing. This chapter exposes the central challenges that non-State actors operating in weak governance States present to existing State-based regulatory initiatives. The extractive industry offers a useful vehicle for this analysis. The barriers to effective non-State actor regulation are magnified in this context, owing to the reliance of resource-rich States on FDI and the instances of prolonged civil strife regularly occurring within their territories. These fragile States often act as a point of confluence among distinct non-State entities whose legal regulation is further complicated by their interplay. Accordingly, the utility of this study's focus on the intersecting roles of MNEs and non-State armed groups will become particularly apparent. The abuses arising from the activities of MNEs decisively illustrate the *practical* failings of existing domestic and international accountability regimes. As for the *theoretical* hurdles to the establishment of direct non-State actor regulation at the international level (the subject of the next chapter), an analysis of non-State armed groups in particular exposes serious flaws.

This chapter contains three substantive sections, beginning with an appraisal of State-centrism in the operation of international human rights and humanitarian law. The second section demonstrates the significant practical obstacles to the achievement of domestic redress for victims of abuses emanating from extractive industries. Its third section discusses mechanisms seeking to regulate non-State actors directly, including 'soft law' initiatives to which multinationals are expected to voluntarily adhere, as well as *ad hoc* agreements made by non-State armed groups. The importance of these models in non-State actor engagement notwithstanding, both clearly lack the coercive bite of judicial enforcement. This final section also examines international criminal law, considering the narrow remit of the ICC, as well as the limited scope for the attribution of direct liability to both collective entities and individuals. In sum, this chapter demonstrates that existing accountability frameworks are unable to effectively respond to the rise of non-State entities. Supplementary soft law and *ad hoc* initiatives provide little certainty, and the international criminal law regime can provide only *ex post facto* redress to victims of the most egregious breaches of international law. As such, there exists a pressing need to establish a robust and effective system of international regulation directly addressing non-State actors.

3.1 State-centrism in international human rights and humanitarian law

In its present form, international law lacks an effective regulatory framework directly addressing non-State actors, despite the rapid expansion in their power and influence in international affairs. This section appraises this position by examining the State-centric operation of human rights and humanitarian law. It is argued that the continuing emphasis placed on the roles and responsibilities of States significantly undermines the application and enforcement of both subsets of public international law and demonstrates the need for substantial normative development if the field is to be responsive to the contemporary challenges posed by non-State actors.

3.1.1 State responsibility in international human rights law

Although recent scholarship frequently suggests that obligations directly addressing non-State actors already exist within widely ratified conventional international law,[1] such observations remain premature and lack substance at both practical and theoretical levels.[2] Although it cannot be denied that a number of provisions acknowledge the potential for these actors to produce adverse effects in the human rights context,[3] States remain the primary entities capable of formally consenting to multilateral treaties[4] and bear direct

---

1 Andrew Clapham, *Human Rights Obligations of Non-State Actors* (Oxford, UK, OUP, 2006) 29; Steven Ratner, 'Corporations and Human Rights: A Theory of Legal Responsibility' (2001) 111 *Yale LJ* 443, 493–4; Jordan J Paust, 'Human Rights Responsibilities of Private Corporations' (2001) 35 *Vand J Transnat'l L* 801, 810–13; Eric Mongelard, 'Corporate Civil Liability for Violations of International Humanitarian Law' (2006) 88 *Int'l Rev Red Cross* 665.

2 Markos Karavias, *Corporate Obligations Under International Law* (Oxford, UK, OUP, 2013) 18–67.

3 Optional Protocol to the Convention on the Rights of the Child on the Involvement of Children in Armed Conflict (25 May 2000) A/RES/54/263, Article 4(1); Convention on the Elimination of All Forms of Discrimination Against Women (18 December 1979) 1249 UNTS 13, Article 2(e); Convention on the Rights of Persons with Disabilities (24 January 2007) A/RES/61/106, Article 4(e); International Convention on the Elimination of All Forms of Racial Discrimination (21 December 1965) 660 UNTS 195, Article 2(1)(d); Convention on the Protection of the Rights of All Migrant Workers and Members of their Families (18 December 1990) A/RES/45/158, Article 16(2).

4 Vienna Convention on the Law of Treaties (23 May 1969) 1155 UNTS 331, Articles 2 and 3 (hereafter VCLT).

responsibility to give effect to such obligations.[5] The position is exemplified by Article 2(1) of the International Covenant on Civil and Political Rights (ICCPR), which mandates State parties to 'respect and ensure to all individuals within [their] territory and subject to [their] jurisdiction the rights recognised in the . . . Covenant'.[6] The Human Rights Committee (HRC) has confirmed that States will only discharge their positive obligations if due diligence is exercised in the protection of individuals,[7] 'not just against violations of the Covenant rights by its agents, but also against acts committed by private persons or entities'.[8]

With regard to individual complaints under the Optional Protocol to the ICCPR, the HRC has held State parties responsible for their failure to protect their populations from the operations of private actors.[9] A salient example is *Lubicon Lake Band v Canada*, where the complainants alleged that their land had been expropriated for commercial development, including oil and gas extraction. The HRC found a breach of Article 27 ICCPR by the State of Canada. Another is *SERAC v Nigeria*,[10] a communication to the African Commission for Human and Peoples' Rights concerning environmental degradation resulting from the conduct of a State oil company that serves as majority shareholder in a joint venture with Shell Petroleum, among others. Although recognising the 'widespread violations perpetrated by the Government of Nigeria and by private actors (be it following its clear blessing or not)',[11] the Commission ultimately affirmed the sole responsibility of the Nigerian State.[12] Similarly, responsibility for the abusive activities of non-State armed groups is said to arise only 'upon the State's own failure to act, the act of armed opposition groups merely constituting the objective condition which gives rise

---

5   Ibid. Article 26.
6   International Covenant on Civil and Political Rights (16 December 1966) 999 UNTS 171, Article 2(1).
7   *Velasquez Rodriguez* (29 July 1988) 28/96 IACtHR, (ser. C) No 4 paras 166–74; Robert P Barnidge, 'The Due Diligence Principle under International Law' (2006) 8 *Int CL Rev* 81.
8   UN Human Rights Commission, 'General Comment No 31[80] – The Nature of the General Legal Obligation Imposed on States Parties to the Covenant' (26 May 2004) UN Doc CCPR/C/21/Rev. 1/Add.13 para 8.
9   *Chief Bernard Ominayak and the Lubicon Lake Band v Canada*, Communication 167/1984, UN Doc CCPR/C/38/D/167/1984 (1990); *Hopu and Bessert v France*, Communication 549/1993, UN Doc CCPR/C/60/D/549/1993/Rev. 1 (1997); *Love et al v Australia*, Communication 983/2001, UN Doc CCPR/C/77/983/2001 (2003); *Ilmari Länsman et al v Finland*, Communication 511/1992, UN Doc CCPR/C/52/D/511/1992 (1994).
10   *Social and Economic Rights Action Centre (SERAC) and Another v Nigeria*, African Commission on Human and Peoples' Rights, Comm Nos 155/96 (2001).
11   Ibid. para 67.
12   Karavias (n 2) 49–52.

to a breach . . . on the part of the State'.[13] Thus, treaty obligations address most non-State actors only indirectly, as a consequence of the obligations held by the State in which they are domiciled. Yet, to term these obligations 'indirect' has been described as 'troubling. The phrase "indirect obligation" actually refers to typical obligations binding on States according to the traditional doctrine of international law'.[14] Thus, at present, the application of conventional international human rights obligations to non-State actors is usually mediated by domestic law.

Despite the attention directed towards the 2003 UN Draft Norms on the Responsibilities of Transnational Corporations,[15] an initiative regarded as an attempt to erode the edifice of State-based regulation, State responsibility continues to receive the primary emphasis where business actors are concerned.[16] The initiative has since been abandoned[17] in favour of the non-binding UN Guiding Principles on Business and Human Rights.[18] During their development, John Ruggie confirmed the primary responsibility of States to protect human rights:[19]

> Some stakeholders believe that the solution lies in a limited list of human rights for which companies would have responsibility, while extending to companies, where they have influence, essentially the same range of responsibilities as States . . . [T]he special Representative has not adopted this formula.[20]

This position was affirmed more recently in an Office of the High Commissioner for Human Rights (OHCHR) consultation 'designed to help States adopt a

13 Liesbeth Zegveld, *Accountability of Armed Opposition Groups in International Law* (Cambridge, UK, CUP, 2002) 182.
14 Karavias (n 2) 12.
15 UN Draft Norms on the Responsibilities of Transnational Corporations and Other Business Enterprises with Regard to Human Rights (2003) UN Doc E/CN.4/Sub.2/2003/12/Rev. 2 (hereafter, UN Draft Norms 2003).
16 David Weissbrodt and Muria Kruger, 'Human Rights Responsibilities of Businesses as Non-State Actors' in Philip Alston (ed), *Non State Actors and Human Rights* (Oxford, UK, OUP, 2005) 318; Jacob Gelfand, 'The Lack of Enforcement in the United Nations Draft Norms: Benefit or Advantage?' in Olivier De Schutter (ed), *Transnational Corporations and Human Rights* (Oxford, UK, Hart, 2006) 315.
17 Pini Pavel Miretski and Sascha-Dominik Bachmann, 'The UN Norms on the Responsibility of Transnational Corporations and Other Business Enterprises with Regard to Human Rights: A Requiem' (2012) 17 *Deankin L Rev* 5.
18 UN Guiding Principles on Business and Human Rights 2011, HR/PUB/11/04 (hereafter UNGPs).
19 Human Rights Council, 'Report of the Special Representative of the Secretary-General on the Issue of Human Rights and Transnational Corporations and Other Business Enterprises' (22 April 2009) UN Doc A/HRC/11/13 para 12.
20 Human Rights Council, 'Report of the Special Representative of the Secretary-General on Issue of Human Rights and Transnational Corporations and Other Business Enterprises, John Ruggie' (7 April 2008) UN Doc A/HRC/8/5 para 6.

more effective and comprehensive approach to judicial remedy and account-ability in cases of business-related human rights abuses'.[21] Thus, it remains contentious to suggest the direct application of any obligations stemming from extant international human rights law to these non-State actors, confirming the vertical conception of human rights as entailing direct obligations for States alone.[22]

Similar pronouncements are apparent in relation to non-State armed groups. In 1999, the Inter-American Commission on Human Rights made clear that it regarded the State as the central component of the human rights regime,[23] having previously found that, 'bringing the acts of armed groups under the American Convention would mean expanding the concept of human rights . . . [I]t was the States' responsibility to decide whether such an expansion is desirable'.[24] Similarly, the Working Group of the UN Commission on Human Rights denied the direct application of human rights treaties to non-State armed groups, finding that only international humanitarian law may bind such groups.[25] Indeed, although it was recognised in 1998 that acts of non-State armed groups resulting in indiscriminate violence and civilian casualties were matters of international concern, it was also suggested that:

> very serious consequences could follow from a rushed effort to address such acts through a vehicle of existing human rights law, not least as it might serve to legitimise actions taken against members of such groups in a manner that violates human rights.[26]

Analogous arguments concerning the direct application of conventional human rights to non-State actors have been made in relation to international custom. It has been suggested that the Universal Declaration on Human

---

21 OHCHR, 'Business and Human Rights: The Accountability and Remedy Project', www.ohchr.org/Documents/Issues/Business/DomesticLawRemedies/OHCHR_ARP_D raftGuidanceConsultation.pdf, accessed 21 April 2016.

22 Eric De Brabandere, 'Non-State Actors and Human Rights: Corporate Responsibility and the Attempts to Formalise the Role of Corporations in the International Legal System' in Jean d'Aspremont (ed), *Multiple Perspectives on Non-State Actors in International Law* (Oxford, UK, Routledge, 2011) 273; Karavias (n 2) 46.

23 Inter-American Commission on Human Rights, 'Third Report on the Human Rights Situation in Colombia' (26 February 1999) OEA/Ser.L/V/II.102 para 5.

24 Zegveld (n 13) 41; Inter-American Commission on Human Rights, 'Annual Report of the Inter-American Commission on Human Rights 1990–1991' (22 February 1991) OEA/Ser.L/V/II.79.rev. 1.

25 UN Commission on Human Rights, 'Report of the Meeting of Special Rapporteurs/ Representatives Experts and Chairpersons of Working Groups of the Special Procedures of the Commission on Human Rights and the Advisory Services Programme' (30 September 1996) UN Doc E/CN.4/1997/3 para 46.

26 UN Commission on Human Rights, 'Report of the Secretary-General on the Minimum Humanitarian Standards' (5 January 1998) UN Doc E/CN.4/1998/87 para 64.

Rights (UDHR),[27] a non-binding instrument that calls upon 'every individual and every organ of society'[28] to promote respect for human rights, has attained customary status.[29] Business actors and non-State armed groups could arguably be defined as organs of society, and thus it has been suggested that they are subject to direct human rights obligations.[30] However, the term 'organ of society' is expressed exclusively in the preamble to the UDHR. Although this instrument has had undeniable impact at both customary and conventional levels, precisely which provisions have attained customary status remains contentious.[31] It has been suggested that the preamble 'has hortatory value and falls short of establishing a legal obligation'.[32] Such a view has also been reflected in international practice.[33] Additionally, the scope of the 'duty' conferred in the preamble is simply to *strive* to promote respect for human rights via *teaching and education*.[34] Thus, although 'organs of society' other than States are *addressed* in the text, it is not established that their duties will mirror those held by States. Rather, a strictly textual approach suggests that any duty conferred will be an educational or promotional one.[35]

Article 29 of the UDHR states that, '[e]veryone has duties to the community in which alone the free and full development of his personality is possible'. Although this too may be seen as evidence of a customary duty addressing non-State actors, it has been argued that any resulting obligations would predominantly relate to natural persons, and that this type of clause 'propagate[s] a generic concept of duties, wanting in clarity, which does not give rise to concrete enforceable legal obligations binding on corporations'.[36] Indeed, subsequent practice (including the adoption of human rights treaties) has largely reaffirmed the State-centric focus of international human rights law. Furthermore, to argue that the UDHR, envisaged at the time of its drafting as a non-binding instrument of primarily moral authority, now binds non-State

---

27 Universal Declaration of Human Rights (10 December 1948) UNGA Res 217A(III) (hereafter UDHR).

28 Ibid. Preamble.

29 Hurst Hannum, 'The Status of the Universal Declaration of Human Rights in National and International Law' (1996) 25 *Ga J Int'l & Comp L* 317.

30 Louis Henkin, 'The Universal Declaration at 50 and the Challenge of Global Markets' (1999) 25 *Brooklyn J Int'l L* 17, 25.

31 International Council on Human Rights Policy, 'Beyond Voluntarism, Human Rights and the Developing International Legal Obligations of Companies' (February 2002) 60 www.ichrp.org/files/reports/7/107_report_en.pdf, accessed 21 April 2016.

32 Karavias (n 2) 77.

33 OHCHR, 'EU Reply to the OHCHR Questionnaire on Responsibilities of Transnational Corporations and Related Business Enterprises with Regard to Human Rights' para 6, www2.ohchr.org/english/issues/globalization/business/docs/replyfinland.pdf, accessed 21 April 2016.

34 UDHR (n 27) Preamble.

35 Karavias (n 2) 78.

36 Ibid. 81.

actors would go against the express intention of States.[37] Thus, although customary international law constitutes another potential avenue to the establishment of non-State actor obligations (and may have utility in other relevant fields, such as international humanitarian law), at present, this is not sufficiently reflected in State practice relating to human rights law.[38] As will be explored in Chapter 4, even if customary law is presumed to establish direct international obligations for non-State actors, deeper theoretical uncertainties relating to legal validity remain.

Whereas human rights provisions often impose due diligence obligations on States to safeguard their populations from private actors, the ILC's Articles on the Responsibility of States for Internationally Wrongful Acts (ASRIWA) 2001 detail specific instances in which the conduct of private entities may be directly attributed to the State. This approach to non-State actor accountability is wholly dependent on the factual connection between the non-State entity and responsible State.[39] The fact that States will be responsible for the abusive acts of their organs and agents,[40] even when acting beyond their official capacity,[41] is non-contentious.[42] States may be held accountable for violations of their international obligations committed vicariously through private actors.[43] There are four key circumstances in which private behaviour will be considered attributable to the State under international law, each of which hinges on the actor's relationship with the State government.[44] First, although the conduct of private entities is not *prima facie* attributable to the State,[45] even when the corporation is wholly owned by the State, or the State possesses a controlling interest in it,[46] the conduct of entities *exercising elements of governmental*

---

37 Olufemi Amao, *Corporate Social Responsibility, Human Rights and the Law: Multinational Corporations in Developing Countries* (Taylor & Francis, 2011) 26.

38 *Kiobel v Royal Dutch Petroleum*, 621 F 3d 148 (2nd Cir 2010) (hereafter, *Kiobel 2010*); Karavias (n 2) 82.

39 Graham Cronogue, 'Rebels, Negligent Support, and State Accountability: Holding States Accountable for the Human Rights Violations of Non-State Actors' (2013) 23 *Duke J Comp & Int'l L* 365.

40 ILC, Articles on Responsibility of States for Internationally Wrongful Acts (2001) UN Doc A/56/49(Vol I)/Corr.4, Articles 4, 5, 6 (hereafter ILC, ASRIWA).

41 Ibid. Article 7.

42 *Ilaşcu and Others v Moldova and Russia* App No 48787/99 (ECtHR 2004) para 319.

43 ILC, ASRIWA (n 40) Article 2; *Costello-Roberts v United Kingdom* App No 13134/87 (ECtHR, 1993) para 27.

44 Inés Tófalo, 'Overt and Hidden Accomplices: Transnational Corporations' Range of Complicity for Human Rights Violations' in De Schutter, *Transnational Corporations and Human Rights* (n 16) 336–9.

45 Robert McCorquodale and Penelope Simons, 'Responsibility beyond Borders: State Responsibility for Extraterritorial Violations by Corporations of International Human Rights Law' (2007) 70 *MLR* 598, 606.

46 ILC, 'Report of the Commission to the General Assembly on the Work of its Fifty-Third Session' (23 April–1 June and 2 July–10 August 2001) Yearbook of the International Law Commission Vol II, UN Doc A/CN.4/Ser.A/2001/Add.1 (2001) 43–8.

authority may be imputed to the State.[47] The relevant conduct must relate to governmental activity and not to other private or commercial activity, though the ILC has not provided precise definitions in this regard.[48] This provision is particularly pertinent given the international trend towards the privatisation of traditionally governmental functions.[49]

The three remaining scenarios are articulated in Articles 8–11. Pursuant to these provisions, certain conduct that does not result directly from the actions of the State, its organs or agents is nonetheless imputed to the State. The least contentious is Article 11, which provides that conduct will be attributable where a 'State acknowledges and adopts the conduct in question as its own'.[50] More problematically, conduct is attributable to the State where an entity operates under its direction or control.[51] Such conduct will rise to this level 'only if it directed or controlled the specific operation and the conduct complained of was an integral part of that operation'.[52] The ICJ, in its *Nicaragua* opinion, which considered whether the conduct of the Contras was attributable to the US, held that:

> despite the heavy subsidiaries and other support provided to them by the United States, there is no clear evidence of the United States having exercised such a degree of control in all fields as to justify the Contras as acting on its behalf.[53]

This restrictive approach has been criticised in international practice,[54] and the ICJ's subsequent *Bosnian Genocide* ruling resorted to a factual analysis demanding that, 'the persons, groups or entities act in "complete dependence" on the State of which they are merely an instrument'.[55] It has been suggested that such a relationship will only be established in a small category of cases, 'either because governments do not typically make many such bald requests, or because corporations do not comply with them'.[56] Thus, although this constitutes an accepted method of achieving redress for non-State actor activity

---

47 ILC ASRIWA (n 40) Article 5.
48 ILC, 'Report to the General Assembly 2001' (n 46) 43.
49 Clapham (n 1) 3; Jennifer A Zerk, *Multinationals and Corporate Social Responsibility: Limitations and Opportunities in International Law* (Cambridge, UK, CUP, 2006) 77–8.
50 ILC, ASRIWA (n 40) Article 11.
51 Ibid. Article 8.
52 ILC, 'Report to the General Assembly 2001' (n 46) 47.
53 *Military and Paramilitary Activities (Nicaragua v United States of America)* (Advisory Opinion) ICJ Reports [1986] para 109.
54 *Prosecutor v Tadić* (Appeals Chamber) IT-94-1-A (15 July 1999) 1541, paras 117 and 137; *Loizidou v Turkey* App No 15318/89 (ECtHR, 1995) paras 23–4.
55 *Bosnian Genocide (Bosnia and Herzegovina v Serbia and Montenegro)* ICJ Reports [2007] para 392.
56 Ratner (n 1) 500.

under the State-based regulatory regime, it is unlikely to aid the majority of victims.[57] Furthermore, Ratner suggests that there may be instances in which 'the company is effectively the superior and the State is the agent'.[58] Although such instances are certainly possible, the ASRIWA do not cater for this inverse scenario. Rather, States are treated as 'superiors' or 'commanders' in their relations with private actors, irrespective of the facts.

Whereas the conduct contemplated by the ASRIWA is contingent on the close proximity between private entity and the State, and accusations of complicity and impunity are levelled at weak governance States with some regularity,[59] violations also result from the basic incapacity or unwillingness of States to regulate their domestic affairs.[60] In this practical context, State-based approaches truly fall apart. The concept of State regulation through municipal law is justified 'on the basis that the State has, at least in theory, the constitutional authority to legislate and regulate such actions to ensure their compliance with its international obligations'.[61] Yet, this approach is often entirely unrealistic. The traditional treatment of non-State actors is staunchly Western and fails to account for the realities of life in weak governance States.[62] With the continuing emphasis placed on the doctrine of State responsibility having been demonstrated, attention now turns to the State-centric operation of international humanitarian law and the challenges presented by non-State armed groups.

3.1.2 State-centricity in international humanitarian law

A conscious separation has been made between international human rights and international humanitarian law. Despite the obvious cross-over in the subject matter they address,[63] both their historical development and the type

57 Cronogue (n 39) 365–88.
58 Ratner (n 1) 493–4.
59 *Doe v Unocal Corp*, 395 F.3d 932 (9th Cir 2002) (hereafter, *Unocal*); Wolfgang Kaleck and Miriam Saage-Maaß, 'Corporate Accountability for Human Rights Violations Amounting to International Crimes' (2010) 8 *JICJ* 699, 704; Tófalo (n 44) 339–48.
60 Eric De Brabandere, 'Human Rights Obligations and Transnational Corporations: The Limits of Direct Corporate Responsibility' (2010) 4 *Hum Rts & Int'l Legal Discourse* 66, 77.
61 David Kinley and Junko Tadaki, 'From Talk to Walk: The Emergence of Human Rights Responsibilities for Corporations at International Law' (2004) 44 *Va J Int'l L* 931, 948; Robert McCorquodale, 'Overlegalising Silences: Human Rights and Non-State Actors' (2002) 96 *ASIL Proc* 384.
62 Dieter Neubert, 'Local and Regional Non-State Actors on the Margins of Public Policy in Africa' in Anne Peters, Lucy Koechlin, Till Förster and Gretta Fenner Zinkernagel (eds), *Non-State Actors as Standard Setters* (Cambridge, UK, CUP, 2009) 36.
63 Jean-Marie Henckaerts, 'Concurrent Application of International Humanitarian Law and Human Rights Law: A Victim's Perspective' in Roberta Arnold and Noelle Quénivet (eds), *International Humanitarian Law and Human Rights Law: Towards a New Merger in International Law* (Leiden, Netherlands, Brill, 2008) 237–68.

of protection they confer are quite distinct.[64] Most notably, some international humanitarian conventions expressly address *all parties* engaged in armed conflicts[65] and, as such, purport to bind both State and non-State actors.[66] Yet, the evolution and contemporary operation of conventional humanitarian law are undeniably State-centric: 'Throughout history, States have determined the rules of engagement in armed conflict . . . Any non-State group was considered within the realm of domestic law and not as a legal international actor'.[67] Prior to the adoption of the 1949 Geneva Conventions, intra-State conflict was regulated on an *ad hoc* basis and categorised into three distinct types according to the intensity of the violence. Rebellions were defined by their limited duration and domestic suppression without resort to military intervention.[68] Insurgencies, on the other hand, involved serious violence over an extended duration and geographical area, coupled with the incapacity of the recognised government to supress the violence.[69] This category was said to give rise to limited rights and obligations for non-State armed groups, the existence of which Lauterpacht restricted to those 'expressly conceded and agreed upon for reasons of convenience, humanity or economic interest',[70] underscoring the relative fluidity of the duties conferred.

The final category of belligerency triggered the application of the laws of war.[71] Oppenheim suggested four discernible criteria indicating belligerency: (1) the existence of civil war accompanied by a state of general hostilities;

64 Konstantinos Mastorodimos, 'The Utility and Limits of International Human Rights Law and International Humanitarian Law's Parallel Applicability' (2009) 5 *Rev Int'l L & Pol* 129; Marco Sassòli and Laura M Olson, 'The Relationship between International Humanitarian and International Human Rights Law Where It Matters: Admissible Killing and Internment of Fighters in Non-International Armed Conflicts' (2008) 19 *Int'l Rev Red Cross*, 599.

65 Geneva Convention for the Amelioration of the Condition of the Wounded and Sick in Armed Forces in the Field (First Geneva Convention) (12 August 1949) 75 UNTS 31; Geneva Convention for the Amelioration of the Condition of Wounded, Sick and Shipwrecked Members of Armed Forces at Sea (Second Geneva Convention) (12 August 1949) 75 UNTS 85; Geneva Convention Relative to the Treatment of Prisoners of War (Third Geneva Convention) (12 August 1949) 75 UNTS 135; Geneva Convention Relative to the Protection of Civilian Persons in Time of War (Fourth Geneva Convention) (12 August 1949) 75 UNTS 287, Common Article 3 (hereafter, Geneva Conventions 1949); Protocol Additional to the Geneva Conventions of 12 August 1949, and relating to the Protection of Victims of Non-International Armed Conflicts (8 June 1977) 1125 UNTS 609, Article 1 (hereafter, Additional Protocol II 1977).

66 Zegveld (n 13) 15.

67 Dawn Steinhoff, 'Talking to the Enemy: State Legitimacy Concerns with Engaging Non-State Armed Groups' (2010) 45 *Tex Int'l LJ* 297, 309.

68 Sandesh Sivakumaran, *The Law of Non-International Armed Conflict* (Oxford, UK, OUP, 2012) 9.

69 Ibid. 10.

70 Hersch Lauterpacht, *Recognition in International Law* (Cambridge, UK, CUP, 1947) 277.

71 Lindsay Moir, *Law of Internal Armed Conflicts* (Cambridge, UK, CUP, 2002) 5–20; Steinhoff (n 67).

(2) occupation and a measure of orderly administration of a substantial part of the territory; (3) observance of the laws and customs of war by the belligerent group operating under a responsible command; and (4) the practical necessity for third-party States to express their attitude to the civil war in question.[72] The scope and content of these criteria have been the subject of much criticism.[73] What is interesting in the context of the present study is the central role played by the State in recognising (or perhaps more appropriately, conceding) the existence of an armed conflict in order to trigger the application of the laws and customs of war.[74] The consequences for States are potentially negative and restrictive: 'recognition is necessarily a sign of weakness of the established government, and any act that publicises this fact would inevitably enhance the prestige of the insurgents to the detriment of the established government'.[75] States are effectively surrendering to the application of international humanitarian law and, as such, may no longer quell uprisings by any means necessary domestically. Recognition is motivated by self-interest, as a means of safeguarding territory or preventing claims from affected third-party States, 'rather than a desire to mitigate the humanitarian suffering of individuals caught up in the conflict'.[76]

Instances of States recognising either insurgency or belligerency, statuses considered to confer direct rights and obligations on non-State armed groups, have been relatively sparse.[77] Although their usage has not been formally ruled out,[78] no instance of such recognition has been recorded since at least 1949, and potentially 1899.[79] This position correlates with the codification of international humanitarian law via the Hague Conventions,[80] the 1949 Geneva Conventions and the Additional Protocols thereto. These instruments aside, the above discussion highlights the State-centric evolution and application of

---

72 Lassa Oppenheim, *International Law, A Treatise* Vol II (Hersch Lauterpacht ed, London, Longmans, Green, 1952) 249–50.
73 Sivakumaran, *Non-International Armed Conflict* (n 68) 11–14.
74 Anthony Cullen, *The Concept of Non-International Armed Conflict in International Humanitarian Law* (Cambridge, UK, CUP, 2010) 20–2.
75 Ti-Chiang Chen, *The International Law of Recognition* (LC Green ed, New York, Praeger, 1951) 371.
76 Sivakumaran, *Non-International Armed Conflict* (n 68) 14–15; Lindsay Moir, 'The Historical Development of the Application of Humanitarian Law in Non-International Armed Conflicts to 1949' (1998) 47 *ICLQ* 337, 343–4.
77 Sivakumaran, *Non-International Armed Conflict* (n 68) 17.
78 Ministry of Foreign Affairs of Colombia, 'Statement of Government of Colombia Regarding the Status of FARC' (June 1999) in Yearbook of International Humanitarian Law, Vol II (December 1999) 441; Robert W Gomulkiewicz, 'International Law Governing Aid to Opposition Groups in Civil War: Resurrecting the Standards of Belligerency' (1988) 63 *Wash L Rev* 43, 44; Mastorodimos (n 64) 301.
79 Sivakumaran, *Non-International Armed Conflict* (n 68) 19.
80 Zoë Howe, 'Can the 1954 Hague Convention Apply to Non-State Actors? A Study of Iraq and Libya' (2012) 47 *Tex Int'l LJ* 403.

the laws of war. Humanitarian considerations proved secondary to State interests. Exactly when the laws of war applied to non-State armed groups was left to the discretion of States, despite the clear erosion of their capacity to ensure the protection of their populations. The potential threats that such groups pose to the sovereignty and territorial integrity of recognised State governments highlight the distinct challenges they present, as well as the diverse political concerns that limit the effective operation of State-centric accountability regimes:[81]

> States have consistently voiced the fear that applying [humanitarian law] to all internal armed conflicts will limit their ability to quell insurgents. This fear was not based on States' desire to use harsh methods or means of combat, but on the law's implications for the legal status of the armed group.[82]

Worryingly, although the International Criminal Tribunal for Rwanda (ICTR) has explicitly stated that, 'the ascertainment of the intensity of a non-international armed conflict does not depend on the subjective judgement of the parties to the conflict',[83] the situation under conventional humanitarian law remains contingent on State interests and recognition.[84] Treaty law is absent a provision detailing the criteria indicative of a non-international armed conflict, and an authoritative definition has proven elusive. Thus, these determinations are made 'according to the political interests of the actors concerned, sometimes in complete variance with the facts on the ground',[85] in spite of the express provision that the application of conventional international humanitarian law 'shall not affect the legal status of non-State armed groups'.[86] Furthermore, the Geneva Conventions are essentially multilateral treaties, and, as such, non-State armed groups are unable to formally consent to the provisions. Thus, the responsibility remains entirely with States to determine when international humanitarian law applies and to ensure adherence to the relevant provisions,[87] irrespective of the wording of the conventions.[88] Although various theories have

---

81 Program on Humanitarian Policy and Conflict Research, 'Empowered Groups, Tested Laws and Policy Options' 24 (Harvard University, 2007) www.hpcrresearch.org/sites/default/files/publications/Report_Empowered_Groups_Nov2007.pdf, accessed 21 April 2016.
82 Steinhoff (n 67) 316.
83 *Prosecutor v Akayesu* (Trial Chamber Judgment) ICTR-96-4-T (2 September 1998) para 603.
84 Andreas Paulus and Mindia Vashakmadze, 'Asymmetrical War and the Notion of Armed Conflict – A Tentative Conceptualisation' (2009) 91 *Int'l Rev Red Cross* 95, 103.
85 Sivakumaran, *Non-International Armed Conflict* (n 68) 155.
86 Geneva Conventions 1949 (n 65) Common Article 3(2).
87 Zegveld (n 13) 225–6.
88 Although States alone may formally ratify the conventions, the wording addresses '*each party* to the conflict': Geneva Conventions 1949 (n 65) Common Article 3; Ratner (n 1) 466.

been formulated to justify the binding quality of international humanitarian law over non-State actors:[89]

> none of them has proved fully satisfactory: either these theories only partially explain this binding character . . . or they gloss over the lack of non-State actors' formal consent . . . [I]t is the requirement of consent, on which the entire edifice of international law is based after all, that should be addressed head-on if the legitimacy of [international humanitarian law] and, hence, the effective compliance with it by non-State actors is to be secured.[90]

This line of argument will be addressed at length in Chapter 4 of this monograph. For now, it suffices to highlight the challenges that non-State actors present to the theoretical validity of international humanitarian law.

A more objective definition of 'armed conflict' has been articulated by the International Criminal Tribunal for the Former Yugoslavia (ICTY) in its 1995 *Tadić* decision:

> an armed conflict exists whenever there is a resort to armed force between States or protracted violence between governmental authorities and organised armed groups, or between such groups within a State.[91]

This definition has generally been accepted as reflecting the threshold for the application of Article 3, common to all four 1949 Geneva Conventions[92] and the sole provision applicable to non-international armed conflict.[93] Although *Tadić* now prescribes a workable definition, recognition of the factual existence of an armed conflict remains bound to the political sensitivities of States. Although international institutions such as the ICJ,[94] UN Security Council,[95]

---

89 See Chapter 4 at Section 4.2; Jann K Kleffner, 'The Applicability of International Humanitarian Law to Organised Armed Groups' (2011) 93 *Int'l Rev Red Cross* 443; Sandesh Sivakumaran, 'Binding Armed Opposition Groups' (2006) 55 *ICLQ* 369.

90 Cedric Ryngaert, 'Non-State Actors in International Humanitarian Law' in d'Aspremont, *Multiple Perspectives* (n 22) 289.

91 *Prosecutor v Tadić* (Decision on the Defence Motion for Interlocutory Appeal on Jurisdiction) IT-93-1-AR72 (2 October 1995) para 70.

92 Paulus and Vashakmadze (n 84) 95.

93 Though note, Additional Protocols I and II 1977 are potentially applicable; Cullen (n 74) 102–7.

94 Final Record of the Diplomatic Conference of Geneva of 1949 (Geneva, 21 April–12 August 1949) Vol I, 361, www.loc.gov/rr/frd/Military_Law/pdf/Dipl-Conf-1949-Final_Vol-1. pdf, accessed 27 November 2015.

95 Charter of the United Nations (26 June 1945) 1 UNTS XVI, Article 39 (hereafter, UN Charter).

UN General Assembly[96] and UN Commission on Human Rights[97] may serve as decision-makers as to whether a conflict exists,[98] it has been suggested that, 'the law of internal armed conflict lacks an independent enforcement mechanism, a body capable of making objective determinations of fact, or a mechanism by which a State or non-State party can be compelled to account for its conduct'.[99] International institutions must also maintain good will to member States.[100] This situation has led to the revocation of determinations on the existence of armed conflict in light of State criticism.[101]

So long as States possess some manner of control over the recognition process, they will be able to deny the existence of the requisite criteria and are likely to deny the engagement of humanitarian law unless it is in their interests to secure its application.[102] The concern expressed by States that the direct application of humanitarian provisions will bolster a group's legal status is:

> typically a façade to mask its true fears of the collateral consequences of recognition . . . State apprehensions concerning engagement are more likely due to the legitimacy implications . . . or a perceived need for the State to maintain its hegemony in the international system.[103]

From a strictly legal standpoint, Clapham has firmly dismissed legitimacy concerns:

> [T]o suggest that the application of international duties to an armed group increases its legitimacy in the eyes of observers has no basis in law and would be hard to demonstrate empirically . . . this argument, like the others,

96 UNGA Res 40/140, 'Situation of human rights and fundamental freedoms in Guatemala' (13 December 1985) UN Doc A/RES/40/140.
97 UNHCR, 'Situation of Human Rights in the Republic of Chechnya of the Russian Federation' Commission on Human Rights, Fifty-Second Session (26 March 1996) UN doc E/CN.4/1996/177, 362–3.
98 Alex Peterson, 'Order out of Chaos, Domestic Enforcement of the Law of Internal Armed Conflict' (2002) 171 *Military L Rev* 1, 67.
99 Zegveld (n 13) 10–13; Sivakumaran, *Non-International Armed Conflict* (n 68) 196.
100 Sivakumaran, *Non-International Armed Conflict* (n 68) 198.
101 UNGA, 'Children and Armed Conflict: Report of the Secretary-General' (10 November 2003) UN Docs A/58/546 and S/2003/1053, Annex II para 61; UNGA, 'Children and Armed Conflict Report of the Secretary-General' (19 April 2004) UN Docs A/58/546/Corr.2 & S/2003/1053/Corr.2.
102 Richard R Baxter, 'Some Existing Problems of Humanitarian Law' (1975) 14 *Mil L & L War Rev* 279, 298; UK Ministry of Defence, *The Manual of the Law of Armed Conflict* (Oxford, UK, OUP, 2004) 384; M. Cherif Bassiouni, 'The New Wars and the Crisis of Compliance with the Law of Armed Conflict by Non-State Actors' (2008) 98 *J Crim L & Criminology* 711, 781–4.
103 Steinhoff (n 67) 317.

depends more on policy preferences of the objector rather than any inherent legal or practical impossibility.[104]

Although the concerns of States as to the legitimising effects of international humanitarian law are highlighted here, it is not suggested that they constitute a *legal* impediment as such. As will later be examined, far more significant theoretical challenges are at play.[105] Yet, the practical significance of this concern is undeniable and should be borne in mind.

Even where recognition is granted, States engaged in non-international armed conflict will be hard pushed to enforce compliance with humanitarian standards, given their weakened governmental and judicial infrastructures and fragmented territorial control.[106] The profound disparity between the provisions regulating international and non-international armed conflict, at the conventional level at least, has further exacerbated this issue, leaving the vast majority of armed conflict under-regulated.[107] Even Common Article 3, which seeks to regulate 'conflict not of an international character, occurring in the territory of one of the High Contracting Parties', has been interpreted as implicitly suggesting that fractious conflict spilling across the borders of multiple States will fall outside its sphere of protection.[108] It has been argued that the Article should be 'evolutively interpreted to apply to any situation of organised armed violence that has been classified as a non-international armed conflict'.[109] Indeed, there is nothing in the *travaux préparatoires* to suggest that the convention was deliberately limited to address conflict occurring on the territory of a single State.[110] The practice of the ICTR appears to corroborate this approach, as its statute permits the prosecution of serious violations of Common Article 3/Additional Protocol II occurring 'in the territory of neighbouring States'.[111] The ICRC has also explicitly stated that non-international armed

---

104 Clapham (n 1) 53.
105 See Chapter 4 at Section 4.2.
106 Nicholas Rost, 'Human Rights Violations, Weak States and Civil War' (2011) 12 *Hum Rts Rev* 417.
107 Orla Marie Buckley, 'Unregulated Armed Conflict: Non-State Armed Groups, International Humanitarian Law, and Violence in Western Sahara' (2012) 37 *NCJ Int'l L & Com Reg* 793, 794.
108 Jean Pictet (ed), 'Commentary to the Fourth Geneva Convention Relative to the Protection of Civilian Persons in Time of War' (ICRC, Geneva, 1958) 36; Elizabeth Holland, 'The Qualification Framework of International Humanitarian Law: Too Rigid to Accommodate Contemporary Conflicts?' (2011) 34 *Suffolk Transnat'l L Rev* 145, 155–81.
109 Jelena Pejic, 'The Protective Scope of Common Article 3: More than Meets the Eye' (2011) 93 *Int'l Rev Red Cross* 189, 199.
110 Ibid. 200.
111 Statute of the International Criminal Tribunal for Rwanda (8 November 1994), Article 1; cf *Prosecutor v Musema* (Trial Chamber) ICTR-96-13-A (27 January 2000) para 247 (hereafter, *Musema*).

conflict 'may occur on the territory of one or more of the High Contracting Parties' and will lead to the obligatory application of Common Article 3.[112]

Similarly, Additional Protocol II 1977, which seeks to develop and supplement Common Article 3, applies only in restrictive circumstances[113] and does not prescribe monitoring from the ICRC.[114] Even in the instances in which the UN Security Council has imposed 'targeted sanctions'[115] on individuals and non-State armed groups responsible for humanitarian atrocities,[116] such measures hinge on consent and implementation by member States,[117] severely affect vulnerable populations[118] and lack due-process guarantees.[119] Aside from the *ex post facto* redress achievable in limited circumstances under the international criminal law regime, as exemplified by the jurisprudence of the ICTY,[120] the Special Court for Sierra Leone (SCSL)[121] and the ICC,[122] the obligation to enforce these limited humanitarian standards falls to States alone.[123] The achievement of redress after the fact is far from ideal, particularly given that the aim of humanitarian regulation is to prevent mass atrocities, rather than to simply punish key perpetrators following their occurrence.[124] These direct

112 'Final Record of the Diplomatic Conference of Geneva of 1949' (Geneva, 21 April–12 August 1949) Vol II-B, 122, www.loc.gov/rr/frd/Military_Law/pdf/Dipl-Conf-1949-Final_Vol-2-B.pdf, accessed 21 April 2016.
113 The protocol addresses groups operating 'under responsible command, control[ling] enough of the territory to carry out sustained military operations'. Additional Protocol II 1977 (n 65) Article 1.
114 Buckley (n 107) 827; Antonio Cassese, *International Law* (Oxford, UK, OUP, 2004) 420.
115 UN Charter (n 95) Article 2(7); Christiane Bourloyannis, 'The Security Council of the United Nations and the Implementation of International Humanitarian Law' (1992) 20 *Denv J Int'l L & Pol'y* 335, 352.
116 Marco Roscini, 'The United Nations Security Council and the Enforcement of International Humanitarian Law' (2010) 43 *Israel L Rev* 330, 346; Sivakumaran, *Non-International Armed Conflict* (n 68) 335.
117 Anne-Marie La Rosa and Caroline Wuezner, 'Armed Groups, Sanctions and the Implementation of International Humanitarian Law' (2008) 90 *Int'l Rev Red Cross* 327, 335–7.
118 UNGA, 'Supplement to an Agenda for Peace' (25 January 1995) UN Doc A/50/60–S/1995/1, para 70.
119 Roscini (n 116) 346.
120 *Prosecutor v Martić* (Trial Chamber) IT-95-11-R61 (8 March 1996); *Prosecutor v Šešelj* (Initial Indictment) IT-03-67 (15 January 2003); *Prosecutor v Babić* (Appeals Judgment) IT-03-72 (18 July 2005).
121 *Prosecutor v Brima, Kamara and Kanu* (the AFRC Accused) SCSL-04-16-T (20 June 2007); *Prosecutor v Issa Hassan Sesay, Morris Kallon and Augustine Gbao* (the RUF accused) (Appeal judgment) SCSL-04-15-A (26 October 2009).
122 *Prosecutor v Thomas Lubanga Dyilo*, ICC-01/04-01/06 (14 March 2012) (hereafter, *Lubanga*).
123 UNSC, 'Security Council Says States Have Primary Responsibility for Protecting Civilians in Conflict' UN Doc SC/10913 (12 February 2013).
124 WJ Fenrich, 'The Law Applicable to Targeting and Proportionality after Operation Allied Force: A View from the Outside' (2000) 3 *YB Int'l Humanitarian L* 53, 79–80.

accountability mechanisms will be further examined in the final substantive section of this chapter. For the time being, it suffices to highlight the practical issues raised by extant international humanitarian and human rights law.

3.2 State-based accountability mechanisms and the challenge of MNEs

The centrality of the State in the operation of international human rights and humanitarian law having been established, this section seeks to assess the efficacy of domestic accountability mechanisms. This analysis is primarily situated in the context of business actors operating within weak governance States. The multinational reach of these entities' operations raises complex questions concerning jurisdictional competence, the selection of appropriate forums and the application of one particular State's domestic law.[125] In lieu of direct legal regulation at the international level, the onus is placed on individual States to provide domestic avenues to effective remedies. Whether the 'host', 'home' or some intermediary State should be tasked with this responsibility is often difficult to ascertain. Although redress is often sought through private law mechanisms, the situation is complicated further by the variety of laws that remain tangentially relevant, including domestic company law, human rights, criminal and employment law. Each of these issues will be explored in turn.

The foregoing analysis highlighted the hesitance of States to concede the application of international humanitarian law, owing to the legitimising effects it is perceived to engender for non-State armed groups considered to directly threaten State sovereignty. Similar concerns were expressed regarding the spread of business actors throughout the 1970s, when foreign-owned companies were viewed:

> as economic agents of their home States, with no particular allegiances to the States in which they chose to invest . . . [and] as a threat to sovereignty . . . because of fears that they might exercise undue influence over the host State's national policies.[126]

Home States too expressed concern regarding the effects of overseas investments on domestic job prospects.[127] Yet, these territorial anxieties have gradually diminished. Instead, business actors have come to be regarded as free agents, tied only to the market.[128] Neo-liberal economic policies, including

---

125 Celia Wells and Juanita Elias, 'Catching the Conscience of the King: Corporate Players on the International Stage' in Alston (n 16) 148.
126 Zerk (n 49) 9–10.
127 Ibid.
128 Milton Friedman, *Capitalism and Freedom* (Chicago, IL, University of Chicago Press, 1962) 132–5.

deregulation, the removal of trade barriers and the promotion of the free market, have gained prominence and placed pressure on developing countries in particular to attract FDI.[129] The economic dependency of many weak governance States on external investment has propagated the unwillingness of States to hold business actors to account.[130] Thus, the variety of political and economic challenges presented by non-State actors is no more apparent than between non-State armed groups and business actors. The challenges presented by the essentially synonymous legal categorisation of these incredibly diverse entities are therefore revealed as a by-product of this analysis. Even if the procedural hurdles inherent in State-based accountability mechanisms can be overcome, nuanced approaches to non-State actor regulation are necessary in order to appropriately respond to the distinct challenges presented by each entity.

A brief note on descriptors is necessary before proceeding. Although numerous terms have been adopted to describe business actors, they have generally been used in an inconsistent and interchangeable manner. Entities are described as 'transnational', 'multinational', and as 'corporations', 'companies' and 'enterprises'. Scholars have attributed various meanings to each of these terms. The term 'transnational' is said to imply '*one* single corporation even if it is composed of corporations with separate identities under the corporation law of the States in which they operate'.[131] Some scholars have distinguished between 'transnational' and 'multinational' entities, adopting the latter where an actor 'engages in *direct investment*, which gives the enterprise not only a financial stake in the foreign venture, but also managerial control'.[132] By implication, a transnational entity would have a single seat of power, usually its place of incorporation or the location of its headquarters.[133] Although the practice of the UN has been fairly inconsistent in this regard,[134] it has generally reflected the view that multinationals are owned and controlled by groups in more than one country, whereas a transnational is controlled by an entity in a single country that operates across State borders.[135] Yet, there is no single

---

129 Ha-Joon Chang, *Globalisation, Economic Development and the Role of the State* (London, Zed Books, 2003) 247.

130 Steven Little and Laureen Snider, 'Examining the Ruggie Report: Can Voluntary Guidelines Tame Global Capitalism?' (2013) 21 *Crit Crim* 177–92.

131 Francis Rigaux, 'Transnational Corporations' in Mohammed Bedjaoui (ed), *International Law: Achievements and Prospects* (The Hague, Netherlands, Martinus Nijhoff, 1991) 121, 124.

132 Peter Muchlinski, *Multinational Enterprises and the Law* (2nd edn, Oxford, UK, OUP, 2007) 12.

133 Zerk (n 49) 146.

134 Muchlinski, *Multinational Enterprises* (n 132).

135 Cynthia Day Wallace, *Legal Control of the Multinational Enterprise, National Regulatory Techniques and the Prospects for International Controls* (Leiden, Netherlands, Brill, 1982) 12; cf Wells and Elias (n 125) 148–9.

authoritative test to determine the nationality of economic entities, and the intricate corporate structures exhibited by many business actors may result in the dispersal of their headquarters, sites of incorporation and shareholders across various States.[136] Accordingly, so-called 'home' States are increasingly difficult to locate, leading some commentators to suggest that the concept is now irrelevant.[137]

Similarly, it has been suggested that the term 'corporation', in contrast with 'enterprise', has been 'used in a relatively limited sense to apply exclusively to entities governed by private law', as opposed to entities that operate, to some degree, under State control.[138] Yet, the term 'enterprise' has been favoured by scholars such as McBeth and Muchlinski, as it is perceived to avoid 'restricting the object of study to incorporated business entities and to corporate groups based on parent–subsidiary relations alone'.[139] Rather, the term 'encompasses a collection of entities working towards a common purpose, and can include many different forms of business organisation'.[140] In the name of pragmatism, the term multinational enterprise will be adopted as the preferred descriptor for the remainder of this study. The following sub-sections examine the operation of accountability mechanisms in both 'home' and 'host' States, demonstrating the impediments to effective non-State actor regulation at the domestic level.

3.2.1 *Challenges to 'host State' accountability*

A host State is simply the 'country in which an entity other than the parent entity is located'.[141] Thus, in basic parent–subsidiary relationships, host countries will house the local arm of a larger entity that is incorporated or headquartered elsewhere. Given the primary responsibility of States to ensure adherence to human rights from all actors within their jurisdiction, the most obvious avenue to redress is via the host State's domestic legal system. The presence of MNEs in such States is often justified on the basis that they provide a catalyst to prosperity and development.[142] Although extractive industries may have

---

136 Zerk (n 49) 149.
137 Clapham (n 1) 200–1.
138 Rigaux (n 131) 121.
139 Muchlinski, *Multinational Enterprises* (n 132) 13.
140 Adam McBeth, *International Economic Actors and Human Rights* (Oxford, UK, Routledge, 2011) 246.
141 UN Commission on Transnational Corporations, 'Draft United Nations Code of Conduct on Transnational Corporations' (7–18 March and 9–21 May 1983) UN Doc E/1983/17/Rev. 1 Annex II, 12 (hereafter, UN Draft Code 1983).
142 Anne Orford, 'Globalisation and the Right to Development' in Alston (n 16) 135; Olubayo Oluduro, *Oil Exploitation and Human Rights Violations in Nigeria's Oil Producing Communities* (Cambridge, UK, Intersentia, 2014) 271.

provided a significant boost to the economies of Western States,[143] mineral-rich developing countries are frequently described as being subject to a resource curse, where '[b]uried oil, gas or mineral wealth acts as a "honey pot" that attracts corruption and stimulates conflicts among local elites seeking to line their own pockets at the expense of the welfare of communities'.[144] Thus, development arguments are difficult to sustain where States lack an accountability framework to ensure the equitable distribution of resource revenues.[145] These States are generally unwilling or incapable of shielding their populations from the abusive operations of MNEs in the first instance, owing to corruption,[146] dependence on FDI or their fragile infrastructures.[147] Accordingly, victims must seek *ex post facto* redress via the initiation of domestic civil, criminal and human rights disputes.[148]

The adverse effects produced by corporate activity do not occur in a vacuum: 'much more common is the situation where a corporation *assists* government, or other actors (local warlords, for example) in violating human rights norms, or provides the opportunity for the violation'.[149] The activities of Anvil Mining in the DRC provide a useful illustration of the factors at play in achieving domestic legal redress in host States. Anvil boasts an extremely complex corporate structure. Its parent is incorporated in Canada, its head office is in Australia, and its subsidiary operating in the DRC is 90 per cent owned by a holding company incorporated in the UK.[150] In October 2004, a minor insurrection led by a rebel group occurred in the village of Kilwa.[151] It is generally agreed that the group was 'set up as pawns in a power play by certain

---

143 Andy Whitmore, 'The Emperor's New Clothes: Sustainable Mining?' (2006) 14 *J Cleaner Prod* 309, 311.

144 Morton Winston, 'Corporate Responsibility for Preventing Human Rights Abuses in Conflict Areas' in Scott Pegg and Jedrzej George Frynas (eds), *Transnational Corporations and Human Rights* (Basingstoke, UK, Palgrave Macmillan, 2003) 82.

145 Geoffrey Chandler, 'The Evolution of the Business and Human Rights Debate' in Rory Sullivan (ed), *Business and Human Rights: Dilemmas and Solutions* (Sheffield, UK, Greenleaf, 2003) 25–6; Denise Humphreys Bebbington and Anthony J Bebbington, 'Extraction, Territory and Inequalities: Gas in the Bolivian Chaco' (2010) 30 *Can J Dev Stud* 259.

146 Oluduro (n 142) 353.

147 Muchlinski, *Multinational Enterprises* (n 132) 104–9.

148 Ibid. 124–5.

149 Andrew J Wilson, 'Beyond Unocal: Conceptual Problems in Using International Norms to Hold Transnational Corporations Liable Under the Alien Tort Claims Act' in De Schutter, *Transnational Corporations* (n 16) 55.

150 Adam McBeth, 'Crushed by an Anvil: A Case Study on Responsibility for Human Rights in the Extractive Industry' (2008) 11 *Yale Hum Rts & Dev LJ* 127, 130.

151 United Nations Organisation Mission in the Democratic Republic of Congo (MONUC), 'Report on the Conclusions of the Special Investigation into Allegations of Summary Executions and Other Violations of Human Rights Committed by the FARDC in Kilwa (Province of Katanga)' (15 October 2004) para 3 (hereafter, MONUC Report 2004).

Congolese politicians'.[152] The following day, members of the Congolese military launched a counter-attack against the group, killing rebels, illegally detaining[153] and massacring vulnerable citizens[154] and looting their properties.[155] Anvil Mining complied with requests from Congolese military leaders for logistical support, providing vehicles, drivers, aeroplanes and food rations.[156] Although there is a tendency in such scenarios to argue that States would engage in these abuses irrespective of corporate involvement, for McBeth, Anvil's role in perpetuating the violations is 'beyond dispute'.[157]

Charges were brought in the Congolese military courts against both the military commanders involved in the 'reprisals' against the insurrectionary group and against Anvil employees.[158] The MNE itself was not charged. Although the prosecutor initially called for life imprisonment for eight of the nine military defendants, all were eventually acquitted.[159] The trial was widely criticised for its assumption of jurisdiction by the military courts and its subsequent ruling. The Special Rapporteur on the Independence of Judges and Lawyers commented, upon his return from the DRC, that, '[m]ilitary justice continues to be tarnished by a very high incidence of military and political interference'.[160] It has even been suggested that the military court's decision was a tactic to insulate the defendants from further criminal proceedings on the grounds of double jeopardy.[161] Although criminal prosecutions were contemplated in Australia, investigations ultimately ceased.[162] Clearly, the judicial systems in many weak governance States can produce insurmountable hurdles to domestic redress. Even where State complicity is not readily apparent, host State litigation has been overlooked owing to 'inadequate protection in municipal law, inability to access the forum, or poor prospects of recovering

---

152 McBeth, 'Crushed by an Anvil' (n 150) 132.
153 MONUC Report 2004 (n 151) paras 26–9.
154 Ibid. paras 30–2.
155 Ibid. paras 33–5.
156 McBeth, 'Crushed by an Anvil' (n 150) 134.
157 Ibid. 135; Tófalo (n 44) 346.
158 *Public Prosecutor v Adémar Ilunga, Sadiaka Sampanda, Anvil Mining Company Congo and Others*, Military Court of Katanga, Congo, RP No 010/2006.
159 McBeth, 'Crushed by an Anvil' (n 150) 143–4.
160 Leandro Despouy, 'Report of the Special Rapporteur on the Independence of Judges and Lawyers: Preliminary Note on the Mission to the Democratic Republic of the Congo' (May 25 2007) UN Doc A/HRC/4/25Add.3 para 3.
161 McBeth, 'Crushed by an Anvil' (n 150) 147–9.
162 Joanna Kyriakakis, 'Australian Prosecution of Corporations for International Crimes' (2007) 5 *J Int'l Crim Just* 809; Global Witness, 'No Justice in Canada for Congolese Massacre Victim as Canada's Supreme Court Dismisses Leave to Appeal in Case Against Anvil Mining' (1 November 2012) www.globalwitness.org/library/no-justice-canada-congolese-massacre-victims-canada%E2%80%99s-supreme-court-dismisses-leave-appeal, accessed 21 April 2016.

compensation'.[163] The endemic procedural irregularities experienced in many host States are often advantageous to MNEs, with competition between governments for business resulting in a 'race to the bottom'.[164]

An example of this phenomenon is visible in Nigeria, where domestic legislation often more readily serves the interests of MNEs than those of its population. The introduction of the Land Use Act (1978) provided that all land in the territory of each Nigerian State is 'vested in the Governor of that State and such land shall be held in trust and administered for the use and common benefit of all Nigerians'.[165] Despite the utilitarian wording of this provision, populations have been deprived of the right to adequate compensation,[166] and land has been procured by governors for use by oil companies,[167] with rent payments made to governors rather than the affected communities.[168] The Act has 'snatched from individuals in the community, families and the communities their inalienable right to property and source of livelihood and turned them into beggars and squatters in their ancestral homes'.[169] This in turn has propagated violence among communities, including instances of rioting, hostage-taking, killing and maiming.[170] A similar scenario has arisen in Ghana, where Newmont Mining Corporation was accused of expropriating the land of vulnerable farming communities without payment of compensation.[171] This, in turn, was justified on the basis that no Act prescribed compensation for the appropriation of land, and all royalty/rent payments are payable, not to 'individual farmers or families, but the traditional authorities'.[172] Under Ghana's State Lands Act (1962), 'every (minerals-rich) land is vested in the government and can be acquired for development. Mining companies therefore do not pay compensation on land *per se* but pay compensation for affected crops and also pay royalties to the central government'.[173] Although Western host States may prove less vulnerable to such exploitation, and may occasionally

163 McBeth, *International Economic Actors* (n 140) 294.
164 Jacqueline Duval-Major, 'One Way Ticket Home: The Federal Doctrine of *Forum Non Conveniens* and the International Plaintiff' (1992) 77 *Cornell L Rev* 650, 675.
165 Land Use Act, Laws of the Federation of Nigeria (1990), Section 1; Oluduro (n 142) 80–3.
166 Ibid. Section 47(2); Rhuks Ako, 'Nigeria's Land Use Act: An Anti-Thesis to Environmental Justice' (2009) 53 *J Afr L* 289.
167 Winston (n 144) 88.
168 Jedrzej George Frynas, 'The Oil Industry in Nigeria: Conflict between Oil Companies and Local People' in Pegg and Frynas (n 144) 102–3.
169 Ibid. 86.
170 Aderoju Oyefusi, 'Oil and the Probability of Rebel Participation among Youths in the Niger Delta of Nigeria' (2008) 45 *J Peace Res* 539.
171 Radu Mares, 'Corporate Responsibility and Compliance with the Law: A Case Study of Land, Dispossession, and Aftermath at Newmont's Ahafo Project in Ghana' (2012) 117 *Bus Soc Rev* 233.
172 Ibid. 239.
173 Ibid. 242.

achieve amicable partnerships between indigenous populations and corporate entities, such instances are undeniably rare.[174]

The operation of civilian courts in many host States has also proven procedurally challenging. Nigerian courts have declined to restrain pollution caused by oil extraction for the explicit reason that it would negatively affect national revenue.[175] Many cases concerning the operations of MNEs are framed in tort law. The superior technical knowledge of oil operations held by MNEs can often impede the ability of plaintiffs to prove that a corporation has acted negligently in violation of accepted environmental standards.[176] Furthermore, the tort of negligence may lend itself more favourably to certain factual circumstances,[177] with instances involving uncontrollable third-party sabotage often falling short of the required threshold.[178] It has been suggested that false claims of sabotage are frequently made by MNEs to avoid liability.[179] Sabotage is also said to be carried out by contractors affiliated with MNEs seeking further clean-up work, 'sometimes with the connivance of oil company staff'.[180] These instances go some way towards '[d]ebunking the long-standing claim of Shell that sabotage is the single most important cause of oil pollution in the Niger Delta'.[181]

Procedural technicalities are initiated by MNEs before Nigerian courts as defensive strategies.[182] The case of *Shell v Enoch*,[183] where a Nigerian community sued for environmental damage resulting from an oil spill, demonstrates this tendency. Shell sought to prevent the plaintiffs from filing a joint action on the basis that the grievance of each individual was distinct. The court concurred, ordering a *non-suit*, but permitted the initiation of separate proceedings by each individual plaintiff. Yet, whereas an entire community may be able to pool the requisite legal fees to bring an action, it is unlikely that an individual would be able to garner the financial resources to take on an MNE alone. In the rare event that fines are incurred by MNEs, and remedial compensation is awarded

---

174 Heike Fabig and Richard Boele, 'Timber Logging in Clayoquot Sound, Canada: Community–Corporate Partnerships and Community Rights' in Pegg and Frynas (n 144) 189–215.

175 *Allar Irou v Shell BP*, Unreported Suit No W/89/71 (High Court of Warri, Nigeria); Olawale Ajai, 'Balancing of Interests in Environmental Law in Nigeria' in Michael Faure and Willemien Du Plessis (eds), *The Balancing of Interests in Environmental Law in Africa* (Pretoria, SA, PULP, 2011) 403.

176 Jedrzej George Frynas, 'Legal Change in Africa: Evidence from Oil-Related Litigation in Nigeria' (1999) 43 *JAfr L* 121, 124; Oluduro (n 142) 167.

177 Frynas, 'Legal Change in Africa' (n 176) 149.

178 Ibid. 127–8.

179 Jedrzej George Frynas, 'Political Instability and Business: Locus on Shell in Nigeria' (1998) 19 *Third World Q* 457, 465.

180 Oluduro (n 142) 139.

181 Ibid. 173.

182 Frynas, 'Legal Change in Africa' (n 176) 149.

183 *Shell v Enoch* (1992) 8 NWLR 335.

to the plaintiffs, the figures are often disproportionately low, hardly covering the cost of litigation.[184] These factors go some way towards explaining the 'forum-shopping' of which victims are often accused.[185]

The domestic company laws of host States have also produced unfortunate effects on avenues to extraterritorial redress. Although such claims will be considered further below, it is useful to highlight the effects of these domestic provisions here. Following independence, the military government of Nigeria introduced the Companies and Allied Matters Act (1968) (CAMA), section 54 of which mandates all corporations registered overseas to reincorporate as Nigerian companies.[186] Although this may be viewed as an attempt by the Nigerian government to assert domestic regulatory control over foreign companies, its effects have been criticised.[187] Pursuant to section 60, this mandatory incorporation does not affect 'the rights or liability of a foreign company to sue or be sued in its name or in the name of its agent', essentially negating the suggested effect of section 54.[188] In practice, section 54 has enabled parent companies to 'deny liability for any adverse consequences . . . since the subsidiary is incorporated and legally recognised as a Nigerian company'.[189] Such factors often play a significant part in the assessment of the proximity in the parent–subsidiary relationship in cases that attempt to pierce the corporate veil.[190] Thus, section 54 provides a legislative aid to the fragmentation of corporate entities, to the potential detriment of vulnerable victims.

Despite these well-documented procedural hurdles, there have been instances of success. Take, for example, the Indonesian litigation against a subsidiary of the US-based Newmont Mining Corporation.[191] Although Indonesian authorities had previously proven reluctant to prosecute corporations domestically,[192] legal proceedings began against the subsidiary company, PT Newmont Minahasa Raya (PTNMR), in March 2005. The civil case, brought by the Indonesian Environment Ministry, sought compensation of US$117.68 million for lost

184 Oluduro (n 142) 181–2.
185 Daniel Dorward, '*Forum Non Conveniens* Doctrine and the Judicial Protection of Multinational Corporations from Forum Shopping Plaintiffs' (1998) 19 *U Pa J Int'l Econ L* 141.
186 Companies and Allied Matters Act (CAMA) Nigeria (1968), section 54(1).
187 Olufemi Amao, 'Corporate Social Responsibility, Multinational Corporations and the Law in Nigeria: Controlling Multinationals in Host States' (2008) 52 *J Afr L* 89, 97.
188 Companies and Allied Matters Act (1990), Laws of the Federation of Nigeria, section 60(b).
189 Amao, 'Corporate Social Responsibility' (n 187) 97; Leslie Mitnick, 'Multinationals Fight Back with the Doctrine of *Forum Non Conveniens*' (1989) 56 *Defence Counsel J* 391, 400.
190 *Mobil Producing (Nig) United v Monokpo* (2003) 18 NWLR 852, 346; *Shell Petroleum Development Company (SPDC) of Nigeria v Dr Pere Ajuwa and Honourable Ingo Mac-Etteli* (27 May 2007) No CA/A/209/06 (Court of Appeal, Abuja Division, Nigeria).
191 Jonathan Hills and Richard Welford, 'Profits, Pollution and Prison: A Case Study of Gold Mining in Indonesia' (2005) 12 *CSR Environ Manage* 105.
192 Alice De Jonge, *Transnational Corporations and International Law: Accountability in the Global Business Environment* (Cheltenham, UK, Edward Elgar, 2011) 131.

income and an additional US$16.3 million for damage to the State's reputation.[193] The case ultimately failed, on the basis that Indonesia had violated the terms of its joint venture with the MNE, which mandated settlement through international arbitration or conciliation. A 'good will' payment of US$30 million was eventually agreed, which PTNMR would distribute to unspecified community programmes over the next decade.[194] The company has also endorsed a number of corporate social responsibility (CSR) initiatives and formulated its own integrated management system to embed human rights standards in future operations.[195] An additional criminal case was filed in 2005 against PTNMR and its director, Richard Ness, for 'unlawful acts including pollution, which caused the indigenous people's environment to be degraded'.[196] However, 15 months later, the District Court of Manado abruptly acquitted both defendants, despite what was perceived by campaigners as strong evidential and NGO support.[197]

Another partial success was achieved by the Indian courts following the Bhopal gas tragedy.[198] The case concerned a chemical plant in Bhopal operated by Union Carbide of India Ltd, a subsidiary that was 50.9 per cent owned by an American parent corporation (Union Carbide Corporation).[199] In 1984, the plant released a substantial quantity of highly toxic pesticide gas into the atmosphere, killing 2,000 people and leaving between 200,000 and 450,000 people with long-term injuries.[200] Common defences were initiated, including accusations of sabotage by disgruntled employees and terrorist groups, but, ultimately, plant equipment was found to be inadequately maintained.[201] Following a period of prolonged litigation, an out-of-court settlement of US$470 million was reached, on the agreement that the parent corporation would be granted immunity from any subsequent actions. The corporation also agreed to invest US$17 million in a new hospital to deal with victims of the

193 Ibid.
194 Jack Morris, *Going for Gold: The History of Newmont Mining Corporation* (Tuscaloosa, AL, University of Alabama Press, 2010) 323.
195 Diego Quiroz-Onate, 'Newmont Mining Corporation: Embedding Human Rights through the Five Star Integrated Management System' in OHCHR, 'United Nations Global Compact: Embedding Human Rights in Business Practice II' (December 2007) 157–66, www.unglobalcompact.org/docs/issues_doc/human_rights/Business_Practices/Newmont %20complete_EHRBP%20II.pdf, accessed 21 April 2016.
196 Adérito de Jesus Soares, 'Reparations for Masyarakat Adat in Indonesia' in Federico Lenzerini (ed), *Reparations for Indigenous Peoples* (Oxford, UK, OUP, 2008) 472.
197 Ibid. 473.
198 Barbara Dinham and Satinath Sarangi, 'The Bhopal Gas Tragedy 1984 to . . .? The Evasion of Corporate Responsibility' (2002) 14 *Environ Urban* 89.
199 Peter Muchlinski, 'Bhopal Case: Controlling Ultrahazardous Industrial Activities Undertaken by Foreign Investors' (1987) 50 *MLR* 545.
200 Loong Wong, 'Revisiting Rights and Responsibility: The Case of Bhopal' (2008) 4 *Soc Resp J* 143, 144.
201 Ibid. 144–5.

disaster. In 1986, an action against the parent was initiated under the US Alien Torts Statute,[202] but the action was rejected on the weighing of public and private interests.[203] Although criminal proceedings were launched against the American company executives, to date, they have not complied with extradition orders.[204] Thus, although lucrative settlements were reached in each of these cases, no formal rulings were rendered against the subsidiaries, parents or company directors, underscoring the difficulty in establishing judicial precedent.

Finally, domestic accountability mechanisms may be embedded in the constitutions of host States. The incorporation of environmental/health rights into State constitutions is a growing practice across the developing world, but is also apparent in the US.[205] Nigeria is one such example. In *Gbemre & Others v Shell Petroleum Development Company*,[206] it was argued that pollution resulting from gas flaring was unconstitutional,[207] having violated the plaintiff's fundamental rights to life, dignity and a healthy environment under the Constitution of the Federal Republic of Nigeria (1999)[208] and the African Charter on Human and Peoples' Rights.[209] Although the express Chapter II rights to a healthy environment enshrined in sections 17(2)(d) and 20 of the Nigerian Constitution are not directly justiciable, a previous ruling indicated that the legislature had 'the power to make them enforceable against government bodies and also private persons including corporations'.[210] The court in *Gbemre* adopted a liberal interpretation of the constitutional right to life/dignity in light of the environmental/health rights enshrined in the African Charter. It was held that Shell's operations constituted a gross violation of the community's human rights, and that existing legislation was inconsistent with both the Nigerian Constitution and the African Charter.[211]

---

202 *Re Union Carbide Corporation Gas Plant Disaster at Bhopal, India*, 809 F.2d 195 (2nd Cir 1987).
203 Allin Seward, 'After Bhopal: Implications for Parent Company Liability' (1987) 21 *Int'l Lawyer* 695.
204 GS Bajpai and Bir Pal Singh, 'The Bhopal Gas Disaster and Corporate Criminal Negligence' in Mangai Natarajan (ed), *International Crime and Justice* (Cambridge, UK, CUP, 2011) 203.
205 Kaniye Ebeku, 'Constitutional Right to a Healthy Environment and Human Rights Approaches to Environmental Protection in Nigeria: Gbemre v. Shell Revisited' (2007) 16 *Rev Eur Community Int'l Environ L* 312, 313–4.
206 *Gbemre v SPDC* (2005) FHC/B/CS/53/05 (Federal High Court of Nigeria).
207 Brown Umukoror, 'Gas Flaring, Environmental Corporate Responsibility and the Right to a Healthy Environment: The Case of the Niger Delta' in Festus Emiri and Gowon Deinduomo (eds), *Law and Petroleum Industry in Nigeria: Current Challenges* (Oxford, UK, African Books Collective, 2009) 54–7.
208 Constitution of the Federal Republic of Nigeria (1999) sections 33(1), 34(1).
209 African Charter on Human and Peoples' Rights (27 June 1981) CAB/LEG/67/3 rev. 5, 21 ILM 58, Articles 4, 16, 24.
210 Oluduro (n 142) 222–31; *Attorney General of Ondo State v Attorney General of the Federation and 35 Others* (7 June 2002) No SC.200/2001 (Supreme Court of Nigeria); Amao, *Corporate Social Responsibility, Human Rights and the Law* (n 37) 135.
211 *Gbemre* (n 206).

It has been suggested that *Gbemre* represents a nascent appreciation of the horizontal application of human rights to non-State actors in Nigeria.[212] Similarly, Amao suggests that human rights approaches to non-State actor accountability often avoid procedural challenges, enabling courts to grant injunctions to safeguard fundamental rights under an enforcement process that is 'much faster than other litigation procedures in Nigeria'.[213] This latter point relates to the fast-track procedure provided by section 46 of the Nigerian Constitution.[214] In 2013, a Dutch court tasked with the application of Nigerian law in a similar case refused to pursue this constitutional route, likely on the basis that the pollution resulted from third-party sabotage.[215] However, one of the key elements of the *Gbemre* decision was that, 'unlike previous cases . . . in which the courts insisted on the proof of "causal connection" . . . the judge . . . ignored the respondent's contention that the . . . activities have no causal connection with any of the reported cases'.[216] Nevertheless, it has been suggested that the case does not yet reflect a strong precedent,[217] though it does demonstrate the potential to resort to the African Charter in order to safeguard rights that are presently non-justiciable in constitutional law.[218]

This appraisal demonstrates the significant challenges to effective non-State actor regulation in many weak governance States. Although resource-rich host States may be obliged to ensure the human rights of their populations in theory, they will typically lack the capacity and infrastructure to protect their citizens in the first instance, and may be unwilling to impose greater domestic regulation or to permit litigation against abusive operations, given their economic dependence on the industries in question. National legislation may have the effect of directly benefitting business actors at the expense of local communities, or of shielding parent companies from direct liability. Where cases do find their way to the courts, civil actions may favour corporate defendants that are able to exploit procedural weaknesses in order to attribute blame to third parties or break up community actions. Even the largest settlements achieved against MNEs have not established precedents, formal legal actions having been hampered by the uneven terms of bilateral investment treaties.[219] Although

---

212 Oluduro (n 142) 400.
213 Amao, 'Corporate Social Responsibility' (n 187) 110.
214 Constitution of the Federal Republic of Nigeria (n 208) section 46.
215 Lee J McConnell, 'Establishing Liability for Multinational Corporations – Lessons from Akpan' (2014) 56 *Int'l JL Manage* 88.
216 Ebeku (n 205) 318.
217 A similar case was dismissed on procedural grounds: *Ikechukwu Opara & Others v Shell Petroleum Development Company Nigeria Ltd and 5 Others* (2005) FHC/PH/CS/518/2005 (Federal High Court of Nigeria).
218 Olufemi Amao, 'The African Regional Human Rights System' in Mashood Baderin and Manisuli Ssenyonjo (eds), *International Human Rights Law: Six Decades after the UDHR and Beyond* (Aldershot, UK, Ashgate, 2010) 250–1.
219 Ryan Suda, 'The Effect of Bilateral Investment Treaties on Human Rights Enforcement and Realisation' in De Schutter, *Transnational Corporations* (n 16) 90–5.

constitutional approaches to human rights claims may offer some promise, the strength of recent precedents is not certain. Thus, in practice, State-based accountability methods are increasingly inadequate. However, this is not the only avenue to domestic redress. Attention now turns to the situation in 'home' States.

3.2.2 Challenges to 'home State' accountability

A clear commercial relationship exists between subsidiary companies operating in host States and their parent corporations, which are often incorporated or domiciled elsewhere. Various questions arise concerning the responsibility of 'home' States to regulate the overseas activities of their so-called 'corporate nationals', and whether there is an appropriate jurisdictional nexus to litigate abuses committed by, or with the assistance of, their foreign subsidiaries.[220] In the affirmative, the attribution of liability to parent corporations for such activities demands careful consideration. It was suggested above that the establishment of an MNE's home State is increasingly problematic, owing to their complex operational structures. Whereas the 1983 UN Draft Code simply provides that a home State is 'the country in which the parent entity is located', this determination is not always so simple.[221] Civil jurisdictions have favoured the 'real seat' theory, which focuses on the actual place of managerial control.[222] Common law States tend to favour the place of incorporation, in line with the *US (Third) Restatement of Foreign Relations Law*.[223] Although the ICJ appears to have adopted the latter approach, it has conceded that, 'in the particular field of diplomatic protection of corporate entities, no absolute test of "genuine connection" has found acceptance . . . and sometimes links with one State have to be weighed with another'.[224]

The difficulty posed by corporate structures is well demonstrated by the ICJ's *Barcelona Traction* Advisory Opinion.[225] Here, Belgium sought to initiate proceedings against Spain for damage resulting from the Spanish government's restrictive foreign business policies. Barcelona Traction was incorporated in Canada and controlled subsidiaries in Spain. The company was controlled by a Belgian parent called Sidro, which was itself controlled by Sofina, the majority shareholders of which were Belgian. To succeed, the Court needed to expose the effective control of the company by its Belgian parent, despite its Canadian

---

220 McCorquodale and Simons (n 45) 598.
221 UN Draft Code 1983 (n 141).
222 Werner Ebke, 'The "Real Seat" Doctrine in the Conflict of Corporate Laws' (2002) 36 *Int'l Lawyer* 1015, 1016.
223 American Law Institute, Restatement (Third) of Foreign Relations Law (1986) §213 (hereafter, US Third Restatement).
224 *Barcelona Traction, Light and Power Company (Belgium v Spain)* (Second Phase) ICJ Reports [1970] para 70 (hereafter, *Barcelona Traction*).
225 Ibid.

incorporation.[226] The ICJ was unwilling, finding Canada to be the proper State to exercise diplomatic protection.[227] The case demonstrates a recurring hurdle to parent company accountability. An entity may be insulated by the separate incorporation of its constituent entities, encapsulating the difficult balancing act between corporate regulation 'and the desire to ensure the effectiveness of company law and the associated economic benefits'.[228] Practical illustrations of such scenarios will be drawn below.

Though MNEs are increasingly considered to be 'stateless' and are no longer perceived as ambassadors of the States in which they are primarily domiciled, home State reputation is still an important factor in corporate regulation.[229] Likewise, concerns surrounding job migration provide an economic incentive to ensure certain minimum standards are met overseas.[230] Yet, the existence of formal international duties mandating corporate oversight by home States remains contentious. From a human rights perspective, it has been suggested that Article 12 of the International Covenant on Economic, Social and Cultural Rights (ICESCR)[231] could reflect an obligation for home States to 'prevent third parties from violating the right [to health] in other countries, if they are able to influence these third parties by way of legal or political means'.[232] However, in its contemplation of the responsibility to protect, the Committee on Economic Social and Cultural Rights expressly refers only to individuals within the particular State's jurisdiction.[233] Although there is room for future evolution in this regard, establishing breaches of such duties would likely prove difficult. At present, it is likely that home State obligations are limited to the 'softer' duties to respect and promote human rights overseas.[234]

Another route concerns the obligation of States to prevent transboundary harm. Pursuant to Article 3 of the Biodiversity Convention, States possess 'the responsibility to ensure that activities within their jurisdiction or control do not cause damage to the environment of other States or areas beyond the limits of

---

226 McBeth, *International Economic Actors* (n 140) 277.
227 *Barcelona Traction* (n 224) 101.
228 McBeth, *International Economic Actors* (n 140) 275.
229 Surya Deva, 'Acting Extraterritorially to Tame Multinational Corporations for Human Rights Violations: "Who Should Bell the Cat?"' (2004) 5 *Melb J Int'l L* 37.
230 Zerk (n 49) 154.
231 International Covenant on Economic, Social and Cultural Rights (16 December 1966) 993 UNTS 3, Article 12.
232 UN Committee on Economic Social and Cultural Rights, 'General Comment 14 – The Right to the Highest Attainable Standard of Health' (11 August 2000) UN Doc E/C. 12/2000/3 para 39; Fons Coomans, 'The Extraterritorial Scope of the International Covenant on Economic, Social and Cultural Rights' (2011) 11 *HRL Rev* 1.
233 Ibid. para 51.
234 Zerk (n 49) 89; Penelope Simons and Audrey Macklin, *The Governance Gap: Extractive Industries, Human Rights and the Home State Advantage* (Oxford, UK, Routledge, 2014) 273–355.

national jurisdiction'.[235] This obligation has been codified by the 1992 Rio Declaration[236] and the ILC's Draft Articles on Transboundary Harm from Hazardous Activities[237] and considered by the ICJ in its *Nuclear Weapons* Advisory Opinion.[238] Yet, aside from the courtesy of providing advance warning of potential hazards, the 'home States of multinationals do not presently appear to be under any requirement . . . to continue regulating the operation and management of those hazards once they are within the jurisdiction of another State'.[239] Moreover, home States are subject to the customary duty of non-intervention in the internal or external affairs of other States, a 'master principle' according to which '[m]atters within the competence of States under general international law are said to be within the reserved domain, the domestic jurisdiction, of States'.[240] Thus, if one adheres to the territorial approach to jurisdiction advanced by the Draft Articles on Transboundary Harm,[241] then 'any assertion of extraterritorial jurisdiction by a State would amount to a violation of international law'.[242] Today, the recognised bases of jurisdictional competence have been subject to some limited expansion, at least in theory.[243] This matter will be briefly explored, before illustration is drawn from practical instances of home State litigation.

3.2.2.1 *Establishing home State jurisdiction*

The *territoriality* principle undoubtedly remains at the heart of determinations concerning jurisdictional competence.[244] It has been suggested that competence may be common to both host and home States on the basis of territoriality, where human rights violations stem from the overseas activities of MNEs.[245] There is certainly justification for this view under the *objective territoriality*

235 Convention on Biological Diversity (5 June 1992) 1760 UNTS 79, Article 3.
236 Rio Declaration on Environment and Development (13 June 1992) 31 ILM 874, Principles 12 and 19.
237 ILC, Draft Articles on the Prevention of Transboundary Harm from Hazardous Activities (2001) UNGOAR Fifty-Sixth Session UN Doc A/56/10, Article 3.
238 *Legality of the Use by a State of Nuclear Weapons in Armed Conflict* (Advisory Opinion) ICJ Reports [1996] 241–242 para 29.
239 Zerk (n 49) 160.
240 Ian Brownlie, *Principles of Public International Law* (7th edn, Oxford, UK, OUP, 2008) 292.
241 ILC, 'Draft Articles on Prevention of Transboundary Harm from Hazardous Activities, with Commentaries' Yearbook of the International Law Commission (2001) Vol II, 150.
242 Muchlinski, *Multinational Enterprises* (n 132) 124.
243 McBeth, *International Economic Actors* (n 140) 281; Sara Seck, 'Home State Responsibility and Local Communities: The Case of Global Mining' (2008) 11 *Yale Hum Rts Dev LJ* 177.
244 Brownlie (n 240) 301.
245 McBeth, *International Economic Actors* (n 140) 281.

principle[246] as applied by the PCIJ in *Lotus*.[247] The case has led to the assertion by States of 'an objective territorial jurisdiction over offences initiated abroad and completed within the jurisdiction'.[248] Thus, although the State where the harm is suffered has objective territorial jurisdiction,[249] where actions originating in a home State have contributed to that harm, that State has a concurrent *subjective* claim to jurisdiction.[250] In this manner, it has been argued that it is the effective control of individuals, even where territorial control is lacking, that is determinative of home State jurisdiction.[251] Although this approach has been endorsed to varying degrees in international jurisprudence, the extent to which a home State can be said to *control* the individuals employed by, and proximate to, a separately incorporated subsidiary or contractor operating extraterritorially remains highly questionable.[252] Rather, it is likely that the nexus would need to border on State agency in order for a State to incur such responsibilities.

Other jurisdictional bases such as the *passive personality*[253] and *protective/ security* principles[254] are probably less relevant to home State jurisdiction for extraterritorial human rights abuses stemming from corporate activity. On the other hand, the *nationality* principle raises another potential justification for the establishment of common jurisdiction: 'in certain cases a State can assert jurisdiction over its nationals abroad. In accordance with this principle, the home State of a MNE could seek to justify jurisdiction over the activities of an overseas unit'.[255] As such, managers exhibiting control over an MNE's overseas operations could be subject to home State laws by way of their nationality. However, the identification of the individuals in overall control of an entity's operations could prove problematic, given the nature of their operational structures. Yet, Muchlinski suggests that, even where home State nationals do not sit on the executive board of a foreign subsidiary, a parent company could exert its nationality as majority shareholder and thus demand compliance with home State laws.[256] Moreover, where subsidiaries have not been subject to separate incorporation, these entities 'retain the nationality of the parent and

---

246 Brownlie (n 240) 301–3.
247 *The Case of the SS 'Lotus' (France v Turkey)* (1927) PCIJ (ser. A) No 10, 18–20 (hereafter, *Lotus*).
248 Muchlinski, *Multinational Enterprises* (n 132) 128.
249 *Lotus* (n 247) 23.
250 McBeth, *International Economic Actors* (n 140) 281.
251 Daniel Augenstein and David Kinley, 'When Human Rights "Responsibilities" Become "Duties": The Extra-Territorial Obligations of States that Bind Corporations' in Surya Deva and David Bilchitz (eds), *Human Rights Obligations of Business: Beyond the Corporate Responsibility to Respect?* (Cambridge, UK, CUP, 2013) 285–6.
252 Ibid. 285–6; Max Schaefer, 'Al-Skeini and the Elusive Parameters of Extraterritorial Jurisdiction' (2011) 5 *EHRLR* 566.
253 Brownlie (n 240) 304.
254 Ibid.
255 Muchlinski, *Multinational Enterprises* (n 132) 127.
256 Ibid.

could, therefore, be subjected to the direct jurisdiction of the home country by reason of their corporate nationality'.[257] On this latter point, it has already been demonstrated that host State legislation may mandate the national incorporation of subsidiary companies, providing another layer of insulation between corporate entities.

Finally, the doctrine of universal jurisdiction, although clearly capable of providing a justification for home State litigation against multinationals, does not rest on the business connections between foreign subsidiaries and parent corporations.[258] Instead, all States are considered to possess jurisdictional competence over specific acts, even 'where such offences are not deemed to constitute threats to the fundamental interests of the prescribing State, or, in appropriate cases, to give rise to effects within its territory'.[259] Despite widespread acknowledgement of the principle, it has been invoked extremely rarely in practice. Even where the doctrine has been central to litigation, the ascription of a definition has been avoided.[260] The general rationale behind the doctrine has been described as 'the international reprobation for certain very serious crimes such as war crimes and crimes against humanity. Its *raison d'être* is to avoid impunity, to prevent suspects of such crimes finding a safe haven in third countries'.[261] The offences capable of giving rise to universal jurisdiction are generally limited to crimes of customary international law or violations of *jus cogens* norms, usually considered to be owed to the entire international community, *erga omnes*.[262] Thus, the extent to which universal jurisdiction may offer an avenue for the prosecution of human rights abuses that fail to reach this magnitude is extremely limited. There is, perhaps, more scope for leaders of non-State armed groups, but, given the predominance of low-intensity armed conflict today, the majority of conduct is unlikely to achieve this threshold.[263]

Many of the instances in which universal jurisdiction has been asserted by a domestic forum have occurred in Belgium. It was in response to these actions that the Congo's Minister of Foreign Affairs, Abdoulaye Yerodia, filed

257 Ibid.
258 Ibid. 140–53.
259 Roger O'Keefe, 'Universal Jurisdiction – Clarifying the Basic Concept' (2004) 2 *JICJ* 745.
260 *Arrest Warrant Case (Democratic Republic of the Congo v Belgium)* ICJ Reports [2002] para 44 (hereafter, *Arrest Warrant Case*).
261 Ibid. para 46; *Eichmann* (1968) 36 *ILR* 26.
262 James Crawford, *Brownlie's Principles of Public International Law* (8th edn, Oxford, UK, OUP, 2012) 468; Gillian Triggs, *International Law: Contemporary Principles and Practices* (Chatsworth Publishing, 2006) 358; *Barcelona Traction* (n 224) 32; Erika De Wet, 'Jus Cogens and Obligations Erga Omnes' in Dinah Shelton (ed), *The Oxford Handbook on Human Rights* (Oxford, UK, OUP, 2013) 553–60.
263 Arturo Carrillo-Suárez, '*Hors de Logique*: Contemporary Issues in International Humanitarian Law as Applied to Internal Armed Conflict' (1999) 15 *Am U Int'l L Rev* 1, 67; Buckley (n 107) 825.

proceedings against Belgium at the ICJ, resulting in its landmark *Arrest Warrant Case*.[264] Two further claims were initiated under the Belgian universal jurisdiction laws, the first pertaining to crimes against humanity allegedly committed by Denis Sassou Nguesso. The French MNE TotalFinaElf was mentioned as a complicit party owing to the logistical support it provided to the main defendant.[265] The second claim was filed by unidentified authors alleging crimes against humanity, 'including acts of torture, arbitrary killings and slavery in Myanmar . . . with TotalFinaElf and two of its executives designated as accomplices'.[266] The actions were widely denounced by the international business community.[267] Furthermore, the decision of the ICJ with regard to the immunity of Yerodia as a State official caused Belgium to revise its laws, which now include a requirement for some other form of jurisdictional link between the accused and the Belgian forum.[268] Despite its historic connection with a former colony, Belgium has no jurisdictional links to the DRC under the territoriality or nationality principles considered above. Although the ICJ did not rule out the potential to exercise universal jurisdiction, the action was enough to shut down this novel piece of Belgian legislation.[269] Thus, not only are the offences that may be prosecuted by virtue of universal jurisdiction incredibly limited, States are reluctant, for diplomatic and economic reasons, to utilise this jurisdictional basis. This avenue to non-State actor accountability is therefore largely unworkable in practice.

3.2.2.2 The challenge of parent–subsidiary relationships

Home States have generally proven reluctant to accept jurisdiction over events occurring wholly overseas.[270] Although a sufficient jurisdictional connection may occasionally be established, procedural matters often preclude the success of proceedings initiated in home States, and corporate structures regularly impede the direct attribution of liability to parent corporations, where the company's major assets usually lie. The case of *Akpan v Royal Dutch Shell (RDS) & Shell Petroleum and Development Company of Nigeria (SPDC)*[271] provides an ideal illustration of these challenges. The case was one of three similar actions

---

264 *Arrest Warrant Case* (n 260).
265 Olivier De Schutter, 'The Accountability of Multinationals for Human Rights Violations in European Law' in Alston (n 16) 288.
266 Ibid.
267 McBeth, *International Economic Actors* (n 140) 282.
268 *Arrest Warrant Case* (n 260) para 51; Steffen Wirth, 'Immunity for Core Crimes? The ICJ's Judgment in the Congo v. Belgium Case' (2002) 13 *EJIL* 877.
269 Crawford (n 262) 469.
270 Seck (n 243).
271 *Akpan v Royal Dutch Shell* (2013) LJN BY9854 (District Court of The Hague) https://milieudefensie.nl/publicaties/bezwaren-uitspraken/final-judgment-akpan-vs-shell-oil-spill-ikot-ada-udo/, accessed 21 April 2016 (hereafter *Akpan Judgment*).

brought jointly by four Nigerian farmers and the Dutch NGO Mileudefensie (Friends of the Earth Netherlands).[272] The applicants sought remediation for environmental damage to their farmlands and fishponds resulting from a number of oil spills occurring between 2004 and 2007. They initiated several civil and human rights claims at the District Court of The Hague against both RDS, which is headquartered in the Netherlands, and its wholly owned Nigerian subsidiary, SPDC. The corporate structure exhibited by these entities is complex and underscores the difficulty in pinpointing the liability of particular business actors. Both operate as part of the Shell Group, with SPDC acting as part of a joint venture with the State-owned Nigerian National Petroleum Corporation, among others. Such relationships are common, with subsidiaries typically maintaining managerial control, and State-owned companies contributing to operational costs.[273] In *Akpan*, the clean-up operation was contracted out to two Nigerian firms, further highlighting the structures that often insulate corporate defendants from liability.

Akpan is notable for the lengths the Dutch court went to in order to establish its jurisdiction over events occurring solely in Nigeria and the separately incorporated subsidiary company, SPDC. The defence raised a number of procedural challenges that, had they been initiated in Nigeria, would likely have led to the case's dismissal. It was argued that: (1) the extraterritorial nature of the case demanded a stringent connection between the causes of action against RDS and SPDC;[274] (2) the claims against the Dutch parent had been initiated solely to establish Dutch jurisdiction over SPDC;[275] (3) the joint action between *Akpan* and the NGO was inadmissible;[276] (4) the plaintiffs' failure to obtain disclosure of internal company documentation rendered the proceedings against the parent certain to fail;[277] and (5) the plaintiffs' ownership of the land in question was disputed.[278]

Somewhat surprisingly, the plaintiffs were able to overcome each of these ancillary challenges, permitting an assessment of the liability of both parent and

---

272 Lee J McConnell, 'Case Comment: Establishing Liability for Multinational Oil Companies in Parent/Subsidiary Relationships' (2014) 16 *Environ L Rev* 50; McConnell, 'Lessons from Akpan' (n 215).

273 Amao, 'Corporate Social Responsibility' (n 187) 94.

274 *Efanga & Oguru v Royal Dutch Shell* (2009) (Motion for the Court to Decline Jurisdiction/Conditional Statement of Defence) Docket No 2009/0579 (13 May 2009) para 75 https://milieudefensie.nl/publicaties/bezwaren-uitspraken/shells-response-to-the-subpoenas, accessed 21 April 2016; *Akpan v Royal Dutch Shell* (2009) (Judgment in Motion Contesting Jurisdiction) (30 December 2009) para 3.7 http://milieudefensie.nl/publicaties/bezwaren-uitspraken/judgment-courtcase-shell-in-jurisdiction-motion-oruma, accessed 21 April 2016 (hereafter, *Akpan Judgment on Jurisdiction*).

275 Ibid. para 80.

276 *Akpan v Royal Dutch Shell* (2011) (Production of Exhibits in the Main Action) (14 September 2011) para 4.3, www.milieudefensie.nl/publicaties/bezwaren-uitspraken/judgment-exhibition-alfred-akpan, accessed 21 April 2016 (hereafter, *Akpan Exhibits*).

277 *Akpan Judgment* (n 271) para 4.3.

278 *Akpan Exhibits* (n 276) para 5.4.

subsidiary on merits. In justification, the court highlighted an 'international trend to hold parent companies of multinationals liable in their own country for the harmful practices of foreign subsidiaries'.[279] Furthermore, it stated that its jurisdiction over the Nigerian subsidiary would not cease, 'even if subsequently . . . hardly any connection [remained] with Dutch jurisdiction'.[280] The court also emphasised its view that, 'the *forum non conveniens* restriction no longer plays any role in today's international private law'.[281] This common law doctrine permits 'the court seised of a case the discretion to decline to exercise jurisdiction because the interests of justice are best served if the trial takes place in another court'.[282] There is no uniform approach to the doctrine's application.[283] The UK test permits its application only where an alternative forum may more suitably serve 'the interests of all the parties and the ends of justice'.[284] Conversely, the US has proven more amenable to balancing public and private interests in its assessment.[285] Particularly concerning is *Piper Aircraft v Reyno*, where the US Supreme Court assigned less weight to the preferences of foreign plaintiffs.[286] This position was later justified in *Wiwa*,[287] not because of:

> bias in favour of US residents . . . [but] because the greater the plaintiff's ties to the plaintiff's chosen forum, the more likely it is that the plaintiff would be inconvenienced by a requirement to bring the claim in a foreign jurisdiction.[288]

Yet, by this logic, equal deference should surely be given to the home State of the multinational, as it is surely 'less inconvenient for a defendant to defend a suit in its home State'.[289]

The reluctance of the court in *Akpan* to consider *forum non conveniens* illustrates a number of recent European developments. First, it reflects the

---

279 *Akpan Judgment* (n 271) para 4.5.
280 Ibid.
281 Ibid. para 4.6.
282 Ronald Brand and Scott Jablonski, *Forum Non Conveniens: History, Global Practice, and Future Under the Hague Convention on Choice of Court Agreements* (Oxford, UK, OUP, 2007) 1.
283 Simons and Macklin (n 234) 331.
284 *Spiliada Maritime v Cansulex Ltd* [1987] AC 460 para 476.
285 Joshua Rose, '*Forum Non Conveniens* and Multinational Corporations: A Government Interest Approach' (1986) 11 *NCJ Int'l L Com Reg* 669; Erin Foley Smith, 'Right to Remedies and the Inconvenience of *Forum Non Conveniens*: Opening US Courts to Victims of Corporate Human Rights Abuses' (2010) 44 *Colum JL Soc Probs* 145; *Gulf Oil v Gilbert* 330 US 501 (Supreme Court 1947) para 508.
286 *Piper Aircraft v Reyno* 454 US 235 (Supreme Court 1981) para 242.
287 *Wiwa v Royal Dutch Petroleum Co* 226 F.3d 88 (2nd Cir 2000).
288 Ibid. para 102.
289 Smith (n 285) 177.

operation of a civil legal system in the Netherlands where *lis pendens* arguments, as codified by the Brussels Regulation[290] and later the Lugano Convention,[291] are often brought instead. Such an argument was dismissed in *Akpan*.[292] Second, the ECJ issued a ruling in 2005 denying the domestic courts of EU member States the option to stay proceedings on the grounds of *forum non conveniens* where the alternative forum was outside the EU.[293] Although extremely positive, it is uncertain as to whether other common law States will follow suit. In addition, this progressive judicial attitude has not been reflected in State practice, the UK government having proposed the reintroduction of the doctrine in its review of the Brussels Regulation.[294]

Although *Akpan* avoided many of the challenges that inhibit litigious success in many host States, the operation of procedural rules in Western home countries can also fundamentally impact the success of claims. While the plaintiffs in *Akpan* maintained that the oil spills resulted from Shell's poor maintenance of a wellhead, the defendants advanced the common defence that they resulted from third-party sabotage. Such circumstances are concerning, given the 'incentive to blame oil pollution on political instability such as sabotage because there is no comprehensive legislation on compensation payments to communities in Nigeria'.[295] Instances of sabotage are often exaggerated.[296] This controversy is recognised by the director general of Nigeria's Federal Environmental Agency, who has suggested a large number of Nigerian oil spills result from outdated pipelines.[297] Furthermore, it is arguable that *Akpan*'s inability to obtain documentation relating to the maintenance of the well impeded the establishment of a causal link between the subsidiary and spill.[298] The attribution of the spill to sabotage meant that the subsidiary's liability was limited to a breach of a duty to secure its facilities against third-party interference.[299] Thus, defence strategies common to oil

---

290 Council Regulation (EC) No 44/2001 on Jurisdiction and the Recognition and Enforcement of Judgments in Civil and Commercial Matters (Brussels Regulation) OJ L012, Article 23.

291 Convention on Jurisdiction and the Recognition and Enforcement of Judgments in Civil and Commercial Matters (Lugano Convention) [2007] OJL339/3, Article 27.

292 *Akpan Judgment on Jurisdiction* (n 274) para 3.4.

293 Case 281/02 *Owusu v Jackson* [2005] ECR 1383; Brand and Jablonski (285) 28–36.

294 UK Ministry of Justice, 'Response to the European Commission Green Paper Relating to the Operation of the Brussels I Regulation in the International Legal Order' (3 September 2009) paras 12–15.

295 Frynas, 'Political Instability' (n 179) 465.

296 Ibid.

297 Gabriel Eweje, 'Environmental Costs and Responsibilities Resulting from Oil Exploitation in Developing Countries: The Case of the Niger Delta' (2006) 69 *J Bus Ethics* 27, 44.

298 In an ancillary hearing, it was submitted that Akpan had a legitimate interest in the production of company documentation under *Wetboek van Burgerlijke Rechtsvordering* (Dutch Civil Procedure Code) (2010) Article 843a. Shell successfully contested this submission. *Akpan Exhibits* (n 276) 4.6.

299 *Akpan Judgment* (n 271) 4.36.

litigation in host States may still undermine claims actioned in Western forums. The export of cases to home States does not grant complete immunity to procedural challenges. Fortunately, the court in *Akpan* felt it was foreseeable that any spill from SPDC's facilities would produce harmful consequences for local populations. The above-ground wellhead had been left unprotected since 1959–60, and, as such, SPDC should have foreseen the risk and taken low-cost measures to reduce the risk of sabotage by sealing the well.[300] Coincidently, SPDC undertook this action following the commencement of proceedings.[301]

Although the liability of the Nigerian subsidiary was established in *Akpan*, the direct attribution of liability to the parent corporation, RDS, met a common, insurmountable hurdle. The plaintiffs submitted that RDS 'exercised influence on SPDC's activities in the region'.[302] It was argued that RDS had assumed a duty of care over SPDC's operations, as the prevention of environmental damage by subsidiary companies was a key policy objective.[303] The recent *Chandler v Cape* case[304] addressed a similar issue: whether the formulation of a health and safety policy by a parent company generated a duty of care for an employee of its subsidiary. The English Court of Appeal held that such a duty may be imposed on a parent for the health and safety of its subsidiary's employees provided: (1) the businesses of the parent and subsidiary were essentially the same; (2) the parent company had more knowledge of health and safety in the industry than the subsidiary; (3) the parent knew of unsatisfactory working conditions at its subsidiary; and (4) the parent knew that its subsidiary or employees would rely on the parent company for protection.[305] In *Akpan*, the Dutch court found that:

> [the] proximity between parent company and the employees of its subsidiary that operates in the same country cannot be unreservedly equated with the proximity between the parent of an international group of oil companies and the [population] in the vicinity of oil pipelines . . . of its subsidiaries in other countries.[306]

Whereas the subsidiary–employee relationship in *Cape* produced a duty of care for a limited group, establishing a duty of care for a parent company of an international oil group for the population proximate to its pipelines would create 'a virtually unlimited group'.[307]

---

300 Frynas, 'The Oil Industry in Nigeria' (n 168) 110.
301 *Akpan Judgment* (n 271) para 4.44.
302 Ibid. 4.27.
303 Ibid.
304 *Chandler v Cape* [2012] EWCA Civ 525.
305 Ibid. para 80; Zerk (n 49) 215–34.
306 *Akpan Judgment* (n 271) para 4.29.
307 Ibid.

Consolidating its dismissal of the *Cape* criteria, the Dutch court found that the two entities were distinct, 'because RDS formulates general policy lines . . . whereas SPDC is involved in the production of oil in Nigeria'.[308] Thus, it could not be assumed that RDS possessed more knowledge of oil production in Nigeria or the protection of the local community. *Cape* did not serve as a precedent. Given the lengths to which the Dutch court went to justify its jurisdiction over both entities, it is somewhat surprising that the court so resolutely dismissed the claims against RDS early in the main action. The finding is also striking in light of Betlem's prophetic suggestion that it may be possible to litigate against Dutch multinationals on a similar private law basis to English cases, 'by constructing the whole case as one involving a lack of supervision by the head office of [an MNE] over its subsidiary abroad'.[309] Nonetheless, there is scope for a further victory against Shell in light of an appeal won by the applicants in December 2015. The ruling demanded disclosure of company documentation initially denied to the *Akpan* claimants and included affirmation of Dutch jurisdiction over RDS.[310] The final outcome of the case is still pending at the time of writing. Moreover, the adoption of laws analogous to the English Modern Slavery Act 2015, section 54 of which requires certain organisations to develop a slavery and human trafficking statement annually, might go some way towards securing ties between parent and subsidiaries in similar cases.[311] The effects of these initiatives are eagerly awaited.

These developments notwithstanding, although home State actions may occasionally proceed beyond jurisdictional and procedural challenges,[312] the achievement of a judgment against a parent for the operations of its subsidiaries abroad remains extremely rare.[313] Although recent pre-trial rulings at the Ontario Superior Court of Justice have indicated that parent corporations may be liable for the actions of their subsidiaries in instances of inadequate supervision, a ruling on merits is required before a precedent is established.[314] Two Canadian Appeal Court decisions have dismissed similar claims in the past.[315]

---

308 Ibid. 4.31.
309 Gerrit Betlem, 'Transnational Litigation against Multinational Corporations before Dutch Civil Courts' in Menno T Kamminga and Saman Zia-Zarifi (eds), *Liability of Multinational Corporations Under International Law* (London, Kluwer, 2000) 286.
310 Friends of the Earth, 'Outcome appeal against Shell' 18 December 2015, www.foei.org/news/outcome-appeal-shell-victory-environment-nigerian-people-friends-earth-netherlands#, accessed 21 April 2016.
311 Modern Slavery Act (2015) section 54.
312 Richard Meeran, 'Access to Remedy: The United Kingdom Experience of MNC Tort Litigation for Human Rights Violations' in Deva and Bilchitz (n 251) 380–2.
313 Zerk (n 49) 206; Sarah Joseph, *Corporations and Transnational Human Rights Litigation* (Oxford, UK, Hart, 2004) 145.
314 *Choc v Hudbay Minerals Inc* (2013) ONSC 1414 (Ontario Superior Court).
315 *Anvil Mining Ltd v Association Canadienne Contre l'Impunité* (2012) QCCA 117 (Québec Court of Appeal); *Piedra v Copper Mesa Mining Corp* (2011) ONCA 191 (Ontario Superior Court).

The principal solicitor in a number of analogous cases has argued that, 'provided there is sufficient involvement in, control and knowledge of the subsidiary operations by the parent, there seems to be no reason in principle why the general principles of negligence should not apply'.[316] Yet, as *Akpan* demonstrates, success is uncommon. Furthermore, in private law cases, 'the synergies with international human rights law are coincidental',[317] and the dismissal or settlement of such cases means that formal decisions against parent companies are rarely rendered.[318]

The recent *Chandler v Cape* decision appears to be the sole exception. Interestingly, Cape was subject to a similar, albeit unsuccessful action in 2002.[319] Having initially determined the case to be actionable in the UK, the initiation of 2,000 further claims in a class action suit prompted the English Court of Appeal to find that the host State (South Africa) was a more appropriate forum.[320] On appeal, these jurisdictional hurdles were overcome,[321] and the responsibility of the parent was postulated by the House of Lords.[322] Yet, the case was ultimately settled out of court for approximately £27 million.[323] It was another decade before a formal precedent was established in the English courts. Similarly, a series of UK-based actions accused Thor Chemicals, a South African manufacturer of mercury-based chemicals, of causing mercury poisoning and three deaths.[324] Criminal proceedings achieved a disappointing £3,000 fine from a local magistrates' court,[325] whereas two further civil actions achieved larger settlements.[326]

Successful actions have been brought against parent companies domiciled in Australia, without dismissal or out of court settlements. In *Barrow and Heys v Colonial Sugar Refinery Ltd*,[327] the employees of an asbestos mine were able to demonstrate that the parent corporation owed a duty of care on the basis that, 'employees of the parent were involved in the supervision of operations

316 Richard Meeran, 'The Unveiling of Transnational Corporations: A Direct Approach' in Michael Addo (ed), *Human Rights Standards and the Responsibility of Transnational Corporations* (The Hague, Netherlands, Springer, 1999) 170.

317 McBeth, *International Economic Actors* (n 140) 297.

318 *Connelly v RTZ* [1998] AC 854.

319 *Lubbe v Cape Plc* [2000] UKHL 41 (hereafter, *Lubbe*).

320 Zerk (n 49) 205.

321 *Lubbe* (n 319) paras 24–36.

322 Ibid. para 20.

323 Zerk (n 49) 205.

324 *Ngcobo v Thor Chemical Holdings Ltd* [1995] TLR 597 (10 November 1995); *Sithole v Thor Chemical Holdings Ltd* [1999] EWCA Civ 706.

325 Richard Meeran, 'The Unveiling of Transnational Corporations' (n 316) 164–6.

326 Zerk (n 49) 205; Thor Chemicals subsequently attempted a demerger, involving the transfer of its offending subsidiaries: Adefolake Adeyeye, *Corporate Social Responsibility of Multinational Corporations in Developing Countries* (Cambridge, UK, CUP, 2012) 33.

327 *Barrow and Heys v Colonial Sugar Refinery (CSR) Ltd* [1988] Unreported, Library No 7231 (Supreme Court of Western Australia); Meeran, 'Access to Remedy' (n 312) 382–6.

at the mine'.[328] However, the parent and subsidiary were operating in the *same country*, rendering the matters of jurisdiction and managerial control far simpler to determine. This is also true of the broadly similar cases of *CSR Ltd v Wren*,[329] and *CSR Ltd v Young*.[330] One notable instance of Australian home State litigation concerning the operations of a foreign subsidiary is *Dagi v BHP*.[331] The suit represented 30,000 indigenous community members against BHP and the operating company of its Ok Tedi mine in Papua New Guinea.[332] The Australian court was unable to deal with claims relating to proprietary damage, nor was it able to address fundamental questions related to environmental human rights, owing to the vague nature of the laws at the time the case was decided.[333] Instead, the case was based on loss of amenity resulting from the disastrous downstream impact of the mining operations.[334] Although it was accepted that there was a serious case to be tried, the parties ultimately signed a settlement agreement that permitted financial compensation to be distributed among the indigenous population and included a commitment to contain the tailings from the mine.[335] BHP's adherence to this commitment has been questioned.[336] Thus, in spite of these small victories, the 2012 *Cape* case remains the only conclusive legal decision rendered in this regard.

3.2.2.3 Extraterritorial litigation in the United States

In addition to regular private law remedies available in Western home States such as the UK and Australia, the US Alien Torts Claims Act (1789) (ATCA) permits non-US citizens to bring claims before federal district courts for acts 'committed in violation of the law of nations or a treaty of the United States'.[337] This novel statute enables actions alleging human rights violations by MNEs to play out in the domestic courts and permits incidents occurring overseas to be heard, provided there is a sufficient nexus between the defendant and the

---

328 Zerk (n 49) 217; Robyn Carroll, 'Corporate Parents and Tort Liability' in Michael Gillooly (ed), *The Law Relating to Corporate Groups* (Annandale, NSW, Federation Press, 1993) 98–9.

329 *CSR Ltd v Wren* [1997] 44 NSWLR 463; [1998] Aust Tort Rep 81–461.

330 *CSR Ltd v Young* [1998] Aust Tort Rep 81–468.

331 *Dagi v Broken Hill Proprietary Company Limited (No 2)* [1997] 1 VR 428 (hereafter, *Dagi*).

332 Stuart Kirsch, 'Mining and Environmental Human Rights in Papua New Guinea' in Pegg and Frynas (n 144) 115–35.

333 *British South Africa Co v Companhia de Moçambique* [1893] AC 602; Per Justice Bryne: '[T]he court will refuse to entertain a claim where it essentially concerns rights . . . to or over foreign land, for these rights arise under the law of the place where the land is situated and can be litigated only in the courts of that place' *Dagi* (n 331) 441.

334 Kirsch (n 332) 118–22.

335 McBeth, *International Economic Actors* (n 140) 295.

336 Ibid. 127.

337 US Alien Tort Claims Act (1789).

US.[338] In *Unocal*, it was submitted that an oil company had assisted the Myanmar government in committing human rights violations.[339] The Myanmar military, acting as security for Unocal, had allegedly 'used forced labour from local villages to provide construction for the pipeline . . . [and] committed acts of murder, torture and rape'.[340] Similarly, in the aforementioned *Wiwa* case, it was alleged that Shell had acted with silent complicity in the execution of an environmental activist, owing to its failure to intercede with the Nigerian government and to petition for his release.[341] Ken Saro-Wiwa had originally been arrested while protesting the environmental effects of the company's operations.[342] In assessment of these claims, the court in *Unocal* adopted an 'aiding and abetting' standard, based on 'knowing practical assistance or encouragement that has a substantial effect on the perpetration of the crime'.[343] The *mens rea* standard demanded 'actual or constructive (i.e. reasonable) knowledge that the accomplice's actions [would] assist the perpetrator in the commission of the crime'.[344] Both cases were ultimately settled out of court following lengthy litigation that indicated a judgment favouring the plaintiffs.[345] To date, no case involving an MNE has ever proceeded to a ruling on merits under ATCA.[346]

The ATCA has suffered practical limitations owing to the common assertion that some element of State action is required in conjunction with the acts of private entities.[347] Actions may only proceed in the absence of State action where the claims relate to a small category of particularly serious offences.[348] This was the approach taken in *Unocal*, the court finding that the crimes of slave trading, forced labour, war crimes and genocide, together with other crimes committed in furtherance of such activities, could be committed by MNEs without State action.[349] It has been argued that this requirement is erroneous and stems from both a misinterpretation of the previous *Filártiga* decision[350] and, by an

---

338 Jonathan Drimmer, 'Human Rights and the Extractive Industries: Litigation and Compliance Trends' (2010) 3 *J World Energy L Bus* 121.

339 *Unocal* (n 59).

340 Kaleck and Saage-Maaß (n 59).

341 Tófalo (n 44) 347; Geoffrey Chandler, 'Oil Companies and Human Rights' (1998) 7 *Bus Ethics* 69; Frynas, 'The Oil Industry in Nigeria' (n 168) 99–114.

342 Zerk (n 49) 23.

343 *Unocal* (n 59) para 951.

344 Ibid. para 952.

345 Ibid. para 939; McBeth, *International Economic Actors* (n 140) 303–4.

346 Simons and Macklin (n 234) 256.

347 Wilson (n 149) 54.

348 US Third Restatement (n 223) §404; *Kadic v Karadic* 70 F.3d 232 (2nd Cir 1995) paras 239–40.

349 *Unocal* (n 59) 945–6.

350 The case concerned torture. Liability was conditional on the offender acting under State instruction under the Torture Declaration 1975: *Filártiga v Peña-Irala*, 630 F.2d 876 (2d Cir 1980).

unfortunate analogy, to the Torture Victim Prevention Act (1991).[351] The State action requirement also raises a difficult balancing act between claims actionable under the ATCA, and those excluded by the Foreign Sovereign Immunities Act (1976)[352] and 'Act of State' doctrine.[353]

More concerning is the impact of the 2013 *Kiobel* judgment,[354] which confirmed a presumption *against* the extraterritorial application of the statute, finding that, 'it would reach too far to say that mere corporate presence suffices'.[355] Echoing *Morrison*,[356] the court found that, 'even where the claims touch and concern the territory of the [US], they must do so with sufficient force to displace the presumption'.[357] As such, this decision could severely restrict the instances in which future cases against MNEs may be heard under ATCA.[358] Furthermore, in an earlier instance, the US Second Circuit Appeals Court held that, '[n]o corporation has ever been subject to any form of liability . . . under the customary law of human rights. Rather, sources of customary international law have . . . explicitly rejected the idea of corporate liability'.[359] Thus, actions against MNEs premised entirely on customary grounds do not form a basis for actions under ATCA, further undermining the utility of this legislation. Yet, although this litigation may spell the end of this novel statutory regime, regular private law mechanisms remain operational.[360] In light of their significant shortcomings, this is likely of little comfort to victims of extraterritorial human rights abuses stemming from corporate activity. Moreover, the very fact that such an archaic statute was revived in this manner underscores the need to establish binding norms of international corporate responsibility.[361]

---

351 Eric Engle, *Private Law Remedies for Extraterritorial Human Rights Violations* (DPhil thesis, University of Bremen, 2006) 70–1.

352 Acts of foreign States are immune from US jurisdiction, subject to the exceptions: US Foreign Sovereign Immunities Act (1976) sections 1605 and 1607.

353 *Duke of Brunswick v King of Hanover* (1848) 2 HL Cas 1.

354 *Kiobel v Royal Dutch Petroleum* (Slip Opinion) 569 US (Supreme Court 2013) (hereafter *Kiobel 2013*).

355 Ibid. 14.

356 *Morrison v National Australia Bank* 561 US 247 (Supreme Court 2010).

357 *Kiobel 2013* (n 354) 1 (Kennedy, J, concurring).

358 *Kiobel* was followed in *Balintulo v Daimler AG* 727 F.3d 174 (2nd Cir 2013); Odette Murray, David Kinley and Chip Pitts, 'Exaggerated Rumours of the Death of an Alien Tort? Corporations, Human Rights and the Remarkable Case of Kiobel' (2011) 12 *Melb J Int'l L* 57.

359 *Kiobel 2010* (n 38) 148.

360 Liesbeth FH Enneking, 'Multinational Corporations, Human Rights Violations, and a 1789 US Statute: A brief exploration of the case of Kiobel v. Shell' (2012) 3 *Nederlands Internationaal Privaatrecht* 396, 400.

361 Mark D Kielsgard, 'Unocal and the Demise of Corporate Neutrality' (2005) 36 *Cal W Int'l LJ* 183, 191; Karavias (n 2) 111.

3.3 The limited reach of 'direct' accountability mechanisms

Thus far, it has been established that international obligations, at least in the field of human rights law, do not address MNES and non-State armed groups directly. In their present form, domestic accountability mechanisms are fraught with procedural obstacles and, as such, are ill-equipped to respond to the contemporary challenges posed by non-State actors. However, these State-centric legal regimes have been supplemented by 'soft law' initiatives as a means of filling this 'governance gap'.[362] Additionally, international criminal law may provide an avenue to hold *individual perpetrators* to account for serious breaches of international law without State involvement.[363] Although both approaches purport to regulate non-State entities directly, their practical operation often remains tied to State concerns, and the legal quality of soft law provisions has been subject to significant debate. These issues are explored in the sub-sections below.

3.3.1 *The international criminal responsibility of non-State actors*

At the time of its substantive codification in the aftermath of the Second World War, international criminal law was considered a revolutionary extension of the international legal system, explicitly recognising the ability of natural persons to possess direct international rights and duties. In the words of the Nuremberg International Military Tribunal (IMT), '[c]rimes against international law are committed by men, not by abstract entities, and only by punishing individuals who commit such crimes can the provisions of international law be enforced'.[364] Although it has been suggested that the doctrine of individual criminal responsibility may diminish the 'conceptual gulf' between individual and collective liability,[365] the practice of the international criminal law regime has not furnished the view that non-State entities as 'juridical persons' are subject to direct rights and obligations more generally.[366] Rather, its reach remains restricted to natural persons whose conduct reaches the threshold of international criminality.[367] As will be demonstrated, these factors severely

---

362 Nicola Jägers, 'Will Transnational Private Regulation Close the Governance Gap?' in Deva and Bilchitz (n 251) 295.
363 William A Schabas, 'State Policy as an Element of International Crimes' (2008) 98 *J Crim L & Criminology* 953.
364 International Military Tribunal at Nuremberg, Judgment and Sentences (1 October 1946) reproduced in (1947) 41 *AJIL* 221.
365 Wells and Elias (n 125) 155.
366 Although the position of 'natural persons' in the international legal system has evolved, the same cannot be said for juridical persons: Roland Portmann, *Legal Personality in International Law* (Cambridge, UK, CUP, 2010) 126–72; Janne E Nijman, *The Concept of International Legal Personality: An Inquiry into the History and Theory of International Law* (The Hague, Netherlands, TMC Asser Press, 2004) 314–22.
367 Olivier De Schutter, 'The Accountability of Multinationals' (n 265) 231.

inhibit the prosecution of collective or corporate non-State actors, including MNEs and non-State armed groups.

It is certainly true that the complicity of company directors in facilitating the Nazi regime was acknowledged alongside that of high-ranking civilian and military officials at Nuremberg.[368] The directors of the IG Farben trust,[369] the Flick trust[370] and the Krupp firm[371] were all indicted before US military tribunals.[372] Similarly, in the 1946 *Zyklon B* case, the owner and general manager of a firm was brought before a British military tribunal.[373] Yet, crucially, it was expressly acknowledged that, 'the corporate defendant . . . is not before the bar of this Tribunal and cannot be subject to criminal penalties in these proceedings . . . But corporations act through individuals'.[374] Although the IMT Charter provided competence to 'declare . . . that the group or organisation of which the individual was a member was a criminal organisation',[375] its jurisdiction was limited *ratione personae* to natural persons.[376] For Karavias, this provision 'cannot in any meaningful manner serve as a precedent in relation to the potential applicability of [international criminal law] to corporations nowadays. The prosecution of members of criminal organisations was a procedure peculiar to the historical context'.[377] Subsequent international practice appears to confirm this position. Provisions relating to the prosecution of criminal organisations were omitted from the contemporary international criminal law regime, as enforced by the ICTY, ICTR[378] and ICC.[379]

---

368 Jonathon Bush, 'The Prehistory of Corporations and Conspiracy in International Criminal Law: What Nuremberg Really Said' (2009) 109 *Colum L Rev* 1094.
369 *Re Krauch and Others* (IG Farben Trial) (1948) 15 AD 678.
370 *Re Flick and Others* (1947) 14 AD 267.
371 *Re Krupp and Others* (1948) 15 AD 627.
372 Kaleck and Saage-Maaß (n 59) 701–2.
373 *Zyklon B Case, Trial of Bruno Tesch and Two Others*, British Military Court, Hamburg (1–8 March 1946) in UN War Crimes Commission, 'Law Reports of Trials of War Criminals' Vol 1 (1947) 93–103, www.loc.gov/rr/frd/Military_Law/pdf/Law-Reports_Vol-1.pdf, accessed 21 April 2016.
374 UN War Crimes Commission, 'Law Reports of Trials of War Criminals – IG Farben and Krupp Trials' Vol X (1949) 52, www.loc.gov/rr/frd/Military_Law/pdf/Law-Reports_Vol-10.pdf, accessed 21 April 2016.
375 Agreement for the Prosecution of Major War Criminals of the European Axis (8 August 1945) 82 UNTS 279, Article 9.
376 Ibid. Article 10.
377 Karavias (n 2) 95.
378 Roman Boed, 'Individual Criminal Responsibility for Violations of Article 3 Common to the Geneva Conventions of 1949 and of Additional Protocol II Thereto in the Case of the International Criminal Tribunal for Rwanda' (2002) 13 *Crim L Forum* 293.
379 Statute of the International Criminal Court (17 July 1998) UN Doc A/CONF.183/9 (hereafter, ICC Statute) Article 25(1); ICTR Statute (n 111) Article 5; Statute of the International Criminal Tribunal for the Former Yugoslavia (25 May 1993) Article 6.

Scholars advocating the international criminal responsibility of non-State entities[380] have highlighted the recourse made to juridical persons during the drafting of the Statute of Rome 1998.[381] Although one draft expressly provided the ICC with the competence to render a judgment over legal persons 'when the crimes committed were committed on behalf of such legal persons or by their agencies', the provision was ultimately omitted.[382] Nonetheless, Clapham has emphasised this resulted from a lack of time during the late stages of the drafting process, rather than objections from representatives.[383] Although commentators have suggested that jurisdiction over legal persons could be affirmed in the future, predictably, the ICC has not pursued such measures.[384] Indeed, the expansion of the ICC's mandate in this manner could foment further political opposition to the Court's very existence.[385] Other objections have emphasised the need for complementarity between national and international spheres, given that the majority of domestic jurisdictions do not permit the criminal prosecution of legal persons,[386] and the inherent difficulties in establishing the *actus reus*[387] and *mens rea* of corporate entities.[388]

Although the first ICC prosecutor was likely correct when he remarked, '[f]ollow the trail of the money and you will find the criminals', given the complex corporate structures boasted by many business actors, the difficulty in pinpointing specific individuals to bear criminal responsibility will be significant.[389] It has been suggested that 'command responsibility', which applies to crimes committed by subordinates operating under the effective

380 Ashifa Kassam, 'Spain's campaigning judge seeks change in law to prosecute global corporations', *The Guardian*, 20 August 2015, www.theguardian.com/world/2015/aug/20/spain-judge-baltasar-garzon-prosecute-global-corporations, accessed 21 April 2016.

381 Clapham (n 1) 245–7; Cristina Chiomenti, 'Corporations and the International Criminal Court' in De Schutter, *Transnational Corporations* (n 16) 288–91.

382 Draft Statute for the International Criminal Court and Draft Final Act, UN Doc A/CONF.183/2/Add.1, Article 23, 49 para 5.

383 Clapham (n 1) 246.

384 De Schutter, 'The Accountability of Multinationals' (n 265) 232.

385 Alice De Jong, 'Transnational Corporations and International Law: Bringing TNCs out of the Accountability Vacuum' (2011) 7 *Crit Perspectives Int'l Bus* 66, 78.

386 Cf Aurora Voiculescu, 'Human Rights and the New Corporate Accountability: Learning from Recent Developments in Corporate Criminal Responsibility' (2009) 87 *J Bus Ethics* 419, 426–7; Karavias (n 2) 103; Chiomenti (n 381) 294; Joana Kyriakakis, 'Corporations and the International Criminal Court: The Complementarity Objection Stripped Bare' (2008) 19 *Crim L Forum* 115.

387 Karavias (n 2) 114.

388 Chiomenti (n 381) 292.

389 Former ICC Chief Prosecutor Luis Moreno Ocampo, reported in: BBC News, 'Firms Face Blood Diamond Probe' (23 September 2003) http://news.bbc.co.uk/1/hi/business/3133108.stm, accessed 21 April 2016; James Podgers, 'Corporations in the Line of Fire: International Prosecutor Says Corporate Officials Could Face War Crimes Charges' (2004) 90 *American Bar Association J* 13.

control of a superior,[390] offers an avenue to exposing company directors to international criminal liability.[391] Commanders may be held criminally responsible for the acts of subordinates in instances of wilful blindness and for their failure to take reasonable measures to prevent or repress crimes that fall within their effective responsibility and control.[392] Although most often utilised to establish responsibility in military command chains, the jurisprudence of the ICTR reflects the conviction of company directors for the crimes of genocide and crimes against humanity on this basis.[393] Yet, it is argued that such avenues are not appropriate to fill the accountability gap with regard to MNEs and non-State armed groups. In armed conflict situations, *ex post facto* criminal proceedings, although potentially useful in providing closure for victims, are hardly ideal. Focus should be placed on the prevention of atrocities, rather than redress. Similarly, given that the corporate structures highlighted above already impede the establishment of tortious liability and compensatory settlements, it is argued that these issues would likely be exacerbated in criminal proceedings.[394] Another limiting factor stems from the small category of acts that fall within the jurisdiction of the ICC. Any suggestion that the competence of the Court could be expanded in the future to include other offences[395] is countered by the limitation of its jurisdiction to 'the most serious crimes of concern to the international community as a whole'.[396] As Chiomenti suggests, '[i]t is difficult to imagine that, except in extreme circumstances ... a corporation ordinarily operating in the industrial, commercial, or services sector, will act as the principal author to commit any of the crimes falling under the jurisdiction of the ICC'.[397]

With regard to non-State armed groups, to date, the international criminal responsibility of these collective entities has not been confirmed.[398] Indeed, it has been argued that non-State actor liability for both crimes against humanity and genocide is further complicated by the requirement that there be some element of State practice or policy.[399] Article 7(2)(a) of the ICC statute stipulates that an attack directed against a civilian population must be 'pursuant

390 ICC Statute (n 379) Article 28(b).
391 McBeth (n 68) 308.
392 ICC Statute (n 379) art 28(b).
393 *Musema* (n 111).
394 Kyriakakis, 'Australian Prosecution' (n 162) 825.
395 It has been suggested that these categories could be expanded to cover serious environmental damage, though such possibilities are modest: Peter Sharp, 'Prospects for Environmental Liability in the International Criminal Court' (1999) 18 *Victoria LJ* 217.
396 ICC Statute (n 379) Article 28(b).
397 Chiomenti (n 381) 299.
398 Cedric Ryngaert and Anneleen Van de Meulebroucke, 'Enhancing and Enforcing Compliance with International Humanitarian Law by Non-State Armed Groups' (2011) 16 *JCSL* 443, 466.
399 Schabas (n 363).

to or in furtherance of a State or organisational policy to commit such an attack'.[400] Thus, it has been suggested that, without some element of State action, individuals would be excluded from liability. Although the leader of a non-State armed group has been successfully prosecuted at the ICC following the conclusion of the protracted *Lubanga* trial,[401] this conviction was achieved under the Article 8 war crimes provision, which is expressly applicable to violations of Common Article 3 committed during non-international armed conflict.[402] Although international jurisprudence has indicated that the State policy requirement has now been abandoned,[403] Schabas suggests that such findings 'were driven more by results-oriented judicial policy . . . than by in-depth analysis of legal authorities, the origins of the concepts, and the object and purpose of genocide and crimes against humanity'.[404] As such, the liability of non-State actors for particular international crimes is potentially extremely limited, further underscoring the State-centric nature of even the most progressive subsets of public international law.

The efficiency of the ICC has also been called into question, it having achieved startlingly few convictions over the first decade of its functioning. Although the operation of the ICTY has proven successful in prosecuting commanders of rebel forces, the limited mandate and jurisdiction of the Court restricts its utility as an accountability mechanism, and the ICTR has been accused of exercising bias by failing to prosecute rebel commanders who have achieved power following the Rwandan genocide.[405] Perhaps most crucially, it is unlikely that the majority of low-intensity armed conflicts will reach the threshold of the crimes over which the ICC and *ad hoc* tribunals hold jurisdiction, and emphasis should be placed on the regulation and prevention of atrocities arising during non-international armed conflict, rather than *ex post facto* redress. As such, it is suggested that this avenue to direct accountability is not particularly suited to the non-State actors contemplated by this monograph.

3.3.2 CSR schemes

During the 1970s, a CSR movement seeking to regulate corporate activity via non-binding (or, at least, non-judicially enforceable) soft law initiatives was

---

400 ICC Statute (n 379) Article 7(2)(a).
401 *Lubanga* (122).
402 ICC Statute (n 379) Article 8(2)(c).
403 *Prosecutor v Jelisic* (Judgment) IT-95-10-T (14 December 1999) para 100; *Prosecutor v Kunarac* (Judgment) IT-96-23/1-A (June 5 2001) para 98.
404 Schabas (n 363) 981.
405 Larissa Van Den Herik, *The Contribution of the Rwanda Tribunal to the Development of International Law* (The Hague, Netherlands, Martinus Nijhoff, 2005) 264; Human Rights Watch, 'Rwanda: Tribunal's Work Incomplete: 25,000 to 45,000 Rwandan Patriotic Front Killings from 1994 Never Addressed' (17 April 2009) www.hrw.org/fr/news/2009/08/17/rwanda-tribunal-s-work-incomplete, accessed 21 April 2016.

established.[406] Although it is beyond the scope of this study to examine in detail the wide variety of CSR schemes operating at the international, regional, national and industrial levels, it is necessary to afford some consideration to the content, practical effects and legal quality of these provisions.[407] Well-known international CSR initiatives include the UN Guiding Principles on Business and Human Rights (UNGPs),[408] UN Draft Norms on Transnational Corporations,[409] OECD Guidelines for Multinational Enterprises[410] and International Labour Organisation (ILO) Tripartite Declaration.[411] For decades, the UN unsuccessfully attempted to formulate a set of provisions reflecting core human rights and labour standards for MNEs.[412] Despite initial enthusiasm surrounding the 2003 UN Draft Norms, John Ruggie commented in 2006 that the exercise had become 'engulfed by its own doctrinal excesses ... it exaggerated legal claims, and conceptual ambiguities created confusion and doubt even among many mainstream international lawyers'.[413] The Draft Norms were at once described as setting 'non-voluntary' standards for MNEs[414] and as a restatement of existing international human rights norms.[415] In light of the foregoing analysis, these two positions are clearly incompatible.[416] Attention has since turned to the UNGPs, the first initiative to receive a formal endorsement from the UN, following Ruggie's Protect, Respect, and Remedy initiative.[417]

Before examining the legal quality of CSR mechanisms, it is useful to appraise their content and efficacy in the context of weak governance States. It has been suggested that overly prescriptive, public international CSR schemes are less likely to be implemented, and that broader, overarching principles are to be favoured.[418] The value in establishing consistent international standards relating

---

406 Emily Carasco and Jang Singh, 'Towards Holding Transnational Corporations Responsible for Human Rights' (2010) 22 *Eur Bus Rev* 432; Zerk (n 49) 15–29; Helen Keller, 'Codes of Conduct and their Implementation' in Rudiger Wolfrum and Volker Roben (eds), *Legitimacy in International Law* (The Hague, Netherlands, Springer, 2008) 219–26.
407 Richard R Baxter, 'International Law in "Her Infinite Variety"' (1980) 29 *ICLQ* 549.
408 UNGPs (n 18).
409 UN Draft Norms 2003 (n 15).
410 OECD Guidelines for Multinational Enterprises, 2011 edn, www.oecd.org/daf/inv/mne/48004323.pdf, accessed 21 April 2016.
411 ILO, *Tripartite Declaration of Principles Concerning Multinational Enterprises and Social Policy* (4th edn, Geneva, 2006) www.ilo.org/wcmsp5/groups/public/--ed_emp/--emp_ent/--multi/documents/publication/wcms_094386.pdf, accessed 21 April 2016.
412 Zerk (n 49) 12.
413 John Ruggie, 'Interim Report of the Special Representative of the Secretary-General on the Issue of Human Rights and Transnational Corporations and Other Business Enterprises' (22 February 2006) UN Doc E/CN.4/2006/97 paras 59 and 65.
414 Weissbrodt and Kruger (n 16) 338; cf Gelfand (n 16) 322–33.
415 Anita Ramasatry, 'Closing the Governance Gap in the Business and Human Rights Arena: Lessons from the Anti-Corruption Movement' in Deva and Bilchitz (n 251) 168.
416 Ruggie 'Interim Report' (n 413) para 60.
417 UNGPs (n 18).
418 Alex Wawryk, 'Regulating Transnational Corporations through Corporate Codes of Conduct' in Pegg and Frynas (n 144) 57.

to MNEs with concomitant monitoring and enforcement mechanisms notwithstanding,[419] most initiatives are wholly reliant on State support for their implementation.[420] The Extractive Industries Transparency Initiative (EITI) is one such example.[421] This UK-based scheme calls for greater transparency between extractive companies and foreign governments, and yet '[t]he exact mode of implementation of the EITI is left to host State parties to determine'.[422] Given the reliance of weak governance States on FDI, the capacity and incentive of States to give effect to these provisions are not guaranteed. Given that States have proven unable or unwilling to enforce hard law standards, CSR may be endorsed as a non-justiciable alternative that can be flaunted without consequence, subject to inconsistent application or ignored altogether.[423]

CSR remains contentious in many weak governance States, given its emergence as a Western construct.[424] Trust plays a major role for vulnerable communities, and MNEs have continually failed to adhere to CSR standards.[425] For decades, CSR schemes in the Niger Delta were absent provisions detailing the developmental roles and responsibilities of MNEs,[426] and many Nigerian CSR programmes have retained an outdated, shareholder-centric focus that fails to account for the views of other stakeholders.[427] Thus, supplementary soft law initiatives have done little to remedy the situation in weak governance States, having failed to provide judicially enforceable regulation and left many communities suspicious of corporate interference. Despite the recent adoption of 'Global Memoranda of Understanding' by companies such as Shell and Chevron, which reflect stronger attempts to engage local communities via multi-stakeholder forums, their implementation has been patchy, and the scope for discussion of environmental issues is limited.[428] The same can be said for the

419 On OECD National Contact Points, see: McBeth, *International Economic Actors* (n 140) 262; Daniel Leader, 'Business and Human Rights – Time to Hold Companies to Account' (2008) 8 *Int'l CLR* 447, 457–8.
420 Gelfand (n 16) 326.
421 Extractive Industries Transparency Initiative (EITI) http://eiti.org/, accessed 21 April 2016.
422 Zerk (n 49) 179.
423 Catherine Coumans, 'Alternative Accountability Mechanisms and Mining: The Problem of Effective Impunity' (2010) 30 *Can J Dev Stud* 27.
424 Gavin Hilson, 'Corporate Social Responsibility in the Extractive Industries: Experiences from Developing Countries' (2012) 37 *Resources Policy* 131, 132.
425 Amao, 'Corporate Social Responsibility' (n 187) 90; Eweje (n 297) 228; Jedrzej George Frynas, 'The False Developmental Promise of Corporate Social Responsibility: Evidence from Multinational Oil Companies' (2005) 81 *Royal Institute Int'l Affairs* 581.
426 Kiikpoye Aaron, 'New Corporate Social Responsibility Models for Oil Companies in Nigeria's Delta Region: What Challenges for Sustainability' (2012) 12 *Progress Dev Stud* 259, 265.
427 Amao, 'Corporate Social Responsibility' (n 187) 99–100; Oluduro (n 142) 306; Coumans (n 423) 38.
428 Aaron (n 426) 267–9.

adherence to and implementation of the UNGPs by these particular MNEs, despite their vocal support for the initiative.[429]

In contrast, industry-level CSR regimes are said to incentivise implementation and compliance through 'ownership of the provisions'.[430] However, wholly private schemes have been described as 'greenwash ... a way of diverting attention from bad press ... [and] as a tactical concession to avoid more stringent legislation at some later stage'.[431] The experience of Guatemalan communities at the Marlin mine highlights these failings. Although the original operator of the mine, Glamis Gold, specifically promised that the project would be a model for responsible operations and advance community development,[432] a number of serious incidents have occurred, including the killing of a local transport contractor and widespread failure to comply with environmental policies.[433] The International Finance Corporation, which funded the venture, has also been accused of failing to engage with indigenous communities prior to its decision to issue funding.[434] This factor represents a 'general problem with the "brand" of CSR being promoted by the extractive industries throughout the developing world', with MNEs raising host community hopes before defaulting on their commitments.[435] Thus, the Marlin project 'provides a clear example of strong public statements by an [extractive] company in support of CSR ... contrasted with on the ground problems and criticism from highly credible external bodies that seem to belie the State commitment to CSR'.[436] There are, of course, some advantages to this style of CSR regulation, including an expedient drafting process, the potential adoption of higher standards than could be achieved via State consensus and the obvious positive

429 Tineke Lambooy, Aikaterini Argyrou and Mary Varner, 'An Analysis and Practical Application of the Guiding Principles on Providing Remedies with Special Reference to Case Studies Related to Oil Companies' in Deva and Bilchitz (n 251) 329–77.
430 Dinah Shelton, 'Law, Non-Law and the Problem of "Soft Law"' in Dinah Shelton (ed), *Commitment and Compliance: The Role of Non-binding Norms in the International Legal System* (Oxford, UK, OUP, 2003) 16.
431 Zerk (n 49) 100–1.
432 World Bank, 'Glamis Gold Ltd's Montana Exploradora Marlin Project in Guatemala', http://web.worldbank.org/WBSITE/EXTERNAL/TOPICS/EXTOGMC/0,,content MDK:20421886~pagePK:210058~piPK:210062~theSitePK:336930,00.html, accessed 21 April 2016.
433 Keith Slack, 'Mission Impossible? Adopting a CSR-Based Business Model for Extractive Industries in Developing Countries' (2012) 37 *Resources Policy* 179, 183.
434 Office of the Compliance Advisor/Ombudsman, 'Assessment of a Complaint Submitted in Relation to the Marlin Mining Project in Guatemala' (September 2005) 28–33, www.cao-ombudsman.org/cases/document-links/documents/CAO-Marlin-assessment-English-7Se p05.pdf, accessed 21 April 2016; International Finance Corporation, 'ILO Convention 169 and the Private Sector' (March 2007) 10, www.ifc.org/wps/wcm/connect/cba339804 88556edbafcfa6a6515bb18/ILO_169.pdf?MOD=AJPERES, accessed 21 April 2016.
435 Hilson (n 424) 134.
436 Slack (n 433).

effects for corporate reputations.[437] Yet these factors are clearly outweighed by weak enforcement mechanisms, a lack of independent oversight, as well as a resistance on the part of MNEs to the adoption of provisions that might result in competitive disadvantages.[438]

On the legal quality of soft law initiatives, Davarnejad has suggested that to describe all CSR initiatives as 'voluntary' is misleading:

> [The term] can only be applied to self-regulating measures such as corporate or industry codes of conduct. The contribution of business representatives to the OECD Guidelines and the ILO Declaration merely demonstrates the[ir] acceptance and approval . . . These codes of conduct are neither 'voluntary' nor self-regulative as they are governmental instruments.[439]

By their nature, it is suggested that initiatives concluded among State parties and intergovernmental organisations *are binding*, but *are not judicially enforceable*.[440] Although this distinction could be written off as pedantic, there is a clear parallel between the lack of enforceability mechanisms in 'binding' or, at least, 'governmental' soft law instruments and 'harder' international law provisions. The lack of enforceability mechanisms is a long-standing criticism leveraged against the entire international legal regime.[441] The separation between what is considered to be hard and soft law is, at its most fundamental level, reflected in the wording of Article 38(1) of the ICJ Statute, which details the competence of the Court to draw on various types of international legal source.[442] This method of determining the sources of international law has been criticised.[443] Yet, in light of criticism regarding enforceability at all levels of international regulation, both hard and soft, the question arises as to what difference there is between the legal quality and practical effects produced by these types of regulatory scheme.

---

437 John Ruggie, 'Business and Human Rights: Treaty Road Not Travelled' (May 2008) *Ethical Corporation* 42–3.
438 Wawryk (n 418) 61–3; Coumans (n 423) 27.
439 Leyla Davarnejad, 'The Impact of Non-State Actors on the International Law Regime of Corporate Social Responsibility: Blessing or Curse?' in Cedric Ryngaert and Math Noortmann, *Non-State Actor Dynamics in International Law: From Law-Takers to Law-Makers* (Aldershot, UK, Ashgate, 2010) 50.
440 Ibid. 54–5.
441 John Austin, *The Province of Jurisprudence Determined* (2nd edn, London, John Murray, 1832) 17–18; James Shand Watson, *Theory and Reality in the International Protection of Human Rights* (The Hague, Netherlands, Martinus Nijhoff, 1999) 4; Douglas Donoho, 'Human Rights Enforcement in the Twenty-First Century' (2006) 35 *Ga J Int'l & Comp L* 1.
442 Brownlie (n 240) 4–5.
443 Jean d'Aspremont, *Formalism and the Sources of International Law: A Theory of the Ascertainment of Legal Rules* (Oxford, UK, OUP, 2012) 148–51.

The preceding chapter contextualised the dominant conception of the State as the primary creator, validator, enforcer and addressee of international law. There is, in principle, a clear difference between constraining the behaviour of States, and non-State entities that are, in theory, subject to the laws prescribed by States. Although there is arguably no theoretical reason precluding sovereign *States* from acting in breach of their international obligations, the activities of MNEs and other actors domiciled within States should, in principle, be far easier to constrain. Clearly, contemporary phenomena have vastly altered the practical reality of this scenario, and it is for this reason that the State-centric view of international law is now open to significant critique. As a means of reconciling this regulatory deficit, recent scholarship has proven increasingly open to embracing 'soft' legal standards. This has resulted in a blurring of the line between hard and soft law standards. A compelling response has been produced by d'Aspremont that calls for a rejuvenation of formal law ascertainment utilising a mixture of Hart's *source* and *social* thesis in order to aid the distinction between law and non-law.[444] Although not expressly adopted by this study, his critique of soft law initiatives such as those introduced by the CSR movement is highly illuminating.[445]

D'Aspremont's criticisms relate to 'effects-based' models of law ascertainment. From this perspective, 'any normative effort to influence international actors' behaviour, at least if it materialises in the adoption of an international instrument, should be considered to be comprised in international law . . . [C]ompliance is elevated to the law-ascertaining yardstick'.[446] The approach is reflected by scholars such as Zerk, who suggests that the distinction:

> between law and CSR is confusing and unhelpful . . . it wrongly assumes that legal compliance is an absolute, whereas in reality there are degrees of compliance and cooperation . . . It also reflects a rather simplistic view of what regulation actually is.[447]

Although there is perhaps some truth to this statement, and observance of law is clearly desirable, it is suggested here that this sentiment conflates the term 'regulation', a catch-all word describing initiatives to curb and monitor behaviour, with *legal* regulation. To say that a provision does not have a legal

---

444 Source thesis refers to the determination of law by reference to pedigreed sources that are valid without recourse to moral values: Joseph Raz, *The Authority of Law* (2nd edn, Oxford, UK, OUP, 2009) 47–8; social thesis refers to Hart's grounding of the rule of recognition (a secondary meta-rule used to ascertain the primary rules of obligation) in the social practice of law applying authorities: d'Aspremont, *Formalism* (n 443) 53–4; Herbert LA Hart, *The Concept of Law* (first published 1961, 3rd edn, Oxford, UK, OUP, 2012) 100–1.
445 D'Aspremont, *Formalism* (n 443) 128.
446 Ibid. 123.
447 Zerk (n 49) 31–2.

quality is not to say that it has no role to play in regulation. Rather, the contention is that the quality of soft law provisions should not be equated with directly binding legal authority. Zerk herself appears to arrive at this same view, finding that, 'the "voluntary versus mandatory" debate is based on the mistaken impression that CSR and law are somehow separate, whereas in reality they are intertwined'.[448]

Yet, Zerk and others suggest that soft law initiatives play an important role in the normative development, clarification and interpretation of international law,[449] and that the growing acceptance of the provisions may lead to their 'hardening'.[450] The process has been welcomed by some as a means of permitting some form of non-State actor participation in the evolution of international law, as evidenced by NGO participation in drafting the text of the UN General Assembly Declaration on the Elimination of all Forms of Violence against Women.[451] For d'Aspremont, 'the deformalisation of law-identification that inevitably accompanies the conceptualisation at the heart of [the soft law] project is meant to be only temporary, since the ultimate aim of these scholars is to re-formalise the identification of those "alternative instruments".'[452] The determination of which instruments have hardened, and when, is problematic. Chinkin suggests three core criteria: the form of the instrument, the intention of the parties and the subject matter addressed by the instrument.[453] It has been suggested that the hardening process is evident in changing perceptions of ICESCR, which contained weak language and no monitoring committee or complaints mechanism when it was first drafted.[454] Yet, the instrument is, and has always been, a major multilateral treaty.[455] D'Aspremont remains highly sceptical of the developmental role purportedly performed by soft law, and of the potential for its future crystallisation. The expansion of both the normative content of international law and attempts to bring new forms of instrumentation and phenomena within the remit of international law has been viewed positively[456] and as a response to an accountability gap between vulnerable communities and those exercising

---

448   Ibid. 35.
449   Davarnejad (n 439) 50–1; Karin Buhmann, 'Integrating Human Rights in Emerging Regulation of Corporate Social Responsibility: The EU Case' (2011) 7 *Int'l JLC* 139.
450   Zerk (n 49) 276–7; Gelfand (n 16) 327; Weissbrodt and Kruger (n 16) 122–47.
451   Christine Chinkin, 'Normative Development in the International Legal System' in Shelton, *Commitment and Compliance* (n 430) 31; Jean d'Aspremont, 'International Law-Making by Non-State Actors: Changing the Model or Putting the Phenomenon into Perspective?' in Ryngaert and Noortmann (n 439) 171–94.
452   D'Aspremont, *Formalism* (n 443) 122.
453   Ibid. 33–4.
454   Ibid. 37–42.
455   Jean d'Aspremont, 'Softness in International Law: A Self-Serving Quest for New Legal Materials' (2008) 19 *EJIL* 1076, 1087.
456   Harold Hongju Koh, 'A World Transformed' (1995) 20 *Yale J Int'l L* ix, xi.

significant power and public authority.[457] However, d'Aspremont suggests that the expansion of new 'legal' materials is ultimately self-serving: an attempt by scholars to stretch the frontiers of their discipline.[458]

> [I]t is not true that international law is a behavioural model to which addressees grow accustomed and finally abide by. International legal rules do not exist simply because States . . . have become habituated to being bound by them . . . the illusory state of non-formal law ascertainment may obfuscate the need to lobby for the adoption of new rules . . . [and] may bring about a feeling that the adoption of legal or non-legal regulations is no longer necessary.[459]

In line with d'Aspremont, this study favours the formal separation between established sources of international law and 'soft law' regulatory initiatives. The peculiarities of 'hard' international law and the practical and theoretical impediments to its direct application to non-State actors will be considered at greater length in Chapter 4 of this monograph. Before proceeding to this argument, and in keeping with the overall approach of this study, voluntary compliance regimes pertaining to non-State armed groups will be examined below.

3.3.3 *Voluntary compliance frameworks for non-State armed groups*

A developing area of regulation broadly analogous to CSR is reflected by the *ad hoc* compliance agreements established between parties to armed conflicts and NGOs. The implementation and judicial enforcement of humanitarian law are generally considered to be at their weakest in non-international armed conflicts, as the mechanisms are not tailored to civil strife.[460] Yet, non-State actor engagement clearly plays an important role in facilitating the compliance of groups that are unable to formally consent to conventional international humanitarian law[461] or may lack the training, knowledge and discipline to ensure adherence to the laws of war.[462] The establishment of agreements, instructions and codes of conduct between non-State armed groups and State parties has

---

457 Christine Chinkin (n 451) 36–7; Davarnejad (n 439) 42.
458 D'Aspremont, *Formalism* (n 443) 132–4; D'Aspremont, 'Softness' (n 455).
459 D'Aspremont, *Formalism* (n 443) 134–5; cf Anthony d'Amato, 'Softness in International Law: A Self-Serving Quest for New Legal Materials: A Reply to Jean d'Aspremont' (2009) 20 *EJIL* 897.
460 Sivakumaran, *Non-International Armed Conflict* (n 68) 532.
461 UNSC, 'Report of the Secretary-General on the Protection of Civilians in Armed Conflict' (29 May 2009) UN Doc S/2009/277 para 39.
462 Steinhoff (n 67) 305.

been practised throughout history.[463] In recent years, there has been an increased willingness on the part of non-State armed groups to adopt commitments, declarations, codes of conduct and memoranda of understanding that are specifically tailored to the circumstances[464] and often make explicit reference to customary international human rights standards.[465]

A scheme led by the Special Representative of the Secretary-General for Children and Armed Conflict has obtained commitments from more than 60 armed groups.[466] This includes a commitment from all political and military leaders in the DRC to implement a five-point plan aimed at ending the recruitment of child soldiers.[467] Unfortunately, a later report to the General Assembly suggests that, although these initiatives serve as advocacy benchmarks, many 'remain unobserved . . . the challenge is to secure systematic monitoring and the application of pressure for enforcement'.[468] Scholars have hinted at a potential role for the UN Security Council in securing the compliance of armed groups via targeted sanctions, travel restrictions, the exclusion of leaders from governmental positions and amnesty provisions.[469] Indeed, the Security Council has voiced an 'intention to consider imposing targeted and graduated measures through country specific resolutions', including bans on the export of military equipment for those who fail to meet commitments or engage in dialogue.[470] A working group was established to review progress by relevant parties and to make recommendations to the Council and other UN bodies.[471] The Security Council also called upon 'all parties concerned to abide by . . . the concrete commitments they have made to the Special Representative of the Secretary-General for Children in Armed Conflict . . . and other United Nations agencies'.[472] Although this coercive approach may encourage increased non-State armed group compliance, the issues surrounding the implementation of UN sanctions highlighted above are likely to persist.

Geneva Call, an international humanitarian organisation[473] dedicated to engaging with non-State armed groups, has had demonstrable success in

---

463 Instructions for the Government of Armies of the United States in the Field (Lieber Code) General Order 100 (24 April 1863); Sivakumaran, *Non-International Armed Conflict* (n 68) 20–9.

464 Clapham (n 1) 288.

465 Jean-Daniel Vigny and Cecilia Thompson, 'Fundamental Standards of Humanity: What Future?' (2002) 20 *Neth Q Hum Rts* 185, 192–4.

466 UNGA, 'Protection of Children Affected by Armed Conflict' (29 August 2003) UN Doc A/58/328, paras 21–2.

467 Ibid. para 21.

468 Ibid. para 22.

469 Clapham (n 1) 289.

470 UNSC Res 1539 (22 April 2004) UN Doc S/RES/1539, para 5.

471 UNSC Res 1612 (26 July 2005) UN Doc S/RES/1612.

472 UNGA, 'Report of the Secretary-General: Children and Armed Conflict' (9 February 2005) UN Docs A/59/695 and S/2005/72, Annexes I and II.

473 Geneva Call, www.genevacall.org/, accessed 21 April 2016.

securing voluntary compliance with some humanitarian standards. Geneva Call's 'Deed of Commitment for Adherence to a Total Ban on Antipersonnel Mines and for Cooperation in Mine Actions' permits signatory non-State armed groups to express commitment to the 1997 Ottawa Convention.[474] As the Convention is a multilateral treaty, non-State actors are not permitted to formally ratify or accede to it.[475] Instead, Geneva Call simply accepts the impossibility of formal treaty ratification and provides an alternative, voluntary method of engagement.[476] In return, the organisation offers implementation support and monitors progress. Thus, the initiative establishes mutually beneficial terms in order to foster non-State actor compliance. In addition, the government of the Republic and Canton of Geneva acts as an officiator by providing a counter-signature and serving as the guardian of the deeds.[477] Non-State armed groups have proven receptive, and it has been suggested that a number of factors, including their belief in the legitimacy of the norms, their dependency on financial/technical support, transnational pressure and the need for internal and external political legitimation, have contributed to their compliance.[478] The initiative has 'also provided a forum for communication . . . It fills a gap in the international legal regime by answering the question of what type of coordinating mechanism might work and where it should be located'.[479] Monitoring takes place on three levels, including self-monitoring through the submission of compliance reports by the armed group itself, through local networks providing third-party specialist knowledge, and follow-up/verification meetings.[480]

Geneva Call demonstrates that engagement with non-State armed groups is both possible and, in some cases, extremely effective,[481] leading commentators to suggest that:

> [i]f armed groups are prepared to take on these human rights obligations, arguments about their non-applicability under international law lose much

---

474 Convention on the Prohibition of the Use, Stockpiling, Production and Transfer of Anti-Personnel Mines and on their Destruction (Ottawa Convention) (18 September 1997) 2056 UNTS 211.

475 Nor does the Convention permit NLMs to declare compliance, as permitted by Protocol I Additional to the Geneva Conventions of 12 August 1949, and relating to the Protection of Victims of International Armed Conflicts (8 June 1977) 1125 UNTS 3; Ryngaert and Meulebroucke (n 398) 448–50.

476 Claudia Hofmann, 'Engaging Non-State Armed Groups in Humanitarian Action' (2006) 13 *Int'l Peacekeeping* 396, 399.

477 Geneva Call (n 473).

478 Stefanie Herr, 'Binding Non-State Armed Groups to International Humanitarian Law, Geneva Call and the Ban of Anti-Personnel Mines: Lessons from Sudan' (Peace Research Institute Frankfurt, 2010) 13–23.

479 Hofmann (n 476).

480 Sivakumaran, *Non-International Armed Conflict* (n 68) 540–1.

481 Buckley (n 107) 830–45.

of their force. States may fear the legitimacy that such commitments seem to imply – but from a victim's perspective such commitments may indeed be worth more than the paper they are written on.[482]

However, Article 6 of the Commitment explicitly renounces any legal effects.[483] As such, there are doubts as to the certainty with which such commitments can be treated, as it is entirely possible for groups to disregard the provisions when adherence is no longer incentivised. Although the number of groups currently engaged in the programme is encouraging,[484] a great deal have yet to sign up, and the fragmented nature of today's non-international armed conflict poses a substantial barrier to access.[485]

For the reasons highlighted above, States remain fearful of bolstering the legitimacy of non-State armed groups threatening their territorial integrity.[486] These political sensitivities can give rise to serious practical challenges. In 2007, the Ethiopian government expelled the ICRC from its territory for engagement with the Ogaden National Liberation Front.[487] Similarly, Afghanistan expelled two EU diplomats for entering talks with the Taliban following US pressure.[488] The UN specifically has been impeded in its attempts to engage with groups in Colombia and Myanmar,[489] likely as a result of the institution's 'formality and prestige'.[490] On the subject of the Kurdistan Workers' Party (PKK), the Turkish government has also explicitly stated that, '[t]he use of terms such as "rebels" or "armed non-State actors" gives the reader a wrong indication about the real nature of a terrorist organisation'.[491] Thus, non-State armed group engagement remains constrained by State interests, irrespective of their capacity to defend their rights to territorial authority and control in practice. The legal quality of the largely voluntary initiatives considered above leads to considerable

482 Clapham (n 1) 294.
483 Geneva Call, 'Deed of Commitment under Geneva Call for Adherence to a Total Ban on Anti-Personnel Mines and for Cooperation in Mine Action' Article 6, www.genevacall.org/wp-content/uploads/dlm_uploads/2013/12/DoC-Banning-anti-personnel-mines.pdf, accessed 21 April 2016.
484 Geneva Call, 'Landmine ban', www.genevacall.org/what-we-do/landmine-ban/, accessed 21 April 2016; Herr (n 478) 5–6.
485 Ryngaert and Meulebroucke (n 398) 450.
486 Steinhoff (n 67) 316–22; Clapham (n 1) 296–9.
487 Sivakumaran, *Non-International Armed Conflict* (n 68) 533.
488 Nicolas Florquin and Elisabeth Decrey Warner, 'Engaging Non-State Armed Groups or Listing Terrorists?' (Disarmament Forum, 2008) 19, www.genevacall.org/wp-content/uploads/dlm_uploads/2013/12/art-13.pdf, accessed 21 April 2016.
489 UNGA, 'Report of the Secretary-General on Children and Armed Conflict' (12 December 2007) UN Docs A/62/609 and S/2007/57, para 158.
490 Sivakumaran, *Non-International Armed Conflict* (n 68) 537.
491 Landmine Monitor, 'Letter from Ambassador Türkekul Kurttekin, Regarding the Status of the PKK' (Geneva, 15 December 2005) www.the-monitor.org/index.php/content/view/full/18609_, accessed 21 April 2016.

uncertainty, given that armed groups could, at any point, breach their agreements without formal legal consequence. As a result, these mechanisms are open to the criticism by concerned State parties that groups will only act in adherence in order to gain international recognition and legitimacy. Yet, despite these issues, the positive examples highlighted above lend credence to the claim that, 'ownership of the law incentivises compliance'.[492] Indeed, this very notion arguably underscores the international obligations held by States, playing a dual role in inducing adherence and providing contractarian validation. It is to this conceptual argument that the next chapter of this monograph will turn.

3.4 Concluding remarks

The legal frameworks presently operating at both the international and domestic levels remain fundamentally State-centric in scope and are ill-equipped to effectively respond to the adverse effects produced by the activities of non-State actors. International human rights law addresses most non-State actors in an indirect fashion, placing due diligence obligations on State parties that are unable to safeguard their populations or lack the appropriate incentives to do so. Even the recently codified regime of State responsibility provides scant opportunities to attribute the conduct of non-State actors to State parties, owing to the restrictive thresholds adopted in international jurisprudence. Although international humanitarian law purports to produce limited duties for all parties to an armed conflict, its operation is substantially undermined by the political sensitivities of States. The situation at the national level does little to fill this accountability vacuum. Concerns relating to governmental corruption and complicity, access to justice and fair trial procedures abound in many weak governance host States. Domestic private law standards inadvertently favour corporate defendants, and legislation often militates against community development while mandating the separate incorporation of foreign companies, thereby shielding parent company assets. On the other hand, home States are not generally considered to owe a duty to prevent abuses emanating from the activities of their corporate nationals on foreign soil. Even if the extensive jurisdictional hurdles can be surmounted, procedural challenges remain potent. To date, only one decision against a parent for the activities of its foreign subsidiary has been formally rendered, and unique avenues to redress provided in the US have been beset by the imposition of erroneous legal standards and are today subject to substantial erosion.

The only path to direct international legal accountability is via the limited competence of the ICC, which has, to date, been plagued by inefficiency and

---

492 Sophie Rondeau, 'Participation of Armed Groups in the Development of the Law Applicable to Armed Conflicts' (2011) 93 *Int'l Rev Red Cross* 649.

lacks the capacity to make determinations against collective entities. Although the prosecution of individual company directors or military commanders remains possible, this approach is largely ill-suited to the actors examined in this study. The identification of responsible individuals within an intricate corporate supply chain would likely present insurmountable difficulties. Similarly, the vast majority of conduct that significantly affects the lives of vulnerable populations is unlikely to reach the threshold of international criminality. Such a regime is incapable of remedying day-to-day, cumulative abuses. Furthermore, the approach is built entirely on *ex post facto* redress. Although it may produce positive effects in terms of compensation and closure for some victims, it does little to advance adequate prevention or management strategies for human rights and humanitarian atrocities, which should receive the primary focus.

Although CSR and other voluntary compliance frameworks have, on occasion, produced desirable effects, their legal quality remains contentious. Such initiatives fail to provide judicially enforceable obligations, and their contribution to the normative development of binding instruments is subject to substantial debate. CSR standards are often viewed cynically by vulnerable communities, and business actors are frequently accused of adopting these provisions as public relations exercises. The schemes also remain strongly tied to the political attitudes of States and their capacity to ensure effective domestic implementation. Similar attitudes have been expressed regarding the adoption of voluntary commitments by non-State armed groups, which have been described as tactical plays for political legitimacy and legal recognition. In sum, the foregoing discussion exposes the practical failings of existing regulatory regimes, which are bolstered by the largely State-centric operation of the international legal system. Advancing this analysis, the next chapter of this monograph draws together the practical and conceptual themes established thus far by examining, in context, the underlying theoretical issues precluding the establishment of direct international obligations for non-State actors.

4 The theoretical scope for direct non-State actor regulation

Thus far, this study has set out the core theoretical components of State-centric scholarship and demonstrated the challenges that are characteristic of the non-State actors that operate in, or are sustained by, extractive industries in weak governance States. It was established that existing avenues to accountability, both domestic and international, remain either the exclusive domain of States or substantially constrained by State concerns. Advancing this analysis, this chapter aims to explore the theoretical potential for the ascription of *direct* international obligations to non-State actors. The political and economic concerns of State parties aside, it has long been suggested that, in today's globalised era of diminishing State power, non-State actors ought to be directly responsible for the adverse human rights impacts they produce.[1] Indeed, some international instruments already purport to bind non-State entities directly.[2] At first sight, the solution is relatively straightforward: simply abandon the classical position that States constitute the principal addressees, and thus subjects, of international law and extend obligations to non-State entities.

---

1 Sarah Joseph, 'Taming the Leviathans: Multinational Enterprises and Human Rights' (1999) 46 *Neth Int'l L Rev* 171, 174; Andrew Clapham, *Human Rights Obligations of Non-State Actors* (Oxford, UK, OUP, 2006) 83; Andrew Clapham, 'Human Rights Obligations of Non-State Actors in Conflict Situations' (2006) 88 *Int'l Rev Red Cross* 491, 523; Yael Ronon, 'Human Rights Obligations of Territorial Non-State Actors' (2013) 46 *Cornell Int'l LJ* 21, 22–5; Markos Karavias, *Corporate Obligations Under International Law* (Oxford, UK, OUP, 2013) 4.

2 Geneva Convention for the Amelioration of the Condition of the Wounded and Sick in Armed Forces in the Field (First Geneva Convention) (12 August 1949) 75 UNTS 31; Geneva Convention for the Amelioration of the Condition of Wounded, Sick and Shipwrecked Members of Armed Forces at Sea (Second Geneva Convention) (12 August 1949) 75 UNTS 85; Geneva Convention Relative to the Protection of Civilian Persons in Time of War (Fourth Geneva Convention) (12 August 1949) 75 UNTS 287; Geneva Convention Relative to the Treatment of Prisoners of War (Third Geneva Convention) (12 August 1949) 75 UNTS 135, Common Article 3 (hereafter, Geneva Conventions 1949); Protocol Additional to the Geneva Conventions of 12 August 1949, and relating to the Protection of Victims of Non-International Armed Conflicts (8 June 1977) 1125 UNTS 609, Article 1 (hereafter, Additional Protocol II 1977).

In the oft-cited words of Rosalyn Higgins, '[w]e have erected an intellectual prison of our own choosing and then declared it to be an unalterable constraint . . . the whole notion of "subjects" and "objects" has no credible reality and . . . no functional purpose'.[3] Yet, as will be demonstrated, the dominant conception of international law engenders certain presumptions for the addressees of international obligations that render the expansion of the *subjects doctrine* neither helpful, nor politically feasible. These presumptions relate to seemingly innate legal capacities, such as law-making competence, political prestige and legitimacy, and will be explored in detail below.[4]

The paucity of international regulation relating to non-international (or internal) armed conflict provides a useful vehicle with reference to which the establishment of direct obligations for non-State actors can be analysed. As such, this chapter will begin by exploring the extent to which non-State armed groups are already subject to direct legal regulation under international humanitarian law, and the theoretical weakness of existing explanations of the validity or binding quality of these provisions. In the latter half of the chapter, it will be argued that the extension of direct obligations is undermined by the peculiarities to which the State-centric conception of international law gives rise, including its heavy reliance on consent for validation and the resulting conflation between addressee and law-maker. The scholarship of Thomas Franck and discursive democracy theorists such as Jürgen Habermas will be drawn upon, and it will be argued that the absence of non-State actor participation in the process of law creation impedes the legitimate extension of direct obligations to those entities and adversely affects their compliance with international standards. Advancing this discussion, the final section of this chapter will assess the practical and theoretical desirability of multi-stakeholder law-making processes, weighing the political concerns of States against potential implications related to the scope, content and quality of international legal rules and structures.

4.1 The direct application of humanitarian law to non-State armed groups

There remains a long-standing disparity between the scope and content of the provisions that govern international and internal armed conflict. Whereas international armed conflict is governed by all four 1949 Geneva Conventions and Additional Protocol I, internal armed conflict is regulated by Common Article 3 and Additional Protocol II alone.[5] Yet, even Additional Protocol II

---

3 Rosalyn Higgins, *Problems and Process: International Law and How We Use It* (Oxford, UK, Clarendon Press, 1994) 49.

4 Jean d'Aspremont, 'The Doctrine of Fundamental Rights of States and the Functions of Anthropomorphic Thinking in International Law' (2015) 4 *CJICL* (forthcoming).

5 Wars of national liberation, which are expressly covered by Additional Protocol I, are internationalised to benefit from the full range of protections under the 1949 Geneva Conventions. These groups are excluded from the present analysis: Protocol Additional to

does not automatically apply in all instances of internal armed conflict. Non-State parties to the conflict will only engage obligations under this instrument when they operate under a 'responsible command, [and] control enough of the territory to carry out sustained military operations'.[6] Moreover, there is no authoritative definition for entities described as 'non-State armed groups'.[7] Such actors are extremely diverse in their size, organisation, motives, goals and resources, and the fluid and fractious nature of their membership compounds this issue. As such, it has been suggested that the majority of low-intensity internal armed conflict engages only the very general provisions contained within Common Article 3.[8] Given that inter-State conflict is increasingly rare, and fragmented civil strife is far more common, this position has been subject to criticism. It has long been argued that there should be a uniform standard of regulation, irrespective of the characterisation of the conflict.[9] This discrepancy in protection further highlights the State-centric operation of international humanitarian law, despite its purported application to non-State armed groups. However, it is not only the application of the provisions particular to *international* armed conflicts that is in doubt. The application of the *entire corpus* of international humanitarian law, including the minimal protection supplied by Common Article 3, may be called into question when one enquires as to the theoretical basis of the validity of these instruments.

The present monograph argues that the direct application of both customary and conventional international law to non-State actors is wholly incompatible with the theoretical underpinnings of State-centric scholarship. Just as primacy was given to MNEs in the preceding discussion of the practical obstacles to State-based non-State actor regulation, it is suggested that the most appropriate vehicle for the present theoretical critique is the application of international humanitarian law to non-State armed groups. This is due, in part, to the express

the Geneva Conventions of 12 August 1949, and relating to the Protection of Victims of International Armed Conflicts (8 June 1977) 1125 UNTS 3, Article 1(4).

6 Additional Protocol II 1977 (n 2) Article 1.

7 For a variety of approaches, see: David Petrasek, 'Ends & Means: Human Rights Approaches to Armed Groups' (International Council on Human Rights Policy, 2000) 5, www. ichrp.org/files/reports/6/105_report_en.pdf, accessed 21 April 2016; Program on Humanitarian Policy and Conflict Research, 'Empowered Groups, Tested Laws and Policy Options' (Harvard University, 2007) 18, www.hpcrresearch.org/sites/default/files/ publications/Report_Empowered_Groups_Nov2007.pdf, accessed 21 April 2016; Claudia Hofmann and Ulrich Schneckener, 'Engaging Non-State Armed Actors in State- and Peace-building: Options and Strategies' (2011) 99 *Int'l Rev Red Cross* 1, 2–3.

8 In *Strugar*, the ICTY omitted the higher threshold in Article 1, Additional Protocol II 1977, though this approach has not been followed in subsequent jurisprudence: *Prosecutor v Strugar* (Trial Judgment) IT-01-42-T (31 January 2005) paras 227–33; Sandesh Sivakumaran, *The Law of Non-International Armed Conflict* (Oxford, UK, OUP, 2012) 66–7.

9 Emmerich de Vattel, *The Law of Nations: Or, Principles of the Law of Nature Applied to the Conduct and Affairs of Nations and Sovereigns* (1758) § 294.

wording of the conventions and judicial commentary dealing with this issue. At present, no international human rights treaties explicitly impose direct obligations on either MNEs or non-State armed groups in the same manner as the Geneva Conventions and Additional Protocols. Given that international law has traditionally maintained a binary distinction between State and non-State entities, it is suggested that the majority of the theoretical analysis below may be applied to MNEs by analogy, despite the vast difference in the economic power and political legitimacy of these actors. Although the logic of State-centric scholarship is followed for present purposes, by implication, it is also argued that a far more nuanced approach is required in developing a workable theoretical model advancing direct non-State actor accountability. Thus, the chapter will critically assess the consequences that State-centric scholarship provokes by adopting its line of reasoning and following it to its logical conclusions.

A short note outlining the orthodox justification for the binding quality of humanitarian law for non-State armed groups is required before proceeding further. Traditionally, non-State armed groups were considered to be bound to the extent that they chose to announce their adherence.[10] Naturally, this approach provides little certainty and permits a group to act in compliance with, or defiance of, a provision, as it pleases. Given that the aim of humanitarian law is to induce certain uniform, minimum standards for the warring parties, this approach is necessarily problematic. As introduced above, some conventional humanitarian provisions address 'all parties to the conflict' and, as such, purportedly affix to non-State actors directly.[11] As the SCSL expressly stated:

> it is well-settled that all parties to an armed conflict, whether States or non-State actors, are bound by international humanitarian law, even though only States may become parties to international treaties.[12]

This position has been described as 'legal heresy but . . . necessary heresy'.[13] Exactly *how* and *why* actors that are unable to formally consent to multilateral treaties are directly bound remains controversial.[14]

Writing in 2002, Zegveld stated that there was no international practice dealing with this question.[15] Perhaps not specifically, but today there exists a

---

10 Sivakumaran, *Non-International Armed Conflict* (n 8) 239.

11 Geneva Conventions 1949 (n 2) Common Article 3.

12 *Prosecutor v Sam Hinga Norman* (Decision on Preliminary Motion Based on Lack of Jurisdiction) SCSL-2004-14-AR72(E) (31 May 2004) para 22.

13 Frédéric Siordet, 'The Geneva Conventions and Civil War' (1950) 3 *Int'l Rev Red Cross Supp* 132, 168.

14 Jann K Kleffner, 'The Applicability of International Humanitarian Law to Organised Armed Groups' (2011) 93 *Int'l Rev Red Cross* 443, 444.

15 Liesbeth Zegveld, *Accountability of Armed Opposition Groups in International Law* (Cambridge, UK, CUP, 2002) 15.

sizeable body of academic commentary and international jurisprudence offering both theoretical and practical justifications for this view.[16] These approaches will be examined in detail below. It is argued that each suffers insurmountable flaws. In spite of growing international practice, there is, at present, no satisfactory theoretical justification for the application of humanitarian provisions to *all* relevant non-State armed groups. The strengths and weaknesses of each of these approaches will be explored in turn. Although this is primarily a theoretical pursuit, practical issues will also be emphasised, as 'a theoretically pleasing approach must not come at the expense of an unacceptable explanation to the armed opposition group . . . thus defeating the very purpose of the exercise'.[17] A deeper theoretical enquiry into the reason for these inherent weaknesses, and how they may be remedied, will then be provided in later sections of this chapter.

4.1.1 *Binding non-State armed groups via State law*

Perhaps the simplest explanation for the direct reach of international humanitarian law to non-State armed groups rests on the principle of *legislative jurisdiction*:[18] the assertion that States ratify international conventions that are directly binding on the national citizens of that State.[19] It is not inferred that the approach is unconvincing by virtue of its simplicity. Indeed, it likely represents the orthodox view on the matter.[20] The approach may be praised for providing an explanation that is not contingent on the consent of the armed groups themselves and is generally compatible with the State responsibility approach to non-State actor regulation.[21] Its origins are apparent in the submissions of State representatives during the drafting of Additional Protocol II 1977. It was suggested by the Soviet delegation during the 1975 Diplomatic Conferences that, if accepted, the Protocol:

> would impose an obligation not only on governments but on those who . . . were engaged in movements against governments. Once adopted, the text would become a national law imposing an obligation on all persons within the territory of the State in question. Any international instrument

---

16 Sandesh Sivakumaran, 'Binding Armed Opposition Groups' (2006) 55 *ICLQ* 369; Veronika Bilkova, 'Treat Them as They Deserve? Three Approaches to Armed Opposition Groups Under Current International Law' (2010) 4 *Hum Rts Int'l & Legal Discourse* 111; Kleffner (n 14) 443–61.
17 Sivakumaran, 'Binding Armed Opposition Groups' (n 16) 370–1.
18 Ibid. 381.
19 Eric David, '*Le droit international humanitaire et les acteurs non étatiques*' (2003) 27 *Collegium* 27, 35.
20 Program on Humanitarian Policy and Conflict Research (n 7) 32.
21 Kleffner (n 14) 445.

signed by a government was binding on all those within its territory . . .
The obligation was in fact for all citizens.[22]

A member of the Belgian delegation reached a similar conclusion, but by reason
of the clear link between Common Article 3 and Additional Protocol II:

> [T]he entire philosophy of the provisions of Common Article 3, whether
> explicitly reaffirmed or not, is included in the Protocol. It is implicit that
> the same applies to the basic sovereign principle that the obligations are
> equally binding on both parties to the conflict.[23]

Indeed, it was even suggested by the ICRC that Common Article 1 of the 1949
Geneva Conventions should contain:

> a formal declaration stating that the . . . undertakings are subscribed to by
> governments in the name of their peoples . . . associating the peoples
> themselves with the duty of ensuring respect . . . [and facilitating] the
> implement[ation] of the present Convention, especially in the case of
> civil war.[24]

Such a declaration was omitted from the final text of the Conventions.

Despite the historical roots of this view, a number of compelling criticisms
have emerged. First, it is unclear whether the obligation arises at the
international or domestic level.[25] The domestic legal systems of 'dualist' States,
such as the UK, do not recognise the direct effect of international obligations
and instead require a piece of implementing legislation to incorporate relevant
provisions into domestic law.[26] Cassese countered this initial criticism, noting
that, '[i]ndisputably, in most States international treaties become part of
domestic law upon ratification, but they bind individuals and State authorities
qua domestic law, and indeed benefit from all the judicial guarantees provided
for by that system'.[27] Thus, although the suggestion that international law

---

22 Official Records of the Diplomatic Conference on the Reaffirmation and Development of
   International Humanitarian Law Applicable in Armed Conflicts (Geneva 1974–1977)
   (Library of Congress, 1979) Vol XIV, 314 paras 21–4.
23 Official Records of the Diplomatic Conference on the Reaffirmation and Development of
   International Humanitarian Law Applicable in Armed Conflicts (Geneva 1974–1977)
   (Library of Congress, 1979) Vol VII, 76.
24 ICRC, Draft Revised or New Conventions for the Protection of War Victims (Geneva,
   May 1948) 5, www.loc.gov/rr/frd/Military_Law/pdf/RC_Draft-revised.pdf, accessed 21
   April 2016.
25 Thomas Fleiner-Gerster and Michael Meyer, 'New Developments in Humanitarian Law:
   A Challenge to the Concept of Sovereignty' (1985) 34 *ICLQ* 267, 268–9.
26 Kleffner (n 14) 446–7.
27 Antonio Cassese, 'The Status of Rebels under the 1977 Geneva Protocol on Non-
   International Armed Conflicts' (1981) 30 *ICLQ* 416, 429.

requires domestic legislative implementation is relatively weak in light of State practice, it is still through the capacity or character of domestic law that the provisions apply to armed groups. As such, it has been suggested that these obligations would not apply, were a non-State armed group to 'declare null and void in a territory under their control [the State's] domestic legislation, and hence the domestic rules incorporating [humanitarian law]'.[28]

Cassese's view is perhaps best reflected in practice by Anzilloti's justification for the *Danzig* Advisory Opinion, discussed in Chapter 2.[29] However, this argument has been disputed on the grounds that international humanitarian instruments:

> are binding on the non-State armed group not through domestic law, but *directly* through international law . . . It is well-accepted that certain treaties create rights and obligations directly upon individuals, irrespective of whether or not they have been incorporated into domestic law.[30]

This is certainly true, as is evidenced by the related field of international criminal law, according to which the violation of norms of fundamental value to the international community may lead to the presumption of individual criminal responsibility.[31] The direct application of treaty rights contained within the Vienna Convention on Consular Relations (VCCR)[32] to individuals has also been demonstrated by the jurisprudence of the ICJ in its *LaGrand* and *Avena* Advisory Opinions.[33] As such, it has been argued that the binding quality of State law upon national citizens:

> which is the centrepiece of the doctrine of legislative jurisdiction, should not be understood narrowly to refer exclusively to legislation through the adoption of rules of domestic law . . . the capacity to legislate also refers to the competence of States to accept [international] rights and obligations . . . for their nationals.[34]

28 Ibid. 430.
29 *Jurisdiction of the Courts of Danzig* Advisory Opinion (1928) PCIJ (ser. B) No 15; Chapter 2 at Section 2.3.
30 Sivakumaran, *Non-International Armed Conflict* (n 8) 241–2; Dieter Fleck, 'The Law of Non-International Armed Conflicts' in Dieter Fleck (ed), *Handbook of International Humanitarian Law* (3rd edn, Oxford, UK, OUP, 2013) 597.
31 ILC, 'Report of the International Law Commission, Second Session: Formulation of the Nuremberg Principles' (5 June–29 July 1950) UN Doc A/1316 para 99; Roland Portmann, *Legal Personality in International Law* (Cambridge, UK, CUP, 2010) 161–2.
32 Vienna Convention on Consular Relations (24 April 1963) 500 UNTS 95.
33 *LaGrand* Case (*Germany v United States of America*) ICJ Reports [2001] 494 para 77; *Case Concerning Avena and Other Mexican Nationals* (*Mexico v United States*) ICJ Reports [2004] 12 para 40; See Chapter 5 at Section 5.2.1.
34 Kleffner (n 14) 448.

Additionally, it has been suggested by Sivakumaran that the manner in which they are bound, whether via an implementing domestic legislative enactment or an international instrument, is of little concern to non-State armed groups.[35] Rather, it is an issue of their participation, or at least consultation, regarding the terms by which armed conflict will be regulated. This issue will be explored further below.

Scholars have highlighted the discrepancy between directly binding individual citizens and directly binding 'groups' or 'corporate' entities.[36] States have objected to the recognition of non-State armed groups as 'parties to the conflict',[37] favouring individual criminal prosecution and leading to the omission of any reference to non-State armed groups as bearers of obligations in the proceedings of the First Periodical Meeting on Humanitarian Law.[38] Such concerns clearly relate to the political and legal legitimacy of non-State armed groups opposing the State.[39] Yet, the view that such groups are bound as individuals 'does not necessarily imply that the rebel "party" is also responsible'.[40] Similarly, for Ryngaert, individual criminal responsibility:

> cannot be used so as to support an argument that there is such a thing as 'collective' criminal responsibility of the entity made up of individuals. If the hypothesis that entities incur international criminal responsibility proves unsubstantiated, so does the hypothesis that those entities are necessarily bound by the substantive norms of international humanitarian law which underlie any criminalisation.[41]

Analogously, the establishment of collective criminality for MNEs has also failed to gain widespread acceptance.[42] Although widespread international practice has confirmed that non-State armed groups are indeed bound as collective entities under the legislative jurisdiction model,[43] the argument presented by

---

35 Sivakumaran, 'Binding Armed Opposition Groups' (n 16) 386.
36 Cedric Ryngaert, 'Non-State Actors in International Humanitarian Law' in Jean d'Aspremont (ed), *Multiple Perspectives on Non-State Actors in International Law* (Oxford, UK, Routledge, 2011) 286–7; Zegveld (n 15) 10.
37 Cassese, 'Status of Rebels' (n 27) 421.
38 Lucius Caflisch, 'Chairman's Report of the First Periodical Meeting on International Humanitarian Law (Geneva 19–23 January 1998)' (1998) 38 *Int'l Rev Red Cross* 366.
39 Denise Plattner, 'The Penal Repression of Violations of International Humanitarian Law Applicable in Non-International Armed Conflicts' (1990) 30 *Int'l Rev Red Cross* 409, 416.
40 Ibid.
41 Ryngaert, 'Non-State Actors in IHL' (n 36) 287.
42 See Chapter 3 at Section 3.3.1.
43 Zegveld (n 15) 10–12; cf M Cherif Bassiouni, 'Criminal Law: The New Wars and the Crisis of Compliance with the Law of Armed Conflict by Non-State Actors' (2008) 98 *J Crim L & Criminology* 711, 739–40; William A Schabas, 'State Policy as an Element of International Crimes' (2008) 98 *J Crim L & Criminology* 953.

Ryngaert does appear to significantly undermine the quality of its theoretical rationale. Geiss has emphasised that, in spite of the focus on the individual elements of obligation:

> the specific substantive obligations of the [armed] group, i.e. of the collectivity as such, have only scarcely been analysed in any depth. This is astounding because, by definition, at least half of the belligerents in the currently most prevalent and most victimising armed conflict . . . are non-State parties.[44]

Crucially, it must be borne in mind that a non-State armed group is 'not merely the sum of all its members, who act as atomised individuals. Rather, organised armed groups (just as States' parties . . .) are identifiable entities with political objectives (broadly conceived) that they pursue by violent means'.[45]

A final theoretical critique of this approach rests on its jurisdictional basis. The legislative jurisdiction method relies heavily on the principle of *active nationality*, in that it makes specific reference to the binding quality of legal rules on the *nationals of consenting States*. Thus, the approach 'fails to explain why [humanitarian] treaty rules are binding in a situation in which an organised armed group is (also) composed of foreign nationals from a State that has not ratified the respective treaty'.[46] This criticism cannot really be applied to provisions such as Common Article 3, given that the 1949 Geneva Conventions boast universal ratification. However, for the more detailed, supplementary provisions contained within Additional Protocol II, this critique could hold water. Additionally, interpretation of the concept of 'nationality', which is likely to be contentious during internal armed conflicts, will clearly impact the doctrine's application. Similar issues have been encountered in establishing the nationality of MNEs, in light of their complex corporate structures. In *Tadić*, the tribunal stated:

> While previously wars were primarily between well-established States, in modern inter-ethnic armed conflicts . . . new States are often created during the conflict and ethnicity rather than nationality may become the grounds for allegiance.[47]

It has been submitted that the text, drafting history and object/purpose of the Conventions suggest that, 'allegiance to a Party to the conflict and,

---

44 Robin Geiss, 'Humanitarian Law Obligations of Organised Armed Groups' in International Institute of Humanitarian Law, *Non-state Actors and International Humanitarian Law* (FrancoAngeli, 2010) 96.
45 Kleffner (n 14) 450.
46 Ibid. 448.
47 *Prosecutor v Tadić* (Appeals Chamber) IT-94-1-A (15 July 1999) para 166.

correspondingly, control by this Party over persons in a given territory, may be regarded as the crucial test'.[48] Although this criticism is certainly compelling, there is no reason as to why one could not adopt a more amenable basis for jurisdiction, such as one based on territoriality, in order to bind all individuals irrespective of national allegiance.[49] This approach may have more utility in relation to MNEs, given that these actors are not usually politically opposed to the State in which they operate. However, the issue of State-based enforcement would likely remain problematic, given the unwillingness of many weak governance States to effectively regulate MNEs for economic reasons.

Even if one were to accept that the legislative jurisdiction doctrine were theoretically satisfactory, it is submitted that it is unworkable in practice.[50] It has been argued that the theory that armed groups are bound by reason of their habitation of the territory of a State that is party to the relevant conventions is 'difficult to uphold . . . [as such] groups seek to exercise public authority, and in doing so, question the authority of the established government, including the government's laws'.[51] The scenario has been cogently described by Baxter:

> The legal problem about [Common Article 3] is that, while a government can bind itself, it cannot bind that 'party to the conflict' which is in rebellion against the lawful government . . . Since the majority of contemporary conflicts are in whole or in part internal, the maximum of legal ordering which can be expected in a great number of conflicts is the one article of the conventions which itself rests upon weak legal grounds.[52]

It has been argued that governmental opposition should not preclude adherence to these conventions, as treaties are concluded by, and attach to, States, rather than incumbent governmental entities.[53] Nevertheless, the identical nature of any domestic implementation legislation likely fuels these objections.[54] Moreover, the equation of non-State armed groups to ordinarily law-abiding citizens 'appears to be somewhat strained, if not entirely neglecting the reality

---

48 Ibid.
49 Ian Brownlie, *Principles of Public International Law* (7th edn, Oxford, UK, OUP, 2008) 300–6.
50 Jean-Marie Henckaerts, 'Binding Armed Opposition Groups through Humanitarian Treaty Law and Customary Law' (2003) 27 *Collegium* 123, 126.
51 Zegveld (n 15) 16.
52 Richard Baxter, 'Forces for Compliance with the Law of War' in Detlev Vagts, Theodor Meron, Stephen M Schwebel and Charles Keever (eds), *Humanizing the Laws of War: Selected Writings of Richard Baxter* (Oxford, UK, OUP, 2013) 154.
53 Dieter Fleck, 'The Law of Non-International Armed Conflicts' in Dieter Fleck and Michael Bothe (eds), *The Handbook of International Humanitarian law* (2nd edn, Oxford, UK, OUP, 2008) 608; Arnold McNair, *The Law of Treaties* (Oxford, UK, Clarendon Press, 1961) 676.
54 Sivakumaran, 'Binding Armed Opposition Groups' (n 16) 386.

of organised groups as challengers to the monopoly of State force that States arrogate for themselves'.[55]

As has already been firmly established in the preceding discussion regarding CSR initiatives, the ownership of rules strongly incentivises compliance with those rules. The same is true for non-State armed groups:[56]

> It is the creation process of the rules that is of concern to them; the party against whom they are in conflict had a say in the formation of the rules by which they are bound and they did not . . . the group will likely regard all laws passed by its opponents as illegitimate, regardless of whether they are domestic or international in nature.[57]

Although this criticism of the legislative jurisdiction approach has been described as 'intuitively appealing', Sivakumaran has suggested that this concern is overstated. Such opposition occurs only rarely in practice, and '[e]ven if the non-State armed group may declare certain State legislation null and void, it tends not to do so of the rules relating to the law of armed conflict'.[58] Indeed, Fleck has highlighted the inclusion of human rights commitments in the policy statements, codes of conduct and unilateral declarations of non-State armed groups.[59] Although this is compelling evidence of the acceptance of these obligations, it essentially represents the orthodox, consent-based view, or relies entirely on *ad hoc* declarations. These instances say very little about the binding quality of the international legal norms, given that non-State armed groups are apparently bound *irrespective* of their formal consent.[60]

Although non-State armed groups may occasionally endorse humanitarian standards, there have been notable examples of outright rejection. For example, the Algerian group Front de Libération Nationale (FLN) expressly stated that it 'did not participate in the Geneva Conventions for the protection of war victims and is not bound by the Conventions'.[61] The NLM of Vietnam refused to apply Common Article 3 because it was 'not bound by the international treaties to which others besides itself subscribed'.[62] A representative of the

---

55 Kleffner (n 14) 446.
56 Sophie Rondeau, 'Participation of Armed Groups in the Development of the Law Applicable to Armed Conflicts' (2011) 93 *Int'l Rev Red Cross* 649, 659.
57 Sivakumaran, 'Binding Armed Opposition Groups' (n 16) 386; Orla Marie Buckley, 'Unregulated Armed Conflict: Non-State Armed Groups, International Humanitarian Law, and Violence in Western Sahara' (2012) 37 *NCJ Int'l L & Com Reg* 793, 804.
58 Sivakumaran, *Non-International Armed Conflict* (n 8) 241–2.
59 Fleck, 'Non-International Armed Conflicts I' (n 30) 597–8; Sivakumaran, 'Binding Armed Opposition Groups' (n 16) 387–91.
60 Zegveld (n 15) 14.
61 Letter from Chef de la Représentation Permanente du FLN du Sud-Vietnam en URSS to Representative of the ICRC (16 October 1965) ICRC Archives BAG 202 223–005, cited and translated in Sivakumaran, *Non-International Armed Conflict* (n 8) 562.
62 ICRC, 'External Activities: Viet Nam' (1965) 5 *Int'l Rev Red Cross* 634, 636.

Colombian group Fuerzas Armadas Revolucionarias de Colombia (FARC), explicitly stated that:

> [i]t is supposed that for one to have to abide by the norms set forth in a pact, one should have participated in its drafting, in its discussion and should be in agreement with its conclusions. We have not been there, were never invited to any forum or event of the international community to discuss this topic.[63]

Yet, although participation by non-State armed groups appears to be instrumental in inducing their compliance, it has been suggested that this process 'instrumentalises the law, [and] will never justify violations of humanitarian rules by armed groups'.[64] Furthermore, Sivakumaran suggests that:

> [t]he legitimacy of rules from the point of view of the armed opposition group has to be balanced against the legitimacy of the armed opposition group from the perspective of the international community. An increase in the former, and a resulting increase in respect for the rules, may result in an increase for the latter.[65]

Such observations demonstrate the link between non-State actor compliance and *political* legitimacy. However, they do not explain the binding quality, or the *legal* legitimacy, of ascribing direct obligations to non-State armed groups under the State-based conception of international law. Thus, the term 'legitimacy' is used in two primary contexts throughout this monograph: (1) in terms of the empirical or social legitimacy that non-State actors are accorded by their acceptance in the context of a political order; and (2) in the legal/normative sense, whereby a law or rule is legitimate on the basis that it 'originates from a formally correct source and/or when it has been adopted in conformity with correct procedures'.[66] As will later be demonstrated, these types of legitimacy are inextricably linked under the dominant theoretical approach. For now, given that, 'the instances of violation or disregard for the provisions of Common Article 3 greatly outnumber the instances of compliance', it is

---

63 'Reaparece Cano' Cambino No 704 (Bogotá, 8–15 November, 1999), cited in Daniel García-Peña Jaramillo, 'Humanitarian Protection in Non-International Conflicts: A Case Study of Colombia' (2000) 30 *Isr YB Hum Rts* 179, 189–90.

64 Rondeau (n 56).

65 Sivakumaran, 'Binding Armed Opposition Groups' (n 16) 386.

66 Anne Peters, Lucy Koechlin and Gretta Fenner Zinkernagel, 'Non-State Actors as Standard Setters: Framing the Issue in an Interdisciplinary Fashion' in Anne Peters, Lucy Koechlin, Till Förster and Gretta Fenner Zinkernagel (eds), *Non-State Actors as Standard Setters* (Cambridge, UK, CUP, 2009) 19; Daniel Bodansky, 'The Concept of Legitimacy in International Law' in Rüdiger Wolfrum and Volker Roben (eds), *Legitimacy in International Law* (The Hague, Netherlands, Springer, 2008) 313–15.

suggested that the legislative jurisdiction model is neither practically nor theoretically viable.[67]

4.1.2 Cassese's Vienna Convention on the Law of Treaties analogy

The second widely cited justification for the binding quality of humanitarian law on non-State armed groups essentially draws from the provisions of the VCLT governing the creation of rights and duties for third-party States.[68] The approach, first propounded by Antonio Cassese, applies these provisions by analogy, in order to explain the conditions under which non-State armed groups will be bound as third parties.[69] Article 36(1) provides that a *right* may be conferred on third parties if this reflects the intention of the parties to the treaty, and the third-party assents. Assent 'shall be presumed so long as the contrary is not indicated, unless the treaty otherwise provides'.[70] The criteria for the creation of a third-party *obligation* are necessarily stricter. Article 35 provides that an obligation may only be created where the parties to the treaty intend the provision to be the means of establishing the obligation and the third party expressly accepts this in writing.[71]

Moreover, this approach attempts to solve the question of legal validity by recourse to the very category of international instrument from which the initial problem arises. The VCLT is *itself* a treaty and, as such, is no more directly applicable to non-State actors than the provisions of conventional international humanitarian law purport to be. This is a fact that Cassese himself acknowledges: '[t]o be sure, this Convention relates only to States, while the customary rules on the matter have a broader scope, in that they govern the effects of treaties on *any international subject* taking the position of a third party *vis-à-vis* a treaty'.[72] Although this is an interesting rebuttal, in light of the elusive nature of customary international law, it will surely be difficult to ascertain which provisions are derived from customary law, and which are not. It has also been suggested by Sivakumaran that:

> even if a custom exists as regards the effect of these rules on States, it does not follow that there is a similar custom with respect to the impact of the rules on entities other than States. The customary rules may be limited *ratione personae*.[73]

---

67 Antonio Cassese, *International Law in a Divided World* (Oxford, UK, Clarendon Press, 1987) 284.
68 Vienna Convention on the Law of Treaties (23 May 1969) 1155 UNTS 331 (hereafter, VCLT).
69 Antonio Cassese, *International Law* (2nd edn, Oxford, UK, OUP, 2004) 129–30.
70 VCLT (n 68) Article 36(1).
71 Ibid. Article 35.
72 Cassese, 'Status of Rebels' (n 27) 423.
73 Sivakumaran, 'Binding Armed Opposition Groups' (n 16) 377.

Yet Cassese maintains that it is appropriate to rely on the Convention alone, given that:

> general international law does not differentiate in this matter between States and other legal persons, as far as the effects of treaties between States are concerned. Secondly, the [VCLT] does not deviate from that law; rather it codifies it and spells it out. Although it explicitly refers to States only ... it does not rule out the applicability of its provisions to other international entities.[74]

Assuming that Cassese is correct, at least for the time being, the VCLT provisions themselves provide some problematic hurdles. First, both articles rely heavily on the intentions of the parties to the treaty. It is beyond the scope of this chapter to provide an in-depth enquiry into the intentions of the State representatives during the drafting of the Geneva Conventions and Additional Protocols.[75] It is already clear in light of the above discussion that the representations made by delegates varied considerably, and Cassese himself concedes that, at least in respect of Additional Protocol II, it is 'probably fair to contend that the view opposed to any extension of legal rights or duties to rebels was far more widespread'.[76] However, he suggests that the ultimate intention of the draftsmen can be discerned via a textual reading of the Protocol, as this represents a crystallised and objective intention, as opposed to the politicised and contradictory representations made by the delegates. Cassese raises three justifications for this view. First, the Protocol should apply directly to non-State armed groups, given that it was intended to 'develop and supplement' Common Article 3[77] without modifying its conditions of application.[78] This justification is based on the view that Common Article 3 indisputably applies to non-State armed groups, despite their inability to ratify the Convention in which it is contained. Although this position may be strongly reflected by international practice, it is something of an anomaly and does not explain the theoretical underpinning for the binding quality of this provision. Yet, it is probably fair to infer, based on the adoption of the inclusive term 'parties to the conflict', that the delegates *intended* Common Article 3 to bind non-State armed groups by the standards of the VCLT.

The second justification for the binding quality of the Protocol rests on the extra conditions for its application, which impose a threshold of organisation/command structure and territorial control.[79] It is submitted that:

74 Cassese, 'Status of Rebels' (n 27) 423.
75 Sivakumaran, *Non-International Armed Conflict* (n 8) 40–53.
76 Cassese, 'Status of Rebels' (n 27) 423.
77 Additional Protocol II 1977 (n 2) Article 1(1).
78 Cassese, 'Status of Rebels' (n 27) 424.
79 Additional Protocol II 1977 (n 2) Article 1(1).

the Protocol only begins to apply when rebels prove they are able to, and do in fact, implement it . . . There would be no reason for insurgents to fulfil the obligations deriving from the Protocol if they could not benefit from the rights it confers, once the Protocol becomes applicable as a result of their compliance.[80]

This approach conflates legal validity with practical compliance. It may also be argued that this view is utopian and disregards the state of affairs on the ground during internal armed conflicts. Although it may be comforting to think of States as strongly motivated by humanitarian concerns, realistically, non-State armed groups directly threaten the territorial control of the State, and, as a result, States are reluctant to admit that such groups meet the conditions for the Protocol's application.[81] These practical concerns aside, it is suggested by Cassese that, if non-State armed groups are considered the direct beneficiaries of rights and obligations under the Protocol, then they are entitled 'to demand from the government in power the full application of the Protocol . . . The very men for whose sake the Protocol has been elaborated are the best equipped to prompt the Government concerned to respect it'.[82] Although this may be so, it has already been established that, in the absence of a credible adjudicator, the attitudes of States remain paramount in the application of humanitarian law.[83]

Cassese's third justification rests on Article 6(5) of the Protocol. This provision requires the parties to the conflict to grant the broadest possible amnesties to those who have participated in the conflict, or been interred or detained.[84] As it may be presumed that this provision will apply to the armed group, if it is successful in overthrowing the recognised government or in managing to secede from the State, then it is:

> logical to maintain that the other rules of the protocol also bind the rebels before that final moment. Otherwise, one could reach the strange conclusion that the Protocol, while it does not grant any legal status to rebels, nevertheless takes them into account once they have attained power.[85]

On this basis, Cassese suggests that a textual reading of the Protocol reflects the intention of the draftsmen that non-State armed groups should be bound

---

80 Cassese, 'Status of Rebels' (n 27) 424–5.
81 Richard Baxter, 'Jus Bello Interno: The Present and Future of Law' in John Norton Moore (ed) *Law and Civil War in the Modern World* (Baltimore, MD, Johns Hopkins Press, 1974) 528; Anthony Cullen, *The Concept of Non-International Armed Conflict in International Humanitarian Law* (Cambridge, UK, CUP, 2010) 55–6; Bilkova (n 16) 122–3.
82 Cassese, 'Status of Rebels' (n 27) 426.
83 See Chapter 3 at Section 3.1.2.
84 Additional Protocol II 1977 (n 2) Article 6(5).
85 Cassese, 'Status of Rebels' (n 27) 427.

directly. Yet, other international instruments, seemingly restricted in their application to State parties, at least on a textual reading, have later been interpreted, on the intention of the drafters, to include non-State armed groups.[86] On the other hand, instruments such as the Optional Protocol to the Convention on the Rights of the Child appear to address non-State actors directly on a textual reading,[87] despite the explicit remarks to the contrary by the drafters.[88] Thus, Cassese's defence of the intention of the parties remains somewhat problematic.

However, the major critique of his approach rests on its ultimate basis in *consent*.[89] Article 34 VCLT provides that, 'a treaty does not create either obligations or rights for a third State without its consent'.[90] Although the consent of non-State armed groups relating to *rights* may be assumed in the absence of contrary evidence, *written* consent is required with regard to the ascription of *obligations*. Although it cannot be denied that many non-State armed groups have expressed their willingness to comply with the provisions in various unilateral declarations,[91] through initiatives such as Geneva Call[92] and other *ad hoc* agreements, such consent is not guaranteed. In addition, their consent has been written off as a façade to gain political legitimacy and has been withheld on the basis of opposition to the recognised State government, or a lack of procedural participation/consultation regarding the terms.[93] Such concerns

---

86 UNESCO, 'Diplomatic Conference on the Second Protocol to the Hague Convention for the Protection of Cultural Property in the Event of an Armed Conflict: Summary Report' (The Hague, 15–16 March 1999) para 36.

87 'Armed groups that are distinct from the armed forces of a State should not, under any circumstances, recruit or use in hostilities persons under the age of 18 years', Optional Protocol to the Convention on the Rights of the Child on the Involvement of Children in Armed Conflict (25 May 2000) A/RES/54/263, Article 4(1).

88 'The prohibition on participation and recruitment should also apply to parties to a non-international armed conflict. *The obligation to ensure compliance with the instrument should rest with the States Parties*' (emphasis added), UNHCR, 'Report of the Working Group on a Draft Optional Protocol to the Convention on the Rights of the Child on Involvement of Children in Armed Conflicts' 54th Session (23 March 1998) UN Doc E/CN.4/1998/102 para 39; Bonnie Docherty, 'Breaking New Ground: The Convention on Cluster Munitions and the Evolution of International Humanitarian Law' (2009) 31 *Hum Rts Q* 959.

89 Ryngaert, 'Non-State Actors in IHL' (n 36) 288.

90 VCLT (n 68) Article 34.

91 Michel Veuthey, 'Learning from History: Accession to the Conventions, Special Agreements and Unilateral Declarations' (2003) 27 *Collegium* 139; Sivakumaran, 'Binding Armed Opposition Groups' (n 16) 389–92.

92 Cedric Ryngaert and Anneleen Van de Meulebroucke, 'Enhancing and Enforcing Compliance with International Humanitarian Law by Non-State Armed Groups' (2011) 16 *JCSL* 443, 448–50; Stefanie Herr, 'Binding Non-State Armed Groups to International Humanitarian Law, Geneva Call and the Ban of Anti-Personnel Mines: Lessons from Sudan' (Peace Research Institute Frankfurt, 2010) 5–9.

93 Dawn Steinhoff, 'Talking to the Enemy: State Legitimacy Concerns with Engaging Non-State Armed Groups' (2010) 45 *Tex Int'l LJ* 297.

surface repeatedly in each of these justifications. These practical concerns aside, Sivakumaran highlights a clear theoretical weakness with Cassese's reliance on the VCLT, both at the conventional level (given the incapacity of armed groups to formally ratify the treaty), and in relation to those provisions that are purported to reflect customary law. The latter will be discussed in further detail below. In light of the above, it is suggested that the present approach suffers from substantial flaws.

4.1.3 Non-State armed groups exercising 'effective power'

A third common justification for the direct application of international humanitarian law to non-State armed groups is perhaps best represented by former ICRC Vice President Jean Pictet's commentaries to the 1949 Geneva Conventions. He posits that, 'if the responsible authority at their head exercises effective sovereignty, it is bound by the very fact that it claims to represent the country, or part of the country'.[94] Whereas the legislative jurisdiction approach seeks to bind non-State armed groups on the basis of law previously enacted or consented to by the *de jure* State government, the focus of this approach is shifted to the *present* and *future* status of the non-State armed group.[95] There are two variants of this view.[96] The first concerns the explicit claim by the non-State armed group in question that it represents the State. This justifies the direct application of international humanitarian law by reason of the law on State succession. The ILC's Articles on State Responsibility provide that the conduct of *successful* insurrectionist groups give rise to State responsibility.[97] As mentioned above, the ratification of an international convention binds the *State*, as opposed to a particular government.[98] Thus, even in the event of a complete political regime change, the obligations incumbent upon the State will remain applicable. However, the present approach stretches this justification one step further. It considers a non-State armed group to be bound by State ratified law even where it simply *purports* to represent the State government.

This approach has been utilised historically, having been adopted in the proceedings following the US Civil War. During the *Trial of Henry Wirz*, it was stated that, 'the moment [the Confederates] asked a place among nations they were bound to recognise and obey those laws international which are and of necessity must be applicable to all'.[99] This approach does not distinguish

---

94 Jean Pictet (ed), 'The Geneva Conventions of 12 August 1949: Commentary, III Geneva Convention Relative to the Treatment of Prisoners of War' (ICRC, Geneva, 1960) 37.
95 Kleffner (n 14) 453.
96 Sivakumaran, 'Binding Armed Opposition Groups' (n 16) 379–80.
97 ILC, Articles on Responsibility of States for Internationally Wrongful Acts (2001) UN Doc A/56/49(Vol I)/Corr.4, Article 10.
98 Fleck, 'Non-International Armed Conflicts II' (n 53) 608.
99 *Trial of Henry Wirz*, US 40th Congress, 2nd Session (House Executive Document No 23, 7 December 1867) 764.

between a group claiming to represent the State government and a group that actually achieves this status. When the latter occurs, 'the principle of succession applies and the rules governing internal armed conflict bind the opposition group, but they do so *qua* the newly formed government and not *qua* the armed opposition group'.[100] Thus, to bind a group merely *claiming* to represent the State, irrespective of the practical reality, is extremely problematic.

The second approach is more implicit, primarily hinging on the criterion of widespread territorial control. By this view:

> non-State armed groups are regarded as independent entities existing side-by-side with the established authorities. This argument recognises the political realities of internal armed conflict and . . . abandons the traditional conception of the State as an impermeable whole.[101]

Yet, the approach has been criticised from a number of angles relating to the elusive definition of non-State armed groups. First, it fails to explain how groups that do not exercise effective territorial control are bound by conventional humanitarian law.[102] Although this may be a criterion for the application of Additional Protocol II, it does not underpin the binding quality of Common Article 3. Second, although this approach subverts the criterion of actually achieving the status of a new governmental regime, in that territorial control would need to be widespread, protracted and consistent in order for a group to gain quasi-governmental status, '*de facto* control of the territory does not necessarily imply a claim to represent the State or part thereof'.[103] The absence of an accepted definition of non-State armed group[104] and the intensely variable nature of their activities and objectives, which range from the fulfilment of quasi-governmental functions[105] to relatively sporadic combatants involved in low-intensity skirmishes, emphasise the limitations of this approach.[106]

100 Sivakumaran, 'Binding Armed Opposition Groups' (n 16) 380.
101 Zegveld (n 15) 15.
102 Ibid.
103 Sivakumaran, 'Binding Armed Opposition Groups' (n 16) 380; Sivakumaran, *Non-International Armed Conflict* (n 8) 239.
104 Nicolas Florquin and Elisabeth Decrey Warner, 'Engaging Non-State Armed Groups or Listing Terrorists? Implications for the Arms Control Community' (Disarmament Forum, 2008) 18, www.genevacall.org/wp-content/uploads/dlm_uploads/2013/12/art-13.pdf, accessed 21 April 2016.
105 Achim Wennmann, 'Economic Dimensions of Armed Groups: Profiling the Financing, Costs, and Agendas and their Implications for Mediated Engagements' (2011) 93 *Int'l Rev Red Cross* 333, 337–8; Kristen Schulze, 'The Free Aceh Movement (GAM): Anatomy of a Separatist Organisation' (East–West Centre, Washington, 2004) 27.
106 Michelle Mack and Jelena Pejic, 'Increasing Respect for International Humanitarian Law in Non-international Armed Conflicts' (ICRC, Geneva, 2008) 11, www.icrc.org/eng/assets/files/other/icrc_002_0923.pdf, accessed 21 April 2016; David McDonough, 'From Guerrillas to Government: Post-Conflict Stability in Liberia, Uganda and Rwanda' (2008) 29 *Third World Q* 357.

Ryngaert has discussed the utility of this method in explaining the binding quality of human rights law more generally, having cautiously supported the idea that non-State armed groups exercising effective territorial control should be subject to 'legitimate expectations' (as distinct from 'binding obligations').[107] Such an approach has been taken in the reports of UN Special Rapporteurs:

> As a non-State actor, the [Liberation Tigers of Tamil Eelam] does not have legal obligations under ICCPR, but it remains subject to the demands of the international community . . . that every organ of society respect and promote human rights.[108]

In some instances, the European Court of Human Rights (ECtHR) has also indicated the directly binding quality of international human rights law in situations of non-international armed conflict, at least in relation to State parties.[109] Although the wording of the Court appeared to confusingly entangle terminology relating to both humanitarian law and human rights law,[110] later judgments seem to suggest that the Court was indeed directly applying human rights law.[111] Sivakumaran has highlighted the fundamental difference between humanitarian law and human rights law: the former promoting the equality of obligations for all parties to the armed conflict; the latter binding only States.[112] Yet, a number of theories, similar to those pertaining to humanitarian law, have been advanced to justify the application of human rights law during internal armed conflict, despite the inability of armed groups to formally consent to the provisions, and the express wording of the treaties. These justifications broadly

---

107 Cedric Ryngaert, 'Human Rights Obligations of Armed Groups' (2008) 41 *RBDI* 355, 374–7.

108 Philip Alston, 'Report of the Special Rapporteur on Extrajudicial, Summary, or Arbitrary Executions – Mission to Sri Lanka' (27 March 2006) UN Doc E/CN.4/2006/53/Add.5 para 25; Philip Alston, Paul Hunt, Walter Kälin and Miloon Kothari, 'Report of the Special Rapporteurs – Mission to Lebanon and Israel' (2 October 2006) UN Doc A/HRC/2/7 para 19.

109 Russian aerial bombardments during a conflict with Chechen rebel groups were held to have violated the right to life: *Isayeva, Yusupova and Bazayeva v Russia* App Nos 57947/000, 57948/00 and 57949/00 (ECtHR, Judgment of 24 February 2005); *Isayeva v Russia* App No 57950/00 (ECtHR, Judgment of 24 February 2005).

110 Giulia Pinzauti, 'The European Court of Human Rights Incidental Application of International Criminal and Humanitarian Law: A Critical Discussion of Kononov v. Latvia' (2008) 6 *JICJ* 1043, 1060; Eriko Tamura, 'The Isayeva Cases of the European Court of Human Rights: The Application of International Humanitarian Law and Human Rights Law in Non-International Armed Conflicts' (2011) 10 *Chinese JIL* 129.

111 *Abuyeva and Others v Russia* App No 27065/05 (ECtHR, Judgment of 2 December 2010) 48 para 3.

112 Sivakumaran, *Non-International Armed Conflict* (n 8) 95; Marco Sassóli and Yuval Shany, 'Should the Obligations of States and Armed Groups under International Humanitarian Law Really Be Equal?' (2011) 93 *Int'l Rev Red Cross* 425.

relate to the principle of equality of obligations/correlative rights, the legitimate expectations of the international community, and the groups' effective territorial control.[113]

The latter reflects UN practice on the matter,[114] and the future extension of direct human rights obligations to non-State actors, limited to those possessing territorial control, has been explored in detail by Ronon.[115] The utilisation of this approach was also readily apparent in *Sadiq Shek Elmi v Australia*, where it was held that the actions of armed groups controlling various regions of Somalia were in contravention of the Convention against Torture, even absent participation by an official of the Somali government.[116] Somalia itself was subject to extreme internal strife and governmental breakdown, and, as a result, governmental officials simply did not exist. Thus, it was suggested that:

> *de facto*, those [armed groups] exercise certain prerogatives that are comparable to those normally exercised by legitimate governments. Accordingly, the members of those [armed groups] can fall, for the purposes of the application of the Convention, within the phrase 'public officials or other persons acting in an official capacity'.[117]

However, on this basis, where armed groups do not exhibit effective territorial control, human rights standards will not apply, despite the aim of human rights law to regulate internal armed conflict in scenarios where humanitarian instruments such as Additional Protocol II do not apply.[118]

It has also been suggested that some regard must be given to the nature of the relationship and the scenario in question when determining the extent of the human rights obligations of non-State armed groups.[119] Ryngaert remains critical of the approach:

> The binding character of human rights obligations for armed groups is based on them being, like governments, in a vertical position of power: those groups exercising territorial control, serve as (quasi-) governments . . . armed conflict, in contrast, is not necessarily based on a situation of governments or government-like actors exercising control over other actors . . . it merely aims at civilising the conduct of warfare.[120]

---

113 Sivakumaran, *Non-International Armed Conflict* (n 8) 95–6.
114 Alston, Hunt, Kälin and Kothari (n 108) para 76.
115 Ronon (n 1) 25–30.
116 *Sadiq Shek Elmi v Australia* Communication 120/1998, UN Doc CAT/C/22/D/ 120/1998 (1999).
117 Ibid. para 6.5.
118 Sivakumaran, *Non-International Armed Conflict* (n 8) 97.
119 Ronon (n 1) 30–1.
120 Ryngaert, 'Non-State Actors in IHL' (n 36) 287.

Thus, Ryngaert concludes that the approach is largely limited to the human rights-oriented provisions of humanitarian law, and specific rules relating to the regulation of occupied territories. In addition, Clapham reiterates the serious practical issues stemming from this theoretical justification, given that, 'one is in reality asking a government to accept that rebels have control of territory and have achieved some sort of authority. Governments have been reluctant to do this'.[121] Claudia Hofmann takes a similar view: '[s]uch a move would signal the inability to exercise effective control over State territory and the admission of a credible challenge to government authority'.[122] As such, it is suggested that this approach is unworkable in the vast majority of cases of internal strife. The effective territorial control argument clearly provides little scope for analogous application in the field of MNE regulation, although the extensive privatisation of traditionally governmental functions stresses the significant public influence that such entities can wield. In these circumstances, it is suggested that the State's 'due diligence' obligations would be engaged, rather than any direct obligations pertaining to the private entities.

4.1.4 Binding non-State armed groups via customary international law

The final approach advanced in justification of the binding quality of humanitarian provisions on non-State armed groups is perhaps the most compelling. It has been said to make the 'heresy' of the orthodox position less blatant, by showing that 'the principles preceded the convention'.[123] The approach may also provide a convincing argument for the application of the entire corpus of international humanitarian law. The argument essentially provides that non-State actors are bound by the principles of customary international law, which may bind all international actors, irrespective of their express consent.[124] In the words of the prosecutor in *Sam Hinga Norman*:

> [c]ustomary international law represents the common standard of behaviour within the international community, thus even armed groups hostile to a particular government have to abide by these laws . . . non-State entities are bound by necessity to the rules embodied in international humanitarian law instruments.[125]

---

121 Clapham, *Human Rights Obligations of Non-State Actors* (n 1) 287.
122 Claudia Hofmann, 'Engaging Non-State Armed Groups in Humanitarian Action' (2006) 13 *Int'l Peacekeeping* 396, 398.
123 Siordet (n 13).
124 Henckaerts, 'Binding Armed Opposition Groups' (n 50) 128; Jelena Pejic, 'The Protective Scope of Common Article 3: More than Meets the Eye' (2011) 93 *Int'l Rev Red Cross* 189, 197–8.
125 *Prosecutor v Sam Hinga Norman* (Decision on Preliminary Motion Based on Lack of Jurisdiction) SCSL-2004-14-AR72(E) (31 May 2004) para 22.

Some scholars have distinguished between the formulation of this approach on the basis of customary international law, and general principles of international law.[126] For example, Fleck states that:

> [c]ustomary international law is based on practice and *opinio juris* of States and binding upon peoples. General principles of law have likewise binding effects upon individuals. Hence, it is safe to say that the rights and duties of States are the rights and duties of people who make up those States. This is in particular relevant for the rules of humanitarian protection.[127]

The *Tadić* decision of the ICTY expressly supported this distinction, finding that the provisions of Additional Protocol II 'can now be regarded as declaratory of existing rules or as having crystallised emerging rules of customary international law, or else as having been strongly instrumental in their evolution as general principles'.[128]

The indeterminacy of the provisions regarded as having solidified as customary international law and as expressing general principles of international law poses substantial problems. Although pronouncements on the subject are evident in international practice,[129] these may be subject to dispute or subjective interpretation, and, as such, it may prove difficult to discern a consensus on the content or quality of such rules.[130] Sivakumaran has dedicated a separate analysis to the general principles approach. He suggests that, although humanitarian standards may be derived from general principles of international law, any provisions that later advance or expand those principles can no longer be regarded as binding on the basis that they derive from a general principle.[131] Where 'no detailed legal provisions exist, general principles fill the gap. Detailed provisions cannot also be general principles at the same time'.[132] The very name of this *general* source of international law infers that it is ill-suited to articulate the entire corpus of detailed provisions relating to international armed conflict, or even Additional Protocol II. For this reason, it is suggested that the customary approach is more convincing.

---

126 Sivakumaran, 'Binding Armed Opposition Groups' (n 16) 371–7.
127 Fleck, 'Non-International Armed Conflicts II' (n 53).
128 *Prosecutor v Tadić* (Decision on the Defence Motion for Interlocutory Appeal on Jurisdiction) IT-93-1-AR72 (2 October 1995) para 117 (hereafter *Tadić*).
129 International Commission on the Inquiry on Darfur, 'Report of the International Commission of Inquiry on Darfur to the United Nations Secretary-General' (Geneva, 25 January 2005) 51 para 173; ibid.
130 Brownlie, *Principles* (n 49) 6–12; Jean d'Aspremont, *Formalism and the Sources of International Law* (Oxford, UK, OUP, 2012) 171.
131 Sivakumaran, 'Binding Armed Opposition Groups' (n 16) 376; Cassese, 'Status of Rebels' (n 27) 423.
132 Sivakumaran, 'Binding Armed Opposition Groups' (n 16) 376–7.

The application of the customary law justification is evident in the Report of the International Commission of Inquiry on Darfur, which expressly stated that the:

> SLM/A [Sudan Liberation Movement/Army] and JEM [Justice and Equality Movement], like all insurgents that have reached a certain threshold of organisation, stability and effective control of territory, possess ILP and are therefore bound by the relevant rules of customary international law on internal armed conflicts.[133]

This formulation of the approach hinges on the suggestion that non-State armed groups possess ILP, and that customary international law binds all international legal persons as a uniform group, irrespective of their express consent. It may be argued, in light of the proliferation of internal armed conflict and the significant threats posed to human rights by non-State armed groups, that the new realities of international life necessitate the expansion of the subjects of international law.[134] The ICJ, in *Reparations* left room for such an expansion.[135] The circular nature of its treatment of this doctrine has been established,[136] and this problematic rationale clearly recurs in the jurisprudence advancing this theoretical justification.[137] For example, the SCSL stated:

> Notwithstanding the absence of unanimity among international lawyers as to the basis of the obligation of insurgents to observe the provisions of Common Article 3 . . . there is now no doubt that this article is binding on States and insurgents alike and that insurgents are subject to international humanitarian law.[138]

Yet, it then proceeded to qualify this statement. The SCSL suggests that, although the armed group is *subject* to humanitarian regulation as a matter of customary international law, this 'does not by itself invest the RUF [Revolutionary United Front] with international personality under international law'.[139] This statement is entirely illogical. The reluctance of the SCSL to recognise, at least in express terms, the ILP of the RUF is demonstrative of concerns surrounding the political status of non-State armed groups, as well as

---

133 International Commission on the Inquiry on Darfur (n 129) 51, para 172.
134 On MNEs, see: Steven Ratner 'Corporations and Human Rights: A Theory of Legal Responsibility' (2001) 111 *Yale LJ* 443, 461.
135 *Reparation for Injuries Suffered in the Service of the United Nations* (Advisory Opinion) ICJ Reports [1949] 178; Bilkova (n 16) 111–17.
136 See Chapter 2 at Section 2.5.1.
137 *Prosecutor v Sesay, Kallon and Gbao* (Appeals Chamber, Decision on Challenge to Jurisdiction: Lome Accord Amnesty) SCSL-04-15-PT-060-II (13 March 2004) para 47.
138 Ibid. para 45.
139 Ibid.

the seemingly innate legal rights and capacities conferred by the *subjects doctrine*.[140] This 'cake-and-eat-it' approach is difficult to square with legal doctrine, as it is not possible for an entity to be subject to a body of law without having legal personality establishing its validity as an addressee.

The reticence of States to imbue non-State armed groups with ILP, however limited, is directly related to concerns surrounding political legitimacy and status. As Clapham suggests:

> governments are often loath to admit that the conditions have been met for the application of this customary international law; for to admit such a situation is seen as an admission that the government has lost a degree of control and an 'elevation' of status of the rebels.[141]

Statements such as those made by the SCSL clearly reflect the similar sensitivities of international adjudicative bodies to this issue. Thus far, the *subjects doctrine* has remained almost exclusively State-centric, save for its limited expansion to natural persons and certain international organisations. It is argued that this hardly reflects a dramatic deviation from traditional doctrine, given the proximity of these entities to, and their exclusive control by, sovereign States. It is submitted that the concerns surrounding the political status of non-State armed groups are directly related to the consequences of the State-centric conception of ILP and its underlying justification for the validity of international law. These consequences primarily result from the conflation between addressee and law-maker discussed at length in Chapter 2 of this monograph. This argument will be advanced further below. For the time being, it suffices to highlight that the ILP of non-State armed groups is likely to be disputed in the majority of cases, thus rendering them incapable of direct address by customary humanitarian law.

It has been suggested that a non-State armed group possessing 'an organised military force, an authority responsible for its acts',[142] and that commits acts exceeding banditry,[143] 'must have attained international legal personality'.[144] Thus, additional to concerns regarding the legitimising effects of ILP, the threshold for attaining this status is also problematic. Under this conception, armed groups that do not meet what are essentially the criteria for the appli-

---

140 Raphaël van Steenberghe, 'Non-State Actors From the Perspective of the International Committee of the Red Cross' in d'Aspremont, *Multiple Perspectives* (n 36) 222–3; Anthea Roberts and Sandesh Sivakumaran, 'Hybrid Sources of Law: Armed Groups and the Creation of International Humanitarian Law' (2011) 37 *Yale J Int'l L* 125, 135–7.

141 Clapham, *Human Rights Obligations of Non-State Actors* (n 1) 272.

142 Pictet (n 94) 36.

143 Ibid.

144 Sivakumaran, 'Binding Armed Opposition Groups' (n 16) 374; Gerald IAD Draper, *The Red Cross Conventions* (New York, Praeger, 1958) 17; Lassa Oppenheim, *International Law: A Treatise* Vol 1 (Ronald Roxburgh ed, 3rd edn, London, Longmans, Green, 1920) 126.

cation of Additional Protocol II will fall outside the scope for the application of customary international law. This, in turn, fails to explain the application of Common Article 3. This issue perfectly elucidates the problems with the binary categorisation of 'State' and 'non-State' actors. Even the sub-category of non-State armed groups is not populated by monolithic entities with the same characteristics, structure, organisation, motives and patterns of behaviour.[145] As such, depending where the line is drawn with regard to the ILP of non-State armed groups, the practical operation of this theory may be unduly restrictive and fail to regulate the majority of internal armed conflicts.

There are still further theoretical issues. For instance, it has been proposed that customary humanitarian obligations should only apply to non-State armed groups to the extent that such groups have customarily adhered to the obligations.[146] Sivakumaran has suggested that such arguments are flawed, in that:

> they suggest that different international legal persons are bound by different customary international rules depending on whether other members of the same class of legal person have acted as if those rules were binding upon them. Yet, custom . . . binds all entities with personality under international law.[147]

There is certainly room for this interpretation, Ryngaert having highlighted the presumption that, 'customary international law binds all actors, and not only States and international organisations'.[148] Yet, is this not simply a reversal of Sivakumaran's prior argument regarding the *ratione personae* nature of customary provisions codified by the VCLT?[149] Perhaps, though, in his defence, it must be admitted that, whereas the VCLT expressly addresses State parties alone, international humanitarian law does at least purport to bind all 'parties to the conflict'. Nevertheless, this remains an interesting theoretical critique that will be addressed in further detail below.

Another issue is that the customary approach imposes on non-State actors only those rules that have crystallised into international custom.[150] It has been submitted that very few provisions applicable to armed conflict will have

---

145 Sivakumaran, *Non-International Armed Conflict* (n 8) 73; Pejic (n 124) 193–7.
146 Sivakumaran, 'Binding Armed Opposition Groups' (n 16) 373; Steenberghe (n 140) 222.
147 Ibid.
148 Ryngaert, 'Non-State Actors in IHL' (n 36) 288.
149 Sivakumaran, 'Binding Armed Opposition Groups' (n 16) 377.
150 There is no comparable international practice relating to MNEs owing to a lack of substantive obligations and *locus standi* before international forums: Cedric Ryngaert, 'Imposing International Duties on Non-State Actors and the Legitimacy of International Law' in Cedric Ryngaert and Math Noortmann (eds), *Non-State Actor Dynamics in International Law: From Law-Takers to Law-Makers* (Aldershot, UK, Ashgate, 2010) 72; The *jus cogens* status of the offences alleged against MNEs has been considered in ATCA litigation: *Tel-Oren v Libyan Arab Republic* 726 F.2d 774 (DC Cir 1984) 794–5.

attained this status. Additional Protocol II makes no explicit reference to custom, on the basis that the development of rules governing internal armed conflict 'only goes back to 1949 and the application of Common Article 3 . . . has not developed in such a way that one could speak of "established custom"'.[151] However, international practice appears to have remedied this situation, and may even address the aforementioned disparity in the regulation of international and internal armed conflicts. For instance, the ICJ, in *Nicaragua*, stated, in reference to its 1949 *Corfu Channel* decision,[152] that the provisions contained within Common Article 3 'constitute a minimum yardstick, in addition to the more elaborate rules which are also to apply to international conflicts; and they are rules which, in the Court's opinion, reflect what the Court in 1949 called "elementary considerations of humanity"'.[153] More recent decisions suggest that many of the humanitarian provisions once only applicable in international armed conflict may now apply irrespective of its character. This was the approach of the ICTY in *Tadić*, where the tribunal ruled that it was:

> preposterous that the use by States of weapons prohibited in armed conflicts between themselves be allowed when States try to put down rebellion by their own nationals on their own territory. What is inhumane, and consequently proscribed, in international wars, cannot but be inhumane and inadmissible in civil strife.[154]

Similar statements were made by the ICTY in *Martić*.[155] Recent multilateral treaties also appear to have adopted this approach. The 1993 Chemical Weapons Convention treats both types of conflict identically by mandating adherence 'under any circumstances'.[156] The 2005 ICRC study on Customary International Humanitarian Law also expressly provides that:

> the gaps in the regulation of the conduct of hostilities in Additional Protocol II have largely been filled through State practice, which has led to the creation of rules parallel to those in Additional Protocol I, but applicable as customary law to non-international armed conflicts.[157]

---

151 Michael Bothe, Karl Josef Partsch and Waldemar Solf, *New Rules for Victims of Armed Conflicts: Commentary on the Two 1977 Protocols Additional to the Geneva Conventions of 1949* (The Hague, Netherlands, Martinus Nijhoff, 1982) 620.

152 *Corfu Channel* (Advisory Opinion) ICJ Reports [1949] 22.

153 *Military and Paramilitary Activities (Nicaragua v United States of America)* (Advisory Opinion) ICJ Reports [1986] 14.

154 *Tadić* (n 128) para 119.

155 *Prosecutor v Martić* (Trial Chamber) IT-95-11-R61 (8 March 1996) para 11.

156 Convention on the Prohibition of the Development, Production, Stockpiling and Use of Chemical Weapons and on their Destruction (13 January 1993) 1974 UNTS 45, Article 1.

157 Jean-Marie Henckaerts and Louise Dowald-Beck, *Customary International Humanitarian Law* Vol 1 (Cambridge, UK, CUP, 2005) xxxv.

Thus, there is much to gain from this approach in terms of ensuring greater standards of regulation for internal armed conflicts, should it prove practically and theoretically sound.

A number of reservations have been expressed regarding this 'levelling' of international humanitarian obligations. The first sensibly cautions that increasing the number of rules applicable to internal armed conflict does not necessarily lead to an increase in compliance or the application of those rules by the groups involved. Many armed groups may feel unable to effectively implement and comply with even the small subset of rules expressly pertaining to internal armed conflict. As such, any additional criteria may prove discouraging if an all-or-nothing approach is adopted.[158] The aforementioned dismissal of the additional conditions for the application of Additional Protocol II in *Strugar*,[159] although not representative of a consensus in international practice, presents a similar issue. Scholars have cautioned that the trend of:

> [i]ncreasing the normative content while simultaneously reducing or removing any threshold brings with it a danger of overloading. At some stage, a tipping point will be reached whereby the normative content overwhelms the capacity of the parties to the conflict.[160]

The 2005 ICRC study confirmed that 161 rules governing international armed conflict were applicable during non-international armed conflict and thus applied directly to non-State armed groups.[161] As such, the customary basis for the extension of classically *international* humanitarian regulation to *non-international* conflicts dramatically compounds this practical concern. Furthermore, it remains to be seen whether States:

> can be duped by experts, NGOs and international criminal tribunals claiming obligations which those States rejected as treaty obligations are in any event part of customary international law. Even less will . . . entities that oppose the whole of the interstate system and the values proclaimed (but only selectively enforced) by the international community.[162]

Thus the general practical utility of the customary approach remains uncertain.

---

158 Sassóli and Shany (n 112).
159 *Strugar* (n 8); *Prosecutor v Limaj, Bala and Musliu* (Trial Judgment) IT-03-66-T (30 November 2005) para 89.
160 Sivakumaran, *Non-International Armed Conflict* (n 8) 67.
161 Pejic (n 124) 205–6; Ron Dudai, 'Closing the Gap: Symbolic Reparations and Armed Groups' (2011) 93 *Int'l Rev Red Cross* 783, 784.
162 Marco Sassóli, 'Transnational Armed Groups and International Humanitarian Law' (Harvard University, 2006) 40, www.hpcrresearch.org/sites/default/files/publications/OccasionalPaper6.pdf, accessed 21 April 2016.

Although international practice appears to indicate that various humanitarian obligations have now attained customary status, it has been suggested that the approach fails to:

> explain how non-State armed groups were bound by various rules before they gained customary status, for example the rules of Additional Protocol II prior to the mid-1990s. Equally, it is unable to explain how armed groups . . . may be prosecuted on the basis of conventional law.[163]

It is only since the proliferation of international adjudicative bodies in the mid 1990s that any real progress has been made in determining the extent of customary international humanitarian law. As such, it would have to be assumed that non-State armed groups had only recently become directly legally obliged to comply with humanitarian regulation. Yet, it is argued here that there is a deeper, more pressing concern that must be dealt with regarding the direct application of customary rules to non-State actors, and that this debate stems from the very foundations of the State-centric conception of international law established in Chapter 2. These matters are considered at length below.

4.2 Legitimacy, participation and State-centrism

Numerous obstacles to the extension of direct international legal obligations to non-State actors have been alluded to throughout the course of this monograph. These challenges primarily relate to the role of *consent* within the decentralised international legal system and the participation of the addressees of international obligations in the process of law creation. The aim of this section is to unpack these criticisms and to explore them in greater depth with the benefit of the foregoing context. The approach of this section is threefold. First, it will establish that certain procedural factors are conducive to compliance at the international level. It was demonstrated in Chapter 2 that the State-centric conception of international law mandates the ascription of certain competences to its legal subjects in the process of law creation.[164] Thus, the sense of obligation and widespread compliance exhibited by many State actors in a consent-based, voluntarist 'legal' system, largely devoid of Austinian coercive enforcement, may be explained by other factors.[165] Utilising the scholarship of Thomas Franck, it will be argued that the sense of participation in the formulation of international legal rules constitutes, for the dominant

---

163 Sivakumaran, *Non-International Armed Conflict* (n 8) 239.
164 See Chapter 2 at Section 2.5.2.
165 Louis Henkin, *How Nations Behave: Law and Foreign Policy* (2nd edn, Cambridge, UK, CUP, 1979) 89; Thomas Franck, *The Power of Legitimacy among Nations* (Oxford, UK, OUP, 1990) 3.

school, one of these legitimating factors and may prove fundamental to securing the compliance of non-State actors.

The second sub-section builds substantially on the first. It is submitted that consent and participation in law-making are theoretical consequences that are necessitated by the State-centric school and are paramount to understanding both the concerns of States relating to the political legitimisation of non-State actors and the absence of a functional system of legal regulation that directly addresses these entities. Although participation and consent may explain actual *compliance*, these factors also play a part in establishing the binding quality of international law, given the parallels that may be drawn at the international level to the terrain of contractual validation. Indeed, compliance and validation are factors that are often conflated in dominant scholarship. In spite of Geiss's assertion that, '[a]nalytical purity will not ensure the breakthrough in terms of ensuring better respect for [humanitarian law]',[166] it is argued that such an endeavour may hold substantial utility in uncovering the criteria essential to inducing non-State actor compliance and in explaining the basis of international legal validity. As Kleffner suggests, '[t]he failure to argue convincingly why and how the law applies to organised armed groups will hinder effective strategies to engage them in the quest to ensure better compliance'.[167] Although primarily theoretical in scope, the third sub-section will examine existing instances of non-State actor participation, in order to better illustrate the practical feasibility of the conceptual arguments advanced and to evaluate their potential flaws.

4.2.1 Understanding compliance at the international level

It was acknowledged above that, although far from perfect, the recent identification of rules of international humanitarian law said to have attained customary status could offer a viable justification for the binding quality of those provisions over non-State actors and may also help to diminish the disparity between the rules engaged in international and internal armed conflict. Yet, as numerous scholars have recognised, '[t]he dilemma remains that even customary law has been exclusively shaped by State practice'.[168] Even representatives of the ICRC engaged in its 2005 Customary International Humanitarian Law study have recognised that the customary approach 'denies the reality that armed opposition groups are important actors in non-international armed conflicts and could play a role in the creation of rules that apply to such conflicts'.[169] As

---

166 Geiss (n 44).
167 Kleffner (n 14) 444.
168 Geiss (n 44); although MNEs may catalyse governmental activity in the development of international law, their participation is always mediated by the State: Stephen Tully, *Corporations and International Lawmaking* (The Hague, Netherlands, Martinus Nijhoff, 2007) 94–5.
169 Henckaerts, 'Binding Armed Opposition Groups' (n 50) 128.

such, it has been suggested that the customary justification for the direct reach of international humanitarian law to non-State actors 'would be even stronger if the practice of armed opposition groups could be taken into account in the formation of customary rules of international humanitarian law applicable in non-international armed conflicts'.[170] The same is true with regard to treaty law. States alone may participate in the creation of conventional international law, and States alone may formally consent to the international obligations contained therein.[171] The question arises as to *why* participation in international law creation should promote the direct application of international law to non-State actors and prove conducive to their compliance. It is argued here that such participation is a peculiar product of the State-centric rationale.

In Chapter 2, the Austinian, positivist critique of the international legal system was introduced. Austin denied that international rules existed as 'law strictly so called', because they lack a centralised, sovereign institution capable of validating rules and enforcing them via coercive sanction.[172] The foundations of this view and some scholarly responses to it have already been discussed.[173] Yet, it is undeniable that the vast majority of States acknowledge international legal norms and boast widespread compliance. Thus, international law is now said to be in its post-ontological era: its mere existence is no longer open to dispute, and yet exactly *how* the system of rules operates and *why* international norms are valid remains contentious.[174] In the words of Thomas Franck, Austin's critique is:

> beyond reproach if one accepts that coercion is a necessary component of law and order. Yet, it is also empirically verifiable that some, indeed *many*, international rules of conduct are habitually obeyed by States . . . Thus, to whatever extent any rules are obeyed in the international system, they must be obeyed due to some factor, or mix of factors, other than the Austinian one.[175]

Franck's scholarship attempted to determine and analyse these other factors that underlie international obligations and induce compliance. An enquiry into these factors will doubtless prove beneficial to identifying, and perhaps overcoming, the challenges that preclude the extension of direct rights and obligations to non-State actors. After all:

---

170 Ibid.
171 Tully (n 168) 149–234.
172 John Austin, *The Province of Jurisprudence Determined* (2nd edn, London, John Murray, 1832) 177.
173 See Chapter 2 at Section 2.3.2.
174 Thomas Franck, *Fairness in International Law and Institutions* (Oxford, UK, OUP, 1998) 6–7.
175 Franck, *Legitimacy Among Nations* (n 165) 20.

[i]f it could be demonstrated that legitimacy validates the international normative order, and that it exerts a pull on States in the direction of uncoerced rule compliance, then we would have a tool for the necessary construction of a world order which . . . could safely postpone or skip, the 'coercive sovereign' stage.[176]

Although this is a virtually impossible task to demonstrate empirically, Franck's aim to reinforce the hypothesis through credible observations based on international practice is commendable and deserves further consideration.

Although his earlier endeavours focused solely on 'legitimacy' (a term that has been variously defined), Franck later articulated a number of compliance-inducing factors under the rubric of *fairness*.[177] Fairness contains within it both procedural and substantive elements. The procedural components are those illustrating 'right process' in the creation and interpretation of law[178] and give rise to what Franck termed 'legitimacy'.[179] Substantive factors are more informed by morality, in particular, the notion of distributive justice.[180] A clear tension exists between procedural factors, which demand stability and order in the law creation process, and substantive factors, which may demand societal change in the pursuit of justice or the equitable allocation of goods, services, rights and duties.[181] As Dworkin suggests, '[e]ven if we . . . based our political activity only on fairness, justice, and procedural due process, we would find the first two virtues sometimes pulling in opposite directions'.[182] For Franck, 'fairness is the rubric under which this tension is managed', and both elements – procedural and substantive – induce compliance at the international level for different reasons.[183]

Recently, scholars such as Cedric Ryngaert have applied similar criteria to the subject of non-State actor regulation. The object of Ryngaert's study is to determine whether 'rules can be legitimate, in the sense of being justified and able to command widespread support, if they are imposed on actors without their consent'.[184] Again, a division is made between procedural and substantive elements. Procedural legitimacy is gained:

> by the participation in the formative process of all actors affected by the norm. Legitimacy then is a function granting adequate participatory rights

176 Ibid.
177 Rüdiger Wolfrum, 'Legitimacy of International Law from a Legal Perspective: Some Introductory Considerations' in Wolfrum and Roben (n 66) 5–7.
178 Franck, *Fairness* (n 174) 25–6.
179 Ibid. 26.
180 Ibid. 8.
181 Ibid. 47.
182 Ronald Dworkin, *Law's Empire* (Oxford, UK, OUP, 1998) 177.
183 Franck, *Fairness* (n 174) 7.
184 Ryngaert, 'Imposing International Duties' (n 150) 69.

or allocating legal personality in the process of law creation, not only to States, but all relevant actors.[185]

On the other hand, substantive legitimacy is gained where a legal norm purports to protect important core values:

> precisely because of the (expected) output of the norm's implementation, the legitimacy of the process of creation of the norm is of lesser relevance. This means that consent of the non-State actor as an addressee of the norm need not be secured, or to a lesser extent.[186]

Such norms are likely to be characterised as *jus cogens*. Whereas, in the ideal, both procedural and substantive elements will be fulfilled,[187] and this scenario should be strived for in international law creation, the two factors are to be regarded as 'communicating vessels'.[188] Clearly, there is much cross-over between Ryngaert's and Franck's approaches, at this level. Yet, a deeper explanation of Franck's approach and its relevance to the study of non-State actors is necessary before proceeding further. It is argued here that Franck's analysis offers a compelling explanation of compliance-inducing factors other than simple command and sanction. As the vast majority of international rules are unlikely to rise to the level of *jus cogens*, and in light of the fundamental indeterminacy of the rules within this category, this discussion will focus on Franck's procedural elements.[189]

4.2.1.1 Franckian procedural legitimacy

Franck identifies several procedural factors that are conducive to what he terms 'legitimacy', defined as:

> a property of a rule or rule-making institution which itself exerts a pull toward compliance on those addressed normatively because those addressed believe that the rule or institution has come into being and operates in accordance with generally accepted principles.[190]

---

185 Ibid. 73.
186 Ibid. 72.
187 Tully (n 168) 96.
188 Ryngaert, 'Imposing International Duties' (n 150) 73.
189 D'Aspremont (n 130) 219–23.
190 Franck, *Legitimacy Among Nations* (n 165) 24.

Franck acknowledges three primary schools of thought relating to legitimacy:[191] (1) the strictly process-based school, advanced by Max Weber;[192] (2) the procedural–substantive school, advanced by Habermas and Rawls;[193] and (3) the neo-Marxist/radical school, which emphasises the realisation of equality, fairness, justice and freedom via legal rules.[194] In line with scholars such as Dworkin, Franck appears to adopt a synergy of all three approaches.[195] Franck's legitimacy consists of four procedural elements that give rise to compliance at the international level: (1) determinacy, (2) symbolic validation, (3) coherence and (4) adherence. The first three factors are relatively straightforward and can be dealt with concisely.

A rule's *determinacy* is evidenced 'either by its textual clarity or by the remedial work of a legitimate clarifying process'.[196] Thus, written rules are likely to be more determinate,[197] so long as they are not so broadly or narrowly drafted as to give rise to absurd results.[198] *Symbolic validation* occurs when 'a signal is used to elicit compliance with a command'.[199] This process may involve certain rituals, similar to the process of royal assent in the English legislative process.[200] Another element is that of pedigree, which demonstrates 'the venerable historic and social origins and continuity of rule standards, and rule making or rule-applying institutions'.[201] This element is readily apparent in the scholarship considered in Chapter 2, which traced the historical and social significance of the sovereign territorial State – the entity from which all international law emanates.[202] Indeed, Franck suggests that, 'a new State's election to membership in the UN is an example of corporate pedigreeing by the international community'.[203] While noting that such genealogical

---

191 Cf Helen Keller, 'Codes of Conduct and Their Implementation' in Wolfrum and Roben (n 66) 256–60.

192 Weber focuses on the legitimacy of the social order/authority: Max Weber, *Economy and Society* Vol 1 (first published 1922, Gyenther Roth and Claus Wittich eds, Berkeley, CA, University of California Press, 2013) 30–2; Franck, *Legitimacy Among Nations* (n 165) 19.

193 Emphasising transparency and procedural participation in rule making: Jürgen Habermas, *Communication and the Evolution of Society* (Thomas McCarthy trans, Boston, MA, Beacon Books, 1979) 185–8; Alan Boyle and Christine Chinkin, *The Making of International Law* (Oxford, UK, OUP, 2007) 24–8.

194 Alan Hyde, 'The Concept of Legitimation in the Sociology of Law' [1983] *Wis L Rev* 379, 419.

195 Dworkin (n 182) 176–224.

196 Franck, *Legitimacy Among Nations* (n 165) 66.

197 D'Aspremont (n 130) 178.

198 Franck, *Legitimacy Among Nations* (n 165) 61–90; ibid 140–1.

199 Franck, *Legitimacy Among Nations* (n 165) 92.

200 Ibid. 91.

201 Ibid. 94.

202 See Chapter 2 at Section 2.2.

203 Franck, *Legitimacy Among Nations* (n 165) 94–5.

significance is of questionable practical utility and is not compelled by logic, Frank suggests that such validation can produce significant compliance-pull,[204] so long as it is 'truthful' or, at the very least, reflects *perceived* reality.[205] Clearly, the political motivations that feed into the recognition of States at the international level undermine this particular process, at least in the eyes of non-State actors exhibiting features proximate to statehood. A rule's *coherence* is bolstered where like scenarios are treated in a manner that is justifiable on principled terms.[206] That is not to say that all scenarios are treated consistently; rather, there must be justifiable reasons for inconsistency.[207] Coherence will induce compliance, and non-compliant actors may even exhibit guilt. Any unreasoned departure from a legitimate rule will also be perceived as a direct threat by third-party States, 'undermining the legitimacy of a rule of which they approve and on which they rely, and ... weakening the fabric of the community's rule system as a whole'.[208] This point brings the present discussion neatly to the central component of Franck's conception of legitimacy and the final one of his procedural compliance-inducing factors.

In his earlier work, Franck departed from strictly contract-oriented explanations of the binding quality of international law, which are based on the mutual consent of parties, emphasising instead the role of *community* in the operation of international law.[209] It is the peculiarity of 'sovereign equality' – the emphasis on equal concern for all members of the international community – that exerts compliance-pull.[210] In Dworkin's words:

> [t]he right of a political community to treat its members as having obligations in virtue of collective community decisions – is to be found not in the terrain of contracts ... but in the more fertile ground of fraternity, community, and their attendant obligations. Political association ... is in itself pregnant of obligation.[211]

These notions are instilled in Franck's fourth criterion of legitimacy, which he terms *adherence*. Here, Franck attempts to demonstrate a normative hierarchy that Hart classically felt was lacking in the international legal system.[212] He attempted to overcome the apparent lack of secondary rules: those that provide an infrastructure regulating the creation, interpretation and application of

204 Ibid. 94.
205 Ibid. 133.
206 Ibid. 144.
207 Ibid. 153.
208 Ibid. 150–1.
209 Ibid. 182.
210 Ibid. 176.
211 Dworkin (n 182) 206.
212 Herbert LA Hart, *The Concept of Law* (3rd edn, Oxford, UK, OUP, 2012) 214.

substantive, primary rules of obligation. Franck suggested that international law exerts a strong compliance pull, and States behave *as if there were a norm hierarchy* of the kind Hart dismissed.[213] In Franck's view, the ultimate rule of recognition stems from community: 'the rule's compliance pull is stronger if the basis of obligation is associational, rather than merely contractual'.[214] As such, he concluded that:

> there are obligations owed by States which they widely recognise as concomitants of community membership and which are accurate predictors of actual State behaviour. There are rules which obligate not because they have been accepted by the individual sovereign State, but because they come with membership in the community of peers. The members of that community relinquish their absolute sovereignty by the very fact of statehood.[215]

The dependency of Franck's legitimacy theory on the 'community of States' makes a direct application to non-State actors somewhat problematic for obvious reasons. At first glance, this aspect of his approach does not advance the argument regarding the participation of non-State actors in the law creation process. Quite the opposite: it arguably reaffirms the statist assumption that obligation and law-making capacity are theoretical consequences of statehood. Yet, his approach could be interpreted as simply reflecting the conceptual proximity between 'statehood' and legal personality established in Chapter 2.[216] Rather than within a community of *States*, perhaps 'adherence' could arise within a community of *international legal persons*. Furthermore, Franck's later work revealed his ultimately contractarian leanings:

> [C]ontractarian theory readily explains the origins, if not the modern nature, of international law and organisation. States, too, have been seen by international legal theory as free and autonomous international 'persons' associating for limited utilitarian purposes in a community to which they delegate certain powers so as to secure, in return, the benefits of peace, order, and mutual support.[217]

Franck even cites Henkin's summary of the State-centric perspective spelled out in Chapter 2 of this monograph: '[i]nter-State law is made, or recognised, or accepted by the will of States. Nothing becomes law for the international system

---

213 Franck, *Legitimacy Among Nations* (n 165) 188.
214 Ibid. 186; cf Ian Scobbie, 'Tom Franck's Fairness' (2002) 13 *EJIL* 909, 917.
215 Franck, *Legitimacy Among Nations* (n 165) 192.
216 See Chapter 2 at Section 2.5.
217 Franck, *Fairness* (n 174) 28.

from any other source'.[218] Thus, Franck's paradigms of 'right process' are characterised as: (1) the sovereign equality of States; (2) the restriction of sovereignty only by consent; (3) the binding quality of consent; (4) that States, engaged in the international community, are bound by its ground rules, regardless of whether consent has been specifically expressed.[219] Crucially, in spite of these *prima facie* State-centric leanings, Franck leaves the door open:[220]

> At present, the term 'global discourse' suggests a conversation between nations. That limited view, however, is wrong. Not only is it inaccurate, overlooking the many actors – multinational corporations . . . service organisations, gender and ethno-culturally specific groups . . . – who are already part of this discourse . . . [but a] discourse solely and exclusively reflecting the views of those who govern nations cannot be expected to produce rules which are fair.[221]

Thus, Franck recognises the expansion of actors relevant to the international community. As will be demonstrated, this awareness fits more readily with the model drawing on discursive democracy theory propounded by Ryngaert and others. At a more fundamental level, Franck's insight into procedural compliance-inducing criteria, as distinct from the Austinian model, is extremely valuable and will find much utility in the remaining sections of this chapter.

4.2.2 *Lessons from discursive democracy scholarship*

There are three core ideas to take away from Franck's thesis: (1) that factors other than coercion may effectively induce compliance with apparently voluntary rules; (2) that the actors relevant to global discourse are expanding and should be accounted for; and (3) that, although community strongly induces compliance in the international system, contractarian notions still underscore international obligation. Thus, the role of the consent of parties to legal norms arguably constitutes a major legitimating procedural factor. As discussed at length in Chapter 2, the underlying justification for the binding quality of international law according to the statist conception, which treats the State as an empirically observable social fact, is the coalescence of the wills of States. All positive international law emanates from the State, which serves as the basis for its validity.[222] Law-making capacity is the exclusive domain of the State, the

---

218 Louis Henkin, *International Law: Politics, Values and Functions* (Recueil des Cours, 1989) 216.
219 Franck, *Fairness* (n 174) 29.
220 Asher Alkoby, 'Non-State Actors and the Legitimacy of International Environmental Law' (2003) 3 *Non-St Actors & Int'l L* 23, 63.
221 Franck, *Fairness* (n 174) 484.
222 On the legitimising qualities of State consent, see: Wolfrum (n 177) 9–21.

primary addressee and original subject of international law. The notions of 'statehood', 'international legal person' and 'law-maker' are essentially synonymous. Without this status, there can be no obligation. Treaties arise from the express consent of States, and international custom arises from their tacit consent, which is implied through their practice and thus their participation in the creation of the law. By this logic, in order for customary international humanitarian law to address non-State armed groups directly, they too must contribute to the process of customary law creation. The proximity between the ILP of States and their supreme status as law-makers explains the reluctance of States to recognise the ILP of non-State actors. Thus, although it is suggested that such an objection is 'not convincing because it confuses personality with legitimacy', it is argued here that this conflation is a *direct consequence* of the dominant theoretical conception of international law.[223]

Scholars such as Portmann have stressed that different theoretical perceptions of international law give rise to various theoretical presumptions with regard to which actors possess law-making capacity.[224] In relation to both the strictly State-centric approach and its modern variants that permit the recognition by States of other entities (usually proximate to States) possessing limited personality, he too emphasises that the law-making capacity of the addressees of legal norms is a necessary theoretical consequence.[225] Similarly, for Ryngaert:

> [d]emanding direct compliance of non-State actors with international obligations can . . . only be justified if those actors have been represented in the adoption process of the rules giving rise to the obligations, or to put it more succinctly, if they are considered as genuine *subjects* of international law.[226]

It is not suggested that this is an ideal scenario, given the myriad of motivations held by such actors that will not always align with the public interest.[227] Rather, this is *one* solution, mandated by the dominant theoretical approach. It will be argued that this is a theoretical consideration lacking from much of the scholarship regarding non-State actor regulation and from widely accepted practical initiatives.

Some elaboration of the theory underlying the call for non-State actor participation is necessary before we proceed further. The contractarian, consensual underpinnings of the State-centric model have been established. Yet, as Dworkin suggests, '[c]onsent cannot be binding . . . unless it is given more

---

223 Kleffner (n 14) 455.
224 Portmann (n 31) 246–7.
225 Ibid. 83.
226 Ryngaert, 'Imposing International Duties' (n 150) 69–70.
227 Keller (n 191) 269; Tully (n 168) 330–5; Roberts and Sivakumaran (n 140) 137.

freely, and with more genuine alternate choice'.[228] It is this matter that emphasises the need for multi-stakeholder discourse in order to secure compliance from non-State actors. Many scholars have emphasised the legitimating role played by discursive (or deliberative) democracy, which entails 'democratic deliberation as un-coerced, other-regarding, reasoned, inclusive and equal debate'.[229] This theoretical approach seems to lend itself to the discussion of consent, international obligation and procedural compliance-inducing factors. In the domestic political context, John Locke's scholarship emphasised the 'state of nature', which detailed man's freedom and equality before the law, 'till by their own consents they make themselves members of some politic society'.[230] Scholars have since emphasised the role of consent in democratic processes and have concluded that, 'the quality of democracy would seem to depend decisively on the quality of its discourses'.[231] Though the theoretical foundations of this approach primarily address individuals within the domestic setting, its scope has been expanded to include non-State actors[232] and emphasised its potential transnational application.[233] Thus, it is submitted that the approach has demonstrable utility in the context of the international legal system.[234] The engagement of actors representing a plurality of viewpoints in the decision-making process is seen as a means of fostering democratic participation and achieving consensus or acceptable decisions among all parties. Utilising this discursive method, actors can:

> justify decisions in a process in which they give one another reasons that are mutually acceptable and generally accessible, with the aim of reaching conclusions that are binding in the present on all . . . but open to challenge in the future.[235]

---

228 Dworkin (n 182) 192–3.

229 Zsuzsanna Chappell, *Deliberative Democracy: A Critical Introduction* (London, Palgrave, 2012) 7; Steven Wheatley, 'Democratic Governance Beyond the State: The Legitimacy of Non-State Actors as Standard Setters' in Peters, Koechlin, Förster and Zinkernagel (n 66) 215–40.

230 John Locke, *Second Treatise on Government* (1690) Ch II, §15; Habermas, *Communication and the Evolution of Society* (n 193) 184.

231 Gerald Mara, *Socrates' Discursive Democracy* (State University of New York Press, 1997) 1–2.

232 Russell Miller, 'Paradoxes of Personality: Transnational Corporations, Non-Governmental Organisations and Human Rights' in Russell Miller and Rebecca Bratspies (eds), *Progress in International Law* (The Hague, Netherlands, Martinus Nijhoff, 2008) 397–8.

233 John S Dryzek, *Deliberative Democracy and Beyond: Liberals, Critics, Contestations* (Oxford, UK, OUP, 2002) 3; Chappell (n 229) 38.

234 Wheatley, 'Democratic Governance' (n 229) 218; cf Allen Buchanan and Robert Keohane, 'The Legitimacy of Global Governance Institutions' in Wolfrum and Roben (n 66) 39.

235 Amy Gutmann and Dennis Thompson, *Why Deliberative Democracy?* (Princeton, NJ, Princeton University Press, 2004) 7.

The legitimating consequences of democratic discourse have been discussed at length by scholars such as Jürgen Habermas. It is beyond the scope of this study to provide a detailed account of Habermas's wide-ranging body of work on this matter, but the elucidation of some key themes is helpful in cognising the consequences of the dominant school's rationale. Habermas seeks to establish an 'intersubjective' form of reasoning based on processes inherent in language and communication.[236] He distinguishes knowledge arising from *rational discourse* among multiple subjects from what he terms *instrumental reason*, where a subject (e.g. a scientist) seeks to understand an object (e.g. nature). Habermas emphasises the emancipatory and legitimating consequences of this discursive, intersubjective form of reason, which aims at shared understanding based on a process that is free from the 'domination' that is characteristic of the subject–object relationship and thus inherent in instrumental reason.[237] Habermas's *discourse principle* illuminates how the validity of norms is to be achieved via discursive procedures emphasising the involvement of all actors *affected* by a disputed norm as participants in a practical discourse.[238] Consent and consensus will not follow 'unless all affected can freely accept the consequences and the side effects that the general observance of a controversial norm can be expected to have for the satisfaction of the interests of each individual'.[239] For Habermas:

> [t]he idea of an agreement that comes to pass among all parties, as free and equal, determines the procedural type of legitimacy of modern times . . . Only the rules and communicative presuppositions that make it possible to distinguish an accord or agreement among free and equals from a contingent or forced consensus have legitimating force today.[240]

Thus, 'discourse' entails a situation in which participants are able to argue on an equal basis, free from coercion or external influences other than the force of the best argument.[241] Involvement in this procedure legitimates legal norms by way of 'rational self-legislation'. In short, the addressees of norms are also taken to be their authors.[242]

Although parliamentary procedure is fundamental to Habermas's vision of discursive democracy, he does not strictly limit citizens to participation by the

236 Ian Johnstone, *The Power of Deliberation: International Law, Politics and Organisations* (Oxford, UK, OUP, 2011) 14.
237 Max Horkheimer and Theodor Adorno, *Dialectic of Enlightenment* (John Cummin trans, London, Verso, 1997).
238 Jürgen Habermas, *Moral Consciousness and Communicative Action* (Cambridge, MA, MIT Press, 1990) 65.
239 Ibid. 93.
240 Habermas, *Communication and the Evolution of Society* (n 193) 185–8.
241 Jürgen Habermas, *Theory of Communicative Action* Vol 1 (Beacon Press, 1984) 25.
242 Jürgen Habermas, *Between Facts and Norms* (Cambridge, MA, MIT Press, 1996) 120.

proxy of elected officials within a public political system.[243] Rather, Habermas takes a broader and more pluralistic view, where the private and broader public spheres can also feed into discourse[244] and, thus, decision-making processes, often via interest groups and civil society institutions.[245] Given the peculiarities of the international legal system discussed throughout this study, it is suggested that Habermas's approach contains clear parallels to the rationale underlying the State-centric conception of international legal validity. Although Habermas's theory is primarily formulated in the domestic context, it may be that his intersubjective, discursive vision of validity can be abstracted and mapped on to the international sphere, where one talks, not of individual citizens, but of States and other international legal persons.[246] Indeed, theorists such as Dryzek have discussed the operation of discursive democracy principles at the international level, emphasising the engagement of a plurality of actors, from States and regional bodies such as the EU, to NGOs, corporate actors and armed resistance movements.[247] Wheatley concurs and offers the compelling suggestion that the identification of participants relevant to law-making discourse at the international level be reframed from those actors *affected* to all those *subjected* to emerging legal norms.[248] This approach continues to emphasise the legitimating consequences arising from the recognition of addressees of legal norms as the authors of those norms. Although Wheatley's primary discussion centres on the role of States as subjects engaged in a law-making process within international organisations such as the UN and other 'non-State' global governance institutions,[249] it is easy to see how the expansion of the *subjects* of international obligations (already apparent in the field of humanitarian law) might, by this logic, necessitate their participation in order to legitimate and induce the compliance of these actors:

> [T]he idea of 'those subjected' includes States and international organisations, corporations and other non-State actors, and individuals – any legal actor may be subject to the authority directives of an autonomous system of law.[250]

243 Cf John Rawls, *Political Liberalism* (New York, Columbia University Press, 2005) 215–16.
244 Habermas, *Between Facts and Norms* (n 242) 365–6.
245 Ibid. 373.
246 Miller (n 232) 397–8.
247 John S Dryzek, *Deliberative Global Politics* (Cambridge, UK, Polity Press, 2006) 60–1; David Victor, Kal Raustialia and Eugene Skolnikoff (eds), *The Implementation and Effectiveness of International Environmental Commitments Theory and Practice* (Cambridge, MA, MIT Press, 1998) 320–1.
248 Steven Wheatley, *The Democratic Legitimacy of International Law* (Oxford, UK, Hart, 2010) 324–6.
249 Ibid. 317–18.
250 Ibid. 326.

No single participatory model can be prescribed; the process may be direct (placing the participation of non-State actors on a par with States) or indirect, via civil society representation of key arguments emerging from – in Harbermasian parlance – the broader 'public sphere'.[251]

Although it has been argued that the interests of many non-State actors are necessarily reflected in the practice of democratic States,[252] for Ryngaert, 'nation-State democracy is definitely not fully acquired yet, leaving the legitimate interests of a sizable portion of the world's non-State actors possibly unaccounted for . . . [and] may silence minority views that are widely shared across national boundaries'.[253] In addition, in the interests of accountability and transparency, it has been suggested that non-State actor participation should not be left to backroom lobbying at the domestic level.[254] Although Habermas was at times sceptical of the ability of collective actors to express a common will,[255] Miller suggests that:

> [i]n a variety of legal contexts . . . we accept that collectives are capable of expressing will and invoking rights . . . Habermas has written to endorse the will-forming impact and potential of broad cultural movements, sometimes loosely referred to as 'civil society'.[256]

Samhat has responded similarly, stating that, 'NGOs and social movements can be representative agents . . . in world politics, implementing tasks and aggregating interests and voices for segments of global policy'.[257] Aside from engagement through civil society representation, the State-centric conception of international law arguably necessitates a more direct form of participation and, by extension, consent of its addressees in the process of law creation. The above analysis of discursive democracy demonstrates a theoretical basis for this view that could yield a number of positive results, in terms of both giving voice to a plurality of relevant actors,[258] better reflecting global political reality,[259] and the refinement of decisions via mutual agreement on the basis of the 'best argument'. In doing so, these procedural factors are likely to legitimise decisions in the eyes of all relevant actors and, therefore, constitute procedural, compliance-inducing factors similar to those advocated by Franck:

251 Ibid. 319.
252 On business actors, see: Tully (n 168) 310–13.
253 Ryngaert, 'Imposing International Duties' (n 150) 74.
254 Ibid.
255 Jürgen Habermas, 'Equal Treatment of Cultures and the Limits of Postmodern Liberalism' (2005) 13 *J Pol Phil* 1, 22.
256 Miller (n 232) 399.
257 Nayef Samhat, 'International Regimes and the Prospects for Global Democracy' (2005) 6 *Whitehead J Diplomacy & Int'l Relations* 179, 186.
258 Ryngaert, 'Imposing International Duties' (n 150) 80.
259 Henckaerts, 'Binding Armed Opposition Groups' (n 50) 128–9.

[H]aving adopted the law and, at the same time, having consented to be bound by that very adoption (as indeed, law-maker and law-taker are synonymous in the horizontal international legal order between States), non-State actors cannot convincingly justify their non-compliance on the grounds of lack of legitimacy of the norm.[260]

The practical feasibility and desirability of this view will be assessed below, before conclusions are drawn.

4.2.3 *Appraising the scope for non-State actor participation in practice*

It has been established that the State-centric conception of international law mandates the consent of its addressees in order to ensure theoretical validity. With regard to custom – the most compelling explanation for the binding quality of humanitarian law in relation to non-State armed groups – tacit consent is partially established by the uniform practice of the addressees of those rules, emphasising the importance of their participation in the process of law creation. Such participation would, in turn, legitimise the direct application of the obligations and may induce compliance. For McCorquodale:

[s]uch developments would be consistent with a better understanding of the international legal system in which the participants are not only States. Non-State actors do participate in the creation, development and enforcement of international law, and . . . [t]his should also strengthen the legitimacy and effectiveness of international law.[261]

Non-State actors already contribute, to varying degrees, to the codification and interpretation of international law. For instance, although hardly a representative sample, 11 non-State armed groups were invited to participate as observers of the drafting of the Additional Protocols to the 1949 Geneva Conventions.[262] Notably, these groups were recognised as NLMs and, as such, demonstrated a high degree of territorial control and organisation. As mentioned above, conflict involving a State and an NLM is 'internationalised' to benefit from the entire corpus of humanitarian law applicable to international armed conflict. Indeed, under Additional Protocol I, NLMs may participate in the Protocol by means

---

260 Ryngaert, 'Imposing International Duties' (n 150).
261 Robert McCorquodale, 'Non-State Actors and International Human Rights Law' in Sarah Joseph and Adam McBeth (eds), *Research Handbook on International Human Rights Law* (Cheltenham, UK, Edward Elgar, 2010) 114.
262 Yves Sandoz, Christophe Swinarski and Bruno Zimmermann (eds), 'Commentaries to the Additional Protocols of 1977 to the Geneva Conventions of 1949' (ICRC, Geneva, 1987) xxix.

of a unilateral declaration to the Swiss Federal Council, the depositary of the Conventions and Protocol.[263]

Similar participatory rights were granted to indigenous peoples under ILO Convention No 169,[264] which permitted indigenous people to 'freely participate . . . at all levels of decision-making'.[265] As Anaya suggests, 'it is evident that this requirement applies not only to decision making within the framework of domestic or municipal processes but also . . . within the international realm', though there are indications that the provision has not been interpreted in this manner.[266] Although there is evidence of indigenous peoples being granted non-voting observer status and participating in the form of statements to the workers' group, Engle has highlighted that:

> indigenous peoples were not permitted to participate directly in ILO conference discussions on the draft . . . While some indigenous peoples participated as representatives of trade unions, and, on rare occasions, indigenous people were permitted to make brief statements to the committee, the process did not provide a formal mechanism for direct indigenous participation.[267]

Similarly, despite the conclusion of 'treaties' between indigenous populations and European settlers historically, it has been suggested that the shift away from natural law, assimilation policies and legal developments in the newly established States 'led to the marginalisation of indigenous peoples in a legal sense'.[268] As such, these instruments are not generally considered to have effect in international law.[269] It is not suggested that indigenous populations or even NLMs offer an ideal parallel to the majority of non-State armed groups, but this analysis demonstrates the discrepancies between even the more politically 'legitimate' territorial non-State actors.

The participation of groups that have not attained NLM status, or are not demonstrably State-like, has rarely been demonstrated in international practice.[270] The nuanced approach taken by Roberts and Sivakumaran in assigning different levels of law-making capacity to different forms of non-State

---

263 Cassese, 'Status of Rebels' (n 27) 420.
264 ILO, Indigenous and Tribal Peoples Convention No 169 (27 June 1989).
265 Ibid. Article 6; Ian Brownlie, *Treaties and Indigenous Peoples* (FM Brookfield ed, Oxford, UK, Clarendon Press, 1992) 65.
266 S James Anaya, *Indigenous Peoples in International Law* (2nd edn, Oxford, UK, OUP, 2004) 154.
267 Karen Engle, *The Elusive Promise of Indigenous Development: Rights, Culture, Strategy* (Duke University Press, 2010) 108.
268 Annika Tahvanainen, 'The Treaty-Making Capacity of Indigenous Peoples' (2005) 12 *Int'l J Minority & Group Rts* 397, 404.
269 Brownlie, *Treaties and Indigenous Peoples* (n 265) 81; ibid 399–404.
270 Roberts and Sivakumaran (n 140) 120–1.

armed group, although entirely sensible on the face of it, is problematic, given the theoretical consequences of the State-centric perspective.[271] On this binary view of States and non-States, 'law-makers and law-takers', the participation of parties engaged in the majority of armed conflict prevalent today is effectively excluded.[272] In order to bridge this gap, academics such as Sivakumaran have proposed the conclusion of a new instrument, drawing together all relevant areas of international law and permitting the active participation of non-State armed groups (including State governments that were, until recently, armed groups) in the process.[273] Yet, the maintenance of the theoretical conflation of addressee and law-maker will likely lead to:

> [t]he over-politicisation of the treaty-making process, the practical difficulties and potential criminal implications of reaching out to groups considered illegal, [and] the possible enhancement of the status of armed groups – against the will of the State – from a common criminal to an 'equal' interlocutor.[274]

It is also unclear as to whether and, in the affirmative, which entities falling within the broad typology of non-State armed groups would be willing or capable to engage peacefully and meaningfully in this manner.

Turning momentarily to MNEs, it was established in the previous chapter that the participation of business actors in the formulation of soft law, including codes of practice, is seen to advance legitimacy and induce compliance with such instruments. A similar voluntary approach has been initiated under the Extractive Industries Transparency Initiative, which offers the potential for multi-stakeholder discourse via an oversight and advisory board composed of 20 members, drawn from governments, the oil and gas industry and civil society.[275] Similarly, multi-stakeholder forums such as the Forest Stewardship Council (FSC) guarantee:[276]

> all participants identical participation conditions . . . [members] are divided into three chambers – economic, social and environmental. Their voices

---

271 Ibid. 119.

272 Math Noortmann and Cedric Ryngaert, 'Non-State Actors: Law-Takers or Law-Makers? Is that the Question?' in Ryngaert and Noortmann (n 150) 195.

273 Sivakumaran, *Non-International Armed Conflict* (n 8) 564–7.

274 Rondeau (n 56) 658.

275 Lucy Koechlin and Richard Calland, 'Standard Setting at the Cutting Edge: An Evidence-Based Typology for Multi-Stakeholder Initiatives' in Peters, Koechlin, Förster and Zinkernagel (n 66) 100–1.

276 Representatives include 'environmental and social non-governmental organisations, the timber trade, forestry organisations, indigenous people's organisations, community forestry groups, retailers and manufacturers and forest certification', Forest Stewardship Council, www.fsc-uk.org/en/about-fsc/what-is-fsc/governance, accessed 21 April 2016.

are equally weighted regardless of the number of participants . . . ensuring parity of representation between Southern and Northern members in each chamber.[277]

The impact of this kind of participation in the context of discursive democracy theories has been explicitly analysed by scholars such as Keller and Bogdandy, both of whom adopt largely Franckian approaches to legitimacy/compliance.[278]

Franck was keen to emphasise his position on the irrelevance of distinctions between law and non-law.[279] It is interesting to question, in this context, why 'hard' international legal provisions are considered to exhibit a compliance-pull rather than soft law provisions. Surely, the participation of multiple stakeholders in the formulation of codes of conduct should act almost as a model for deliberative democracy in miniature? The suggested answer offered here relates back to Franck's reliance on the nature of community:

> Obligation . . . is uniquely rooted in the notion of community . . . it can . . . arise as a concomitant of status, but only after an association has reached an advanced stage of development. A 'community' differs from a rabble, first, in that it is an organised system of interaction in accordance with rules, while a rabble typically involves unstructured, standardless interactions between actors whose conscious relationship to one another is limited to the circumstance of casual proximity.[280]

Thus, it could be argued that the continuity and communitarian peer pressure expected by members of the 'international community' (at present, States and some IOs) is not present in the primitive association of stakeholders feeding into soft law codes. In addition, the impact of non-compliance on the future application and content of 'hard' international legal standards is not reflected at the soft law level. As such, there is less concern relating to the erosion of core standards in the field of soft law.

In the absence of the capacity of non-State actors to formally consent to multilateral treaties, it was suggested above that one of the more compelling theoretical explanations for the extension of direct obligations to non-State armed groups was via custom. Sivakumaran has suggested, in line with the analysis above, that, '[i]ncorporating their practice into the formation of custom would counter this argument and give them a sense of ownership of the rules,

---

277 Stéphane Guéneau, 'Certification as a New Private Global Forest Governance System: The Regulatory Potential of the Forest Stewardship Council' in Peters, Koechlin, Förster and Zinkernagel (n 66) 386.
278 Keller (n 191) 254–98; Armin von Bogdandy, 'Codes of Conduct and the Legitimacy of International Law' in Wolfrum and Roben (n 66) 299–307.
279 Franck, *Legitimacy Among Nations* (n 165) 27–40.
280 Ibid. 196.

potentially making them less willing to break the rules'.[281] As Zegveld highlights, Article 38 of the ICJ Statute does not specify that evidence of custom must solely concern State practice.[282] Indeed, during the *Tadić* appeal case, the ICTY expressly stated that the practice of the insurgents was 'instrumental in bringing about the formation of the customary rules'.[283] Yet, the ICRC, during the course of its 2005 Study on Customary Humanitarian Law, stated that the legal significance of non-State armed group practice remained unclear.[284] In addition, scholars such as Meron have suggested that the primary focus on *opinio juris* in establishing custom weights customary principles in favour of how the State has *represented itself*, rather than actual practice.[285]

Discussion of customary international law brings in the secondary element of Ryngaert's procedural–substantive approach to the legitimacy of international legal rules. As mentioned above, rules that had attained *jus cogens* status and were generally considered to be owed *erga omnes* to the entire international community, were to be considered legitimate *regardless* of consent or participation in their creation, owing to the substantive quality of the norms.[286] It has been suggested that, in the absence of procedural participation for non-State actors:

> our best bet is . . . to rely on the legitimacy inherent in the substantive content of [international humanitarian] rules. After all, even if one has not been involved in the formation process of a given provision, a rule may still be compelling and perceived to safeguard one's interest.[287]

Although this is certainly one manner in which direct obligations could be imposed on non-State actors without their consent, it is suggested that the approach falls victim to recurring criticisms regarding indeterminacy, derivation from natural law principles, and the limited scope and content of norms that have achieved this status. For example, the level of protection provided by *jus cogens* norms would not match that of the corpus of law applicable in international armed conflicts. As such, it is suggested that substantive legitimacy is of limited utility here.

The influence of international organisations such as the ICRC in the articulation of customary international law standards, and of NGOs and civil

---

281 Sivakumaran, 'Binding Armed Opposition Groups' (n 16) 375.

282 Zegveld (n 15) 26; Tully (n 168) 92–3.

283 *Tadić* (n 128) para 108.

284 Jean-Marie Henckaerts, 'Study on Customary International Humanitarian Law: A Contribution to the Understanding and Respect for the Rule of Law in Armed Conflict' (2005) 87 *Int'l Rev Red Cross* 175, 179–80.

285 Theodor Meron, 'Is International Law moving towards Criminalisation?' (1998) 9 *EJIL* 18, 28.

286 Ryngaert, 'Imposing International Duties' (n 150) 72.

287 Geiss (n 44) 96.

society groups, is undeniable.[288] In spite of the ICRC listing the practice of non-State armed groups under 'other practice' in its 2005 study, it nevertheless 'mentions statements made by armed groups in order to justify the customary nature of some [humanitarian] rules binding on those groups'.[289] The ICRC has even been granted observer status at the UN General Assembly.[290] Although the special status of bodies such as the UN and ICRC as institutional mechanisms of the international legal system goes some way to explaining the somewhat anomalous position they occupy, it is clear that non-State actors may contribute considerably to the oversight and interpretation of international law. Such a role was envisaged for NGOs under the 2003 UN Draft Norms for Transnational Corporations, which were to be subject to 'periodic monitoring, verified by the United Nations . . . This monitoring shall be transparent and independent and take into account input from stakeholders (including non-governmental organisations)'.[291] Miller describes this as 'a remarkable parenthetical. It formally incorporates NGOs in the enforcement of the norms . . . codifying the monitoring and reporting role NGOs have assumed in many international human rights regimes'.[292]

Treaty monitoring bodies such as the International Committee on Economic and Social Rights[293] and Committee on the Elimination of Discrimination against Women[294] are already able to receive written and oral submissions from NGOs, though these 'participatory modalities . . . are variable, conditional, unspecific and discretional'.[295] During the 1992 Rio Conference, the ratio of NGO participants to State officials was 1:1.[296] Steer highlights that, '[t]he drafting of the Rome Statute was also influenced by the participation of NGOs, which were observing and lobbying during the entire process . . . the formation

288 On potential contributions of NGOs to the formation of customary international law: Isabelle Gunning, 'Modernising Customary International Law' (1991) 31 *Va J Int'l L* 211, 222–34.

289 Steenberghe (n 140) 222.

290 UNGA Res 45/6, 'Observer status for the International Committee of the Red Cross' (16 October 1990) UN Doc A/RES/45/6; Christian Koenig, 'Observer Status for the International Committee of the Red Cross at the United Nations: A Legal Viewpoint' (1991) 31 *Int'l Rev Red Cross* 37.

291 UN Sub-Commission on the Promotion and Protection of Human Rights, 'Commentary on the Norms on the Responsibilities of Transnational Corporations and Other Business Enterprises with Regard to Human Rights' (2003) UN Doc E/CN.4/Sub.2/2003/38/Rev. 2 para 16.

292 Miller (n 232) 391.

293 UN Committee on Economic Social and Cultural Rights, 'Rules of Procedure of the Committee, XVII' UN Doc E/C.12/1990/4/Rev. 1, Rule 69.

294 UN Committee on the Elimination of Discrimination against Women, 'Rules of Procedure for the Optional Protocol to the Convention on the Elimination of All Forms of Discrimination against Women, XVI' UN Doc A/56/38, Rule 83(3)-(4).

295 Tully (n 168) 15.

296 Alkoby (n 220) 34.

of the normative content is driven by non-State participants'.[297] Although they are usually precluded from the formal treaty-making process,[298] their roles in advocating the adoption of international instruments and throughout the drafting process are significant.[299] Additionally, international jurisprudence has permitted the participation of various EU agencies and NATO in the disclosure of documents to the *ad hoc* international criminal tribunals[300] and the submission of *amicus* briefs before the ICJ.[301] Thus, non-State actor participation already feeds into the creation and clarification of international law.

Nevertheless, there are a number of criticisms relating to the participation of non-State actors in the international law-making process, not least those relating to the political legitimisation of non-State armed groups highlighted above. One major concern relates to the *desirability* of the direct participation of actors whose motives may lie outside the public interest.[302] Miller notes that the discrepancy between the participation by NGOs and business actors is usually justified on the basis that the latter group 'are capable of violating international law, and, at the same time, unaccountable for the power they exercise'.[303] Yet, he argues that this polarity in the granting of participatory

297 Cassandra Steer, 'Non-State Actors in International Criminal Law' in d'Aspremont, *Multiple Perspectives* (n 36) 300.

298 On customary entitlements of NGOs to observer status within law-making institutions: Steve Chanovitz, 'Non-Governmental Organisations and International Law' (2006) 100 *AJIL* 348, 370; cf Anne Peters, Till Förster and Lucy Koechlin, 'Towards Non-State Actors as Effective, Legitimate and Accountable Standard Setters' in Peters, Koechlin, Förster and Zinkernagel (n 66) 494.

299 Theo van Boven, 'The Role of Non-Governmental Organisations in International Human Rights Standard-Setting: A Prerequisite of Democracy' (1990) 20 *Cal W Int'l LJ* 207; Menno T Kamminga, 'The Evolving Status of NGOs under International Law: A Threat to the Inter-State System?' in Gerard Kreijen, Marcel Brus, Jorris Duursma, Elizabeth De Vos and John Dugard (eds), *State, Sovereignty, and International Governance* (Oxford, UK, OUP, 2002) 394–9.

300 *Prosecutor v Kordić & Čerkez* (Order for the Production of Documents by the European Community Monitoring Mission and its Member States) IT-95-14/2-T (4 August 2000); *Prosecutor v Milutinović & Others* (Decision on Request of the North Atlantic Treaty Organisation for Review, Appeals Chamber) IT-05-87AR108bis1 (15 May 2006); Guido Acquaviva, 'Non-State Actors from the Perspective of International Criminal Tribunals in d'Aspremont', *Multiple Perspectives* (n 36) 185–203; Steer (n 297) 296–7.

301 *International Status of South West Africa* (Advisory Opinion, Pleadings) ICJ Reports [1949] 324; *Legal Consequences of the Construction of a Wall in the Occupied Palestinian Territory* (Advisory Opinion) ICJ Reports [2004] 142; Anna Dolidze, 'The Arctic Sunrise and NGOs in International Judicial Proceedings' (American Society of International Law Insight, 2014) www.asil.org/insights/volume/18/issue/1/arctic-sunrise-and-ngos-international-judicial-proceedings, accessed 21 April 2016; Gleider Hernández, 'Non-State Actors from the Perspective of the International Court of Justice' in d'Aspremont, *Multiple Perspectives* (n 36) 141–63; Tully (n 168) 242–5.

302 Boyle and Chinkin (n 193) 125–49.

303 Miller (n 232) 393.

rights for some actors and not others is arbitrary, on the grounds that similar criticisms could be brought against NGOs. Indeed, certain NGOs have been accused of political bias owing to their links with States, and the 'broad accreditation rules of international organisations potentially allow [MNEs] to masquerade as NGOs'.[304] Although NGOs and international organisations are often linked to States in terms of their funding, '[t]he paradoxical international treatment of NGOs and [MNEs] . . . is only justifiable if the ever-less persuasive distinction between the two as non-profit and for-profit entities is sustained'.[305] Related is the concern that such participation would erode existing international legal principles and hinder the progressive development of international human rights standards on the grounds of economic or political self-interest.[306]

These concerns undoubtedly present serious practical obstacles to the direct participation of non-State actors in the international law-making process. The heterogeneity of influential actors could also prove problematic,[307] and, as Chappell points out, increased deliberation does not necessarily mean more democratic outcomes:

> it will be well organised groups, whether they are NGOs, pressure and protest groups or even terrorist organisations that are most able to shape deliberative discourse to their own advantage. But these groups will not necessarily be representative of global discourse in general. They may receive high pay-offs from the issues they represent . . . Groups with diffuse costs and benefits will find it much less easy to set up effective collective organisations.[308]

Indeed, as Ryngaert suggests:

> [s]tating that non-State actors ought to be consulted, when regulation is contemplated by the international community is one thing. It is quite another to devise formal rules of non-State actor participation . . . across the whole range of international norm making processes and institutions.[309]

The manner in which participation is given effect is perhaps the central issue. If all relevant actors were able to participate in the same manner that States presently formulate international law, the above concerns would no doubt be

---

304 Peters, Förster and Koechlin (n 298) 519; Alkoby (n 220) 47–50.
305 Miller (n 232) 396.
306 Jonathan Charney, 'Transnational Corporations and Developing Public International Law' (1983) 32 *Duke LJ* 748, 772–3; Roberts and Sivakumaran (n 140) 137–8.
307 Thomas Kleinlein, 'Non-State Actors from an International Constitutionalist Perspective: Participation Matters!' in d'Aspremont, *Multiple Perspectives* (n 36) 45–6.
308 Chappell (n 229) 38; Tully (n 168) 330–5.
309 Ryngaert, 'Imposing International Duties' (n 150) 81.

pronounced. If participation were to take place under an institutional infrastructure, with the views of many stakeholders feeding into 'civil society', in the manner that Habermas envisages, then perhaps the inequalities in wealth and social power of various actors could be tamed.[310]

For Habermas, the process of communicative action procedurally limits the influence of the elements of strategic action that stem from power and wealth.[311] Thus:

> communicatively acting subjects commit themselves to coordinating their action plans on the basis of consensus that depends in turn on their reciprocally taking positions on, and intersubjectively recognising, validity claims . . . only those reasons count that all the participating parties together find acceptable.[312]

In a more practical context, Habermas's approach permits relevant actors to:

> capitalise on their social power and convert it into political power only insofar as they can advertise their interests in a language that can mobilise convincing reasons and shared value orientations . . . Public opinions that can acquire visibility only because of an undeclared infusion of money or organisational power lose their credibility as soon as these sources of social power are made public.[313]

Such an approach seems to have been implemented within the aforementioned Forest Stewardship Council, though whether such an initiative could be transferred to the public level is uncertain.[314]

How such a system would look in practice is, necessarily, highly speculative: 'there is no unified system of global institutions within which a fair and effective allocation of institutional responsibilities can be devised'.[315] Whether the system would resemble that of the present NGO structure, which arguably 'bring[s] non-State values into the international system', is doubtful.[316] It is unlikely that non-State actors would perceive this as true participation.[317] In the words of the indigenous participants during the ILO conferences:

310 Habermas, *Between Facts and Norms* (n 242) 366–7.
311 Miller (n 232) 401.
312 Habermas, *Between Facts and Norms* (n 242) 119.
313 Ibid. 364.
314 Guéneau (n 277) 403.
315 Buchanan and Keohane (n 234) 41.
316 Gaelle Breton-Le Goff, 'NGOs Perspectives on Non-State Actors' in d'Aspremont, *Multiple Perspectives* (n 36) 259.
317 David Held, *Democracy and the Global Order* (Cambridge, UK, Polity Press, 1995) 181.

[w]e did not come here to be passive observers while diplomats, labour leaders and executives decided what to do with us. We did not come here to give your deliberations our tacit approval by our presence.[318]

The legitimacy of any international institutions involved would also need to be established and accepted by relevant stakeholders.[319] Both State and non-State values would need to be reflected on an equal playing field. The broadening of international conferences to include representatives of non-State actors, similar to that reflected in the institutional support within the UN and EU during the formulation of the Kimberly Process, constitutes one suggestion,[320] though the initiative has been subject to criticism by NGOs.[321]

Another, perhaps more utopian, proposal by De Burca suggests that participation in transnational governance be structured 'in a way that keeps the circle of participants *continuously open* and that sets incentives to generate the fullest degree of participation possible'.[322] This 'democracy-striving' approach is then tested in the context of international financial institutions and the Poverty Strategy Reduction Programme, which, according to De Burca, 'provides an embryonic example of the democratic-striving approach . . . for the transnational domain'.[323] Yet, if a potentially infinite number of stakeholders must be accounted for, there is a clear risk that standard setting could be 'killed by an accountability paralysis . . . a reasonable balance between the need for adequate input and swift decision-making must be struck'.[324] As a middle ground, Miller has suggested that the tripartite structure of the ILO could provide an inclusive Habermasian forum for the participation of a variety of stakeholders.[325] How the efficacy of such approaches should be assessed and evaluated also raises complex questions and is, at present, under-explored. Should the level of participation or the implementation of a multi-stakeholder process be indicative of success or failure, or should attention be on outcomes and impact?[326] It is likely that each method would produce variable and perhaps conflicting views.

---

318 Leonard Crate, 'Representative of the International Organisation of Indigenous Resource Development' International Labour Conference, 76th Session (Geneva, 1989) 31/6, cited in Engle (n 267) 109.

319 Buchanan and Keohane (n 234) 26–62.

320 Nils Rosemann, 'Code of Conduct: Tool for Self-Regulation for Private Military and Security Companies' (Geneva Centre for the Democratic Control of Armed Forces, Occasional Paper No 15, 2008) 35.

321 Ian Smillie, 'Blood Diamonds and Non-State Actors' (2013) 46 *Vand J Transnat'l L* 1003, 1019.

322 Griánne de Burca, 'Developing Democracy Beyond the State' (2008) 46 *Colum J Transnat'l L* 221, 253–4.

323 Ibid. 256–7.

324 Peters, Förster and Koechlin (n 298) 530; Tully (n 168) 95–6.

325 Miller (n 232) 404; Ryngaert, 'Imposing International Duties' (n 150) 85.

326 Koechlin and Calland (n 275) 106–9.

Moreover, although illustrative of the conceptual problem, the potential participatory roles of indigenous populations and MNEs cannot be conflated with those of non-State armed groups. The willingness and capacity of these intensely variable groups to peacefully participate alongside other international actors that have been recognised or imbued with some degree of political or social legitimacy are highly problematic. Yet, this is the scenario demanded by the prevailing theoretical conception. Envisioning a generalizable, catch-all approach is one of the most fundamental challenges presented by the topic of non-State actor regulation, given the simple, binary differentiation between States and non-State actors ascribed by traditional doctrine. Remaining optimistic, Ryngaert urges that the move towards reform of the State-centric system should not be stayed on the basis of such doubts, for 'immature inclusive democracy is still better than no democracy at all'.[327] Yet, whereas some progress may be feasible in relation to MNEs, the same can hardly be said for the vast majority of non-State armed groups. Whether this approach is at all workable is highly debatable. Its effects on the normative content of international law are also uncertain. Yet, these are the results yielded when the methodology of the State-centric school is followed to its logical conclusions. Whether international scholarship should continue to adhere to this model in light of its practical and theoretical effects is an important question, with potential implications for the future normative development of the field.

4.3 Concluding remarks

The novel legal relationship between non-State armed groups and the international humanitarian law regime provides a useful lens through which the ascription of direct rights and duties to non-State actors may be examined. Though non-State armed groups are incapable of formal ratification or accession to the conventional provisions that expressly address them, they are still expected to comply with these international obligations. It was argued that each of the four broad justifications for the binding quality of these rules suffers insurmountable flaws at both theoretical and practical levels. The approach with the most utility was the one that asserted the binding quality of international rules that have attained customary status. This justification has the added benefit of supplementing the current disparity in the regulation of internal and international armed conflicts. Although the reservations surrounding the increase in the normative content of humanitarian provisions governing internal armed conflict are acknowledged, an extension of the rules relating to the protection of prisoners of war and civilians is arguably preferable, given the proliferation of internal armed conflicts.

327 Ryngaert, 'Imposing International Duties' (n 150) 83; cf Joseph Weiler, 'The Geology of International Law – Governance, Democracy and Legitimacy' (2004) 64 *Heidelberg J Int'l L* 547, 552.

A recurring critique of the aforementioned approaches related to the role of *consent* in the validation of international law, and the deficit in the procedural participation of non-State actors in the law-making process. Consent and participation are necessarily related, in terms of both practical compliance and theoretical validity. Drawing on the themes established in Chapter 2, it was argued that the State-centric view, which cites the 'coalescence of the wills of States' as the ultimate source of international law, necessitates the participation of its addressees in the process of law creation. The consent of the addressees establishes binding international obligations, and their participation incentivises this consent (and thus compliance) procedurally. This conflation partially explains the reticence of State parties to establish direct obligations for non-State actors. From the statist perspective, this process would imbue actors posing direct threats to a State's territorial integrity with State-like political prestige and law-making capacities. This insight permitted an exploration of the practical and theoretical consequences of these presumptions. It was argued that discursive democracy scholarship has substantial utility in light of the peculiarities generated by the State-centric method. This approach emphasises the advantages of multi-stakeholder discourse, which gives rise to significant benefits in terms of providing a voice to a plurality of actors and viewpoints usually overlooked during the law-making process, better reflecting global political reality, and refining contentious provisions via discursive processes. Participation by addressees is not only a theoretical presumption of State-centric scholarship. Through adherence to discursive democratic processes, any resulting provisions will be legitimised in the eyes of all relevant actors, leading to widespread consent and compliance-pull – a view supported by Franck.

Two models were contemplated in the evaluation of the existing instances of non-State actor participation in the creation and interpretation of international law. The first pertained to the representation of multi-stakeholder views via civil society institutions. It was suggested that such an approach was problematic in that non-State actors may perceive their participation as being merely passive or tacit. Naturally, there are concerns that direct participation in the manner traditionally reserved for States will lead to the further politicisation of the law-making process, the erosion of existing standards and the dominance of views outside the public interest. Although this disparity in the balance of power may be rectified under Habermas's vision of an ideal communicative scenario, the practicalities of devising effective non-State actor participation at all levels of the international law-making process are undeniably utopian. Although there are potential advantages to greater democratic governance at the international level, it is not suggested that this approach represents the ideal scenario. Rather, it is a product of the dominant State-centric methodology. If a functional system of non-State actor regulation is to be devised without departing from this theoretical model, it would appear that some form of non-State actor consultation and participation is necessitated. The question remains as to whether there is some other theoretical perspective that could permit the extension of direct obligations to non-State actors without their participation, and whether the desirability and practical application of this approach should be favoured over the State-centric model. It is to this question that the next chapter of this monograph will turn.

5 Abandoning the State

Towards an alternative theoretical framing

The foregoing chapters of this monograph have critically examined the extant approaches to the legal regulation of non-State actors. It has been argued that State-based methods are an ineffective means of securing non-State actor accountability, particularly in weak governance States. In addition, the theoretical scope for the attribution of direct international obligations to non-State actors is extremely limited by traditional doctrine. The consequences of this view, which bolsters a largely contractarian vision of a decentralised international legal system based on the consent of sovereign States, include the conflation of the creators of international law with the addressees of the resulting duties. This presupposition has effectively excluded non-State actors from the direct reach of international law. It has led to widespread concern that politically dubious non-State actors will be legitimised if they are considered the direct addressees of international rights and duties.

Even if these political concerns were overcome, this conflation arguably necessitates the conferral of international law-making capacity on non-State actors, as a means of both squaring the expansion of the international community with the theoretical presumptions of traditional scholarship and inducing their compliance in practice. Although such initiatives may advance global democratisation, the design, practical implementation and desirability of such participatory procedures remain contentious. Advancing this analysis, this chapter examines the utility of an alternative theoretical explanation of the structure and functioning of the international legal system and will evaluate its potential practical effects in relation to non-State actor regulation.

Having pursued the logic of the State-centric approach to its limits, this chapter adopts a theoretical model that may be inclusive of other influential international actors. It will demonstrate that the fundamentals of the Pure Theory of Law, as developed by the Austrian positivist Hans Kelsen, may offer a theoretically sounder means of directly binding non-State actors at the international level, free from presumptions relating to the political legitimacy and law-making capacity of addressees. Contrary to dominant scholarship, this chapter will demonstrate that, if international law is detached from the 'sovereign' State, with presumptions regarding the natural competences that stem from 'legal personality' thereby erased and replaced instead by the conclusion that international legal norms both define the State and determine the actors that those norms address, it is theoretically possible to conceive of a legal system in which non-State actors are regulated directly. To date, Kelsen's approach has not achieved mainstream popularity in international legal scholarship.[1] Indeed, the Pure Theory of Law has been subject to practical and theoretical criticism, both from within the legal tradition[2] and from scholars of the emergent realist school of international relations.[3] These concerns will be addressed over the course of this chapter. Yet, although the Pure Theory of Law may be unable to offer definitive answers on the issue, it is argued that the approach finds significant utility, both as an inclusive theoretical framing that could permit the attribution of direct international obligations to non-State entities without entailing law-making consequences, and as a critical lens through which the flaws of the State-centric school may be further examined. Finally, in keeping with the approach of the preceding chapters, the practical application of the theory will be evaluated in light of recent international developments, particularly those relating to non-State armed groups and MNEs.

5.1 The Pure Theory of Law as an alternative theoretical model

The Pure Theory of Law serves as the foundational model for Hans Kelsen's conception of the structure and operation of legal orders. It is a general theory of positive law, applicable to both the international and domestic spheres.[4] Indeed, it will be demonstrated that the unique manner in which Kelsen's theory

---

1 Alexander Somek, 'Stateless Law: Kelsen's Conception and its Limits' (2006) 26 *OJLS* 753, 754; Jochen von Bernstorff, *The Public International Law Theory of Hans Kelsen* (Cambridge, UK, CUP, 2010) 278.

2 Hersch Lauterpacht, 'Kelsen's Pure Science of Law' in Elihu Lauterpacht (eds), *International Law: Collected Papers of Hersch Lauterpacht* Vol 2 (Cambridge, UK, CUP, 1970) 424–31; Herbert LA Hart, 'Kelsen's Doctrine of the Unity of Law' in Herbert LA Hart, *Essays in Jurisprudence and Philosophy* (Oxford, UK, OUP, 1983) 309–42; Herbert LA Hart, *The Concept of Law* (2nd edn, Oxford, UK, Clarendon Press, 1997) 232–7; Lon Fuller, *The Law in Quest of Itself* (Clark, NJ, The Lawbook Exchange, 1999) 66–95; Stanley Paulson and Bonnie Litschewski-Paulson (eds), *Normativity and Norms: Critical Perspectives on Kelsenian Themes* (Oxford, UK, OUP, 1999); Richard Tur and William Twining (eds), *Essays on Kelsen* (Oxford, UK, Clarendon Press, 1986).

3 Carl Schmitt, *Political Theology: Four Chapters on the Theory of Sovereignty* (George Schwab trans, Cambridge, MA, MIT Press, 1985) 18–35; Hedley Bull, 'Hans Kelsen and International Law' in Tur and Twining (n 2) 336; Hans Morgenthau, 'Positivism, Functionalism and International Law' (1940) 34 *AJIL* 260, 275; Casper Sylvesta, 'Realism and International Law: The Challenge of John H Herz' (2010) 2 *Int'l Theory*, 410; Martti Koskenniemi, *The Gentle Civiliser of Nations: The Rise and Fall of International Law 1870–1960* (Cambridge, UK, CUP, 2002) 465–509.

4 Hans Kelsen, *The Pure Theory of Law* (Max Knight trans, 2nd edn, Berkeley, CA, University of California Press, 1970) 1.

unifies the national and international into a single, monistic legal order constitutes one of his thesis's core concepts, which, in turn, has the effect of tailoring its application to the regulation of non-State actors. This section will begin by providing a working definition of the Pure Theory of Law and will broadly contextualise its aims and methodological approach. It will then proceed to examine the application of the theory in relation to three key subject areas: (1) the definition of the State, (2) the definition of sovereignty and (3) legal monism. In light of the theory's generality, it would be impossible to provide a detailed analysis of every sphere of its application. Yet, it is argued that, in relation to these three areas, the theory's application to the topic of non-State actor regulation is particularly evident. Furthermore, these areas will draw together and give new relevance to many of the concepts considered in preceding chapters. Thus, in addition to detailing Kelsen's handling of these subjects, the deconstructive and constructive potential of the Pure Theory of Law will be demonstrated. Kelsen was intensely critical of both natural law *and* State-centric positivist scholarship, and, as a result, it has been suggested that his theory's 'utter consistency is an ideal basis for the immanent critique of international law'.[5] At the same time, an alternative theoretical model will be proposed in the wake of Kelsen's dissection of traditional doctrine. It will be argued that this conception may provide a more logical underpinning to the operation of international law at large and, thus, to the direct regulation of non-State actors.

5.1.1 *Defining the Pure Theory of Law*

Prior to an appraisal of the manner in which the Pure Theory of Law might apply in the context of the direct regulation of the non-State actors in international law, it is necessary to contextualise the aims of Kelsen's project. At its core, the Pure Theory of Law attempts to establish a science of law that is founded on a strict separation between '*is*' and '*ought*':[6]

> The Pure Theory of Law is a theory of positive law ... its exclusive purpose is to know and to describe its object. The theory attempts to answer the question what and how the law *is*, not how it ought to be ... It is called a 'pure' theory of law, because it only describes the law and attempts to eliminate from the object of this description everything that is not strictly law: Its aim is to free the science of law from alien elements.[7]

---

5 Jörg Kammerhofer, 'The Benefits of the Pure Theory of Law for International Lawyers, or: What use is Kelsenian Theory' (2006) 12 *Int'l Theory* 5, 24.
6 Philip Allott, *Health of Nations: Society and Law Beyond the State* (Cambridge, UK, CUP, 2002) 83 para 3.26.
7 Kelsen, *Pure Theory* (n 4).

Although the dichotomy between *is* and *ought* found its formulation in the philosophy of Hume[8] and Kant,[9] it has been suggested that Kelsen was the first to demonstrate a consistent adherence to this distinction.[10] The Pure Theory of Law is a formalist theory, in the sense that it attempts to strip out foreign influences from fields such as psychology, sociology, ethics and political theory that have polluted legal scholarship.[11] Kelsen argued that the influence of these divergent disciplines gives rise to the methodological inconsistencies that result from the conflation of *is* and *ought*,[12] of empirical and normative science.[13]

The legal system is strictly defined as a system of 'norms'. A norm describes a particular behaviour that *ought* to occur, as entirely distinct from the actual fulfilment of the act prescribed in empirical reality.[14] Thus, whereas the object of legal science is purely descriptive (an elaboration of what the law *is*), the legal norms it seeks to identify are merely the prescriptive (*ought*) statements enacted by law-creating authorities.[15] 'A statement to the effect that something ought to occur is a statement about the existence and contents of a norm, not a statement about natural reality i.e. actual events in nature.'[16] As such, nonconformity with the content of a norm in the empirical realm will not lead to its negation. Consider the norm 'all murderers ought to receive life sentences'. It does not follow that all murderers will actually be caught and appropriately sentenced in empirical reality, and the nonconformity of the norm with reality alone does not in every instance negate the norm in question. This position naturally leads to questions concerning the relationship between the 'validity' and 'effectiveness' of legal norms. Whereas the former relates to the binding quality of the norm (that individuals *ought* to behave as prescribed), the latter is clearly dependent on real-world conformity with a normative prescription.[17] Thus, these concepts are distinct, yet necessarily related.

> A norm is considered valid only on the condition that it belongs to a system of norms, to an order which, on the whole, is efficacious. Thus, efficacy is

8 David Hume, *A Treatise of Human Nature* Vol II (first published 1738, London, Thomas & Joseph Allman, 1817) Bk III, Pt I, 154–72.
9 Immanuel Kant, *The Critique of Pure Reason* (first published 1781, Norman Kemp Smith trans, Macmillan 1963) 313.
10 Kammerhofer, 'The Benefits of the Pure Theory of Law' (n 5) 11–12.
11 Gustav Bergmann and Lewis Zerpy, 'The Formalism in Kelsen's Pure Theory of Law' (1945) 55 Ethics 110, 130; Roland Portmann, *Legal Personality in International Law* (Cambridge, UK, CUP, 2010) 173.
12 Kelsen, *Pure Theory* (n 4); Hans Kelsen, *Introduction to the Problems of Legal Theory* (first published 1934, Bonnie Litschewski-Paulson and Stanley Paulson trans, Oxford, UK, Clarendon Press, 2002) 7–8.
13 Kammerhofer, 'The Benefits of the Pure Theory of Law' (n 5) 16.
14 Kelsen, *Pure Theory* (n 4) 6.
15 Hans Kelsen, *General Theory of Law and State* (first published 1945, Andres Wedberg trans, Cambridge, MA, Harvard University Press, 1949) 45.
16 Ibid. 36–7.
17 Ibid. 39.

a condition of validity; a condition, not a reason of validity. A norm is not valid because it is efficacious; it is valid if the order to which it belongs is, on the whole, efficacious.[18]

Kelsen advocated the view that legal norms were valid even absent the capacity to enforce them individually.[19] Thus, although a minimally efficacious legal order is necessary for a valid normative order to operate, this efficacy is not the reason that the order is valid.[20] Ebenstein helpfully elaborates this relationship, highlighting that some minimal degree of 'tension' between real-world compliance and non-compliance with legal norms is necessary to conceive of law as a normative order. If all norms were complied with in practical reality, the notion of 'ought' would collapse into 'is', as the resulting normative position – that one ought to behave as one actually behaves – is no norm at all, but rather a description of reality.[21]

Similarly, if norms were completely unobserved to the extent that they were entirely ineffective, the requisite tension would be lacking. Although Kelsen does not define the minimum conditions of tension necessary, in most cases, the principle should cause no issues and, in marginal cases, will depend on 'qualitative analyses of prevailing patterns of behaviour'.[22] But the crucial point remains: this minimal efficacy will not *in itself* determine the validity of a normative order. It simply provides the conditions necessary to conceive a system of norms at all. The ultimate locus of normative validity finds its roots in the *Grundnorm*, a notion that will be explored in greater depth below. For the time being, it suffices to note that norms remain valid even if there are individual instances of non-compliance that go unpunished.[23] In the context of the international sphere, this is particularly pertinent. Kelsen viewed the international legal order as primitive,[24] particularly in terms of its enforcement mechanisms, but individual instances of non-compliance did not undermine its overall efficacy, nor did its minimal efficacy determine international law's validity.[25] Rather, some minimal level of tension between the spheres of *is* and *ought* is necessary to conceive of separate empirical and normative realms in the first place.

The approach of this study, which has weighed the quality of theoretical explanations relating to the regulation of non-State actors against the political

18 Ibid. 42.
19 Ibid. 23–6.
20 Ibid. 42.
21 William Ebenstein, 'The Pure Theory of Law: Demythologizing Legal Thought' (1971) 59 *CLR* 617, 641–2.
22 Ibid.
23 Ibid. 46.
24 Kelsen, *Pure Theory* (n 4) 323.
25 Hans Kelsen, *Collective Security under International Law* (US Government Printing Office, 1957) 14, 23–6.

and economic realities of international practice, could be accused of the very methodological impurity to which Kelsen was opposed.[26] Yet, prior analysis attempted to critically discuss the efficacy of the State-centric conception of international law *on its own terms* and was thus beholden to different methodological constraints. Any attempt in this chapter to elaborate the practical effects facilitated by the adoption of the Pure Theory of Law as a methodological device in no way seeks to conflate the validity of legal norms with their specific content, practical operation and efficacy. This chapter simply aims to weigh an alternative theoretical justification for legal validity against the overall effectiveness of the legal order, a principle that Kelsen considers fundamental.[27] Indeed, Kelsen was keen to emphasise that a strict adherence to his methodological separation could prove mutually beneficial to empirical sciences:

> Nor let it be said that the jurist may not also undertake sociological, psychological, or historical studies . . . These are necessary; except that the jurist . . . must never incorporate the results of his explanatory examination into his construction of normative concepts.[28]

As such, manifestations of the Pure Theory of Law in international practice and the extent to which an effective system of direct non-State actor regulation could be realised under Kelsen's approach will be considered below. While doing so, no conclusions as to the *validity* of the legal norms will be derived from this practical analysis.

Two further related concepts that are fundamental to the operation of the theory require elaboration before we proceed with an analysis of its consequences for non-State actors. The first relates to the structure of the normative legal order. If norms do not strictly depend on their practical efficacy, questions arise as to the locus of their validity. Kelsen's response rests on his conception of the legal order as a normative hierarchy.[29] A norm's validity rests on its creation in conformity with a hierarchically higher norm, rather than a social fact.[30] This point is particularly relevant in the context of this study, given the emphasis placed by the dominant positivist school on the emergence of law from the factually conceived State. For Kelsen, no *is* proposition can establish

---

26 Cf Hidemi Suganami, 'Understanding Sovereignty through Kelsen/Schmitt' (2007) 33 *Rev Int'l Stud* 511, 521; Alexander Somek, 'Kelsen Lives' (2007) 18 *EJIL* 439; Kelsen, *General Theory of Law and State* (n 15) 221.

27 Kelsen, *Pure Theory* (n 4) 212; Kelsen, *General Theory of Law and State* (n 15) 213–17.

28 Hans Kelsen, *Hauptprobleme der Staatsrechtslehre, entwickelt aus der Lehre von Rechtssatz* (2nd edn, Tübingen, Germany, Mohr, 1923) 42, cited and translated in Bernstorff (n 1) 45–56.

29 Kelsen, *General Theory of Law and State* (n 15) 110.

30 Hans Kelsen, 'On the Basic Norm' (1957) 47 *CLR* 107, 108.

legal validity, as no normative *ought* statements may be derived from empirical facts.[31] Thus, every norm may be traced back to a supra-ordinated norm that created it: what Kelsen called the basic norm or *Grundnorm*.[32] The *Grundnorm* 'contains nothing but the determination of a norm-creating fact, the authorisation of a norm-creating authority or . . . a rule that stipulates how the general and individual norms of the order based on the basic norm are to be created'.[33] The validity of this norm is presupposed,[34] and, in that sense, it is the only non-positive legal norm, as it does not derive its validity from a higher source.[35] The actual *content* of the *Grundnorm* is empty; it serves a purely validating, procedural function:[36]

> The basic norm supplies only the reason for validity, but not at the same time the content of the norms constituting the system. Their content can only be determined by the acts by which the authority authorised by the basic norm, and the authorities authorised by this authority, create the positive norms of this system.[37]

In the context of public international law, treaties derive their validity from a general norm obliging States to act in conformity with treaty obligations (*pacta sunt servanda*), which in turn may be conceived as subordinate to a more general norm of customary law. 'The basic norm, therefore, must be a norm which countenances custom as a norm-creating fact, and might be as follows: "The States ought to behave as they have customarily behaved".'[38] Thus, the *Grundnorm* permits legal scholars to view systems of law, the particular content of which is positively defined by the law-makers, in purely normative terms. It is sufficient at this stage to sketch the function of the *Grundnorm* in broad terms. Given the foundational significance of the doctrine in the Pure Theory of Law, it will be subject to further elaboration and critical discussion below.[39]

31 Jörg Kammerhofer, *Uncertainty in International Law: A Kelsenian Perspective* (Oxford, UK, Routledge, 2011) 201.

32 Bernstorff (n 1) 81.

33 Kelsen, *Pure Theory* (n 4) 196.

34 Ibid. 203; Kelsen, *General Theory of Law and State* (n 15) 110–12; Kelsen, 'On the Basic Norm' (n 30).

35 Kelsen vehemently opposed the equation of the *Grundnorm* to natural law validation: Kelsen, *Pure Theory* (n 4) 217–19; Kelsen, 'On the Basic Norm' (n 30) 109; cf Bruno Simma, 'The Contribution of Alfred Verdross to the Theory of International Law' (1995) 6 *EJIL* 33; Bernstorff (n 1) 154–5.

36 Kelsen, *Pure Theory* (n 4) 198; Bernstorff (n 1) 160–5.

37 Kelsen, *Pure Theory* (n 4) 197.

38 Kelsen, *General Theory of Law and State* (n 15) 369; on customary law formation from the perspective of the Pure Theory of Law: cf Kammerhofer, *Uncertainty* (n 31) 59–86; Bernstorff (n 1) 170–2.

39 See below at Section 5.1.2.5.

In light of the above, it is clear that norms both regulate their own creation and prescribe the process by which legal norms are made. Norm application and norm creation are essentially synonymous concepts.[40] An addressee's duties and competences are prescribed by the norms in question, which in turn derive their validity from hierarchically higher norms. In international law, the relevant legal norms related to law creation prescribe that States have the competence to formulate international legal norms. No status or prestige in social reality is to be derived from these competences, as such concerns relate to the realm of empirical science (*is*). No factual or sociological 'person' or 'entity' is to be derived either. A legal person is simply:

> the personified concept of the unity of a bundle of legal duties and legal rights . . . *all* subjects of law – even if their inclusion in a legal order seems fundamental to its working – are constituted by the law itself through the content of the legal order.[41]

Viewed in this way, legal personality is simply a fictive device employed for the description of legal phenomena. Clearly, all legal norms prescribe the behaviour of natural human beings in the empirical realm. Yet, from the perspective of the Pure Theory of Law, natural persons are only relevant to the extent that they are subject to legal rights and duties. This is because 'the legal person is not a separate entity besides "its" duties and rights'.[42] The acts of natural persons, to the extent that their behaviour engages or corresponds with legal norms, may be imputed or ascribed to 'collective' juristic persons such as the State, which are also defined entirely in normative terms: as normative orders comprising the unity of bundles of rights and duties.[43] As will be demonstrated, the consequences stemming from this theoretical perspective are fundamental to the dissolution of the view that States are the principal actors that may be subject to international duties,[44] as well as presumptions relating to the international law-making capacities of the addressees of international law and, thus, the political legitimacy accorded to them. Naturally, the conception of the legal order as a unitary, hierarchical order of norms strongly favours a monist view that permits State sovereignty to break 'free of its doctrinally cemented anchor . . . uniting international law and national law into a monistic legal cosmos was a central precondition for a new, objective edifice of international law'.[45] The

---

40 Hans Kelsen, *Principles of International Law* (New York, Rinehart, 1952) 304; Kelsen, *Pure Theory* (n 4) 71.
41 Kammerhofer, 'The Benefits of the Pure Theory of Law' (n 5) 33; Kelsen, *Pure Theory* (n 4) 172–3.
42 Kelsen, *General Theory of Law and State* (n 15) 93.
43 Ibid. 97–8.
44 Bernstorff (n 1) 83.
45 Ibid.

application and consequences of this view in relation to non-State actors will be elaborated below.

One final preliminary remark is necessary. It has been established that the Pure Theory of Law seeks to distinguish legal norms from other normative orders such as morality and theology. The question arises as to the delineating features of legal norms that merit this stringent distinction.[46] In answering it, Kelsen revives a long-standing argument relating to the description of the international order as a system of 'law improperly so-called'.[47] He emphasised the distinct manner in which legal norms prescribe coercive sanctions in response to '*delicts*' or legally determined wrongs.[48] Although moral, ethical and religious normative systems may also prescribe sanctions in instances of non-compliance, Kelsen observed that they are essentially indirect or transcendental in character, rather than being socially organised and directly enacted, as is the case for the legal order.[49] Thus, it is the socially imminent nature of legal sanctions that distinguishes law from other normative orders. The study of law should only pertain to such systems.

The utilisation of the 'coercive sanction' doctrine as the litmus test to distinguish between legal and non-legal norms raises a number of problems when relayed to the monist conception of law advanced by Kelsen. The international legal order has long been criticised for its lack of a centralised coercive power and the parallel concern that the establishment of such a body would establish a tyrannical world State.[50] The Vienna School responded to this criticism by drawing on Kaltenborn, who had defended the quality of international law by envisaging a decentralised system in which 'States themselves were legislators and judges and war international law's ultimate enforcement'.[51] As distinct from the legal duty of States to make reparations,[52] the international community, primarily through the conduct of the injured party,[53] fulfils the criterion of coercive sanction in a decentralised manner by way of war and reprisals.[54] In this sense, the international legal order holds a monopoly on the use of force, which is only permitted as a sanction in response to a delict.[55] Thus, in a sense, international law is placed above the State: the legal order entirely regulates the use of force. For Kelsen, to deny the monopoly

---

46 Kelsen, *Pure Theory* (n 4) 31.
47 John Austin, *The Province of Jurisprudence Determined* (2nd edn, London, John Murray, 1832) 17–18.
48 Kelsen, *General Theory of Law and State* (n 15) 328.
49 Ibid. 20; Kelsen, *Pure Theory* (n 4) 27–30.
50 Adolf Lasson, *Princip und Zukunft des Völkerrechts* (Berlin, W Hertz, 1837) 23; Bernstorff (n 1) 85.
51 Koskenniemi, *The Gentle Civiliser* (n 3) 26; Bernstorff (n 1) 85–6.
52 Kelsen, *General Theory of Law and State* (n 15) 329.
53 Kelsen, *Principles of International Law* (n 40) 13.
54 Kelsen, *General Theory of Law and State* (n 15) 330.
55 Ibid. 331–6.

of force held by the legal order is to deny the existence of international law.[56] As will be demonstrated, this consequence has significant effects in relation to the direct regulation of non-State actors.

The Kantian leanings of Kelsen's work are exposed in this element of the Pure Theory of Law.[57] His promotion of the monopolisation of the use of force by an objective, universal legal order can be seen to practically advance, by consequence, an approximation of Kant's perpetual peace.[58] The principle that war is forbidden except as a sanction and the principle of non-intervention are generally accepted today, the ILC having recently affirmed Kelsen's view in express terms.[59] Naturally, a number of critiques have been mounted against Kelsen's utilisation of coercive sanction as a means of distinguishing between legal and non-legal norms, by realists, international relations scholars and even students of the Pure Theory of Law.[60] The role of these criticisms in fundamentally undermining Kelsen's overall theoretical project, and the neo-Kelsenian approaches that have arisen in response, will be discussed in further detail below. For now, it suffices to highlight Kelsen's reliance on the Austinian model as a core attribute of his theoretical approach.

5.1.2 *Applying the Pure Theory of Law to non-State actors*

Having sketched the core concepts underpinning the Pure Theory of Law, this section demonstrates the consequences that the approach entails in the context of public international law. As will become apparent, the utter consistency of Kelsen's method enables many of the inconsistencies and 'untenable fictions' underscoring State-centric scholarship to be dispelled.[61] The result is a conception of the international legal system that is at once theoretically receptive to the extension of direct obligations to non-State actors and absent undesirable consequences relating to law-making capacity. What will become clear is that the role of individuals/natural persons, in which respect the edifice of State-centric scholarship has already been eroded, is key to Kelsen's theoretical liberation.

---

56 Ibid. 336.
57 Cf Alida Wilson, 'Is Kelsen Really a Kantian?' in Tur and Twining (n 2) 37–64; Hillel Steiner, 'Kant's Kelsenianism' in Tur and Twining (n 2) 65–75.
58 Immanuel Kant, *The Metaphysics of Morals* (first published 1797, Mary Gregor trans, Cambridge, UK, CUP, 2003) 119, §61; cf Lars Vinx, *Hans Kelsen's Pure Theory of Law: Legality and Legitimacy* (Oxford, UK, OUP, 2007) 177–207; Danilo Zolo, 'Hans Kelsen: International Peace through International Law' (1998) 9 *EJIL* 306.
59 ILC, 'Report of the International Law Commission Fifty-Third Session' (23 April–1 June and 2 July–10 August 2001) UN Doc A/56/10, 324; Jörg Kammerhofer, 'Kelsen – Which Kelsen? A Reapplication of Pure Theory to International Law' (2009) 22 *LJIL* 225, 230.
60 Kammerhofer, 'Which Kelsen?' (n 59); Kammerhofer, *Uncertainty* (n 31).
61 Utilising this term invokes the neo-Kantian scholarship of Hans Vaihinger, who cautioned against the use of a device that consciously contradicts reality for the purpose of comprehending reality. For Kelsen, this is precisely the approach of State-centric scholarship: Portmann (n 11) 188.

5.1.2.1 *Redefining States and ILP*

In Chapter 2, the perception of the State in classical scholarship was explored. The reliance of these scholars on the historical prestige of States, conceived as social facts and consisting of empirically observable criteria, was examined.[62] The historiographical justifications for the primacy of States, and the ill-defined nature of their constituent features were critically analysed. Advancing this discussion, the unique manner in which the Pure Theory of Law conceives of the addressees of legal norms serves a useful critical function in the further evaluation of the dominant theoretical perspective. This critique is premised on Kelsen's strict adherence to the methodological separation of empirical and normative science. In its wake, the Pure Theory of Law frees international law from the dogma of State-centric doctrine, perceiving all addressees in purely juristic terms and constructing an open conception of ILP, free from presumptions relating to political status or legal competences.[63] By reducing the State to a body corporate, free of ideology and mysticism, and placing it on par with any other international actor, Kelsen's 'identity thesis' represents the first step in the conception of an international legal system that is receptive to the direct imputation of legal obligations to non-State actors.[64]

Kelsen considered 'legal sociology', an approach that attempts to derive the existence and validity of law from social facts, as a methodological abomination.[65] This was particularly so in relation to the State.[66] Yet, the scholarship that attained dominance in nineteenth century Europe and, it has been argued, underlies much of the contemporary discourse[67] explicitly maintained a duality in its perception of the State, both as a juristic entity and as one that was conceivable in social, psychological and historical terms:[68]

> Law . . . is assumed to regulate the behaviour of the State, conceived as a kind of man or superman, just as law regulates the behaviour of men. The duality of the State and law is in fact one of the cornerstones of modern political science and jurisprudence . . . The State as a legal community is not something apart from its legal order, any more than the corporation is distinct from its constitutive order.[69]

62 See Chapter 2 at Section 2.4.
63 Portmann (n 11).
64 Kelsen, *Pure Theory* (n 4) 286.
65 Bernstorff (n 1) 45.
66 Kelsen, *General Theory of Law and State* (n 15) 182; Kelsen, *Pure Theory* (n 4) 285.
67 See Chapter 2 at Section 2.2.
68 Jo Eric Khushal Murkens, *From Empire to Union: Conceptions of German Constitutional Law since 1871* (Oxford, UK, OUP, 2013) 19–20; Duncan Kelly, 'Revisiting the Rights of Man: Georg Jellinek on Rights and the State' (2004) 22 *LHR* 493; Koskenniemi, *The Gentle Civiliser* (n 3) 242.
69 Kelsen, *General Theory of Law and State* (n 15) 182; Kelsen, *Pure Theory* (n 4) 100.

For the Pure Theory of Law, the empirical element of the State is only the collective of natural persons behaving.[70] Legal sociology is simply 'parasitical upon normative jurisprudence'.[71] As Koskenniemi summarises:

> members of a group mediate their relations through . . . a system of norms, and come to think of themselves as a State by reference to it. But . . . the State's existence is a matter of definition independent of any "feeling of association": it is a juridical notion which then offers through metaphor . . . a point of identification for the group.[72]

Thus, Kelsen's methodological division between *is* and *ought* permits the State to be conceived of only as a legal order that establishes the relations between a group of natural persons and mediates their behaviour. 'The sociological concept of an actual pattern of behaviour, oriented to the legal order is not a concept of the State, it presupposes the concept of the State, which is a juristic concept.'[73] Crucially, the juristic concept does not presuppose the sociological.[74] However, although Kelsen denied the factual existence of the State in terms of its relevance to legal scholarship, he did not deny social reality:

> These facts do not lose their reality if it is asserted that their 'State'-quality is nothing but the result of an interpretation. These facts are the actions of human beings, and these actions are acts of the State only insofar as they are interpreted according to a normative order, the validity of which has to be presupposed.[75]

Accordingly, Kelsen's purely normative perception of the State advances the view that natural persons are the ultimate addressees of international law in the empirical realm. The content of norms addressing 'States' as juristic persons is determined by the international legal order, and the personal element of the duty (i.e. the particular individual required to act as the State's agent in complying with the norm) is determined by the legal sub-order of the State.[76] In this way, behaviour can be *imputed* or ascribed to the State as a juristic person, but this entails neither the existence of a factual State entity, nor a necessary connection between the factual State and the validity of the norm. As will be elucidated below, this approach lays the foundations for the direct application of international law to non-State actors.

---

70   Ibid.
71   Vinx (n 58) 12.
72   Koskenniemi, *The Gentle Civiliser* (n 3) 243, fn 231.
73   Kelsen, *General Theory of Law and State* (n 15) 189.
74   Ibid. 183.
75   Ibid. 189; cf Somek, 'Stateless Law' (n 1) 761–2.
76   Kelsen, *Principles of International Law* (n 40) 97–9.

Kelsen defended his thesis against a number of critiques propounded by traditional scholarship. Leaving aside his critique of the sociological conception of the State momentarily, Kelsen formulated a scathing response to the assertion of a real, psychological unity between the members of a State, a form of collective consciousness in which citizens possessed an identical state of mind.[77] He found this position to be highly unlikely, 'except in relatively small groups whose extension or membership would also be constantly changing'.[78] Kelsen was particularly critical of the view that the State possessed a separate will, over and above that of its subjects.[79] He viewed the sociological and psychological explanations of the State and its 'sovereign will' as reified abstractions[80] – metaphorical fictions that had been personified and anthropomorphised as real:[81]

> Behind a tree, a dryas, behind a river, a nymph, behind the moon, a moon-goddess, behind the sun, a sun-god. Thus, we imagine behind the law, its hypostatised personification, the State, the god of law. The dualism of law and State is an animistic superstition. The only legitimate dualism here is that between the validity and efficacy of the legal order.[82]

Such a phenomenon was noted by Hume[83] and, later, Nietzsche, who commented that even the natural scientist looks:

> only for metamorphoses of the world in man; he wrestles for an understanding of the world as a human-like thing and . . . regards the whole world as connected to man, as an infinitely broken echo of an original sound, that of man; as a manifold copy of an original picture, that of man.[84]

In this respect, although receptive to Freud's analysis relating to the emancipation of the individual,[85] Kelsen was critical of his psychological conception of

---

77 See Chapter 2 at Section 2.2; Janne E Nijman, *The Concept of International Legal Personality: An Inquiry into the History and Theory of International Law* (The Hague, Netherlands, TMC Asser Press, 2004) 113.

78 Kelsen, *General Theory of Law and State* (n 15) 184; Somek, 'Stateless Law' (n 1) 759.

79 Kelsen, *General Theory of Law and State* (n 15) 185.

80 Nijman (n 77) 161.

81 On this point, Kelsen exhibits clear influence from the scholarship of Ernst Mach and Fitz Mauthner: Allan Janik and Stephen Toulmin, *Wittgenstein's Vienna* (London, Weidenfeld & Nicolson, 1973) 123; ibid 161–2.

82 Kelsen, *General Theory of Law and State* (n 15) 191; Nijman (n 77) 184–7.

83 David Hume, 'The Natural History of Religion' in David Hume, *Essays and Treatises on Several Subjects* (Edinburgh, Millar, Kincaid & Donaldson, 1758) 492.

84 Friedrich Nietzsche, *Werke in Drei Bänder* (Schlechter, 1966) 316, translated in Stewart Guthrie, *Faces in the Clouds: A New Theory of Religion* (Oxford, UK, OUP, 1993) 63.

85 Drawing on Le Bon, Freud analysed the individual's loss of independence as part of a mass: Sigmund Freud, *Group Psychology and the Analysis of the Ego* (James Strachey trans, The Hogarth Press, 1949) 82.

the State as an abstract idea fulfilling the function of a leader in a socially organised but leaderless group.[86] The role of the individual as the ultimate addressee of all legal norms proved crucial to Kelsen's reformulation of the doctrine of ILP.[87] Similarly, his opposition to the psychological conception of the State will be examined further below in relation to the sovereign authority of the State and its theoretical relation to the binding quality of international law. These factors underlie the utility of the Pure Theory of Law in expanding the reach of international law to address non-State actors.

Returning briefly to sociology, Kelsen also formulated a thorough response to the assertion that the interactions of individual citizens are rooted in a social reality that is separate from the legal sphere. Even in the early twentieth century, Kelsen recognised that citizenship was not the only group membership to which a person could belong. Indeed, there are numerous communities operating both within the State and, as a result of globalisation, trans-nationally:[88]

> State borders are no hindrance to relationships between people . . . The State is presupposed as a juristic unit when the problem as to its sociological unity is formulated . . . [T]he interaction theory does not offer any tenable answer to this problem, and it would seem that any attempted positive solution must involve the same type of political fiction.[89]

In keeping with his framing of the State in purely normative terms, Kelsen redefined the 'empirical' characteristics of the State quantified by the Montevideo Convention simply as 'spheres of validity' established by law.[90] Thus, a State is not an area of territory, a government, a permanent population or an amalgam of these physical properties. All factual elements commonly recognised as constituting the State must be capable of being presented as properties of the legal order. It is the *norm* defining a State's territory that is relevant to the study of law, rather than the *actual* territory.[91]

The normative conception of the State proves extremely enlightening with respect to the almost tautological definition of ILP provided by the ICJ in its

---

86 Ibid. 81–100; Hans Kelsen, 'The Conception of the State and Social Psychology with Special Reference to Freud's Group Theory' (1924) 5 *Int'l J Psycho-Analysis* 1, 20; Nijman (n 77) 103–5, 169–71.

87 'The idea that [Kelsen] simply did away with the concept of ILP is . . . not correct . . . the human being and international law are connected in the concept of legal personality', Nijman (n 77) 188; clear parallels are visible in: Hersch Lauterpacht, *International Law and Human Rights* (New York, Praeger, 1950) 27; Philip Allott, 'Reconstituting Humanity – New International Law' (1992) 3 *EJIL* 219.

88 Kelsen, *General Theory of Law and State* (n 15) 183.

89 Ibid. 184.

90 Montevideo Convention on the Rights and Duties of States (26 December 1933) 165 LNTS 17, Article 1; Bernstorff (n 1) 53.

91 Kelsen, *General Theory* (n 15) 189.

Reparation Advisory Opinion.[92] That an entity is perceived as an international legal person to the extent that it is so defined by positive law makes perfect sense under the logic of Pure Theory.[93] That different entities might be the addressees of varying rights and obligations is not at all problematic[94] and need not be expressed in terms such as 'full' or 'limited' legal personality: juristic persons are simply devices employed to describe legal phenomena, in particular, the referral or imputation[95] of norms regulating human behaviour to a legal 'order' or 'corporation' such as, but not necessarily exclusively, the State.[96] Via the strict separation of *is* and *ought*, the Pure Theory of Law is able to strip away the mythologised notions of the State as a manifestation of collective psychic will, thereby freeing the doctrine of ILP from the political or moral connotations it carried under State-centric scholarship. The consequences of this theoretical critique in the context of non-State actor regulation should now become clear. Kelsen's conception of international personality is entirely open and neutral;[97] it entails no presumptions as to the political or moral status of the entity, nor presumptions as to which rights and capacities a subject of international law 'possesses'.[98] These factors are the irrelevant results of methodological inconsistencies or are determined by the legal normative order, respectively. As legal personality is simply the unity of a bundle of norms, international obligations may conceivably be imputed to *any* entity as a juristic person: to *any* non-State actor.

Kelsen spoke expressly of the attribution of 'legal personality' to generic corporate bodies[99] and even armed groups exercising effective territorial control:

> By the effective control of the insurgent government over part of the territory and people of the State involved in civil war, an entity is formed which indeed resembles a State in the sense of international law. This is of great importance as far as the extent of responsibility of the insurgent government is concerned.[100]

92 *Reparation for Injuries Suffered in the Service of the United Nations* (Advisory Opinion) ICJ Reports [1949] (hereafter, *Reparation*).
93 Ibid. 179; for Kammerhofer, the Court erred in its phrasing: 'The "capacity" *qua* validity of norms establishing duties and rights creates legal personality, not vice versa', Kammerhofer, 'The Benefits of the Pure Theory of Law' (n 5) 36.
94 'The subjects of law in any legal system are not necessarily identical in their nature or in the extent of their rights', *Reparation* (n 92) 178.
95 Stanley Paulson, 'Hans Kelsen's Doctrine of Imputation' (2001) 14 *Ratio Juris* 47.
96 Kelsen, *Principles of International Law* (n 40) 98.
97 Portmann (n 11) 175.
98 Ibid. 177; Kelsen, *Principles of International Law* (n 40) 148–9; Jean d'Aspremont, 'The Doctrine of Fundamental Rights of States and the Functions of Anthropomorphic Thinking in International Law' (2015) 4 *CJICL* (forthcoming).
99 Kelsen, *Principles of International Law* (n 40) 98.
100 Kelsen, *General Theory of Law and State* (n 15) 230.

Although, in the latter case, personality has been formulated on the basis of the group's similarity to the legal order of the State (and, as such, arguments relating to the regulation of only 'State-like' entities may be raised),[101] this analogy is purely illustrative.[102] By detaching international law from the State, Kelsen frees the doctrine of legal personality and permits the legal process to ascribe direct international obligations regulating the behaviour of individuals to any entity as a juristic person.[103] This consequence demonstrates the utility of the Pure Theory of Law as a means of establishing legal personality for entities such as MNEs and non-State armed groups and, thus, in underscoring the establishment of international obligations directly binding upon non-State actors more generally. Yet, this normative conceptualisation of the State is merely the first step in the application of Kelsen's theoretical project to non-State actors.[104] The Pure Theory of Law's treatment of sovereignty, the binding quality of international law, the structure of the international legal system, and law-making processes will be considered further below.

5.1.2.2 *Sovereignty and law-making capacity*

The above analysis demonstrates a crucial consequence of the Pure Theory of Law's methodology in the context of non-State actor regulation. Specifically, Kelsen was able to reduce the State from a sociologically conceived, factual entity to a 'personified fiction' resulting from the imputation of legal norms ultimately addressing individuals. Thus, the doctrine of ILP was reconceived as an open concept, no longer restricted to States. Developing this application, this section addresses concerns relating to the authority, binding quality and creation of international law. Although these matters have been examined at length throughout this study, in the present context, they are necessarily linked with Kelsen's methodological approach and with the monist conception of a single, objective legal order. The effects of the Pure Theory of Law in relation to these concepts will be further elaborated throughout the course of the remaining sub-sections, in order to comprehensively demonstrate the liberation of the treatment of non-State actors from the constraints of traditional scholarship.

The doctrine of sovereignty and its relationship with the binding quality of international law were broadly introduced in Chapter 2.[105] It was acknowledged that the notion of sovereignty has been ascribed a diverse range of definitions, likely as an attempt to square traditional statist doctrine with developments in

---

101 See Chapter 4 at Section 4.2.3.
102 Kelsen, *Principles of International Law* (n 40) 98, 158–88.
103 Jörg Kammerhofer, 'Non-State Actors from the Perspective of the Pure Theory of Law' in Jean d'Aspremont (ed), *Multiple Perspectives on Non-State Actors in International Law* (Oxford, UK, Routledge, 2011) 59; Nijman (n 77) 172.
104 Somek, 'Stateless Law' (n 1).
105 See Chapter 2 at Section 2.3.

international law.[106] For Kelsen, sovereignty indicates a supreme authority within a legal sphere, 'above which there can be no higher authority limiting the function of the sovereign entity'.[107] Thus, the question of how States, as apparently sovereign entities, are constrained by international law naturally arises.[108] The dominant answer in Kelsen's era, which remains widely accepted today, draws on the principle of 'self-obligation' or 'auto-limitation':[109]

> The autonomous individual legislates for herself. Acting within the international sphere, the sovereign State is in an analogous position. It legislates for itself and its capacity to do so – its autonomy – is the exhaustive explanation for why it is bound.[110]

This justification for the binding quality of international law directly relates to the discussion in Chapter 4 relating to the State-centric conflation of the addressees of international obligations with the creators of international legal norms by way of an essentially contractarian rationale.[111] Kelsen recognised the popular view that international law was created by 'treaty' (or contract) alone, either via conventional or customary international law, the latter serving as a 'tacit' treaty.[112] According to this classical view, consent is derived from the 'coalescence of wills' of sovereign States.[113] The consequences of this view in relation to the direct regulation of non-State actors arguably necessitate the express or tacit consent and thus participation of those actors in the international law-making process, as the preceding discussion relating to discursive democracy and legitimation explored.[114]

The response of the Pure Theory of Law follows the logic of its critique of the duality of the State as both a normative order and social fact:

> The problem of the so-called auto-obligation of the State is one of the pseudo-problems that result from the erroneous dualism of State and law … [T]here is no difficulty at all, unless the person of the State … is

---

106 Bernstorff (n 1) 62.
107 Kelsen, *Principles of International Law* (n 40) 108.
108 Ibid. 108–9.
109 'It does not exhaust the nature of law that it is the will of the State, for it is not the will of the State as such that is law, but the binding will of the State', Georg Jellinek, *Die rechtliche Natur der Staatenverträge* (Vienna, Hölder, 1880) 6, cited and translated in Bernstorff (n 1) 30; Stephen Hall, 'The Persistent Spectre: Natural Law, International Order and the Limits of Legal Positivism' (2001) 12 *EJIL* 269, 277–84.
110 Koskenniemi, *The Gentle Civiliser* (n 3) 204.
111 See Chapter 4 at Section 4.2.
112 Kelsen, *General Theory of Law and State* (n 15) 351.
113 Kelsen, *Principles of International Law* (n 40) 315.
114 Ibid. 317.

hypostatised into a super-individual being, and one then speaks of
obligations and rights of the State in the same sense . . . as individuals.[115]

The Pure Theory of Law requires the separation of the notion of sovereignty
from the pseudo-psychological will of the State. Indeed, sovereignty, seen as a
primordial or natural competence of States, was seen as an untenable 'symptom
of the anarchy of jurisprudential terminology . . . which loves to present as
subjective "right" all content that has any legal relevance or content that was
desired as legally relevant'.[116] But, for the Pure Theory of Law, the State is
neither rooted in social fact, nor empirical manifestations of power and
authority, nor collective psychology, nor historicism. The notion of 'natural
rights' preceding positive law and attaching to certain categories of legal
persons is therefore theoretically unjustifiable.[117] The law-creating function of
States is simply prescribed by a higher norm, or, more specifically, such a
competence is assigned by the law to an individual, in their capacity as an agent,
and then imputed to the State legal order. Thus, the conflation between
addressee and law-maker is completely dissolved by the application of the theory.
Law-creating competence may be imputed to *any* entity. It just so happens that,
at present, this core function in the international legal system is primarily
prescribed to States.[118] In the domestic context:

> [a] command is binding, not because the individual commanding has an
> actual superiority . . . but because he is 'authorised' or 'empowered' to issue
> commands of a binding nature. And he is 'authorised' or 'empowered' only
> if a normative order, which is presupposed to be binding, confers on him
> this capacity, the competence to issue binding commands.[119]

The same is true at the international level.

Under the logic of the Pure Theory of Law, the consent-based, self-
obligating, contractarian explanations of legal validity are rendered irrelevant.
Kelsen illustrated this in the practical context of State succession, remarking
that the conception of customary international law as a 'tacit' treaty was:

115 Kelsen, *General Theory of Law and State* (n 15) 197–8.
116 Hans Kelsen, *Das Problem der Souveränität und die Theorie des Völkerrechts* (2nd edn,
     Tübingen, Germany, Mohr, 1928) 555, cited and translated in Bernstorff (n 1) 63; Hans
     Kelsen, 'The Principle of Sovereign Equality of States as a Basis for International
     Organisation' (1944) 53 *Yale LJ* 207, 212.
117 German (*Volksgeist*) and French (*solidarité social*) sociological conceptions of the State
     cannot 'be proved in a scientific way. Both are assumptions of social metaphysics . . . [and]
     are very similar to the natural-law doctrine', Kelsen, *Principles of International Law* (n 40)
     309–10; d'Aspremont, 'The Doctrine of Fundamental Rights of States' (n 98).
118 Bernstorff (n 1) 174.
119 Kelsen, *General Theory of Law and State* (n 15) 31.

an obvious fiction motivated by the desire to trace back all international law to the 'free will' of the State and thereby maintain the idea that the State is 'sovereign' . . . [This view] does not serve the purpose for which it was devised.[120]

For example, that a newly formed State cannot escape the validity of general international law demonstrates that international law is not formulated entirely in contractual circumstances and may apply irrespective of a State's 'will', consent or participation.[121] Similarly, it is possible to prescribe obligations to new States created via treaty, as is observable in the (admittedly exceptional) cases of the Free City of Danzig[122] and Vatican City.[123] But, more crucially:

> [e]ven if all international law had the character of contractual law, it would still not be possible to maintain the idea that the States are sovereign because they are not subject to a superior legal order restricting their free will . . . [because a] treaty concluded by two States can have a legal effect . . . only if there is a general norm by which the treaty is qualified as a norm-creating fact.[124]

Thus, the validation of a contract presupposes a higher norm (such as *pacta sunt servanda*) establishing that contractual/treaty agreements be adhered to.[125] Accordingly, the legal order regulates its own creation via the application of a superior, validating norm. Binding quality is not derived from the consent or natural status of the addressee, but from the legal order itself, which ultimately finds its basis in the *Grundnorm*.[126] The theoretical justification for the overall validity of the *Grundnorm* will be considered in greater depth below.[127]

In criticism, it has been suggested that the Pure Theory of Law leads to a 'chicken and egg' scenario in relation to the origin of international law. If one considers the doctrine *pacta sunt servanda* to derive its validity from customary international law, as Kelsen did, then it may be argued that, in order for the

---

120 Ibid. 351.
121 Kelsen, *Principles of International Law* (n 40) 312.
122 Treaty of Versailles (28 June 1919) British and Foreign State Papers (1919) Vol CXIII (HM Stationery Office, 1922), Article 104.
123 Lateran Treaty (11 February 1929) 130 British and Foreign State Papers 791.
124 Kelsen, *General Theory of Law and State* (n 15) 354.
125 Kelsen, *Principles of International Law* (n 40) 314.
126 'With respect to its reason of validity, the conventional international law is inferior to the customary international law . . . The binding force of customary law rests . . . on the hypothesis that international custom is a law-creating fact. This hypothesis may be called the basic norm . . . it is presupposed by jurists interpreting legally the conduct of States', Kelsen, *Principles of International Law* (n 40) 314.
127 See below at Section 5.1.2.5.

behaviour of States to generate custom, States must have factually existed prior to international law. Kelsen denied this assertion. He argued it was possible that primitive social groups developed *simultaneously* with the establishment of international law (a view explored in Chapter 2), and, 'even if the existence of States really preceded the existence of international law, the *historical* relation between national and international legal orders does not preclude the *logical* relation which, it is maintained, exists between their reasons of validity'.[128] Once international law was established, the domestic and international legal systems must necessarily form part of a monistic legal order validated by the *Grundnorm*. Thus, on the establishment of international law, national legal orders may, as a matter of logic, take their position below it in a hierarchical system.[129]

More will be said on this matter in the remaining sub-sections below. For now, it suffices to highlight that the logic of the Pure Theory of Law appears to solve many of the complex doctrinal issues relating to the direct regulation of non-State actors. The prestige surrounding 'international legal personality', linked with a historically based, sociological/empirical view of the State that exerts a 'sovereign will', is stripped away. Concerns surrounding the political legitimacy of addressees are invalid. In addition, the subjects of international law are uncoupled from law creation and, thus, from contractarian explanations of validity.[130] Although Kelsen's approach was criticised for ignoring the social reality of State power and its ties to the validity of law, his innovative approach foreshadowed the diminishing power of the State in the wake of globalisation.[131] Any relevant actor may be a subject. Thus, non-State actors may 'possess' ILP. Any entity may act as law creator. Thus, non-State actors may be ascribed law-making competence. Yet, unlike the approach utilised in Chapter 4, this is not strictly necessary in order to establish an obligation. Legal validity is not contingent on consent or participation. As such, '[e]ven if prevailing international law left it up to the States to determine the organs authorised to conclude a treaty, this was an allocation of competency that emanated from international law.'[132] Everything is derived from the normative hierarchy of the legal order. Particularly illustrative of this point is the fact that the average, individual human person, the ultimate addressee of every legal norm, has clearly had no direct personal correspondence with the State agent involved in the drafting or conclusion of the treaty.[133] Thus, according to the Pure Theory

---

128 Kelsen, *Principles of International Law* (n 40) 418–19 (emphasis added).
129 Ibid.; Kelsen, *General Theory of Law and State* (n 15) 370.
130 Hall (n 109) 299–300; Bernstorff (n 1) 68.
131 Peter Caldwell, *Popular Sovereignty and the Crisis of German Constitutional Law: The Theory & Practice of Weimar Constitutionalism* (Duke University Press, 1997) 90–7; Somek, 'Stateless Law' (n 1) 769–70; Bernstorff (n 1) 66.
132 Bernstorff (n 1) 174.
133 Kelsen, 'On the Basic Norm' (n 30) 110; Kelsen, *Introduction to the Problems of Legal Theory* (n 12) 45–6; Nijman (n 77) 190; Vinx (n 58) 211–14; Sandrine Baum, *Hans Kelsen and the Case for Democracy* (Colchester, UK, European Consortium for Political Research Press, 2013) 1–63.

of Law, nothing precludes the establishment of directly binding international obligations for non-State actors. Advancing this argument, the next sub-section will address related concerns from both Kelsenian scholars and external critics relating to the establishment of a monist hierarchy of legal norms.

5.1.2.3 *Validity and the monist legal order*

A number of consequences stem from the Pure Theory of Law's unique revision of the concept of sovereignty outlined above. These effects must be critically discussed before we proceed further. It has been established that the validity of normative claims cannot logically be derived from empirical facts. Instead, the source of their validity must also be normative. Kelsen ultimately roots the validity of all legal norms in a single presupposed basic norm. A monist view of the legal order must be adopted as a necessary consequence. This is because all legal norms, distinguished from other normative spheres on the basis of their prescription of socially imminent coercive sanctions, necessarily belong to the same normative hierarchy.[134] Thus, although States may be authorised to create international law, it is international law itself that provides this empowerment. As such, the sovereignty of the ultimate foundation of legal validity, the *Grundnorm*, and the primacy of international law over domestic law appear to be the logical consequences of the Pure Theory of Law.[135] Yet, interestingly, Kelsen recognised that there was in fact a *choice* between the primacy of the municipal and international legal orders.[136] It is this claim to which we now turn.

Kelsen's *choice hypothesis* proceeds from two potential postulates. The legal order is either: (1) a monist system in which the international sphere is superior, and the national legal order derives its validity therefrom;[137] or (2) a monist system in which a *single* national legal order is superior, and the international sphere is validated by that State's recognition.[138] The second view essentially denies or ignores the validity of the legal orders of all other States.[139] The validity of international law may only be conceived from the perspective of a single State; every State establishes the validity of international law, and thus of every other external State, via its own, individual, national legal order.[140] Although Kelsen openly admitted that this view was compatible with the Pure Theory of Law,[141] he stated that:

---

134 Kelsen, *General Theory of Law and State* (n 15) 373.
135 Kelsen, *Principles of International Law* (n 40) 412.
136 Bernstorff (n 1) 105.
137 Kelsen, *Pure Theory* (n 4) 336.
138 Ibid. 333.
139 'Since the legal existence of other States also rests on recognition by one's own State, the legal system of one's own State must be imagined as extending over the legal systems of other States', Kelsen, *Introduction to the Problems of Legal Theory* (n 12) 115.
140 Kelsen, *Pure Theory* (n 4) 333.
141 Ibid. 338–44; Bernstorff (n 1) 106.

> [t]he dogma of sovereignty, resulting in the primacy of the legal system of
> one's own State, corresponds completely to a subjectivistic view that
> ultimately collapses into solipsism, the view that would comprehend the
> single individual, the 'I', as the centre of the world.[142]

Kelsen's preference for the primacy of the international order is evident in
his analysis of the apparent 'equality of States',[143] in that the primacy of the
national legal order would result in all other State legal orders, as well as
international law, being conceived as derived legal sub-orders of the legal order
of a single State:[144]

> The sovereignty of one State excludes the sovereignty of every other State
> . . . Most exponents of these views do not think them out to their last
> consequences . . . the theorist's own State [is] the sovereign centre of the
> world. But this philosophy is incapable of comprehending other States as
> equal to the philosopher's own State.[145]

In light of these responses and the aims of this study, the primacy of international law is favoured. This approach advances the liberation of international
law from the State-centricity of legal personality, law-making capacity and
binding quality and, as such, advances the theoretical scope for the direct
international regulation of non-State entities.

There are two further matters relating to the monist structure of the
international order proposed by the Pure Theory of Law that have proven
problematic. These have been broken down into two further sub-sections in
order to maintain clarity. Although these critiques may, at times, seem
somewhat divorced from the topic of non-State actors, they are recurring issues
that threaten to undermine the application of the Pure Theory of Law as a
whole. As such, it is important to assess whether these criticisms present
insurmountable challenges that fundamentally undermine its methodology and
thus negate its utility in the context of non-State actors. Moreover, they bring
full circle many of the arguments addressed in Chapter 2 of this study relating
to the source and binding quality of international law, which have proven a
persistent source of disagreement among scholars.

5.1.2.4 Monism and coercion

It has been established that Kelsen's adoption of the Austinian 'coercive order'
paradigm enables scholars to delineate the norms that are relevant to legal study

---

142 Kelsen, *Introduction to the Problems of Legal Theory* (n 12) 116.
143 Kelsen, 'The Principle of Sovereign Equality' (n 116) 212; Joseph Kunz, 'The Vienna
     School and International Law' (1934) 11 *NYU LQ Rev* 307, 401.
144 Bernstorff (n 1) 106.
145 Kelsen, *General Theory of Law and State* (n 15) 386; Somek, 'Kelsen Lives' (n 26) 422.

and thus enables law to exist within a unified order, absent conflicts with other normative spheres.[146] At the international level, the Pure Theory of Law treats war and reprisals as decentralised coercive sanctions, a position that has been criticised for recognising neither the political dimensions to these acts,[147] nor the distinction between acts of self-defence and sanction.[148] According to Kelsen's *bellum justum* principle, coercive force may only be resorted to in response to an international wrong or delict. This position has been criticised by Kelsen scholars on the basis that it violates the *is/ought* dichotomy:

> To make law's existence dependent on coercive elements – which are designed to guarantee its effectiveness – in effect means making it dependent on a factual occurrence . . . Kelsen could be read as making that mistake (i) by stipulating the 'coercive order' paradigm and (ii) by making the validity of a legal system dependent on (not equivalent to!) its continued effectiveness.[149]

As will be demonstrated, Kammerhofer's neo-Kelsenian interpretation of the theory is able to circumvent this flaw in a manner wholly consistent with Kelsen's project.

The coercive order paradigm was a foundational concept in the Pure Theory of Law, and, thus, its dismissal leads to the dissolution of the monistic unity of law that Kelsen argued was a logical by-product of his method.[150] As a consequence, insoluble conflicts between norms may arise.[151] The acceptance that more than one normative order (i.e. law, morals, ethics) can be valid in a given sphere dissolves the unity of law as an object of knowledge.[152] As coercion no longer differentiates the legal order from other normative orders, the *Grundnorm* cannot constitute the locus of validity that determines the necessary connection between international law and a subordinate order, such as domestic law.[153] The validity of domestic law, it could be claimed, is delegated by a *moral* or *theological* norm, rather than a higher legal order. This revelation is:

> an incredibly destructive force, and the *very possibility of normative systems could be denied*. On the other hand, it could have an incredibly *constructive*

---

146 Kelsen, *General Theory of Law and State* (n 15) 373, 376.
147 Carl Schmitt, *The Concept of the Political* (first published 1927, Chicago, IL, University of Chicago Press, 2008) 54.
148 Kammerhofer, 'Which Kelsen?' (n 59) 245; Derek Bowett, *Self-Defence in International Law* (Manchester, UK, Manchester University Press, 1958) 119; Somek, 'Kelsen Lives' (n 26) 421.
149 Kammerhofer, 'Which Kelsen?' (n 59) 239–40.
150 Ibid. 240.
151 Hans Kelsen, *General Theory of Norms* (first published 1979, Michael Hartney trans, Oxford, UK, OUP, 1991) 215.
152 Kammerhofer, 'Which Kelsen?' (n 59) 241.
153 Ibid. 243.

effect, gluing together the most unlikely norms and normative systems
. . . a unity of all norms, under the general *Grundnorm* repeated in every
particular *Grundnorm*: norms are to be observed, or, in other words, norms
are norms.[154]

Thus, the primary problem becomes one invented by traditional positivism: the
elevation of one 'true' body of law above all other normative orders. Under
Kammerhofer's neo-Kelsenian conception, law lies in a continuum with all other
normative orders. Even particular categories of law need not derive from the
same *Grundnorm* in perfect unity, because all norms are unified under a general
Grundnorm, whereas particular *Grundnorms* determine their *specific* sphere of
validity.

For instance, although Kelsen provides a workable relationship between
customary and conventional international law,[155] the two need not necessarily
'be one normative order, but a number of different normative orders "held
together" by an empirical classification'.[156] Although this well-reasoned line of
argument may appear at first sight to be fairly catastrophic for the Pure Theory
of Law, which has been built on the strict separation of law from other
normative orders, all it is doing, in effect, is recognising that multiple normative
orders may be valid simultaneously; perhaps not in the view of their respective
or 'particular' normative orders, but this does not by consequence lead to their
invalidation. Rather, the Pure Theory of Law may now claim stricter adherence
to its methodology, which liberated the creation and application of law from
an anthropomorphised State and, thus, advanced the possibility of direct non-
State actor regulation. Kammerhofer's work demonstrates that, although the
Pure Theory of Law, when strictly applied, can be severely deconstructive of
even Kelsen's interpretation of the structure of legal orders, it nevertheless leaves
his analysis of the State, legal personality, sovereignty and law-making largely
untouched.[157] The validity of law remains disconnected from the State. Socio-
psychological and historical explanations of the State as the bearer of a 'sovereign
will' possessing innate rights and duties remain untenable methodological
breaches of the *is/ought* dichotomy. Thus, for the purposes of this study, the
Pure Theory of Law remains theoretically viable.

5.1.2.5 *The Pure Theory of Law as natural law*

The final issue stemming from the above discussion of monism is likely the most
common criticism advanced against the Pure Theory of Law: that it is essentially

---

154   Ibid.
155   Kelsen, *Principles of International Law* (n 40) 314.
156   Kammerhofer, 'Which Kelsen?' (n 59) 247; Kammerhofer, 'The Benefits of the Pure Theory
       of Law' (n 5) 52–3.
157   Ibid. 53–5.

natural law.[158] The basis of the validity of all law in a presupposed basic norm that cannot be positively determined has been equated with the presupposition of binding commandments from the divine. As Lloyd cogently surmised, the *Grundnorm* is 'rather like the idea of the world supported by an elephant, the rules not permitting you to ask what supports the elephant'.[159] Similarly, for Hall, Kelsen does not solve the fundamental issues that stem from positive law, but 'simply tidies them up and relocates them'.[160] Kelsen himself stated that, '[i]f one wishes to regard [the *Grundnorm*] as an element of natural-law doctrine . . . very little objection can be raised'.[161] From this statement, one could infer that Kelsen's quest to rid jurisprudence of all natural law elements was substantially flawed; rather, he was guilty of the very methodological duality exhibited by Grotius.[162] Yet, he did offer some important points of qualification:

> [T]he theory of the basic norm may be considered a natural law doctrine in keeping with Kant's transcendental logic. There still remains the enormous difference which separates, and forever must separate, the transcendental conditions of all empirical knowledge and consequently the laws prevailing in nature on the one side from the transcendent metaphysics beyond all experience on the other.[163]

Thus, Kelsen conceived a real difference between a norm that 'simply makes possible the cognition of positive law as a meaningful order, and a natural law doctrine which proposes to establish a just order beyond, and independent of, all positive law'.[164] Although the basic norm may serve the same *validating* function as that of a naturalist principle of 'absolute justice', and although its existence also lies beyond positivist determination, its purpose is entirely different, and its content is *entirely empty*.[165] The basic norm simply makes the cognition of positive legal norms possible; it is the lens through which norms are discernible. It is simply the idea of the ideal; an expression of pure *ought*, without which one could not even perceive a norm as an *ought* claim:[166]

158 Verdross' conception of the Pure Theory of Law invoked natural law: Alfred Verdross, 'Die allgemeinen Rechtsgrundsätze des Völkerrechts' in Alfred Verdross, *Gesellschaft, Staat, und Recht. Untersuchungen zur Reinen Rechtslehre. Festschrift für Hans Kelsen* (The Hague, Netherlands, Springer, 1931) 358; Bernstorff (n 1) 154–5; Kammerhofer, *Uncertainty* (n 31) 210–35.
159 Dennis Lloyd, *The Idea of Law* (revised edn, London, Penguin, 1981) 194.
160 Hall (n 109) 300.
161 Kelsen, *General Theory of Law and State* (n 15) 437.
162 See Chapter 2 at Section 2.1.1.
163 Kelsen, *General Theory of Law and State* (n 15) 437–8.
164 Ibid.
165 Bernstorff (n 1) 115–16.
166 Kammerhofer, *Uncertainty* (n 31) 259.

> Just as the State is not an entity different from the law but is to be . . .
> explained away, as the unification of the normative functions of law, the
> basic norm is not something actually willed by any real or imaginary being
> . . . but merely the function of making possible a normative interpretation
> of a 'modally different substratum'.[167]

As such, the basis of the Pure Theory of Law is a value-neutral presumption of
normative legal validity necessary for the cognition of a positively defined legal
order, and not a theological ideal with prescribed, substantive moral content.[168]

   Kelsen's theoretical project involved maintaining the 'normativity' of law
inherent within the natural law theoretical tradition, while rejecting appeals to
an ultimate moral basis for the system of norms. At the same time, Kelsen seeks
to retain the positive determination of the content of legal norms, while
rejecting the inseparability of law and fact maintained by dominant positivist
jurisprudence.[169] Thus, the peculiarity of Kelsen's theory lies in its claim to
formulating a strictly normative theory of positive law, rooted neither in
empirical facts nor in naturalist absolutes. The manner in which Kelsen justified
this position varied throughout his career.[170] His appeals to Kant's theory of
knowledge during his long classical phase have been subject to significant
scholarly analysis.[171] This argument proceeds from the claim that a similar
presupposition to that of the *Grundnorm* is necessary in the field of the natural
sciences. For example, even the sensual perception of events occurring in
empirical reality in terms of 'cause and effect' would either present us:

> directly with the metaphysics of infinity, or a 'first cause' must be pre-
> supposed in order that the series be complete . . . we may assume a first
> cause as a limiting idea, knowing that no such entity exists or even could
> exist.[172]

Yet the presupposition of 'causality' as a lens through which the mind can
perceive the empirical world is necessary to the validity of scientific claims.[173]
As such, 'every scientific endeavour legitimately makes assumptions or presup-
positions that are in some sense "ultimate" but are often left unexpressed.'[174]

---

167 Richard Tur, 'The Kelsenian Enterprise' in Tur and Twining (n 2) 154.
168 Ibid. 155.
169 Stanley Paulson, 'The Neo-Kantian Dimension of Kelsen's Pure Theory of Law' (1992)
     12 *OJLS* 320.
170 Stanley Paulson, 'Four Phases in Hans Kelsen's Legal Theory? Reflections on a
     Periodisation' (1998)18 OJIS 153.
171 Kelsen, *Pure Theory* (n 4) 202.
172 Tur, 'The Kelsenian Enterprise' (n 167) 169.
173 William Ebenstein, *The Pure Theory of Law* (New York, AM Kelley, 1969) 150–2.
174 Hamish Ross, 'Hans Kelsen and the Utopia of Theoretical Purism' (2001) 12 KCLJ 174,
     193.

On this reading, the *Grundnorm* (and more specifically the notion that Kelsen terms 'imputation')[175] serves, in Kantian parlance, as a *synthetic a priori* notion that makes the cognition of law as a unified normative order possible.[176] Ebenstein provides perhaps the most lucid expression of this argument:

> [A] self-contained natural science becomes metaphysics when it attempts to consider the origin of nature by means of concepts which permit it to treat only the processes within nature . . . We can say that natural science becomes metaphysics when it attempts to discuss the creation of the natural universe, and that jurisprudence goes beyond the normative sphere when it attempts to discuss the creation of the world of law . . . Just as self-contained natural science can say nothing of its own nature but must presuppose it as a hypothesis, self-contained legal science has its hypothesis in the basic norm.[177]

This justification is consistent with the distinction drawn above between the Pure Theory of Law and natural law. The *Grundnorm* is 'a methodological maxim, a norm of method which is ontologically neutral . . . [It] simply makes evident the limits of human knowledge generally, and the limits of positive, normative legal knowledge in particular'.[178] The basic norm is an epistemological device necessary for the cognition of legal norms;[179] it 'cuts off the possibility of moving beyond acceptable metaphysics to illusory speculation about the nature of the will which logically correlates to the basic norm'.[180] The *Grundnorm* is Pure Theory's 'big bang'. There is no need to ask who willed the *Grundnorm*, or to locate that will in a deity, the supernatural or an absolute subject. It must simply and pragmatically be presumed by anyone seeking to adopt a normative view of law.

It must be acknowledged that the strength of this Kantian justification has been subject to cogent criticism.[181] Perhaps the most incisive is advanced by Paulson, who highlights the difficulties in the wholesale replication of the structure of the Kantian proof for the *a priori* nature of the category of causality in natural science in relation to normative science. This is because one cannot have knowledge of the empirical world unconditioned by *a priori* categories such as causality. If one is to agree that we perceive the natural world through

---

175 Kelsen treats 'imputation' as analogous to 'causality' in natural science: Hans Kelsen, 'Causality and Imputation' (1950) 61 *Ethics* 1.

176 Cf Ebenstein, 'Demythologizing Legal Thought' (n 21) 628–39; Ross (n 174) 192.

177 Ebenstein, *Pure Theory* (n 173) 151.

178 Tur, 'The Kelsenian Enterprise' (n 167) 170; ibid 32.

179 Kelsen, *Pure Theory* (n 4) 72, 202–5.

180 Tur, 'The Kelsenian Enterprise' (n 167) 174.

181 Wilson (57) 37; Stanley Paulson, 'The Neo-Kantian Dimension (n 169) 322–32; Uta Bindreiter, *Why Grundnorm? A Treatise on the Implications of Kelsen's Doctrine* (The Hague, Netherlands, Springer, 2002) 24–8.

sense experience at all, one must *of necessity* agree that our perception is conditioned by causality. Whether the same claim can be made for knowledge of the law is open to dispute, for, to experience law is not to demand that one must perceive law in purely normative terms. It is, after all, feasible that one might experience law as necessarily connected to social facts (*is*), as contended by dominant positivist scholarship. Although there is scope for Kelsen to formulate a neo-Kantian variant of this proof that begins with the claim that one experiences legal norms as a 'given' and, in order to cognise them, one must, by necessity, presuppose the category of 'imputation' just as 'causality' must be presupposed for the cognition of the empirical world, it may be contended that we *do not* experience law *qua* norms as a given object of study. Accordingly, there is nothing to prevent the sceptic from claiming that we experience law *qua* fact. Thus, it is only if one accepts the normative view of law that one can rely on the Kantian (or at least neo-Kantian)[182] justification of the *Grundnorm* as an *a priori* condition of legal knowledge. There is, therefore, *a choice*.

This analysis reveals that, although the category of imputation might be successfully formulated as a necessary transcendental premise for the cognition of law in normative terms, its object (law *qua* norms) is not of necessity a given in the same way that raw sense data are a given in natural science. Rather, one is left with an empty formal category that is not oriented towards a particular object of study.[183] Thus, cognition of law, taken as a system of norms, demands that we posit the validity of norms via the *Grundnorm* as an *a priori* category of knowledge,[184] but this is not strictly *necessary*.[185] Kammerhofer lucidly exposes the crux of the issue. When natural science attempts to explain its 'given' object of study (empirical reality), it attempts to do something that is impossible for normative theory:

> because here the theory through the creation of the intellectual super-structure determines its object: the ought. A purported 'given' that does not satisfy the criteria of normative theory is not a 'given' of normative scholarship . . . The choice is existential, because everyone cognising norms has already made the choice, even if they are not aware that they have done it. It is an expression of our existential freedom to choose our own dogmas and is thus most profound.[186]

182 Geert Edel, 'The Hypothesis of the Basic Norm: Kelsen and Hermann Cohen' in Paulson and Litschewski-Paulson (n 2) 195–219.

183 Stefan Hammer, 'A Neo-Kantian Theory of Knowledge in Kelsen's Pure Theory of Law' in Paulson and Litschewski-Paulson (n 2) 185–90.

184 On the defensibility of this view in light of Cohen's neo-Kantian philosophy, see: Edel (n 182) 212–19; Kammerhofer, *Uncertainty* (n 31) 259–61.

185 Paulson, 'The Neo-Kantian Dimension' (n 169) 331–2.

186 Kammerhofer, *Uncertainty* (n 31) 260–1.

Although this revelation undermines the *necessity* of a purely normative conception of law, the foregoing analysis is not necessarily fatal. Rather, Kelsen's claim to uniqueness in solving the antinomy between natural and positive law is undermined, and the Pure Theory simply 'takes its place alongside other normativist legal theories . . . perhaps best understood as offering *a legal point of view*'.[187] Although admittedly somewhat underwhelming, this is all that is necessary in the context of this study. It is beyond the scope of this work to embark on further critical discussion of this point, the topic having been treated in considerable detail by Kelsen scholars. Although it may not be possible to definitively compel readers to adopt this normative view, it is hoped that the more modest claim that the perspective lends itself strongly to the context of non-State actor regulation is at least *compelling*. The adoption of a normative view has utility, both as a deconstructive, critical methodology that further exposes the weakness of traditional doctrine, and as a potential theoretical foundation that is responsive to contemporary challenges faced by public international law and upon which the direct international regulation of non-State entities may be constructed. Thus, the practical impediments to the State-based regulation of non-State actors stemming from the unwillingness or incapacity of weak governance States to safeguard human rights may be overcome, at least in theory. The feasibility of the practical utilisation of the theory will be explored below in the final substantive section of this chapter.

5.2 Appraising the practical utility of the Pure Theory of Law

With the theoretical suitability of the Pure Theory of Law to the topic addressed by this monograph having been sketched, the remainder of this chapter seeks to evaluate the contemporary relevance of the theory in light of international practice relating to non-State actors. It was acknowledged above that Kelsen's perspective never gained widespread acceptance in international legal scholarship, and yet, '[m]uch of modern public international law appears to coincide with his ideas and aspirations'.[188] Esteemed jurists such as Antonio Cassese have emphasised the influence of Kelsen's monistic theory as 'an admirable theoretical construction . . . in advance of its time', which has had significant influence on the role of international law in regulating the behaviour of States and their officials.[189] In recent years, new formalist theoretical approaches have been the subject of much academic consideration. D'Aspremont's scholarship, based on a post-modern Hartian theoretical model, embraces a return to formal methods

---

187 Paulson, 'The Neo-Kantian Dimension' (n 169) 332; Joseph Raz, *The Authority of Law* (first published 1979, 2nd edn, Oxford, UK, OUP, 2009) 140–5; Bindreiter (n 181) 90–5.

188 Somek, 'Kelsen Lives' (n 26) 417–18; Charles Leben, 'Hans Kelsen and the Advancement of International Law' (1998) 9 *EJIL* 287.

189 Antonio Cassese, *International Law* (2nd edn, Oxford, UK, OUP, 2004) 216.

of law identification in light of the rise of soft law, new governance initiatives and indeterminacy in the formulation of custom and general principles of international law.[190] Similarly, Kammerhofer's neo-Kelsenian approach seeks to resolve the inconsistencies exposed by his constructive criticism of Kelsen's formalism.[191] Having further stratified the Pure Theory of Law, Kammerhofer's approach permits its theoretical effects relating to the nature of the State, sovereignty and the imputation of legal norms to non-State actors to find firmer, more consistent foundations. D'Aspremont and Kammerhofer have recently collaborated on an edited collection that includes detailed analysis of the influence of Kelsenian positivism in public international law.[192]

Another explicit endorsement of the Pure Theory of Law's novel treatment of ILP is evident in the work of Roland Portmann, who advocates a hybrid of Kelsenian formalism and the individualist scholarship of Lauterpacht.[193] The compatibility of the two approaches is readily evident, in that Kelsen viewed legal personality as 'merely a point of attribution, after pausing at which, international law continued on its way . . . and ultimately addressed the individual human being'.[194] In line with Kelsen, Portmann finds that there are no *a priori* legal persons (with the exception of individuals),[195] and no entities are of necessity *excluded* from being legal persons.[196] The addressees of legal obligations are prescribed by legal norms, and, by the same token, there are no presumed, substantive competences stemming from legal personality, including law-making capacity.[197] Thus, *recognition* of the legal personality of non-State entities by States is irrelevant, as mere recognition does not produce any legal consequence.[198] At the same time, recognition by judicial bodies may serve an evidentiary purpose, clarifying those actors that are the addressees of international obligations. Portmann suggests that pronouncements by the ICTY that the ICRC is bound by a customary rule of confidentiality may be viewed in this manner.[199]

190 Jean d'Aspremont, *Formalism and the Sources of International Law: A Theory of the Ascertainment of Legal Rules* (Oxford, UK, OUP, 2012).
191 Kammerhofer, 'Which Kelsen?' (n 59) 225.
192 Jean d'Aspremont and Jörg Kammerhoder (eds), *International Legal Positivism in a Post-Modern World* (Cambridge, UK, CUP, 2015).
193 Portmann (n 11) 271–81; Nijman (n 77) 457–73.
194 Nijman (n 77) 450.
195 '[T]here is a rebuttable presumption that individuals possess personality in international law when crimes and basic human rights are concerned', Portmann (n 11) 273.
196 Ibid. 272.
197 Ibid. 274–5.
198 Ibid. 272.
199 *Prosecutor v Simic and Others* (Decision on the Prosecution Motion under Rule 73) IT-95-9 (27 July 1999), para 46.

Although the imputation of direct obligations to non-State actors is not theoretically excluded by the formalist approach, the types of existing obligation that may be interpreted in this manner are likely to be fairly minimal:

> In general, it may be more difficult to find convincing arguments for the application of . . . ordinary custom to non-State actors, for they have historically been developed in relation to States and analogy may be delicate.[200]

One exception may be the rules of customary international humanitarian law.[201] Although the rules applicable to conflicts between two or more States have traditionally been more detailed and robust, recent recognition that such rules are applicable in instances of internal armed conflict may circumvent the exclusively State-centric subject matter of those rules.[202] Furthermore, it cannot be denied that, in relation to *jus cogens* norms, 'there is a presumption for their direct application towards individuals. In so far as analogy with individual human beings is not precluded on logical grounds, this also holds true for other non-State actors, for example private corporations'.[203] The practical feasibility of this position, which is born of Kelsenian logic, will be assessed below in the remaining sub-sections of this chapter.

5.2.1 *Manifestations in international practice*

The lack of a sound theoretical basis for the attribution of direct international obligations to non-State armed groups was considered at length in Chapter 4 of this study.[204] According to the Pure Theory of Law, the existence of such duties is not at all problematic. The addressees and validity of international law are no longer tied to the creators of those rules. As such, it may be concluded that the existing rules of non-international armed conflict directly bind non-State armed groups, even absent their express consent. By the same token, there is nothing to prevent the elaboration of further international obligations addressing non-State armed groups, in the form of new multilateral treaties, or via international custom. Yet, the position regarding MNEs is somewhat different. To date, no analogous direct international obligations have been established, except those relating to individuals under international criminal law.

---

200 Portmann (n 11) 280.
201 See Chapter 4 at Section 4.1.4.
202 *Prosecutor v Martić* IT-95-11-R61 (8 March 1996) para 11; Jean-Marie Henckaerts and Louise Dowald-Beck, *ICRC, Customary International Humanitarian Law* Vol 1 (Cambridge, UK, CUP, 2005) xxxv.
203 Portmann (n 11) 280.
204 See Chapter 4 at Section 4.2.

There are, however, a number of practical illustrations in international jurisprudence that appear to recognise the feasibility of the direct regulation of MNEs by way of the Pure Theory's formalist logic. The ICJ's *LaGrand* Advisory Opinion is one such example.[205]

In *LaGrand*, it was held that a provision of the VCCR created direct rights for individuals.[206] Although the PCIJ's *Free City of Danzig* decision[207] has been considered virtually identical in principle to *LaGrand*,[208] it is suggested that the dualist reading outlined in Chapter 2 renders the former's position on individual rights and obligations far more ambiguous.[209] *LaGrand* concerned an action between the US and Germany relating to two German brothers who were alleged to have been involved in an armed robbery that resulted in one fatality.[210] The brothers were convicted of first-degree murder and sentenced to death. It was conceded by the US authorities that, throughout all proceedings,[211] no information had been provided to the brothers relating to consular assistance pursuant to Article 36(1)(b) VCCR.[212] Domestic challenges on the grounds of *habeas corpus* initiated by the brothers were not permitted during subsequent proceedings, as federal courts may only consider legal arguments that have previously been presented. Given the brothers' ignorance as to their rights to consular assistance, no such challenge was permitted.[213] Both brothers were executed prior to the ICJ's ruling, despite an order to stay proceedings until the Court had passed a verdict.[214]

The case continued at the ICJ posthumously. The German government submitted that the US authorities had violated both Germany's rights and the individual rights of the LaGrand brothers under Article 36(1)(b) VCCR.[215] Article 36(2) requires domestic law to give full effect to Article 36(1)(b).[216] Thus, the failure of the US to assess the LaGrand brothers' *habeas corpus* claims

---

205 *LaGrand Case (Germany v United States of America)* ICJ Reports [2001] (hereafter, *LaGrand*); Robert Jennings, 'The LaGrand Case' (2002) 1 *Int'l Cts & Tribunals* 13.
206 Vienna Convention on Consular Relations (24 April 1963) 500 UNTS 95 (hereafter, VCCR).
207 *Jurisdiction of the Courts of Danzig* (Advisory Opinion) 1928 PCIJ (ser. B) No 15.
208 James Crawford, *The ILC's Articles on Responsibility of States: Introduction, Text and Commentaries* (Cambridge, UK, CUP, 2002) 209.
209 Chapter 2 at Section 2.2.
210 *LaGrand* (n 205) para 14.
211 Ibid. para 16.
212 VCCR (n 206) Article 36(1)(b).
213 *LaGrand* (n 205) para 23.
214 Ibid. paras 29–34.
215 '[T]he United States . . . violated its international legal obligations to Germany, in its own right and in its right of diplomatic protection of its nationals', ibid para 11(1).
216 'The rights referred to in paragraph (1) of this article shall be exercised in conformity with the laws and regulations of the receiving State, subject to the proviso, however, that the said laws and regulations must enable full effect to be given to the purposes for which the rights accorded under this article are intended', VCCR (n 206) Article 36(2).

could be seen to breach their direct rights as individuals.[217] The ICJ, citing precedents relating to treaty interpretation, rather than the direct effect of treaties on individuals, relied on the express text of the provision:[218]

> [T]his subparagraph ends with the following language: 'The said authorities shall inform the person concerned without delay of *his rights* under this paragraph' ... The clarity of these provisions, viewed in their context, admits of no doubt ... the Court concludes that Article 36, paragraph 1 creates individual rights, which ... may be invoked in this Court by the national State of the detained person.[219]

There was no rebuttable presumption relating to whether individuals may or may not be the direct addressees of treaties; rather, it depended entirely on the content of the legal rule in question.[220] Additionally, it was unnecessary to bolster the importance of the individual application of the right by virtue of its 'status' or 'prestige' as a human right, as Germany had sought to argue.[221]

Clearly, the ICJ's approach in *LaGrand* correlates with Kelsen's theoretical perspective, and, in this regard, the case has been cited as illustrating the death of Anzilotti's *Mavrommatis* fiction.[222] The Court affirmed its position in *Avena*.[223] There is no reason, according to the Pure Theory of Law, preventing the imputation of direct international rights and obligations to collective or corporate actors either. Indeed, subsequent instances of international investment arbitration have indicated that arbitrators 'do not consider individuals (understood to encompass corporations) as mere beneficiaries of rights

---

217 The US maintained that, although such provisions *benefited* individuals, they did not confer direct rights; *LaGrand* (n 205) para 76.
218 *Acquisition of Polish Nationality* (1923) PCIJ (Ser. B) No 7, 20; *Competence of the General Assembly for the Admission of a State to the United Nations* (Advisory Opinion) ICJ Reports [1950] 8; *Arbitral Award of 31 July 1989 (Guinea-Bissau v Senegal)* (Advisory Opinion) ICJ Reports [1991] 69–70, para 48; *Territorial Dispute (Libyan Arab Jamahiriya/Chad)* (Advisory Opinion) ICJ Reports [1994] 25, para 51.
219 *LaGrand* (n 205) para 77.
220 Portmann (n 11) 202–3.
221 Cf *LaGrand* (n 205) para 78; Right to Information on Consular Assistance in the Framework of Güarantees of the Due Process Law (1 October 1999) OC-16/99 IACtHR, (ser. A) No 16, paras 85–7.
222 Alain Pellet, 'The Second Death of Euripide Mavrommatis? Notes on the International Law Commission's Draft Articles on Diplomatic Protection' (2008) 7 *Int'l Cts & Tribunals* 33.
223 *Case Concerning Avena and Other Mexican Nationals (Mexico v United States)* ICJ Reports [2004] para 40; a number of domestic decisions contradicting the ICJ's logic have been rendered: *Sanchez-Llamas v Oregon*, 548 US 331 (Supreme Court 2006); *The Queen v Van Bergen* (2000) 261 AR 387 (Alberta Court of Appeal) para 15; Carsten Hoppe, 'Implementation of LaGrand and Avena in Germany and the United States: Exploring a Transatlantic Divide in Search of a Uniform Interpretation of Consular Rights' (2007) 18 *EJIL* 317.

contained in bilateral or multilateral investment treaties that are actually held by their State of nationality, but as the direct holders of these international rights'.[224] Similar arguments have been discussed by Muchlinski, who recognises the evolution of international norms dealing with corporations, investments and MNE–State contracts.[225] He cites as examples the *Texaco v Libya* and *Revere Copper* arbitrations,[226] which demonstrated the direct application of international law to MNEs in relation to bilateral investment treaties, though it is conceded that such an approach has not found uniform support in arbitral awards.[227]

Citing the judgments in *Mondev International Ltd* and *SGS v Philippines*,[228] Portmann concludes that, '[b]y referring to *LaGrand*, these tribunals appear to have affirmed direct rights of corporations under international investment treaties . . . [i]n doing so, they have manifested [Kelsen's] formal conception of international legal personality'.[229] Muchlinski has taken a critical view on this line of argument, though his remarks do not align with Kelsenian logic, which conceives of international personality as being wholly determined by the content of legal norms, as opposed to a doctrine entailing particular presumptions that give rise to 'full' or 'partial' personality. Muchlinski suggests that, 'the fact that States choose to give international legal rights or obligations to non-State actors does not require full international personality for the latter . . . There is no need to extrapolate international personality from this process'.[230] Yet, according to the Pure Theory of Law, this is *exactly* how legal personality comes about: the addressees of norms are determined during the law-making process, which remains primarily a competence of States, at present. A recent illustration in line with the approaches in *Texaco*[231] and *Revere Copper* is apparent in *Amco v*

224 Portmann (n 11) 204; Markos Karavias, *Corporate Obligations Under International Law* (Oxford, UK, OUP, 2013) 157–63.
225 Peter Muchlinski, 'Multinational Enterprises in International Law: Creating "Soft Law" Obligations and "Hard Law" Rights' in Cedric Ryngaert and Math Noortmann (eds), *Non-State Actor Dynamics in International Law: From Law-Takers to Law-Makers* (Aldershot, UK, Ashgate, 2010) 10–12; August Reinisch, 'The Changing International Legal Framework for Dealing with Non-State Actors' in Philip Alston (ed), *Non State Actors and Human Rights* (Oxford, UK, OUP, 2005) 37–89; Robert McCorquodale, 'An Inclusive International Legal System' (2004) 17 *LJIL* 477, 490–2.
226 An agreement between Texaco and Libya was subjected to international law as the contract expressly referred to principles of international law: *Texaco v Libya* (1978) 17 ILM 1; Julien Cantegreil, 'The Audacity of the Texaco/Calasiatic Award: René-Jean Dupuy and the Internationalisation of Foreign Investment Law' (2011) 22 *EJIL* 441; *Revere Copper* (1978) 17 ILM 1321.
227 Muchlinski, 'Multinational Enterprises' (n 225) 12.
228 *Mondev International Ltd v United States* (2002) 42 ILM 85 para 116; *Société Générale de Surveillance (SGS) v Republic of the Philippines* (Decision on Objections to Jurisdiction, 2004) 8 ICSID Reports 518 para 154.
229 Portmann (n 11) 204.
230 Muchlinski, 'Multinational Enterprises' (n 225) 13.
231 Cantegreil (n 226) 453–4.

Indonesia,[232] which applied international law to a contract between an MNE and the State of Indonesia, simply because the relevant article of the International Centre for the Settlement of Investment Disputes (ICSID) Convention stipulated so.[233]

Analogously, it has been convincingly argued by Karavias that internationalised functional contracts concluded between international organisations and corporate entities may contain international obligations directly addressing MNEs.[234] In particular, he highlights contracts for resource exploration under the 1982 Law of the Sea Convention between the International Seabed Authority and corporations,[235] and private loan agreements between business actors and the International Bank for Reconstruction and Development.[236] In both these scenarios:

> all stages of the contractual relationship, i.e. conclusion, performance, breach of contract, and dispute settlement are subject to international law. Such internationalisation is founded on the consent of States, as expressed in the international agreements structurally covering the contract between the international organisation and the corporation . . . thus submitting the bundles of bilateral contractual relationships to international law.[237]

The key point is that, in line with the Pure Theory of Law, the addressees of these norms are stipulated by the norms themselves. Personality is not restricted to States, and, thus, Kelsenian logic can both explain the formulation of bodies of international norms directly addressing corporations and leaves open the possibility of imputing human rights obligations to them, their lack of participation in the process of law creation notwithstanding. Although the instances evidencing the direct regulation of corporations may be underdeveloped at present, with specific rights and duties constrained to particular spheres or largely mediated via internationalised contracts, there is no limit to their expansion. Indeed, as a theoretical framing for these recent developments, the Pure Theory of Law is a perfect fit.[238]

232 *Amco Asia Corporation & Others v The Republic of Indonesia* (Resubmitted Case: Award on the Merits, 1990) 1 ICSID Reports 569.
233 Convention on the Settlement of Investment Disputes Between States and Nationals of Other States (18 March 1965) 575 UNTS 159, Article 42(1).
234 Karavias (n 224) 117–63.
235 Convention on the Law of the Sea (10 December 1982) 1833 UNTS 2; The International Seabed Authority's 2000 Regulations on Prospecting and Exploration for Polymetallic Nodules in the Area demand compliance with the 1982 UN Convention on the Law of the Sea. These regulations are incorporated into any resulting contracts with corporate actors: International Seabed Authority, 'Fact Sheet: Contractors for Seabed Exploration', www.isa.org.jm/files/documents/EN/Brochures/2014/ISAContractors.pdf, accessed 23 April 2016; Karavias (n 224) 120–5.
236 Ibid. 144.
237 Ibid. 162.
238 Leben (n 188) 303–4.

5.2.2 *Responding to realist criticism*

The above instances of international practice evidencing broad alignment with the Pure Theory of Law notwithstanding, it has been argued that the approach is particularly vulnerable to realist criticism. Although it would be impossible to explore every facet of realist critique advanced by this diverse tradition, some of the main concerns relating to the practical operation of international law under the theory will be addressed.[239] The Pure Theory of Law has long been accused of ignoring the political and social realities of international life, a consequence arising from its strict adherence to the *is/ought* dichotomy and, thus, its division of the empirical and normative realms.[240] Carl Schmitt famously remarked that, 'unity and purity are easily attained when the basic difficulty is emphatically ignored and when, for formal reasons, everything that contradicts the system is excluded as impure'.[241] Yet, although the Pure Theory of Law seeks to strip out what it deems extraneous considerations from the study of law, it cannot be accused of failing to respond to political and social realities. Indeed, it was arguably formulated as a consequence of these realities. Kelsen theorised:

> the equation of law with the State against the backdrop of the particular political situation of the Dual Monarchy, and, subsequently, of the Austrian Republic's polluted political atmosphere . . . the Pure Theory sought a legal answer to the (contemporary) problems concerning the identity of the State, political stability and threatened democracy . . . This legal theoretical exercise was therefore as much a socio-political and ethical political exercise.[242]

Yet, with this recognition came renewed criticism that Kelsen's work failed to completely eliminate the pollution stemming from subjective value judgements.[243] Rather, his work was a reflection of his own political predilections, concealed by a façade of objectivity.[244] The paradox of Kelsen's project and the ideological consequences it engenders – including the defence of democracy,

---

239 Todd Landman, *Protecting Human Rights: A Comparative Study* (Washington, DC, Georgetown University Press, 2005) 13–22; Martti Koskenniemi, 'Carl Schmitt, Hans Morgenthau, and the Image of Law in International Relations' in Michael Byers (ed), *The Role of Law in International Politics: Essays in International Relations and International Law* (Oxford, UK, OUP, 2001) 17–34; Koskenniemi, *The Gentle Civiliser* (n 3) 413–509.
240 The neo-realist school of international relations has been described as 'virtually law-blind . . . little more than pure theory stood on its head', Sylvesta (n 3) 440.
241 Schmitt, *Political Theology* (n 3) 21.
242 Nijman (n 77) 190–1; Bernstorff (n 1) 6.
243 Sylvesta (n 3) 416.
244 David Dyzenhaus, *Legality and Legitimacy, Carl Schmitt, Hans Kelsen, and Herman Heller in Weimar* (Oxford, UK, Clarendon Press, 1997) 104.

tolerance and moral relativism – must be acknowledged and may even aid its full comprehension.[245] But, it cannot be said that his logical, consistent, purely formal approach relies on these ideals for external validation. The Pure Theory of Law can, in principle, be mapped on to any legal order capable of normative presentation.

A more concerning area of weakness relates to the enforcement of international law, a factor that is evidently problematic irrespective of theoretical framing, owing in part to its decentralised nature. Yet, it is worth considering the effects of the Pure Theory of Law on the enforceability of international rules in order to assess current realities relating to non-State actor regulation and to forecast future developments. The role of international law in the monopolisation of the use of force was discussed above. This principle underscores Kelsen's monist conception of the legal order, according to which States possess the competence to act as agents of the international community, utilising coercive force only in response to a delict. However, despite the equality of all States to determine breaches and issue sanctions, there is clearly a wide asymmetry between their respective economic and military resources:[246]

> Where collective security is absent, the States, for their individual security, follow the policy of armaments, alliances and the balance of power. Under such a system a 'weak' State can hardly go to war or take reprisals against a more powerful State, whereas the latter may abuse its power.[247]

As such, dominant global powers may be more able to protect and represent their interests internationally. Moreover, superpowers may be free to operate as they please, unrestrained by even collective enforcement,[248] as a bully in a system of universal hypocrisy.[249] Given the emphasis placed on the vulnerability of many weak governance States to effectively respond to the challenges presented by increasingly powerful non-State actors, this factor is of pressing concern.

The scenario is perhaps best illustrated by Hedley Bull, who criticised Kelsen's presentation of war as a simple binary between those States committing delicts and those imposing sanctions, thereby ignoring the question of actual

---

245 Nijman (n 77) 166.
246 Kelsen, *Principles of International Law* (n 40) 14.
247 Joseph Kunz, 'Sanctions in International Law' (1960) 54 *AJIL* 324, 325.
248 US exceptionalism exemplifies this issue: John Quigley, 'The United States' Withdrawal from International Court of Justice Jurisdiction in Consular Cases: Reasons and Consequences' (2009) 19 *Duke J Comp & Int'l L* 263; Sarah Sewall and Carl Kaysen (eds), *The United States and the International Criminal Court: National Security and International Law* (Oxford, UK, Rowman & Littlefield, 2000).
249 Somek, 'Kelsen Lives' (n 26) 430.

'might'.[250] Kelsen does appear to address these concerns, though his response is quite undeveloped. He recognises that, during war, overpowering an opponent by force is often viewed as implicit in the intention of both parties, but responds that it is 'hardly possible to deny that the attacked State may have only the intention to defend itself, without overpowering the aggressor'.[251] This argument is not particularly compelling.[252] That the international legal order holds a monopoly on the use of force does not prevent a superpower from defying this norm, nor does it aid the injured State or States in enforcing sanctions against such an aggressor.[253] Hans Morgenthau, one of the fathers of realism in international relations, similarly stated that:

> [i]nternational law owes its existence to identical or complementary interests of states, backed by power as a last resort, or, where such identical interests do not exist, to a mere balance of power which prevents a State from breaking these rules of international law. Where there is neither community of interests nor balance of power, there is no international law.[254]

By emphasising that, 'sanctions be not only enacted but actually effective for legal rules to have reality', Morgenthau acknowledged the importance of the relative interests and power of national orders in international relations.[255] In his more socio-legal work, and quite distinct from the strict methodology underscoring his Pure Theory of Law, Kelsen recognised the primitive nature of the international legal system.[256] He felt that determinations relating to the legality of the use of force should be left to an international court of compulsory jurisdiction[257] and did not consider the centralisation of the enforcement of coercive sanctions particularly necessary:[258]

---

250 'The force monopoly of which Kelsen speaks . . . is a monopoly in law, not in political fact . . . aspirations are not themselves enough to bring changes about', Bull (n 3) 330.
251 Kelsen, *Principles of International Law* (n 40) 31.
252 Zolo (n 58) 314–16.
253 Aggressors acting without legal empowerment are essentially invisible to the discipline of law: Kelsen, *General Theory of Norms* (n 151) 103; although States may violate norms *prohibiting* aggression, this says little about the ability of the international community to respond: Morgenthau, 'Positivism, Functionalism and International Law' (n 3); Noberto Bobbio, 'Kelsen and Legal Power' in Paulson and Litschewski-Paulson (n 2) 499–500.
254 Morgenthau, 'Positivism, Functionalism and International Law' (n 3).
255 Koskenniemi, *The Gentle Civiliser* (n 3) 458.
256 Kelsen, *Pure Theory* (n 4) 323.
257 Hans Kelsen, 'Compulsory Adjudication of International Disputes' (1943) 37 *AJIL* 397; Bernstorff (n 1) 191–224.
258 Realists such as Carr also note that the lack of centralisation and enforcement of international law does not 'deprive it of the title to be considered as law', Edward H Carr, *The Twenty Years' Crisis* (first published 1939, Basingstoke, UK, Palgrave Macmillan, 2001) 160–1.

[C]ases where the law remains unenforced because the delinquent is more powerful than his opponent may be frequent ... Nevertheless, the importance of a centralisation restricted to the establishment of tribunals without the centralisation of the execution of the sanction should not be underestimated.[259]

For Kelsen, the chance of adherence to law was far stronger in instances in which the situation could be adjudicated by a centralised judicial body, irrespective of the capacity to enforce a ruling.[260] In addition, Kelsen viewed the formal justice of law that demands:

[its] general and predictable application independent of power resources and morality ... [as] a means to address and argue about shared standards and fundamental experiences of injustice within the only communicative medium that – by way of its formality – is capable of transcending power asymmetries and idiosyncratic preferences.[261]

More recently, Somek has advanced a similar argument, issuing a defence from the perspective of the Pure Theory of Law. He highlights the rise of 'rationalist' American scholarship in international law and international relations, which suggests that, 'the shape of international society can be explained by looking at [the State as] a composite unity that uses scarce resources and engages in cooperation in order to attain its own ends'.[262] For scholars such as Goldsmith and Posner, in the absence of a reason for States to adhere to international law when it is contrary to their interests, international law rests on that self-interest alone.[263] It does not constrain the activity of States, but is the reflection of the combined effects of State conduct: '[i]nternational law emerges from States' pursuit of self-interested policies on the international stage. International law is ... endogenous to State interests. It is not a check on State self-interest; it is a product of State self-interest'.[264] As such, States abide by rules as they please and cannot be forced or compelled to act in compliance.

Noting the Hegelian character of such arguments and their proximity to the idealisations dispelled by the Pure Theory of Law, Somek argues that States cannot be reduced to undifferentiated unitary actors, as rational entities with

259 Kelsen, *Collective Security* (n 25) 14.
260 Kelsen cites the conclusion of alliance treaties as a means of overcoming the issue of powerful opponents: ibid. 39–42.
261 Bernstorff (n 1) 258.
262 Somek, 'Kelsen Lives' (n 26) 415.
263 Jack Goldsmith and Eric Posner, *The Limits of International Law* (Oxford, UK, OUP, 2005) 9; cf Robert Keohane, 'Rational Choice Theory and International Law: Insights and Limitations' (2002) 31 *J Leg Stud* 307.
264 Goldsmith and Posner (n 263) 14.

complete and uniform preferences.[265] 'Realism in international law is often idealism with regard to the power of States or the discernibility of the collective interest.'[266] According to the Pure Theory of Law, the principle that States *ought to behave as they have customarily* is all that underlies the validity of customary international law. The explanation of customary law via other phenomena such as social solidarity creates a 'doubled' or 'hypostatised' element separate to the purely normative requirement.[267] For Somek, this observation is:

> highly relevant to currently fashionable attempts to construct public international law from the vantage point of reasons for compliance . . . such theories are theories of validity in disguise, for what they are really concerned with are *good* reasons to abide by international obligations . . . Compliance theories, consequently, are confronted with a recurring dilemma. They are either empirically indeterminate, or overcharged with idealisations, that is, attributions to agents of reasons that are taken to be 'the right reasons'.[268]

Although Somek's analysis is salient, and although Kelsen's theoretical approach may liberate the validity of international law and the doctrine of ILP from its classical constraints, the creation of international norms alongside their adjudication and enforcement is, at present, left largely to States. This is particularly true with regard to non-State actors that have yet to be granted standing before a centralised international judicial body. Although Kelsen provides scope to alter this scenario, it is uncertain whether State governments will be compelled to move international law in this direction.

Although the interests of States should not be treated as uniform, rational or consistent, the economic system under which the majority of States function will surely introduce an element of predictability in their amenability to the regulation of entities that boast significant economic influence.[269] Such general concerns relating to enforcement and compliance with international legal norms are not to cast doubt on the presumptive validity of minimally efficacious legal orders, nor are they utilised to interpret, derive or deny any legal normative content. They simply highlight potential restraints on the advancement of legal norms and enforcement measures taken by States, the

265 Somek, 'Kelsen Lives' (n 26) 446.
266 Ibid. 451.
267 Kelsen, *Principles of International Law* (n 40) 308–11.
268 Somek, 'Kelsen Lives' (n 26) 448; Oona Hathaway and Ariel Lavinbuk, 'Rationalism and Revisionism in International Law' (2005) 119 *Harv L Rev* 1404; Bernstorff (n 1) 269.
269 Bernstorff cautions against the conflation of economic rationality with legal rationality in light of underdeveloped institutional frameworks at the international level: Bernstorff (n 1) 269; Kelsen, *Collective Security* (n 25) 253–5.

competence for which is prescribed by legal norms.[270] Paine's optimism in this regard is refreshing:

> True, we need to be cognizant that the powerful will retain the ability to act contrary to existing law, but ... legal validity ... can offer a useful medium for critiquing the actions of the powerful and should not be given up too quickly, even when confronted with the ability of the powerful to displace existing law.[271]

The scope for the generation of binding international obligations directly addressing non-State actors remains. Yet, the extant system of decentralised enforcement, coupled with an asymmetry in the capacity and willingness of States to effectively enforce international obligations, generates uncertainty as to its practical implementation. A recent initiative in this regard will be considered below, before conclusions are drawn.

5.2.3 Laying the groundwork for a binding business and human rights treaty

The realist criticism levied against the Pure Theory of Law notwithstanding, it has been demonstrated that valid international obligations can be established for non-State actors. Indeed, such duties already exist for non-State armed groups. In recent years, the business and human rights dialogue has shifted back to hard law standards, evidenced by the desire of weak governance States in particular to establish directly binding international obligations for business actors.[272] Much of the recent debate has been inspired by the turbulent Ecuador–Chevron litigation, which concerned an accusation by Ecuadorian villagers that Texaco (later acquired by Chevron) had contaminated an oilfield between 1964 and 1992.[273] Perhaps surprisingly, given the lengthy discussion in Chapter 3 relating to the procedural challenges that arise in respect of such litigation, the Ecuadorian Supreme Court, in November 2013, upheld an

270 Kammerhofer, *Uncertainty* (n 31) 129–31.
271 Joshua Paine, 'Review Essay: Kelsen, Normativity and Formal Justice in International Relations' (2013) 26 *LJIL* 1037, 1048.
272 Human Rights Council, 'Republic of Ecuador: Statement on behalf of a Group of Countries at the 24th Session of the Human Rights Council, Transnational Corporations and Human Rights' (Geneva, September 2013) http://business-humanrights.org/media/documents/statement-unhrc-legally-binding.pdf, accessed 23 April 2016; Olubayo Oluduro, *Oil Exploitation and Human Rights Violations in Nigeria's Oil Producing Communities* (Cambridge, UK, Intersentia, 2014) 309–11; Sarah Joseph, 'Taming the Leviathans: Multinational Enterprises and Human Rights' (1999) 46 *Neth Int'l L Rev* 171, 174.
273 Christopher Whytock, 'Chevron–Ecuador Case: Three Dimensions of Complexity in Transnational Dispute Resolution' (2012) 106 *ASIL Proc* 425.

earlier finding that Chevron was liable, ordering the corporation to pay billions of dollars in compensation.[274] Having initially contended, on the basis of the doctrine of *forum non conveniens*, that the Ecuadorian courts were better suited to hear the action, Chevron subsequently argued the case should be heard in the US. Consequently, since 2011, there has been additional protracted litigation in US courts[275] and a 2015 ruling by the Supreme Court of Canada permitting the claimants to pursue enforcement of the Ecuadorian award of damages under Canadian jurisdiction.[276] The case is ongoing, and its outcome remains uncertain.

In light of these struggles, a statement was submitted at the 24th session of the HRC on behalf of Ecuador, the African Group, the Arab Group and a number of other States, emphasising the need to establish:

> a legally binding framework to regulate the work of transnational cor-
> porations and to provide appropriate protection, justice and remedy to
> the victims of human rights abuses directly resulting from or related to the
> activities of some transnational corporations and other business enter-
> prises.[277]

The initiative has received resounding support from more than 100 NGOs[278] and has been followed up by a workshop, convened by Ecuador, during the 25th session of the HRC.[279] This was followed, in June 2014, by a resolution establishing the need for further elaboration on the subject of a legally binding

274 *Aguinda v Chevron-Texaco*, Case No 11–1150 (3 January 2012) (Appellate Panel, Ecuador), http://chevrontoxico.com/assets/docs/2012-01-03-appeal-decision-english.pdf, accessed 23 April 2016; for Chevron's successful bilateral investment arbitration, requiring Ecuador to suspend enforcement of any judgment against Chevron: *Chevron Corporation and Texaco Petroleum Corporation v Republic of Ecuador*, UNCITRAL, PCA Case No 2009–23 (First Interim Award, 25 January 2012) at 16–17; Alexandra Valencia, 'Ecuador High Court Upholds Chevron Verdict, Halves Fine' *Reuters* (13 November 2013) www.reuters.com/article/2013/11/13/us-chevron-ecuador-idUSBRE9AC0YY20131113, accessed 23 April 2016.

275 *Chevron Corporation and Texaco Petroleum Corporation v Republic of Ecuador*, UNCITRAL, PCA Case No 2009–23 (Order of the US District Court in the *Republic of Ecuador v Stratus Consulting Inc*, 29 May 2013); case documentation is available at: International Treaty Arbitration, www.italaw.com/cases/257, accessed 23 April 2016.

276 *Chevron Corp v Yaiguaje* (2015) SCC 42.

277 Human Rights Council, 'Republic of Ecuador: Statement' (n 272).

278 Stop Corporate Impunity, 'Statement to the Human Rights Council in Support of the Initiative of a Group of States for a Legally Binding Instrument on Transnational Corporations' (13 September 2013) www.stopcorporateimpunity.org/?p=3830, accessed 23 April 2016.

279 Olivier De Schutter, 'Human Rights and Transnational Corporations: Paving the Way for a Legally Binding Instrument' (Geneva, 11–12 March 2014) www.ohchr.org/Documents/Issues/Food/EcuadorMtgBusinessAndHR.pdf, accessed 23 April 2016.

treaty directly addressing business actors.[280] This type of initiative has antecedence in the agreement to explore the possibility of creating a specific treaty regulating private military and security companies.[281] The conception of international law advanced by the Pure Theory of Law eliminates traditional doctrinal constraints as to which actors may be the addressees of international rights and duties, as well as concerns stemming from contractarian explanations of legal validity. Thus, the existing rules of conventional and customary international humanitarian law that directly address non-State armed groups are entirely consistent with Kelsen's approach, and there is no legal or doctrinal barrier to prevent States from pursuing similar measures relating to MNEs. That said, enduring questions remain concerning the willingness of States to adopt such measures in light of their financial dependency and the role of corporations in 'backroom lobbying'.[282] Business actors may publicly support binding instruments only to exercise their influence domestically in order to temper more stringent regulations that might have otherwise been expressed in soft law.[283] In recent years, NGOs have detailed the negative effects of corporate lobbying on the implementation of US legislation relating to the regulation of conflict minerals.[284] Furthermore, although the establishment of direct law-making capacity for non-State actors is not ruled out under the Pure Theory of Law, the willingness of States to cede this competence and the desirability of any resulting direct corporate influence remain contentious.

John Ruggie's response to Ecuador's initiative has been mixed, having pragmatically highlighted the diverse legal issues related to the sphere of business and human rights:

---

280 Human Rights Council, 'Elaboration of an International Legally Binding Instrument on Transnational Corporations and other Business Enterprises with Respect to Human Rights', 26th Session (25th June 2014) UN Doc A/HRC/26/L.22/Rev. 1.

281 Human Rights Council Res 15/26 (7 October 2010) A/HRC/RES/15/26.

282 Cedric Ryngaert, 'Imposing International Duties on Non-State Actors and the Legitimacy of International Law' in Ryngaert and Noortmann (n 225) 74; Arthur Nelsen, 'TTIP: Chevron Lobbied for Controversial Legal Rights as "Environmental Deterrent"', *The Guardian* (London, 26 April 2016) www.theguardian.com/environment/2016/apr/26/ttip-chevron-lobbied-for-controversial-legal-right-as-environmental-deterrent?CMP=share_btn_tw, accessed 29 April 2016.

283 Stefanie Khoury and David Whyte, 'The Rarefied Politics of Global Struggles: Corporations, Hegemony and Human Rights' in Wilem de Lint, Marinella Marmo and Nerida Chazal (eds), *Crime and Justice in International Society* (Oxford, UK, Routledge, 2014) 238.

284 Global Witness, 'Are Electronics Companies Trying to Have it Both Ways on Conflict Minerals Legislation?', *Global Witness* (London, 2012) www.business-humanrights.org/media/documents/comment-piece-global-witness-on-companies-and-coc-nam-may-2012.doc, 23 April 2016; Business & Human Rights Resource Centre, 'Press Release: Electronics Companies Responses to Allegations that their Industry Associations Undermine Conflict Minerals Legislation' (1 August 2012) www.business-humanrights.org/media/documents/press-release-conflict-minerals-legislation-aug-2012-final.pdf, accessed 23 April 2016; *National Association of Manufacturers v Securities and Exchange Commission*, No 13–5252 (DC Cir, 14 April 2014).

Even with the best of 'political will,' the crux of the issue is that the category of business and human rights is not so discrete an issue-area as to lend itself to a single set of detailed treaty obligations. It includes complex clusters of different bodies of national and international law . . . any attempt to aggregate them into a general business and human rights treaty would have to be pitched at such a high level of abstraction that it is hard to imagine it providing a basis for meaningful legal action.[285]

Ruggie has also previously expressed concern that the establishment of such a treaty might set too low a ceiling.[286] How such an instrument might look remains contentious. Scholars such as Ramasatry, largely echoing Ruggie's apprehensions, have drawn analogy from the anti-corruption/bribery movement and instead advocated a number of narrower treaties establishing corporate liability for specific conduct, particularly in the fields of mineral extraction and illegal logging.[287] Although this middle ground may go some way towards addressing Ruggie's concerns, the present Anti-Corruption Convention, despite emphasising the liability of legal persons,[288] is still framed entirely in terms of State responsibility.[289] Given the unwillingness and incapacity of weak governance States to give effect to such provisions, it is suggested that this approach would fall victim to the same issues detailed in Chapter 3.

Although Ruggie's criticisms could be written off as unduly pessimistic, many of his observations are cogent. It is unlikely that the form and content of international human rights obligations directly addressing corporate actors could simply mirror those presently addressed to States. As Nollkaemper suggests, '[i]t may not be possible to solve the legal problems created by a shift in authority from the public to the private sphere by a wholesale and non-discriminate transfer of public international law norms to the private sphere'.[290]

---

285 John Ruggie, 'A UN Business and Human Rights Treaty?', Harvard Kennedy School (28 January 2014) 3, www.hks.harvard.edu/m-rcbg/CSRI/UNBusinessandHumanRights Treaty.pdf, accessed 23 April 2016; Michael Addo, UN Working Group on Business and Human Rights, 'Human Rights and Transnational Corporations: Paving the Way for a Legally Binding Instrument' (Geneva, 11–12 March 2014) 4, www.ohchr.org/ Documents/Issues/Business/WGStatementEcuadorWorkshop12Mar2014.pdf, accessed 23 April 2016.

286 John Ruggie, *Just Business: Multinational Corporations and Human Rights* (London, Norton, 2013) 64.

287 Anita Ramasatry, 'Closing the Governance Gap in the Business and Human Rights Arena: Lessons from the Anti-Corruption Movement' in Surya Deva and David Bilchitz (eds), *Human Rights Obligations of Businesses: Beyond the Corporate Responsibility to Protect* (Cambridge, UK, CUP, 2013) 162–89.

288 United Nations Convention against Corruption (31 October 2003) UN Doc A/58/422, Article 26.

289 Ibid.

290 André Nollkaemper, 'Responsibility of Transnational Corporations in International Environmental Law: Three Perspectives' in Gerd Winter (ed), *Multilevel Governance of Global Environmental Change* (Cambridge, UK, CUP, 2006) 196.

Whereas broadly negative obligations to respect human rights may easily lend themselves to application in the corporate context,[291] obligations demanding positive action to advance or fulfil the realisation of human rights may prove more problematic.[292] Given that the extent of obligations is determined by their framing rather than their content, the redundancy of the binary separation often maintained between positive and negative duties is revealed under the Pure Theory of Law.[293] For instance, although economic, social and cultural obligations are classically conceptualised as inherently positive, demanding progressive realisation via the provision by addressees of funding and necessary infrastructure, the same rights could be reframed to reflect the differential duties of private actors. It is possible to conceive of an obligation to *refrain* from the use of land in a manner that produces negative effects on the health of proximate populations. Although a positive duty to carry out impact assessments may be implicit within this framing, this type of demand is already codified within existing soft law regimes.[294]

Another issue demanding normative development relates to the scope of the duties. Extant human rights duties are currently delineated by a spatial dimension, that of a State's jurisdiction, conceived as being primarily territorial in nature.[295] As business actors do not control territory in the same manner as a State, or even a non-State armed group, alternative frontiers will need to be established in order to delimit corporate responsibility. The principle of 'due diligence' is one such standard, incorporated to a significant degree in Ruggie's UNGPs.[296] Others have emphasised the responsibility of actors for human rights to the extent that they fall within their 'sphere of influence'[297] or the actors exercise functional 'control' over individuals.[298] The latter approach is perhaps the most compelling and is evidenced by the jurisprudence of the ECtHR. The

291 Steven Ratner, 'Corporations and Human Rights: A Theory of Legal Responsibility' (2001) 111 *Yale LJ* 443, 517.
292 Karavias (n 224) 168–72.
293 Ben Saul, David Kinley and Jaqueline Mowbray, *The International Covenant on Economic, Social and Cultural Rights: Cases, Materials, and Commentary* (Oxford, UK, OUP, 2014) 1–2; Ruth Gavison, 'On the Relationships between Civil and Political Rights and Social and Economic Rights' in Jean-Marc Coicaud, Michael W Doyle and Anne-Marie Gardner (eds), *The Globalisation of Human Rights* (Tokyo, UN University Press, 2003) 23.
294 UN Guiding Principles on Business and Human Rights 2011, HR/PUB/11/04, Commentary to Principle 18 (hereafter, UNGPs).
295 *Al-Skeini v United Kingdom* App No 55721/07 (ECtHR 2011) para 130; Karavias (n 224) 85–9.
296 UNGPs (n 294) Principle 17(a); cf Sabine Michalowski, 'Due Diligence and Complicity: A Relationship in Need of Clarification' in Deva and Bilchitz (n 287) 218–42.
297 Human Rights Council, 'Clarifying the Concepts of "Sphere of Influence" and Complicity"' 8th Session (15 May 2008) A/HRC/8/16, 4; cf Karavias (n 224) 172–4.
298 Control may be over persons, premises, territory or vessels: *Al-Saadoon & Mufdhi v United Kingdom* App No 61498/08 (ECtHR 2009); *Al-Skeini* (n 295); *Medvedyev and others v France* App No 3394/03 (ECtHR 2010).

Court expressly acknowledged, in *Al-Skeini*, that jurisdiction does not arise solely on a spatial basis, as exhibited where a State exercises control 'over the buildings, aircraft or ship in which the individuals [are] held. What is decisive in such cases is the exercise of physical power and control over the persons in question'.[299] This statement notwithstanding, the Court has been notoriously inconsistent in its justifications for the establishment of jurisdiction. In most cases purporting to establish jurisdiction based on control over persons, there has existed a parallel spatial ground upon which jurisdiction could equally have been established. For instance, in *Al-Skeini*, the Court stressed the significance of the public powers exercised by the UK in parts of Iraq. In *Al-Jedda*, a judgment delivered on the same day as *Al-Skeini*, jurisdiction was expressly derived from the UK's control over buildings in which the victims were present.[300] The Court's tendency to conflate personal and spatial jurisdictional principles in this regard breeds significant uncertainty, and, given that practice in this area is yet to solidify in relation to States and their agents, no firm conclusions may be drawn.

The potential for the proposed treaty to address both States and non-State actors simultaneously raises further conceptual questions relating to the division of responsibility among multiple duty-bearers. Although each actor will be independently responsible for solitary breaches of primary obligations, the issue becomes more complex where the conduct of multiple actors jointly contributes to the breach of a single provision. International law suffers from a general underdevelopment in relation to its secondary rules in this regard, as demonstrated by the scholarship of the SHARES project, led by Nollkaemper and Jacobs.[301] Although Article 47 ASRIWA contemplates the scenario in which two States are jointly responsible for the same internationally wrongful act,[302] there is a distinct lack of guidance or practice in relation to the operation of this provision.[303] How might this deficiency be overcome? One approach might be to adopt a rule structure within the proposed treaty that facilitates a conceptual distinction between the wrongful conduct of multiple parties. Such a model would need to approach responsibility in a holistic fashion, incorporating existing regimes that are external to the proposed treaty. For instance, the attribution model of responsibility outlined in Chapter 3, which provides limited scope to attribute the conduct of a non-State party to a State

---

299 *Al-Skeini* (n 295) para 136; *Andreou v Turkey* App No 45653/99 (ECtHR 2008).

300 *Al-Jedda v United Kingdom* App No 27021/08 (ECtHR 2011) para 85; Marko Milanovic, 'Al-Skeini and Al-Jedda in Strasbourg' (2012) 23 *EJIL* 121, 131.

301 André Nollkaemper and Dov Jacobs, 'Shared Responsibility in International Law: A Conceptual Framework' (2013) 34 *Mich J Int'l L* 359.

302 ILC, Articles on Responsibility of States for Internationally Wrongful Acts (2001) UN Doc A/56/49(Vol I)/Corr.4, Article 47 (hereafter, ASRIWA).

303 Nollkaemper and Jacobs (n 301) 393; Annemarieke Vermeer-Künzli, 'Invocation of Responsibility' in André Nollkaemper and Ilias Plakokefalos (eds) *Principles of Shared Responsibility in International Law* (Cambridge, UK, CUP, 2014) 252–4.

where the State directs or controls the private conduct giving rise to the breach, will undoubtedly continue to perform some role. But what of the situation where the relevant conduct does not meet the threshold for attribution to the State, or where a non-State actor serves as the principal wrongdoer, and the State's contribution is secondary? The inclusion of complicity provisions that derive responsibility from the principal wrongdoer's conduct rather than attributing the wrongful conduct to a secondary party could prove useful in responding to this regulatory gap.[304]

As a legal concept, complicity is already subject to codification at the international level in Article 16 ASRIWA.[305] The ILC's primary mandate was to codify *secondary* rules of international law that serve to bridge the gap between breaches of primary duties, the determination of liability and the assignment of appropriate remedies. Nonetheless, it has been convincingly argued that Article 16 constitutes a separate primary rule of obligation.[306] There is an implicit acknowledgement of this reading in the ILC's commentaries, which provide, 'the assisting State is responsible for its own act in deliberately assisting another State to breach an international obligation by which they are both bound. It is not responsible as such for the act of the assisted State'.[307] Even if one were to dispute on conceptual grounds the framing of this *general* complicity rule in this way, this does not preclude the development of specific *lex specialis* rules within the proposed treaty.[308] Indeed, provisions of the 1948 Genocide Convention have also been read, in light of the instrument's object and purpose, as implying complicity provisions conceived as primary rules to refrain from complicit conduct.[309] This framing of complicity rules as primary obligations may circumvent issues surrounding the allocation of concurrent responsibility to multiple parties for a single wrongful act. Instead, two separate rules have been breached, entailing separate responsibility – for instance, the direct breach of an obligation against torture by a non-State actor, and the breach of a distinct provision to refrain from complicit conduct by a State.

304 Helmut Philipp Aust, *Complicity and the Law of State Responsibility* (Cambridge, UK, CUP, 2011) 188; Georg Nolte and Helmut Philipp Aust, 'Equivocal Helpers – Complicit States, Mixed Messages and International Law' (2009) 58 *ICLQ* 1, 8.

305 ASRIWA (n 302) Article 16.

306 Miles Jackson, *Complicity in International Law* (Oxford, UK, OUP, 2015) 148–50; Christian Tams, 'All's Well that Ends Well – Comments on the ILC's Articles on State Responsibility' (2002) 62 *ZaöRV* 759, 746; Ulf Linderfalk, 'State Responsibility and the Primary–Secondary Rules Terminology – The Role of Language for an Understanding of the International Legal System' (2009) 78 *Nordic J Int'l L* 53, 58–72.

307 ILC, 'Draft Articles on Responsibility of States for Internationally Wrongful Acts with Commentaries' Yearbook of the International Law Commission (2001) Vol II, 67.

308 Aust (n 304) 200.

309 *Application of the Convention on the Prevention and Punishment of the Crime of Genocide (Bosnia and Herzegovina v Serbia and Montenegro)* (Merits) [2007] ICJ Rep 43 para 167; Jackson (n 306) 203.

General ambiguities remain in relation to the level of contribution and *mens rea* required to engage complicity provisions.[310] With regard to the latter, the Inter-American Court and Commission have adopted a due diligence threshold that requires only *support* or *toleration* of the wrongful conduct.[311] Such a threshold is arguably unnecessarily low, given that such conduct will likely engage separate due diligence obligations within extant human rights conventions, at least for States. Recognition of this factor enables one to conceive of separate breaches of primary obligations within the proposed treaty by the principal actor, and a breach of a distinct due diligence provision within an altogether separate treaty regime by a State. Thus, taken in aggregate, existing State responsibility regimes may respond to yet another level of the governance gap and aid the conceptual distinction between wrongful acts by multiple wrongdoers.

The potential utility of such a rule structure notwithstanding, questions remain as to the actual apportionment of responsibility among multiple wrongdoers. In this regard, the inclusion of a joint and several liability clause may prove to be useful. Although the acceptability of this domestic private law concept in the context of international law has been subject to debate,[312] scholars such as Noyes and Smith and Vandenhole have endorsed the doctrine in light of its pervasive municipal use and conceptual compatibility with human rights law.[313] The adoption of such provisions at the international level is visible in both the Law of the Sea Convention and the Space Liability Convention.[314] Notably, both instruments seek to hold multiple parties jointly and severally liable for their contributions to the same *damage* or *harmful outcome*. This framing is distinct from Article 47 ASRIWA, which seeks to hold multiple parties responsible for a *single wrongful act*. Presumably, the harmful outcome could arise from a number of *separate* breaches, were the rule structure advanced above adopted. Article 4(2) of the Space Liability Convention provides that contributions to any damages awarded are to be apportioned between the

---

310 Mark Gibney, 'Litigating Transnational Human Rights Abuses' in Wouter Vandenhole (ed), *Challenging Territoriality in Human Rights Law* (Oxford, UK, Routledge, 2015) 93–8; Vladyslav Lanovoy, 'Complicity in an Internationally Wrongful Act' in Nollkaemper and Plakokefalos (n 303) 140; Jackson (n 306) 158; Nolte and Aust (n 304) 12–15.

311 *Riofrío Massacre* (6 April 2001) IACommHR No 62/01 para 48; *Mapiripán Massacre* (Colombia) (15 September 2005) IACtHR (Ser. C) No 134 para 98a.

312 Christian Tams, 'Countermeasures against Multiple Responsible Actors' in Nollkaemper and Plakokefalos (n 303) 327–9.

313 John Noyes and Brian Smith, 'State Responsibility and the Principle of Joint and Several Liability' (1988) 13 *Yale J Int'l L* 225; Wouter Vandenhole, 'Shared Responsibility of Non-State Actors: A Human Rights Perspective' in Noemi Gal-Or, Cedric Ryngaert and Math Noortmann (eds), *Responsibilities of the Non-State Actor in Armed Conflict and the Market Place: Theoretical and Empirical Findings* (Leiden, Netherlands, Brill, 2015) 56.

314 UN Convention on the Law of the Sea (1982) 1833 UNTS 3, Article 139; Convention on International Liability for Damage Caused by Space Objects (1972) 961 UNTS 187, Articles 4 and 5 (hereafter, Space Liability Convention).

parties, 'in accordance to the extent they were at fault; if the extent of the fault cannot be established, compensation shall be apportioned equally among them'.[315] Although such determinations would require complex assessments of causation, it is suggested that the conceptual separation of breaches facilitated by the aforementioned framework of rules might provide a basis on which the nature of particular breaches might be distinguished, and the level of responsibility allocated to each wrongdoer might be delimited. This possibility notwithstanding, the absence of an international adjudicative body of compulsory jurisdiction in which States and non-State actors could pursue one another for contributions to any damages awarded presents a significant challenge.

This acknowledgement leads the present discussion neatly to the question of how the proposed instrument ought to be enforced. Should a treaty monitoring body be established with reporting requirements, the very States prone to human rights abuses at the hands of MNEs are unlikely to possess the capacity to comply with such obligations or to enforce the reporting duties of actors within their territory.[316] It is clear in the statement submitted by Ecuador that avenues for remediation and redress ought to be provided under the binding regulatory framework proposed. Ruggie and others have stressed the need for elaboration as to whether such enforcement would take place at the domestic level, in which case it would clearly be vulnerable to many of the flaws highlighted in Chapter 3, or whether an 'international court for corporations' should be established.[317] In a similar vein, a draft statute for a World Court of Human Rights, which grants standing not only to individuals but also to non-State actors, has been developed by Nowak and Kozma.[318] Unfortunately, in this case, the standing of non-State actors is contingent upon a declaration of their consent, a factor that is rendered entirely unnecessary from the perspective of the Pure Theory of Law.[319] Similar proposals have recently been advanced by practitioners such as Claes Cronstedt, who has discussed the

---

315 Space Liability Convention (n 314) Article 4(2).
316 Ruggie, *Just Business* (n 286).
317 Ruggie, 'A UN Business and Human Rights Treaty?' (n 285); Peter Muchlinski, 'Beyond the Guiding Principles? Examining New Calls for a Legally Binding Instrument on Business and Human Rights', Institute for Business and Human Rights (15 October 2013) www.ihrb.org/commentary/guest/beyond-the-guiding-principles.html, accessed 23 April 2016.
318 Manfred Nowak and Julia Kozma, 'Research Project on a World Human Rights Court' (University of Vienna, June 2009) http://bim.lbg.ac.at/files/sites/bim/World%20Court%20of%20Human%20Rights_BIM_0.pdf, accessed 23 April 2016; Martin Scheinin, 'International Organisations and Transnational Corporations at a World Court of Human Rights' (2012) 3 *Global Policy* 488.
319 Nowak and Kozma (n 318) 45.

potential structure and operation of an International Tribunal on Business and Human Rights, though its rulings would not be legally binding.[320]

Kelsen often emphasised the significance of centralised judicial bodies in determining the precise content of the often-abstract sphere of international law, even absent the correlative power to ensure adherence to decisions.[321] Indeed, the enforcement of legal norms is not an essential property of their validity as a result of his theoretical adherence to the *is/ought* dichotomy. Yet, actual enforcement is clearly desirable, and decisions rendered by a 'World Court' would likely fall to the weak governance States that harbour the majority of victims. In the alternative, major international cooperation would be required. Whether the enforcement of the binding treaty would require the adoption of bilateral or multilateral measures between host and home States of MNEs to ensure that decisions are rendered is an area ripe for further analysis in this regard. In his socio-legal work, and entirely separate to his theoretical model, Kelsen relied heavily on the cooperation of the 'Great Powers' in the enforcement of international obligations:

> If it were possible to obtain, for a treaty such as that suggested, the ratification of the United States, Great Britain, China and the Soviet Union, it would be almost certain that these great powers would conscientiously respect the stipulations of the treaty . . . [and] would render any serious violation unlikely . . . They are the 'power behind the law' for which those realists who conceive of the law as a mere ideology of force might enquire.[322]

This position is undeniably utopian.[323] Although States can theoretically accord:

> supranational competences to an overarching body, or even, under exceptional circumstances . . . sign off their sovereign statehood altogether . . . the growth of international cooperation is a slow process because States would generally be hesitant to reduce the legal freedoms they enjoy.[324]

In addition, scholars such as Boyle and Harrison have proven resistant to the idea of a specialised international environmental court, on the basis of the sheer variety of laws relevant to environmental disputes. The judges of such a court would require a wide-ranging grasp of international law, rendering them no

---

320 Claes Cronstedt and David Ronnegard, 'International Tribunal on Business & Human Rights' (September 2013) www.l4bb.org/news/tribunal.pdf, accessed 23 April 2016.
321 Kelsen, *Collective Security* (n 25) 14; Bernstorff (n 1) 219.
322 Hans Kelsen, *Peace Through Law* (Chapel Hill, NC, University of North Carolina Press, 1944) 66.
323 Zolo (n 58) 321.
324 Suganami (n 26) 527.

different, in effect, to those at the ICJ.[325] Given the strong parallels between environmental degradation and the operations of MNEs, as well as the variety of laws contemplated in Chapter 3, similar practical concerns could be expressed in relation to a World Court on Business and Human Rights.

This is an important realist factor that hampers the practical implementation of Kelsen's theory. Although there is nothing preventing the extension of direct obligations to non-State actors in theory, the political willingness of State governments is not guaranteed. After all, these bodies remain the primary legislators and are often substantially economically dependent on MNEs for employment and capital. Although it is theoretically possible under the Pure Theory of Law to open up international law creation to other international actors, thereby circumventing these political concerns, this too would be dependent on States' willingness to surrender this competence. As such, Suganami suggests that:

> the Kelsenian conception of State sovereignty is relatively benign, or at least neutral, with respect to the possibility of furtherance of international goals[.] [T]hat may be a sufficient reason for doubting the relevance of the Keslenian conception to the practice of international politics.[326]

Whether the enforcement of the binding treaty would require the adoption of bilateral or multilateral measures between host and home States of MNEs to ensure that decisions are rendered is an area ripe for further analysis in this regard. One may sensibly ask what use establishing the theoretical validity of international law is when it may remain largely unenforced in practice. Kelsen's answer would likely stress the primitive nature of the current international legal system and the scope for practical solutions to develop in time. Retrospect reveals that his optimism regarding the establishment of the UN system was somewhat misplaced. However, the present monograph demonstrates that the manner in which the issue of non-State actor regulation is framed theoretically may have profound consequences on its practical operation. As such, it is argued that there is significant utility in establishing more robust theoretical foundations, even in the absence of an effective enforcement mechanism at present.

5.3 Concluding remarks

The methodology advanced by the Pure Theory of Law provides a valuable critical lens through which the failings of dominant scholarship can be further

---

325 Alan Boyle and James Harrison, 'Judicial Settlement of International Environmental Disputes: Current Problems' (2013) 4 *J Int'l Disp Settlement* 245, 274–5.
326 Suganami (n 26) 527.

evaluated and establishes a robust theoretical foundation that is more receptive to the formulation of direct international obligations for non-State actors. Kelsen's model adopts a strict separation between *is* and *ought* in order to advance legal scholarship in the direction of a purely normative science. The consequences of this view are pervasive and strike at the heart of State-centric doctrine, which bases the creation and validity of international law on the consent of sovereign States, conceived as empirically observable, socio-psychological entities possessing certain natural competences. This persistent contractarian notion has rendered the direct regulation of non-State entities largely unfeasible. Its scholarship has politicised the concept of ILP by treating it as synonymous with 'statehood', thereby necessitating the ascription of law-making competences to all subjects of international obligations. Even if a multi-stakeholder system of law-making were feasible in practice, it was suggested that such an initiative may negatively affect the quality and content of international legal norms. The Pure Theory of Law circumvents these political anxieties and practical effects. If international law is conceived as sovereign, with its validity derived from a hypothetical basic norm, the mythology of State-centric scholarship can be abandoned. Instead, it is the legal order that determines its creators and addressees, and, as such, the notion of ILP is left entirely open. The international legal order may impute obligations to non-State actors without their participation or consent. Thus, the Pure Theory of Law is able to reconcile the binding quality of the existing framework of customary and conventional international humanitarian law, which directly addresses non-State armed groups, and offers scope to develop a similar binding accountability regime addressing MNEs.

However, although there are no doctrinal impediments to the creation of binding international obligations for non-State actors or the expansion of the entities involved in the process of international law creation, such competences are, at present, largely imputed to State actors. Thus, even if Kelsen's model were to offer a defensible theoretical foundation for the advancement of direct non-State actor regulation, in practice, it remains largely constrained to the political will of State governments. The recent initiative led by Ecuador is encouraging in this regard. The potential utility of the rule structure suggested above notwithstanding, the initiative raises complex questions concerning the normative development of the field, and there are enduring uncertainties as to the capacity of international treaties to capture the complexity of corporate human rights regulation. Similar questions remain as to the enforcement framework underpinning a directly binding treaty. The international legal system is presently absent an appropriate institutional infrastructure to deal with the adjudication of direct breaches emanating from collective non-State actors of the type contemplated in the present study. Were a new body established, the enforcement of any judgments attained, while raising major public relations concerns for the actors involved, would likely fall to the very States that are unable or unwilling to enforce domestic judgments to this effect. In the alternative, a system of multilateral or bilateral enforcement demanding significant international cooperation would be necessary.

This discussion demonstrates the continuing complexity of direct non-State actor regulation, which, in many respects, transcends the theoretical lens adopted to examine it. Although Kelsen's approach is extremely useful in piercing the mythology surrounding the structure and operation of international law, thereby freeing legal validity and ILP from the constraints of State-centric scholarship, the international legal order is currently heavily reliant on States for the purposes of creating, enforcing and adjudicating international human rights standards. Thus, although the Pure Theory of Law offers scope to alter this scenario, its practical realisation remains uncertain. Yet, history demonstrates that the establishment of treaty regimes absent functional enforcement mechanisms can, in time, ossify into advanced institutionalised systems. As a result, it is submitted that there is value in laying the conceptual groundwork for a set of valid legal standards against which the acts of both States and non-State actors may be directly measured and critiqued.

6 Conclusion

The breadth of the practical and theoretical uncertainties clouding the direct legal regulation of non-State actors is substantial. Despite heightened scholarly interest in the field in recent decades, much of it in response to international phenomena such as globalisation, privatisation and the proliferation of internal armed conflict, few workable solutions have emerged. An overarching aim of this work has been to critically examine the dominant treatment of non-State actors, which has developed in an inconsistent, piecemeal fashion, by subjecting it to a degree of consistent methodological scrutiny largely absent from the majority of scholarship addressing the topic. Adopting as an analytical tool the adverse effects produced by the intersection of non-State armed groups and MNEs in weak governance States, the study sought to expose compelling insights that are conceptually robust, in that they are both informed by, and responsive to, contemporary realities. It is recognised that there is clear value in regularly appraising the feasibility and desirability of potential solutions against this context, in order to prevent the work from proceeding uncritically into the warren of abstract theory. Such an endeavour has proven a complex path to tread, given that a central thread of this study has related to abstract explanations for international legal validity. Through the adoption of this approach, it has been demonstrated that the theoretical framing assumed can demand substantial practical consequences when its underlying logic is strictly followed.

The general malleability of the dominant statist model of legal validity has been subject to extensive discussion. Although the lengthy contextualisation provided in Chapter 2 of this study may have, at first, seemed superfluous, the trajectory of this monograph demonstrates that a thorough discussion of these doctrinal foundations can shed significant light on seemingly insurmountable practical challenges and is critical to the formulation of alternative solutions. The fluid, ill-defined nature of the objective criteria taken to denote 'statehood' prove highly problematic on a number of levels, particularly for a school that hinges the validity of international law on what is, in reality, an intensely variable category of international actors. It has been acknowledged that the categorisation of the vast plurality of 'non-State' entities under a single heading was excessively reductive and, thus, obstructive to their effective regulation. Yet, a parallel argument may be made with regard to 'State' actors. The diversity of entities recognised as fulfilling the criteria for statehood further highlights the illogic of this binary classification. The consequences are pervasive and particularly demonstrable in the context of ILP. 'Statehood' is treated as virtually synonymous with ILP by dominant scholarship. Naturally, the definitional inadequacy of one term produces serious effects for the other. Similarly, the temporal continuity of States once 'recognised' as members of the international community, in spite of a lapse in efficacy and/or constituent features, further underscores the doctrine's flaws and divorces it from the empirical reality on which it apparently depends. It is essential to the State-centric school to be able to draw precise distinctions, particularly in contentious cases, between which entities may be considered States and which may not. That this model is unable to define the most central component of its conception of international law is symptomatic of its redundancy. Yet, it is not only the decline in State power, the increase in internal armed conflict and the rise of non-State actors over the course of the last century that have diminished the validity of this theoretical model, although these events have undoubtedly brought its flaws to the fore. The historiographical justifications for the primacy of the role of States in the international legal system are similarly problematic. In spite of the retrospective significance attributed to seventeenth and eighteenth century doctrinal shifts, it was argued that such events are prone to subjective interpretation – particularly when divorced from their social and historical contexts – and that recourse to this level of genealogical argument is ultimately a rather inadequate remedy for doctrinal uncertainties.

In spite of these deep conceptual issues, the empirical determination of statehood remains central to dominant scholarship's justification for the creation and binding quality of international law in a largely decentralised international legal system. The lasting influence of late-nineteenth- and early-twentieth-century German and Italian academics was examined in this regard. It was during this period that Hegelian notions of the State as an empirically observable social fact imbued with historical prestige became common place. The demonstrable failings of the State-based regulatory initiatives that are born of this method at the domestic level and in the spheres of international humanitarian, human rights and criminal law were comprehensively established in Chapter 3 of this study. Although some recent progress has been made at the international level with the adoption of soft law and *ad hoc* initiatives, these schemes are absent a judicial enforcement mechanism, and their role in advancing the formulation of binding norms is highly contentious. Moreover, the later chapters of this monograph revealed that this State-centricity underscores legitimacy concerns in two particular contexts.

The first relates to the political legitimisation of entities recognised as international legal persons, as direct addressees of legal obligations. These anxieties surrounding the 'status' that ILP apparently confers is rooted in the State-centric school's conflation of this doctrine with statehood. Once established, a State is imbued with the natural competence to create international law and enter into international relations, irrespective of practical realities. Such competences are almost *natural* in origin: they are the uncontested product of historical lineage and social power and enable State actors to express their will to shape and be bound by the law. This theoretical deification of the territorial State explains the general reluctance to impute international obligations directly to non-State entities, particularly those that are considered politically dubious. The second dimension to legitimacy also concerns this conflation between addressee and law-maker, but this time relates to the legal legitimacy of international obligations. In the absence of a supreme, centralised executive body able to enact and coercively enforce international law, consent plays a key role in the formulation, validation and compliance-pull of international legal norms. The rationale is contractarian: the addressees validate the law via their consent. States are able to consent directly to multilateral treaties. Consent to customary international law may be *tacit*, largely emanating from State practice. Consent is often incentivised by participation in the creation of legal provisions. As such, in order for non-State actors to be bound, they too must consent to those provisions and participate in their creation. Participation is particularly key in relation to the establishment of custom for obvious reasons. In support of this argument, this study drew on the work of scholars such as Thomas Franck, Jürgen Habermas and Cedric Ryngaert, whose scholarship emphasises the desirability of participation for the legitimisation of the imposition of direct duties on non-State actors via adherence to due process. Franck's scholarship demonstrated that greater compliance could be incentivised in a legal system devoid of Austinian coercive sanction through procedural factors such as participation in law creation. It explained the parallel concerns expressed by non-State armed groups and their reticence to accept laws determined entirely by the State party to which they were politically opposed. The discursive democracy scholarship drawn upon supplemented this finding, emphasising the virtues of multi-stakeholder decision-making at the international level, giving voice to a plurality of relevant viewpoints, better reflecting social and political reality at the international level, and formulating the most desirable decision for all relevant parties.

At the same time, it was acknowledged that the involvement of actors such as MNEs, which wield enormous economic power and may not act in the public interest, is not entirely appropriate. The same could be said for extremist or terrorist factions of non-State armed groups. It is also likely that States will be reluctant to cede these competences. Yet, according to the logic of the dominant school, this is a necessary measure both for the validation of direct duties and in terms of incentivising compliance, a factor already acknowledged by soft law and *ad hoc* initiatives. The practicalities of implementing a system that could serve as an effective forum for international decision-making and, at the same time, democratically represent the views of all relevant stakeholders are necessarily speculative. In addition, the potential impact of such a system on the quality and normative content of international law as it stands is uncertain, and any reduction in standards relating to non-State actors would clearly be antithetical to their inclusion. Thus, the weaknesses of the concepts upon which dominant scholarship relies produce potential ramifications in practice: they preclude the advancement of directly enforceable international obligations for non-State actors, give rise to political sensitivities and ignore social reality. The contribution of this study is, therefore, most demonstrable in its detailed examination of theoretical conceptions of international law and the consequences they engender in the field of non-State actor regulation. These foundational issues are all too often overlooked and may have discernible practical impact in terms of regulatory efficacy. The study offers two distinct solutions: one (described above) follows the logic of State-centric scholarship, and the other demands a theoretical reconceptualization of the structure and operation of the international legal system. Although the desirability and feasibility of both approaches remain somewhat contentious, it was argued that the latter approach is more theoretically compelling and may be more conducive to the establishment of a direct international accountability regime for non-State actors.

This approach was examined in the final substantive chapter of this study, which utilised the components of the Pure Theory of Law as both a critical tool to dispel the doctrinal flaws of the mainstream positivist model and as a potential theoretical framing for direct non-State actor regulation, free from consequences relating to law-making capacity. The approach adopts a methodological distinction between the realms of *is* and *ought*, between the empirical and normative spheres of validity. Law is conceived as a product of the latter – a formally complete hierarchy of norms, the validity of which does not depend on the historical/social prestige or psychological will of an empirical State entity. Instead, States are framed in purely legal normative terms. The State is simply the national legal order. No natural status or competences attach to these personified normative orders; rather, their competences in relation to law creation are determined by the legal order itself and imputed to the State legal order. Legal personality is an open concept that is not determined by certain vague criteria with an apparently empirical basis, but is simply prescribed by the particular content of the relevant norm; it is the product of being an addressee of the norm in question. Thus, the ascription of direct duties to non-State armed groups under international humanitarian law is no longer problematic and does not demand their active participation in law creation. Nor is it inconceivable that MNEs may one day be subject to similar substantive regulation, at least in theory.

It cannot be denied that there are a number of theoretical issues that have persistently plagued the Pure Theory of Law, with most criticism centring on the elusive nature of the basic norm. Yet, it has been argued that the basic norm is often misconceived. The neo-Kantian explanation of its purpose as a methodological lens through which legal norms may be perceived, analogous to the role of causality in natural science, is, by and large, defensible. Although this concept lies beyond positive determination, and it must be conceded that a strictly normative view of the law is not, of necessity, the *only* way of perceiving legal validity, for the purposes of this study, the Pure Theory of Law has substantial utility. It both frees non-State actor regulation from the limitations of classical doctrine and, arguably, rests on a single (albeit fundamental) fiction, as opposed to the dense mythology of traditional scholarship. The recent resurgence in Kelsenian scholarship has offered precise, logical rebuttals to many persistent challenges, including Kelsen's reliance on a coercive order paradigm, and realist critiques seeking to equate practical compliance with legal validity. Yet, although the Pure Theory of Law offers a more logical *theoretical* basis for the direct regulation of non-State actors, practical efficacy is also clearly desirable. Although the *validity* of legal norms is entirely detached from the 'will' and 'consent' of territorial States, at present, the competences to *create* and *enforce* international law lie largely with States. Their political willingness to impute international obligations directly to the non-State actors upon which they are economically dependent is uncertain, as is their capacity to enforce such provisions without a robust system of international courts and tribunals to make determinations or sufficient international cooperation to enforce potential judgments.

The Ecuadorian initiative notwithstanding, complex doctrinal questions remain as to the future normative development of international human rights law in relation to the delimitation of corporate obligations, absent the spatial frontier of territorial jurisdiction. Although some suggestions have been advanced as to how the scope and content of any resulting rules might be framed, precisely how international law will develop to respond to scenarios entailing the allocation of responsibility among multiple and diverse duty-bearers remains to be seen, despite a recent and overdue surge in scholarly attention. Ultimately, no theoretical perspective is without its challenges. It is no doubt the case that political and economic dynamics transcending any one legal scholar's particular methodological framing will be the ultimate deciding factors in determining the future content, addressees and practical implementation of international law. Yet, this does not mean that one must also abandon legal validity. It is submitted that there is inherent value in attempting to solve these doctrinal dilemmas, even absent an enforcement process in the short term. The articulation of a compelling theoretical framing that is receptive to non-State actor regulation may aid in establishing the groundwork for the evolution of a direct accountability regime. This process may also fortify legal scholarship as a means to critique the abusive acts of both State and non-State actors. Nonetheless, although far from hopeless, the exact shape of non-State actor regulation remains unclear. What is clear is that, without a robust international accountability framework for non-State actors, the human rights abuses that stem from resource extraction in weak governance States will continue to occur.

Selected bibliography

Books

Abiad, N, *Sharia, Muslim States and International Human Rights Treaty Obligations: A Comparative Study* (London, British Institute of International and Comparative Law, 2008).

Adeyeye, A, *Corporate Social Responsibility of Multinational Corporations in Developing Countries: Perspectives on Anti-Corruption* (Cambridge, UK, CUP, 2012).

Akashi, K, *Cornelius Van Bynkershoek: His Role in the History of International Law* (The Hague, Martinus Nijhoff, 1998).

Allott, P, *Health of Nations: Society and Law Beyond the State* (Cambridge, UK, CUP, 2002).

Amao, O, *Corporate Social Responsibility, Human Rights and the Law: Multinational Corporations in Developing Countries* (Oxford, UK, Taylor & Francis, 2011).

Amerasinghe, CF, *Principles of the Institutional Law of International Organisations* (2nd edn, Cambridge, UK, CUP, 2005).

Anaya, SJ, *Indigenous Peoples in International Law* (2nd edn, Oxford, UK, OUP, 2004).

Anghie, A, *Imperialism, Sovereignty and the Making of International Law* (Cambridge, UK, CUP, 2007).

Anzilotti, D, *Cours de droit international* (Paris, Librarie de Recueil Sirey, 1929).

Anzilotti, D, *Teoria generale della responsabilità dello stato nel diritto internazionale* (1902).

Aristotle, *Politics* (350 BC, Jowett, B trans, New York, Dover, 2000).

Aristotle, *Rhetoric* (Roberts WR trans, Oxford, UK, Clarendon Press 1924).

Armstrong, D, Farrell, T and Lambert, H, *International Law and International Relations* (2nd edn, Cambridge, UK, CUP, 2012).

Aust, HP, *Complicity and the Law of State Responsibility* (Cambridge, UK, CUP, 2011).

Austin, J, *The Province of Jurisprudence Determined* (2nd edn, London, John Murray, 1832).

Baum, S, *Hans Kelsen and the Case for Democracy* (Colchester, UK, European Consortium for Political Research Press, 2013).

Beales, D, *The Risorgimento and the Unification of Italy* (London, George Allen & Unwin, 1971).

Bederman, DJ, *International Law in Antiquity* (Cambridge, UK, CUP, 2001).

Bergbohm, C, *Staatsverträge und Gesetze als Quellen des Völkerrechts* (1877).

Bernstorff, JV, *The Public International Law Theory of Hans Kelsen* (Cambridge, UK, CUP, 2010).

Berolzheimer, F, *The World's Legal Philosophies* (Clark, NJ, The Lawbook Exchange, 1929).

Bindreiter, U, *Why Grundnorm? A Treatise on the Implications of Kelsen's Doctrine* (The Hague, Netherlands, Springer, 2002).

Bodin, J, *Six Books of the Commonwealth* (first published 1576, Tooley, MJ trans, New York, Barnes & Noble, 1967).

Bothe, M, Partsch, KJ and Solf, WA, *New Rules for Victims of Armed Conflicts: Commentary on the Two 1977 Protocols Additional to the Geneva Conventions of 1949* (The Hague, Netherlands, Martinus Nijhoff, 1982).

Bowett, DW, *Self-Defence in International Law* (Manchester, UK, Manchester University Press, 1958).

Boyle, A and Chinkin, C, *The Making of International Law* (Oxford, UK, OUP, 2007).

Brand, RA and Jablonski, SR, *Forum Non Conveniens: History, Global Practice, and Future Under the Hague Convention on Choice of Court Agreements* (Oxford, UK, OUP, 2007).

Breuilly, J, *The Formation of the First German Nation-State: 1800–1871* (London, Macmillan, 1996).

Brierly, JL, *The Law of Nations* (first published 1928, 6th edn, Oxford, UK, Clarendon Press, 1963).

Brownlie, I, *Principles of Public International Law* (7th edn, Oxford, UK, OUP, 2008).

Brownlie, I, *Treaties and Indigenous Peoples* (Brookfield FM ed, Oxford, UK, Clarendon Press, 1992).

Caldwell, PC, *Popular Sovereignty and the Crisis of German Constitutional Law: The Theory & Practice of Weimar Constitutionalism* (Durham, NC, and London, Duke University Press, 1997).

Carr, EH, *The Twenty Years' Crisis* (first published 1939, Basingstoke, UK, Palgrave Macmillan, 2001).

Cassese, A, *International Law* (2nd edn, Oxford, UK, OUP, 2004).

Cassese, A, *International Law in a Divided World* (Oxford, UK, Clarendon Press, 1987).

Chang, H, *Globalisation, Economic Development and the Role of the State* (London, Zed Books, 2003).

Chappell, Z, *Deliberative Democracy, A Critical Introduction* (London, Palgrave, 2012).

Charlesworth, H and Chinkin, C, *The Boundaries of International Law: A Feminist Analysis* (Manchester, UK, Manchester University Press, 2000).

Chen, T, *The International Law of Recognition* (Green, LC ed, New York, Praeger, 1951).

Cicero, *The Republic* (54 BC).

Clapham, A, *Brierly's Law of Nations: An Introduction to the Role of International Law in International Relations* (7th edn, Oxford, UK, OUP, 2012).

Clapham, A, *Human Rights Obligations of Non-State Actors* (Oxford, UK, OUP, 2006).

Clark, JF, *African Stakes of the Congo War* (Basingstoke, UK, Palgrave Macmillan, 2004).

Clarke, L, *Public–Private Partnerships and Responsibility Under International Law: A Global Health Perspective* (Oxford, UK, Routledge, 2014).

Crawford, J, *Brownlie's Principles of Public International Law* (8th edn, Oxford, UK, OUP, 2012).

Crawford, J, *The Creation of States in International Law* (Oxford, UK, OUP, 2007).

Crawford, J, *The ILC's Articles on Responsibility of States: Introduction, Text and Commentaries* (Cambridge, UK, CUP, 2002).

Creveld, MV, *The Rise and Decline of the State* (Cambridge, UK, CUP, 1999).

Cullen, A, *The Concept of Non-International Armed Conflict in International Humanitarian Law* (Cambridge, UK, CUP, 2010).

Curtin, PD, *Cross-Cultural Trade in World History* (Cambridge, UK, CUP, 1984).

D'Aspremont, J, *Formalism and the Sources of International Law: A Theory of the Ascertainment of Legal Rules* (Oxford, UK, OUP, 2012).

De Jonge, A, *Transnational Corporations and International Law: Accountability in the Global Business Environment* (Cheltenham, UK, Edward Elgar, 2011).

Degan, VD, *Developments in International Law: Sources of International Law* (The Hague, Netherlands, Martinus Nijhoff, 1997) 27–8.

DeLupis, ID, *The International Legal Order* (Aldershot, UK, Ashgate, 1994).

Draper, GIAD, *The Red Cross Conventions* (New York, Praeger, 1958).

Dryzek, JS, *Deliberative Democracy and Beyond: Liberals, Critics, Contestations* (Oxford, UK, OUP, 2002).

Dryzek, JS, *Deliberative Global Politics: Discourse and Democracy in a Divided World* (Cambridge, UK, Polity Press, 2006).

Du Plessis, W, *The Balancing of Interests in Environmental Law in Africa* (Pretoria, SA, PULP, 2011).

Dworkin, R, *Law's Empire* (Oxford, UK, OUP, 1998).

Dyzenhaus, D, *Legality and Legitimacy, Carl Schmitt, Hans Kelsen, and Herman Heller in Weimar* (Oxford, UK, Clarendon Press, 1997).

Ebenstein, W, *The Pure Theory of Law* (New York, AM Kelley, 1969).

Edwards, A, *Violence Against Women and International Human Rights Law* (Cambridge, UK, CUP, 2011).

Engle, K, *The Elusive Promise of Indigenous Development: Rights, Culture, Strategy* (Durham, NC, and London, Duke University Press, 2010).

Evans, MD, *Religious Liberty and International Law in Europe* (Cambridge, UK, CUP, 2008).

Falk, RA, *Law in an Emerging Global Village: A Post-Westphalian Perspective* (New York, Transnational, 1998).

Franck, T, *Fairness in International Law and Institutions* (Oxford, UK, OUP, 1998).

Franck, T, *The Power of Legitimacy Among Nations* (Oxford, UK, OUP, 1990).

Friedman, M, *Capitalism and Freedom* (Chicago, IL, University of Chicago Press, 1962).

Fuller, LL, *The Law in Quest of Itself* (Clark, NJ, The Lawbook Exchange, 1999).

Gerber, CF, *Grundüge des Deutschen Staatsrechts* (1880).

Gierke, O, *Das Wesen der Menschlichen Verbände* (1902).

Gill, G, *The Nature and Development of The Modern State* (Basingstoke, UK, Palgrave Macmillan, 2003).

Giorgetti, C, *A Principled Approach to State Failure: International Community Actions in Emergency Situations* (Leiden, Netherlands, Brill, 2010).

Goldsmith, JL and Posner, EA, *The Limits of International Law* (Oxford, UK, OUP, 2005).

Grewe, WG, *The Epochs of International Law* (revised edn, Berlin, De Gruyter, 2000).

Grotius, H, *De jure belli ac pacis libri tres* (first published 1625, Kelsey, FW trans, Oxford, UK, Clarendon Press, 1925).

Gutmann, A and Thompson, D, *Why Deliberative Democracy?* (Princeton, NJ, Princeton University Press, 2004).

Habermas, J, *Between Facts and Norms* (Cambridge, MA, MIT Press, 1996).

Habermas, J, *Communication and the Evolution of Society* (McCarthy, T trans, Boston, MA, Beacon Books, 1979).

Habermas, J, *Moral Consciousness and Communicative Action* (Cambridge, MA, MIT Press, 1990).

Hall, WE, *A Treatise on International Law* (Higgins, AP ed, 7th edn, Oxford, UK, Clarendon Press, 1917).

Halleck, HW, *Halleck's International Law* Vol 1 (Baker, GS ed, 2nd edn, London, Kegan Paul, 1878).

Hart, HLA, *The Concept of Law* (first published 1961, 2nd edn, Oxford, UK, Clarendon Press, 1997).

Hart, HLA, *The Concept of Law* (first published 1961, 3rd edn, Oxford, UK, OUP, 2012).

Hegel, WF, *Philosophy of Right* (1821).

Held, D, *Democracy and the Global Order* (Cambridge, UK, Polity Press, 1995).

Henkin, L, *How Nations Behave: Law and Foreign Policy* (2nd edn, Cambridge, UK, CUP, 1979).

Henkin, L, *International Law: Politics, Values and Functions* (Recueil des Cours, The Hague, Martinus Nijhoff, 1989).

Herik, L, *The Contribution of the Rwanda Tribunal to the Development of International Law* (The Hague, Netherlands, Martinus Nijhoff, 2005).

Herodotus, *Histories* (440 BC, Aubrey de Sélincourt trans, London, Penguin, 1954).

Higgins, R, *International Law and the Avoidance, Containment and Resolution of Disputes* (Recueil des Cours, Leiden, Netherlands, Brill, 1991).

Higgins, R, *Problems and Process: International Law and How We Use It* (Oxford, UK, Clarendon Press, 1994).

Hobbes, T, *De Cive* (first published 1642, Tuck, R and Sliverthorne, M eds, Cambridge, UK, CUP, 1998).

Hobbes, T, *Leviathan*, (first published 1651, Tuck, R ed, Cambridge, UK, CUP, 1996).

Hollis, DB, *The Oxford Guide to Treaties* (Oxford, UK, OUP, 2012).

Horkheimer, M and Adorno, T, *Dialectic of Enlightenment* (John Cummin trans, London, Verso, 1997).

Hume, D, *A Treatise of Human Nature* (first published 1738, London, Thomas & Joseph Allman, 1817).

Igwe, UT, *Communicative Rationality and Deliberative Democracy of Jürgen Habermas: Toward Consolidation of Democracy in Africa* (London, LIT-Verlag, 2004).

Jackson, M, *Complicity in International Law* (Oxford, UK, OUP, 2015).

Janik, A and Toulmin, S, *Wittgenstein's Vienna* (London, Weidenfeld & Nicolson, 1973).

Jellinek, G, *Allemeine Staatslehre* (Berlin, Häring, 1905).

Jellinek, G, *Die Rechtliche Natur der Saatenvertrage* (Vienna, Hölder, 1880).

Jennings, R and Watts, A (eds), *Oppenheim's International Law* (9th edn, London, Longmans, Green, 1992).

Johnstone, I, *The Power of Deliberation: International Law, Politics and Organisations* (Oxford, UK, OUP, 2011).

Joseph, S, *Corporations and Transnational Human Rights Litigation* (Oxford, UK, Hart, 2004).

Kammerhofer, J, *Uncertainty in International Law: A Kelsenian Perspective* (Oxford, UK, Routledge, 2011).

Kant, I, *The Critique of Pure Reason* (first published 1781, Smith, NK trans, London, Macmillan, 1963).

Kant, I, *The Metaphysics of Morals* (first published 1797, Gregor, M trans, Cambridge, UK, CUP, 2003).

Karavias, M, *Corporate Obligations Under International Law* (Oxford, UK, OUP, 2013).

Karpat, KH, *Studies on Ottoman Social and Political History: Selected Articles and Essays* (Leiden, Netherlands, Brill, 2002).

Kauffmann, E, *Das Wesen Völkerrechts und die Clausula rebus sic stantibus* (Tübingen, Germany, Mohr, 1911).

Kelsen, H, *Collective Security Under International Law* (US Government Printing Office, 1957).

Kelsen, H, *General Theory of Law and State* (first published 1945, Wedberg, A trans, Cambridge, MA, Harvard University Press, 1949).

Kelsen, H, *General Theory of Norms* (first published 1979, Hartney, M trans, Oxford, UK, OUP, 1991).

Kelsen, H, *Hauptprobleme der Staatsrechtslehre, entwickelt aus der Lehre von Rechtssatz* (2nd edn, Tübingen, Germany, Mohr, 1923).

Kelsen, H, *Introduction to the Problems of Legal Theory* (first published 1934, Litschewski-Paulson, B and Paulson, SL trans, Oxford, UK, Clarendon Press, 2002).

Kelsen, H, *Peace Through Law* (Chapel Hill, NC, University of North Carolina Press, 1944).

Kelsen, H, *Principles of International Law* (New York, Rinehart, 1952).

Kelsen, H, *The Pure Theory of Law* (Knight, M trans, 2nd edn, Berkeley, CA, University of California Press, 1970).

Klabbers, J, *An Introduction to International Institutional Law* (2nd edn, Cambridge, UK, CUP, 2009).

Knight, WSM, *The Life and Works of Hugo Grotius* (No 4, Grotius Society Publications, London, Sweet & Maxwell, 1925).

Korhonen, O, *International Law Situated: An Analysis of the Lawyer's Stance towards Culture, History and Community* (London, Kluwer Law International, 2000).

Koskenniemi, M, *From Apology to Utopia: The Structure of International Legal Argument* (Cambridge, UK, CUP, 2006).

Koskenniemi, M, *The Gentle Civiliser of Nations: The Rise and Fall of International Law 1870–1960* (Cambridge, UK, CUP, 2002).

Kreijen, G, Brus, M, Duursma, J, De Vos, E and Dugard, J (eds), *State, Sovereignty, and International Governance* (Oxford, UK, OUP, 2002).

Kreijen, G, *State Failure, Sovereignty and Effectiveness: Legal Lessons from the Decolonisation of Sub-Saharan Africa* (The Hague, Netherlands, Martinus Nijhoff, 2004).

Kunz, JL, *On the Theoretical Basis of the Law of Nations* (London, Sweet & Maxwell, 1919).

Laband, P, *Das Staatsrecht des Deutschen Reiches* (first published 1880, 5th edn, Aalen, Germany, Scientia, 1964).

Laham, N, *Crossing the Rubicon: Ronald Reagan and US Policy in the Middle East* (Aldershot, UK, Ashgate, 2004).

Lalonde, S, *Determining Boundaries in a Conflicted World: The Role of Uti Possidetis* (London, McGill-Queen's University Press, 2002).

Landman, T, *Protecting Human Rights: A Comparative Study* (Washington, DC, Georgetown University Press, 2005).

Lasson, A, *Princip und Zukunft des Völkerrechts* (Berlin, W Hertz, 1837).

Lauterpacht, H, *International Law and Human Rights* (New York, Praeger, 1950).

Lauterpacht, H, *Recognition in International Law* (Cambridge, UK, CUP, 1947).

Lauterpacht, H, *The Development of International Law by the International Court* (Cambridge, UK, CUP, 1982).

Lauterpacht, H, *The Development of International Law by the Permanent Court of International Justice* (London, Longmans, Green, 1934).

Lawrence, TJ, *The Principles of International Law* (New York, Heath, 1895).

Lidenfeld, DF, *The Practical Imagination: The German Sciences of State in the Nineteenth Century* (Chicago, IL, University of Chicago Press, 2008).

Lloyd, D, *The Idea of Law* (revised edn, London, Penguin, 1981).

Locke, J, *Second Treatise on Government* (1690).

McBeth, A, *International Economic Actors and Human Rights* (Oxford, UK, Routledge, 2011).

McNair, AD, *The Law of Treaties* (Oxford, UK, Clarendon Press, 1961).

Moir, L, *Law of Internal Armed Conflicts* (Cambridge, UK, CUP, 2002).

Morgenthau, H, *Politics Among Nations* (New York, McGraw-Hill, 1948).

Morris, CW, *An Essay on the Modern State* (Cambridge, UK, CUP, 2002).

Morris, JH, *Going for Gold: The History of Newmont Mining Corporation* (Tuscaloosa, AL, University of Alabama Press, 2010).

Muchlinski, P, *Multinational Enterprises and the Law* (2nd edn, Oxford, UK, OUP, 2007).

Murkens, JEK, *From Empire to Union: Conceptions of German Constitutional Law since 1871* (Oxford, UK, OUP, 2013).

Neff, SC, *Justice Among Nations: A History of International Law* (Cambridge, MA, Harvard University Press, 2014).

Nijman, JE, *The Concept of International Legal Personality: An Inquiry into the History and Theory of International Law* (The Hague, Netherlands, TMC Asser Press, 2004).

Nussbaum, A, *A Concise History of the Law of Nations* (London, Macmillan, 1954).

O'Connell, DP, *International Law* Vol 1 (London, Stevens, 1965).

Oluduro, O, *Oil Exploitation and Human Rights Violations in Nigeria's Oil Producing Communities* (Cambridge, UK, Intersentia, 2014).

Oppenheim, L, *International Law, A Treatise* Vol II (Lauterpacht, H ed, London, Longmans, Green, 1952).

Oppenheim, L, *International Law: A Treatise* Vol I (Roxburgh, R ed, 3rd edn, London, Longmans, Green, 1920).

Oppenheim, L, *The Future of International Law* (Oxford, UK, OUP, 1921).

Oshionebo, E, *Regulating Transnational Corporations in Domestic and International Regimes: An African Case Study* (Toronto, University of Toronto Press, 2009).

Parlett, K, *The Individual in the International Legal System: Continuity and Change in International Law* (Cambridge, UK, CUP, 2011).

Paz, RY, *A Gateway Between a Distant God and a Cruel World: The Contribution of Jewish German-Speaking Scholars to International Law* (The Hague, Netherlands, Martinus Nijhoff, 2012).

Pegg, S, *International Society and the de facto State* (Aldershot, UK, Ashgate, 1989).

Plato, *The Republic* (380 BC, Jowett, B trans, New York, Dover, 2000).

Pollock, F, *Essays in the Law* (London, Macmillan, 1922).

Polybius, *The Histories* (Waterfield, R trans, Dewald, C ed, Oxford, UK, Oxford World Classics, 2008).

Portmann, R, *Legal Personality in International Law* (Cambridge, UK, CUP, 2010).

Pufendorf, S, *De Jure Nature et Gentium Libri Octo* (1729).

Pulzer, P, *Germany 1870–1945 – Politics, State Formation and War* (Oxford, UK, OUP, 1997).

Raič, D, *Developments in International Law Vol 43: Statehood and the Law of Self-Determination* (The Hague, Netherlands, Martinus Nijhoff, 2002).

Rawls, J, *Political Liberalism* (expanded edn, New York, Columbia University Press, 2005).

Raz, J, *The Authority of Law* (first published 1979, 2nd edn, Oxford, UK, OUP, 2009).

Raz, J, *The Concept of a Legal System – An Introduction to the Theory of Legal System* (2nd edn, Oxford, UK, Clarendon Press, 1980).

Reinisch, A, *International Organisations Before National Courts* (Cambridge, UK, CUP, 2000).

Renton, D, Seddon, D and Zellig, L, *The Congo: Plunder and Resistance* (London, Zed Books, 2007).

Riall, L, *The Italian Risorgimento – State, Society and National Unification* (Oxford, UK, Routledge, 1999).

Robertson, G, *Crimes Against Humanity: The Struggle for Global Justice* (London, Penguin, 2006).

Ruggie, JG, *Just Business: Multinational Corporations and Human Rights* (London, WW Norton, 2013).

Russell, FH, *The Just War in the Middle Ages* (Cambridge, UK, CUP, 1977).

Saul, B, Kinley, D and Mowbray, J, *The International Covenant on Economic, Social and Cultural Rights: Cases, Materials, and Commentary* (Oxford, UK, OUP, 2014).

Sawyer, B and Sawyer, PH, *Medieval Scandinavia: From Conversion to Reformation, Circa 800–1500* (Minneapolis, MN, University of Minnesota Press, 1993).

Schmitt, C, *Political Theology: Four Chapters on the Theory of Sovereignty* (George Schwab trans, Cambridge, MA, MIT Press, 1985).

Schmitt, C, *The Concept of the Political* (first published 1927, Chicago, IL, University of Chicago Press, 2008).

Schneewind, JB, *The Invention of Autonomy: A History of Modern Moral Philosophy* (Cambridge, UK, CUP, 1997).

Scott, JB, *The Catholic Conception of International Law* (Clark, NJ, The Lawbook Exchange, 2007).

Shaw, M, *Title to Territory in Africa: International Legal Issues* (Oxford, UK, OUP, 1986).

Simons, P and Macklin, A, *The Governance Gap: Extractive Industries, Human Rights and the Home State Advantage* (Oxford, UK, Routledge, 2014).

Sivakumaran, S, *The Law of Non-International Armed Conflict* (Oxford, UK, OUP, 2012).

Skinner, Q, *The Foundations of Modern Political Thought* (Cambridge, UK, CUP, 1978).

Smith, A, *An Inquiry into the Nature and Causes of the Wealth of Nations* (1776).

Somos, M, *Secularisation and the Leiden Circle* (Leiden, Netherlands, Brill, 2011).

Spiermann, O, *International Legal Argument in the Permanent Court of International Justice* (Cambridge, UK, CUP, 2005) 170.

Stolleis, M, *Public Law in Germany 1800–1914* (New York, Berghahn Books, 2001).

Strayer, JR, *On the Medieval Origins of the Modern State* (Princeton, NJ, Princeton University Press, 1972).

Stumpf, CA, *The Grotian Theology of International Law: Hugo Grotius and the Moral Foundations of International Relations* (Berlin, De Gruyter Publishing, 2006).

Suarez, F, *De Legibus, ac Deo Legislatore* (Williams, GL trans, Oxford, UK, Clarendon Press, 1944).

Teschke, B, *The Myth of 1648: Class, Geopolitics, and the Making of Modern International Relations* (London, Verso Press, 2003).

Toyoda, T, *Theory and Politics of the Law of Nations: Political Bias in International Law Discourse of Seven German Court Councillors in the Seventeenth and Eighteenth Centuries* (The Hague, Netherlands, Martinus Nijhoff, 2011) 31–5.

Triepel, H, *Völkerrecht und Landesrecht* (Leipzig, Germany, CL Hirschfeld, 1899).

Triggs, G, *International Law: Contemporary Principles and Practices* (Chatsworth, 2006).

Tully, S, *Corporations and International Lawmaking* (The Hague, Netherlands, Martinus Nijhoff, 2007).

Tuori, K, *Ratio and Voluntas: The Tension Between Reason and Will in Law* (Aldershot, UK, Ashgate, 2011).

UK Ministry of Defence, *The Manual of the Law of Armed Conflict* (Oxford, UK, OUP, 2004).

Vattel, E, *The Law of Nations: Or, Principles of the Law of Nature Applied to the Conduct and Affairs of Nations and Sovereigns* (1758).

Verdross, A, *Die Verfassung der Völkerrechtsgemeinschaft* (The Hague, Netherlands, Springer, 1926).

Vickers, M, *The Albanians: A Modern History* (London, IB Tauris, 2006).

Vinx, L, *Hans Kelsen's Pure Theory of Law: Legality and Legitimacy* (Oxford, UK, OUP, 2007).

Vitoria, F, *De Indis et De Jure Belli Reflectiones* (first published 1532, Bate, JP trans, Nys, E ed, New York, Oceana, 1963).

Vitoria, F, *De Potesate Civili* (1528).

Voegelin, R, *Published Essays 1922–1928* (Columbia, MO, University of Missouri Press, 2003).

Wallace, CD, *Legal Control of the Multinational Enterprise, National Regulatory Techniques and the Prospects for International Controls* (Leiden, Netherlands, Brill, 1982).

Watson, JS, *Theory and Reality in the International Protection of Human Rights* (The Hague, Netherlands, Martinus Nijhoff, 1999).

Weber, M, *Economy and Society* Vol 1(first published 1922, Roth, G and Wittich, C eds, Berkeley, CA, University of California Press, 2013).

Wheatley, S, *The Democratic Legitimacy of International Law* (Oxford, UK, Hart, 2010).

Wheaton, H, *Elements of International Law* (Phillipson, C ed, 5th edn, London, Stephens, 1916).

Wilde, R, *International Territorial Administration: How Trusteeship and the Civilizing Mission Never Went Away* (Oxford, UK, OUP, 2010).

Wolff, C, *Jus Gentium Methodo Scientifica Pertractum* (1749).

Wood, N, *Cicero's Social and Political Thought* (Berkeley, CA, University of California Press, 1988).

Zegveld, L, *Accountability of Armed Opposition Groups in International Law* (Cambridge, UK, CUP, 2002).

Zerk, JA, *Multinationals and Corporate Social Responsibility: Limitations and Opportunities in International Law* (Cambridge, UK, CUP, 2006).

Edited collections

Addo, M (ed), *Human Rights Standards and the Responsibility of Transnational Corporations* (The Hague, Netherlands, Springer, 1999).

Alfredsson, G, Grimheden, J *et al* (eds), *International Human Rights Monitoring Mechanisms, Essays in Honour of Jakob Th. Möller* (2nd revised edn, The Hague, Netherlands, Martinus Nijhoff, 2009).

Alston, P (ed), *Non-State Actors and Human Rights* (Oxford, UK, OUP, 2005).

Arnold, R and Quénivet, NNR (eds), *International Humanitarian Law and Human Rights Law: Towards A New Merger in International Law* (Leiden, Netherlands, Brill, 2008).

Baderin, MA and Ssenyonjo, M (eds), *International Human Rights Law: Six Decades After the UDHR and Beyond* (Aldershot, UK, Ashgate, 2010) 250–1.

Bedjaoui, M (ed), *International Law: Achievements and Prospects* (The Hague, Netherlands, Martinus Nijhoff, 1991).

Begg, I, Peterson, J and Weiler, JHH (eds), *Integration in an Expanding European Union: Reassessing the Fundamentals* (London, Blackwell, 2003).

Bianchi, A (ed), *Non-State Actors and International Law – The Library of Essays in International Law* (Aldershot, UK, Ashgate, 2009).

Brecht, A, 'Sovereignty' in Speier, H and Kahler, A, *War in Our Time* (London, WW Norton, 1939) 58–77.

Byers, M (ed), *The Role of Law in International Politics: Essays in International Relations and International Law* (Oxford, UK, OUP, 2001).

Cane, P and Kritzer, HM (eds), *The Oxford Handbook of Empirical Legal Research* (Oxford, UK, OUP, 2010).

Coicaud, JM, Doyle, MW and Gardner, AM (eds), *The Globalisation of Human Rights* (Tokyo, UN University Press, 2003).

Cook, RJ (ed), *Human Rights of Women: National and International Perspectives* (Philadelphia, PA, University of Pennsylvania Press, 1994).

Craven, MCR, Fitzmaurice, M and Vogiatzi, M (eds), *Time, History and International Law* (The Hague, Netherlands, Martinus Nijhoff, 2007).

Crawford, J, Pellet, A and Olleson, S (eds), *The Law of International Responsibility* (Oxford, UK, OUP 2010).

D'Aspremont, J (ed), *Multiple Perspectives on Non-State Actors in International Law* (Oxford, UK, Routledge, 2011).

D'Aspremont, J and Kammerhoder, J (eds), *International Legal Positivism in a Post-Modern World* (Cambridge, UK, CUP, 2015).

De Lint, W, Marmo, M and Chazal, N (eds), *Crime and Justice in International Society* (Oxford, UK, Routledge, 2014).

De Schutter, O (ed), *Transnational Corporations and Human Rights* (Oxford, UK, Hart, 2006).

Deva, S and Bilchitz, D (eds), *Human Rights Obligations of Businesses: Beyond the Corporate Responsibility to Protect* (Cambridge, UK, CUP, 2013).

Emiri, F and Deinduomo, G (eds), *Law and Petroleum Industry in Nigeria: Current Challenges* (Oxford, UK, African Books Collective, 2009).

Evans, MD (ed), *International Law* (2nd edn, Oxford, UK, OUP, 2006).

Evans, MD (ed), *International Law* (3rd edn, Oxford, UK, OUP, 2010).

Fassbender, B and Peters, A (eds), *The Oxford Handbook of the History of International Law* (Oxford, UK, OUP, 2012).

Fleck, D (ed), *Handbook of International Humanitarian Law* (3rd edn, Oxford, UK, OUP, 2013).

Fleck, D and Bothe, M (eds), *The Handbook of International Humanitarian law* (2nd edn, Oxford, UK, OUP, 2008).

Follesdal, A, Peters, B *et al* (eds), *The Legitimacy of International Human Rights Regimes: Legal, Political and Philosophical Perspectives* (Cambridge, UK, CUP, 2013).

Gal-Or, N, Ryngaert, C and Noortmann, M (eds), *Responsibilities of the Non-State Actor in Armed Conflict and the Market Place: Theoretical and Empirical Findings* (Leiden, Netherlands, Brill, 2015).

Gillooly, M (ed), *The Law Relating to Corporate Groups* (Annandale, NSW, Federation Press 1993).

Goldstein, J and Keohane, RO (eds), *Ideas and Beliefs, Institutions, and Political Change* (Ithaca, NY, Cornell University Press, 1993).

Grewe, WG (ed), *Fontes Historiae Iuris Gentium: Sources Relating to the History of the Law of Nations* Vol 2 (Berlin, De Gruyter, 1988).

Hart, HLA, *Essays in Jurisprudence and Philosophy* (Oxford, UK, OUP, 1983).

Higgins, R, *Themes and Theories, Selected Essays, Speeches and Writings in International Law* Vol 1 (Oxford, UK, OUP, 2009).

Hume, D, *Essays and Treatises on Several Subjects* (Edinburgh, Millar, Kincaid & Donaldson, 1758).

Joseph, S and McBeth, A (eds), *Research Handbook on International Human Rights Law* (Cheltenham, UK, Edward Elgar, 2010).

Josselin, D and Wallace, W (eds), *Non-State Actors in World Politics* (Basingstoke, UK, Palgrave Macmillan, 2001).

Kamminga, MT and Zia-Zarifi, S (eds), *Liability of Multinational Corporations Under International Law* (London, Kluwer, 2000).

Kingsbury, B and Straumann, B (eds), *The Roman Foundations of the Law of Nations: Alberico Gentili and the Justice of Empire* (Oxford, UK, OUP, 2010).

Klosko, G (ed), *The Oxford Handbook of the History of Political Philosophy* (Oxford, UK, OUP, 2011).

Lauterpacht, E (ed), *International Law: Collected Papers of Hersch Lauterpacht* Vol 1 (Cambridge, UK, CUP, 1970).

Lauterpacht, E (ed), *International Law: Collected Papers of Hersch Lauterpacht* Vol 2 (Cambridge, UK, CUP, 1975).

Lenzerini, F (ed), *Reparations for Indigenous Peoples: International and Comparative Perspectives* (Oxford, UK, OUP, 2008).

Lesaffer, R (ed), *Peace Treaties and International Law in European History* (Cambridge, UK, CUP, 2004).

Lesaffer, R (ed), *The Twelve Years Truce (1609): Peace, War and Law in the Low Countries at the Turn of the 17th Century* (The Hague, Netherlands, Martinus Nijhoff, 2014).

Miller, RA and Bratspies, RM (eds), *Progress in International Law* (The Hague, Netherlands, Martinus Nijhoff, 2008).

Moore, JN (ed), *Law and Civil War in the Modern World* (Baltimore, MD, Johns Hopkins Press, 1974).

Natarajan, M (ed), *International Crime and Justice* (Cambridge, UK, CUP, 2011).

Nollkaemper, A and Plakokefalos, I (eds), *Principles of Shared Responsibility in International Law* (Cambridge, UK, CUP, 2014).

Onuf, N, *International Legal Theory: Essays and Engagements 1966–2006* (Oxford, UK, Routledge, 2008).

Orakhelashvili, A (ed), *Research Handbook on the Theory and History of International Law* (Cheltenham, UK, Edward Elgar, 2011).

Paulson, SL and Litschewski-Paulson, B (eds), *Normativity and Norms: Critical Perspectives on Kelsenian Themes* (Oxford, UK, OUP, 1999).

Pegg, S and Frynas, JG (eds), *Transnational Corporations and Human Rights* (Basingstoke, UK, Palgrave Macmillan, 2003).

Peters, A, Koechlin, L, Förster, T and Zinkernagel, GF (eds), *Non-State Actors as Standard Setters* (Cambridge, UK, CUP, 2009).

Ragazzi, M (ed), *International Responsibility Today: Essays in Memory of Oscar Schachter* (Leiden, Netherlands, Brill, 2005).

Rawlings, R, Leyland, P and Young, A, *Sovereignty and the Law: Domestic, European and International Perspectives* (Oxford, UK, OUP, 2013).

Roxani, M, Sabra, A and Sijpesteijn, P (eds), *Histories of the Middle East* (Leiden, Netherlands, Brill, 2010).

Rubin, B (ed), *Conflict and Insurgency in the Contemporary Middle East* (Oxford, UK, Routledge, 2009).

Ryngaert, C and Noortmann, M (eds), *Non-State Actor Dynamics in International Law: From Law-Takers to Law-Makers* (Aldershot, UK, Ashgate, 2010).

Sewall, SB and Kaysen, C (eds), *The United States and the International Criminal Court: National Security and International Law* (Oxford, UK, Rowman & Littlefield, 2000).

Shelton, D (ed), *Commitment and Compliance: The Role of Non-binding Norms in the International Legal System* (Oxford, UK, OUP, 2003).

Shelton, D (ed), *The Oxford Handbook on Human Rights* (Oxford, UK, OUP, 2013).

Speier, H and Kahler, A, *War in Our Time* (London, WW Norton, 1939).

Sullivan, R (ed), *Business and Human Rights: Dilemmas and Solutions* (Sheffield, UK, Greenleaf, 2003).

Tur, R and Twining, W (eds), *Essays on Kelsen* (Oxford, UK, Clarendon Press, 1986).

Vagts, DF, Meron, T, Schwebel, SM and Keever, C (eds), *Humanizing the Laws of War: Selected Writings of Richard Baxter* (Oxford, UK, OUP, 2013).

Vandenhole, W (ed), *Challenging Territoriality in Human Rights Law* (Oxford, UK, Routledge, 2015).

Victor, DG, Raustialia, K and Skolnikoff, EB (eds), *The Implementation and Effectiveness of International Environmental Commitments Theory and Practice* (Cambridge, MA, MIT Press, 1998).

Wellens, K (ed), *International Law: Theory and Practice* (The Hague, Netherlands, Martinus Nijhoff, 1998).

Winter, G (ed), *Multilevel Governance of Global Environmental Change – Perspectives from Science, Sociology and Law* (Cambridge, UK, CUP, 2006).

Wolfrum, R and Roben, V (eds), *Legitimacy in International Law* (The Hague, Netherlands, Springer, 2008).

Journal articles

Aaron, KK, 'New Corporate Social Responsibility Models for Oil Companies in Nigeria's Delta Region: What Challenges for Sustainability' (2012) 12 *Progress Dev Stud* 259.

Acquaviva, G, 'Subjects of International Law: A Power-based Analysis' (2008) 38 *Vand J Transnat'l L* 345.

Ako, RT, 'Nigeria's Land Use Act: An Anti-Thesis to Environmental Justice' (2009) 53 *J Afr L* 289.

Alkoby, A, 'Non-State Actors and the Legitimacy of International Environmental Law' (2003) 3 *Non-State Actors & Int'l L* 23.

Allott, P, 'Reconstituting Humanity – New International Law' (1992) 3 *EJIL* 219.

Alston, P, 'The Myopia of the Handmaidens: International Lawyers and Globalisation' (1997) 8 *EJIL* 442.

Amao, OO, 'Corporate Social Responsibility, Multinational Corporations and the Law in Nigeria: Controlling Multinationals in Host States' (2008) 52 *J Afr L* 89.

Aziz, D, 'Global Public–Private Partnerships in International Law' (2012) 2 *Asian JIL* 339.

Barnidge, P, 'The Due Diligence Principle under International Law' (2006) 8 *Int'l CL Rev* 81.

Bartels, S, Scott, J, Leaning, J, Mukwege, D, Lipton, R and VanRooyen, M, 'Surviving Sexual Violence in Eastern Democratic Republic of the Congo' (2010) 11 *J Int'l Women's Stud* 37.

Bassiouni, MC, 'Criminal Law: The New Wars and the Crisis of Compliance with the Law of Armed Conflict by Non-State Actors' (2008) 98 *J Crim L & Criminology* 711.

Baxter, RR, 'International Law in "Her Infinite Variety"' (1980) 29 *ICLQ* 549.

Baxter, RR, 'Some Existing Problems of Humanitarian Law' (1975) 14 *Mil L & L War Rev* 279.

Beaulac, S, 'Emer de Vattel and the Externalisation of Sovereignty' (2003) 5 *J Hist Int'l L* 237.

Beaulac, S, 'The Westphalian Model in Defining International Law: Challenging the Myth' (2004) 8 *Aust J Leg Hist* 181.

Bebbington, DH and Bebbington, AJ, 'Extraction, Territory and Inequalities: Gas in the Bolivian Chaco' (2010) 30 *Can J Dev Stud* 259.

Bederman, DJ, 'The Souls of International Organisations: Legal Personality and the Lighthouse at Cape Spartel' (1996) 36 *Va J Int'l L* 275.

Bergmann, G and Zerpy, L, 'The Formalism in Kelsen's Pure Theory of Law' (1945) 55 *Ethics* 110.

Bickley, LS, 'US Resistance to the International Criminal Court: Is the Sword Mightier than the Law?' (2000) 14 *Emory Int'l L Rev* 213.

Bilkova, V, 'Treat Them as They Deserve? Three Approaches to Armed Opposition Groups under Current International Law' (2010) 4 *Hum Rts & Int'l Legal Discourse* 111.

Binion, G, 'Human Rights: A Feminist Perspective' (1995) 17 *Hum Rts Q* 509.

Bismuth, R, 'Mapping a Responsibility of Corporations for Violations of International Humanitarian Law Sailing Between International and Domestic Legal Orders' (2010) 38 *Denv J Int'l L & Pol'y* 203.

Boed, R, 'Individual Criminal Responsibility for Violations of Article 3 Common to the Geneva Conventions of 1949 and of Additional Protocol II Thereto in the Case of the International Criminal Tribunal for Rwanda' (2002) 13 *Crim L Forum* 293.

Bourloyannis, C, 'The Security Council of the United Nations and the Implementation of International Humanitarian Law' (1992) 20 *Denv J Int'l L & Pol'y* 335.

Boven, TV, 'The Role of Non-Governmental Organisations in International Human Rights Standard-Setting: A Prerequisite of Democracy' (1990) 20 *Cal W Int'l LJ* 207.

Boyle, A and Harrison, J, 'Judicial Settlement of International Environmental Disputes: Current Problems' (2013) 4 *J Int'l Disp Settlement* 245.

Buckley, OM, 'Unregulated Armed Conflict: Non-State Armed Groups, International Humanitarian Law, and Violence in Western Sahara' (2012) 37 *NCJ Int'l L & Com Reg* 793.

Buhmann, K, 'Integrating Human Rights in Emerging Regulation of Corporate Social Responsibility: The EU Case' (2011) 7 *Int'l JLC* 139.

Burgis, M, 'Faith in the State? Traditions of Territoriality, International Law and the Emergence of Modern Arab Statehood' (2009) 11 *J Hist Int'l L* 37.

Bush, JA, 'The Prehistory of Corporations and Conspiracy in International Criminal Law: What Nuremberg Really Said' (2009) 109 *Colum L Rev* 1094.

Butkevych, O, 'History of Ancient International Law: Challenges and Prospects' (2003) 5 *J Hist Int'l L* 189.

Caflisch, L, 'Chairman's Report of the First Periodical Meeting on International Humanitarian Law (Geneva 19–23 January 1998)' (1998) 38 *Int'l Rev Red Cross* 366.

Cantegreil, J, 'The Audacity of the Texaco/Calasiatic Award: René-Jean Dupuy and the Internationalisation of Foreign Investment Law' (2011) 22 *EJIL* 441.

Carasco, EF and Singh, JB, 'Towards Holding Transnational Corporations Responsible for Human Rights' (2010) 22 *Eur Bus Rev* 432.

Carrillo-Suárez, A, '*Hors de Logique*: Contemporary Issues in International Humanitarian Law as it Applies to Internal Armed Conflict' (1999) 15 *Am U Int'l L Rev* 1.

Cass, DZ, 'Navigating the Newstream: Recent Critical Scholarship in International Law' (1996) 65 *Nordic J Int'l L* 341.

Cassese, A, 'The Status of Rebels Under the 1977 Geneva Protocol on Non-International Armed Conflicts' (1981) 30 *ICLQ* 416.

Castellino, J, 'Territory and Identity in International Law: The Struggle for Self-Determination in the Western Sahara' (1999) 28 *Millennium J Int'l Stud* 523.

Chandler, G, 'Oil Companies and Human Rights' (1998) 7 *Bus Ethics* 69.

Chanovitz, S, 'Non-Governmental Organisations and International Law' (2006) 100 *AJIL* 348.

Charney, JI, 'Transnational Corporations and Developing Public International Law' (1983) 32 *Duke LJ* 748.

Chinkin, C, 'A Critique of the Public/Private Dimension' (1999) 10 *Eur J Int'l L*, 387.

Clapham, A, 'Human Rights Obligations of Non-State Actors in Conflict Situations' (2006) 88 *Int'l Rev Red Cross* 491.

Clapham, C, 'Degrees of Statehood' (1998) 24 *Rev Int'l Stud* 143.

Clavier, S, 'Contrasting Franco-American Perspectives on Sovereignty' (2008) 14 *Ann Surv Int'l & Comp L* 1.

Collier, P and Hoeffler, A, 'On Economic Causes of Civil War' (1998) 50 *Oxf Econ Pap* 563.

Conklin, WE, 'The Myth of Primordialism in Cicero's Theory of *Jus Gentium*' (2010) 23 *LJIL* 479.

Coomans, F, 'The Extraterritorial Scope of the International Covenant on Economic, Social and Cultural Rights in the Work of the United Nations Committee on Economic Social and Cultural Rights' (2011) 11 *Hum Rts L Rev* 1.

Copelon, R, 'Recognising the Egregious in the Everyday: Domestic Violence as Torture' (1994) 25 *Colum Hum Rts L Rev* 291.

Coumans, C, 'Alternative Accountability Mechanisms and Mining: The Problem of Effective Impunity' (2010) 30 *Can J Dev Stud* 27.

Crawford, J, 'The ILC's Articles on the Responsibility of States for Internationally Wrongful Acts: A Retrospect' (2002) 96 *AJIL* 874.

Cronogue, G, 'Rebels, Negligent Support, and State Accountability: Holding States Accountable for the Human Rights Violations of Non-State Actors' (2013) 23 *Duke J Comp & Int'l L* 365.

Cutler, AC, 'Critical Reflections on the Westphalian Assumptions of International Law and Organisation: A Crisis of Legitimacy' (2001) 27 *Rev Int'l Stud* 133.

D'Amato, A, 'Softness in International Law: A Self-Serving Quest for New Legal Materials: A Reply to Jean d'Aspremont' (2009) 20 *EJIL* 897.

D'Aspremont, J, 'Softness in International Law: A Self-Serving Quest for New Legal Materials' (2008) 19 *EJIL* 1076.

D'Aspremont, J, 'The Doctrine of Fundamental Rights of States and the Functions of Anthropomorphic Thinking in International Law' (2015) 4 *CJICL* (forthcoming).

Daboné, Z, 'International Law: Armed Groups in a State-Centric System' (2011) 93 *Int'l Rev Red Cross* 395.

David, E, 'Le droit international humanitaire et les acteurs non étatiques' (2003) 27 *Collegium* 27.

De Brabandere, E, 'Human Rights Obligations and Transnational Corporations: The Limits of Direct Corporate Responsibility' (2010) 4 *Hum Rts & Int'l Legal Discourse* 66.

De Brabandere, E, 'Non-state Actors, State-Centrism and Human Rights Obligations' (2009) 22 *LJIL* 191, 192.

De Burca, G, 'Developing Democracy Beyond the State' (2008) 46 *Colum J Transnat'l L* 221.

De Jong, A, 'Transnational Corporations and International Law: Bringing TNCs out of the Accountability Vacuum' (2011) 7 *Crit Perspectives Int'l Bus* 66.

De Moraes Farias, PF, 'Silent Trade: Myth and Historical Evidence' (1974) 1 *History in Africa* 9.

De Vito, D, 'Rape as Genocide: The Group/Individual Schism' (2008) 9 *Hum Rts Rev* 361.

Del Vecchio, G, 'Grotius and the Foundation of International Law' (1962) 37 *NYU L Rev* 260.

Demos, R, 'Paradoxes in Plato's Doctrine of the Ideal State' (1957) 7 *Classical Q* 164.

Deva, S, 'Acting Extraterritorially to Tame Multinational Corporations for Human Rights Violations: "Who Should Bell the Cat?"' (2004) 5 *Melb J Int'l L* 37.

Devine, DJ, 'Requirements of Statehood Re-examined' (1971) 34 *MLR* 410.

Dinham, B and Sarangi, S, 'The Bhopal Gas Tragedy 1984 to . . .? The Evasion of Corporate Responsibility' (2002) 14 *Environ Urban* 89.

Dixon, R, 'Rape as a Crime in International Humanitarian Law: Where to from Here?' (2002) 13 *EJIL* 697.

Docherty, B, 'Breaking New Ground: The Convention on Cluster Munitions and the Evolution of International Humanitarian Law' (2009) 31 *Hum Rts Q* 959.

Domingo, R, 'Gaius, Vattel, and the New Global Law Paradigm' (2011) 22 *EJIL* 627.

Domingo, R, 'The Crisis of International Law' (2009) 42 *Vand J Transnat'l L* 1543.

Donoho, D, 'Human Rights Enforcement in the Twenty-First Century' (2006) 35 *Ga J Int'l & Comp L* 1.

Dorward, DJ, '*Forum Non Conveniens* Doctrine and the Judicial Protection of Multinational Corporations from Forum Shopping Plaintiffs' (1998) 19 *U Pa J Int'l Econ L* 141.

Drimmer, J, 'Human Rights and the Extractive Industries: Litigation and Compliance Trends' (2010) 3 *JWEL & B* 121.

Dudai, R, 'Closing the Gap: Symbolic Reparations and Armed Groups' (2011) 93 *Int'l Rev Red Cross* 783.

Duval-Major, J, 'One Way Ticket Home: The Federal Doctrine of *Forum Non Conveniens* and the International Plaintiff' (1992) 77 *Cornell L Rev* 650.

Ebeku, KSA, 'Constitutional Right to a Healthy Environment and Human Rights Approaches to Environmental Protection in Nigeria: Gbemre v. Shell Revisited' (2007) 16 *Rev Eur Community Int'l Environ L* 312.

Ebke, WF, 'The "Real Seat" Doctrine in the Conflict of Corporate Laws' (2002) 36 *Int'l Lawyer* 1015.

Elshtain, JB, 'Sovereign God, Sovereign State, Sovereign Self' (1991) 66 *Notre Dame L Rev* 1355.

Enneking, LFH, 'Multinational Corporations, Human Rights Violations, and a 1789 U.S. Statute: A brief exploration of the case of Kiobel v. Shell' (2012) 3 *Nederlands Internationaal Privaatrecht* 396.

Eulau, HHF, 'Theories of Federalism under the Holy Roman Empire' (1941) 35 *APSR* 643.

Eweje, G, 'Environmental Costs and Responsibilities Resulting from Oil Exploitation in Developing Countries: The Case of the Niger Delta' (2006) 69 *J Bus Ethics* 27.

Fenrich, WJ, 'The Law Applicable to Targeting and Proportionality after Operation Allied Force: A View from the Outside' (2000) 3 *YB Int'l Humanitarian L* 53.

Fleiner-Gerster, T and Meyer, MA, 'New Developments in Humanitarian Law: A Challenge to the Concept of Sovereignty' (1985) 34 *ICLQ* 267.

Fox, GH, Nolte, G, Roth, BR and Stacy, H, 'Sovereignty: Essential, Variegated, or Irrelevant' (2005) 99 *ASIL Proc* 387.

Fox, M, 'Child Soldiers and International Law: Patchwork Gains and Conceptual Debates' (2005) 7 *Hum Rts Rev* 27.

Freedman, J, 'Tackling the Tin Wars in DR Congo' (2011) 24 *Mineral Economics* 45.

Frohnen, BP, 'A Problem of Power: The Impact of Modern Sovereignty on the Rule of Law in Comparative and Historical Perspective' (2012) 20 *Transnat'l L & Contemp Probs* 599.

Frynas, JG, 'Legal Change in Africa: Evidence from Oil-Related Litigation in Nigeria' (1999) 43 *J Afr L* 121.

Frynas, JG, 'Political Instability and Business: Locus on Shell in Nigeria' (1998) 19 *Third World Q* 457.

Frynas, JG, 'The False Developmental Promise of Corporate Social Responsibility: Evidence from Multinational Oil Companies' (2005) 81 *Royal Institute Int'l Affairs* 581.

Goldberg, P and Kelly, N, 'International Human Rights and Violence Against Women' (1993) 6 *Harv Hum Rts J* 195.

Gomulkiewicz, RW, 'International Law Governing Aid to Opposition Groups in Civil War: Resurrecting the Standards of Belligerency' (1988) 63 *Wash L Rev* 43.

Green, F, 'Fragmentation in Two Dimensions: The ICJ's Flawed Approach to Non-State Actors and International Legal Personality' (2008) 9 *Melb J Int'l L* 47.

Greenen, S and Claessens, K, 'Disputed Access to the Gold Sites in Luhwindja, Eastern Democratic Republic of the Congo' (2013) 51 *JMAS* 85.

Gross, L, 'The Peace of Westphalia 1648–1948' (1948) 42 *AJIL* 20.

Gunning, IR, 'Modernising Customary International Law' (1991) 31 *Va J Int'l L* 211.

Guy, NC, 'Fixing the Frontiers? Ethnography, Power Politics, and the Delimitation of Albania 1912–1914' (2005) 5 *Studies in Ethnicity and Nationalism* 27.

Habermas, J, 'Equal Treatment of Cultures and the Limits of Postmodern Liberalism' (2005) 13 *J Pol Phil* 1.

Hall, S, 'The Persistent Spectre: Natural Law, International Order and the Limits of Legal Positivism' (2001) 12 *EJIL* 269–70.

Hannum, H, 'The Status of the Universal Declaration of Human Rights in National and International Law' (1996) 25 *Ga J Int'l & Comp L* 317.

Harding, C, 'Statist Assumptions, Normative Individualism, and New Forms of Personality: Evolving a Philosophy of International Law for the Twenty First Century' (2001) 1 *Non-State Actors & Int'l L* 107.

Hathaway, OA and Lavinbuk, AN, 'Rationalism and Revisionism in International Law' (2005) 119 *Harv L Rev* 1404.

Henckaerts, J, 'Study on Customary International Humanitarian Law: A Contribution to the Understanding and Respect for the Rule of Law in Armed Conflict' (2005) 87 *Int'l Rev Red Cross* 175.

Henkin, L, 'The Universal Declaration at 50 and the Challenge of Global Markets' (1999) 25 *Brooklyn J Int'l L* 17.

Hills, J and Welford, R, 'Profits, Pollution and Prison: A Case Study of Gold Mining in Indonesia' (2005) 12 *CSR Environ Manage* 105.

Hilson, G, 'Corporate Social Responsibility in the Extractive Industries: Experiences from Developing Countries' (2012) 37 *Resources Policy* 131.

Hofmann, C, 'Engaging Non-State Armed Groups in Humanitarian Action' (2006) 13 *Int'l Peacekeeping* 396.

Hofmann, C and Schneckener, U, 'Engaging Non-State Armed Actors in State- and Peace-building: Options and Strategies' (2011) 99 *Int'l Rev Red Cross* 1.

Holland, E, 'The Qualification Framework of International Humanitarian Law: Too Rigid to Accommodate Contemporary Conflicts?' (2011) 34 *Suffolk Transnat'l L Rev* 145.

Hollis, DB, 'Why State Consent Still Matters – Non-State Actors, Treaties and the Changing Sources of International Law' (2005) 23 *Berkeley J Int'l L* 137.

Hoppe, C, 'Implementation of LaGrand and Avena in Germany and the United States: Exploring a Transatlantic Divide in Search of a Uniform Interpretation of Consular Rights' (2007) 18 *EJIL* 317.

Howe, Z, 'Can the 1954 Hague Convention Apply to Non-State Actors? A Study of Iraq and Libya' (2012) 47 *Tex Int'l LJ* 403.

Hyde, A, 'The Concept of Legitimation in the Sociology of Law' (1983) *Wis L Rev* 379.

Ip, EC, 'Globalisation and the Future of the Law of Sovereign State' (2010) 8 *ICON* 636.

Janis, MW, 'Individuals as Subjects of International Law' (1984) 17 *Cornell Int'l LJ* 61.

Jaramillo, DGP, 'Humanitarian Protection in Non-International Conflicts: A Case Study of Colombia' (2000) 30 *Isr YB Hum Rts* 179.

Jennings, R, 'The LaGrand Case' (2002) 1 *Int'l Cts & Tribunals* 13.

Joseph, S, 'Taming the Leviathans: Multinational Enterprises and Human Rights' (1999) 46 *Neth Int'l L Rev* 171.

Kahn, P, 'The Question of Sovereignty' (2004) 40 *Stan J Int'l L* 259.

Kaleck, W and Saage-Maaß, M, 'Corporate Accountability for Human Rights Violations Amounting to International Crimes' (2010) 8 *J Int'l Crim Just* 699.

Kälin, W, 'Late Modernity: Human Rights Under Pressure?' (2013) 15 *Punishment & Society* 397.

Kammerhofer, J, 'Kelsen – Which Kelsen? A Reapplication of Pure Theory to International Law' (2009) 22 *LJIL* 225.

Kammerhofer, J, 'The Benefits of the Pure Theory of Law for International Lawyers, or: What Use Is Kelsenian Theory' (2006) 12 *Int'l Theory* 5.

Kammerhoffer, J, 'The Armed Activities Case and Non-State Actors in Self-Defence Law' (2007) 20 *LJIL* 89.

Kapelus, P, Hamann, R and O'Keefe, E, 'Doing Business with Integrity: The Experience of AngloGold Ashanti in the Democratic Republic of the Congo' (2005) 57 *Int'l Social Science J* 119.

Kelly, D, 'Revisiting the Rights of Man: Georg Jellinek on Rights and the State' (2004) 22 *LHR* 493.

Kelly, MJ, 'Pulling at the Threads of Westphalia: "Involuntary Sovereignty Waiver" – Revolutionary International Legal Theory or Return to Rule by the Great Powers?' (2005) 10 *UCLA J Int'l L & Foreign Aff* 361.

Kelsen, H, 'Causality and Imputation' (1950) 61 *Ethics* 1.

Kelsen, H, 'Compulsory Adjudication of International Disputes' (1943) 37 *AJIL* 397.

Kelsen, H, 'On the Basic Norm' (1957) 47 *CLR* 107.

Kelsen, H, 'The Conception of the State and Social Psychology with Special Reference to Freud's Group Theory' (1924) 5 *Int'l J Psycho-Analysis* 1.

Kelsen, H, 'The Principle of Sovereign Equality of States as a Basis for International Organisation' (1944) 53 *Yale LJ* 207.

Kennedy, D, 'A New Stream of International Law Scholarship' (1988) 7 *Wis Int'l LJ* 1.

Kennedy, D, 'International Law and the Nineteenth Century: History of an Illusion' (1997) 17 *Quinnipiac L Rev* 99.

Keohane, RO, 'Rational Choice Theory and International Law: Insights and Limitations' (2002) 31 *J Leg Stud* 307.

Kielsgard, MD, 'Unocal and the Demise of Corporate Neutrality' (2005) 36 *Cal W Int'l LJ* 183.

Kinley, D and Tadaki, J, 'From Talk to Walk: The Emergence of Human Rights Responsibilities for Corporations at International Law' (2004) 44 *Va J Int'l L* 931.

Kleffner, JK, 'The Applicability of International Humanitarian Law to Organised Armed Groups' (2011) 93 *Int'l Rev Red Cross* 443.

Koenig, C, 'Observer Status for the International Committee of the Red Cross at the United Nations: A Legal Viewpoint' (1991) 31 *Int'l Rev Red Cross* 37.

Krassner, SD, 'The Hole in the Whole: Sovereignty, Shared Sovereignty and International Law' (2004) 25 *Mich J Int'l L* 1075, 1077.

Kunz, J, 'Sanctions in International Law' (1960) 54 *AJIL* 324.

Kunz, J, 'The Vienna School and International Law' (1934) 11 *NYULQ Rev* 307.

Kyriakakis, J, 'Australian Prosecution of Corporations for International Crimes' (2007) 5 *J Int'l Crim Just* 809.

Kyriakakis, J, 'Corporations and the International Criminal Court: The Complementarity Objection Stripped Bare' (2008) 19 *Crim L Forum* 115.

La Rosa, A and Wuezner, C, 'Armed Groups, Sanctions and the Implementation of International Humanitarian Law' (2008) 90 *Int'l Rev Red Cross* 327.

Lafont, C, 'Accountability and Global Governance: Challenging the State-Centric Conception of Human Rights' (2010) 3 *Ethics & Global Politics* 193.

Leader, D, 'Business and Human Rights – Time to Hold Companies to Account' (2008) 8 *Int'l CLR* 447.

Leben, C, 'Hans Kelsen and the Advancement of International Law' (1998) 9 *EJIL* 287.

Lee, EY, 'Early Development of Modern International Law in East Asia – With Special Reference to China, Japan and Korea' (2002) 4 *J Hist Int'l L* 42.

Lesaffer, R, 'Argument from Roman Law in Current International Law: Occupation and Acquisitive Prescription' (2005) 16 *EJIL* 25.

Lesaffer, R, 'The Grotian Tradition Revisited: Change and Continuity in the History of International Law' (2002) 73 *Brit YB Int'l L* 10.

Lewis, E, 'Organic Tendencies in Medieval Political Thought' (1938) 32 *APSR* 849.

Linderfalk, U, 'State Responsibility and the Primary-Secondary Rules Terminology – The Role of Language for an Understanding of the International Legal System' (2009) 78 *Nordic J Int'l L* 53.

McBeth, A, 'Crushed by an Anvil: A Case Study on Responsibility for Human Rights in the Extractive Industry' (2008) 11 *Yale Hum Rts & Dev LJ* 127.

McCarthy, T, 'Kantian Constructivism and Reconstructivism: Rawls and Habermas in Dialogue' (1994) 105 *Ethics* 44.

McConnell, LJ, 'Establishing Liability for Multinational Corporations – Lessons from Akpan' (2014) 56 *Int'l JL & Manage* 88.

McConnell, LJ, 'Case Comment: Establishing Liability for Multinational Oil Companies in Parent/Subsidiary Relationships' (2014) 16 *Environ L Rev* 50.

McCorquodale, R, 'An Inclusive International Legal System' (2004) 17 *LJIL* 477.

McCorquodale, R, 'Beyond State Sovereignty: The International Legal System and Non-State Participants' (2006) 8 *Int'l L Rev Colomb* 103.

McCorquodale, R, 'Overlegalising Silences: Human Rights and Non-State Actors' (2002) 96 *ASIL Proc* 384.

McCorquodale, R and Simons, P, 'Responsibility Beyond Borders: State Responsibility for Extraterritorial Violations by Corporations of International Human Rights Law' (2007) 70 *MLR* 598.

McDonough, DS, 'From Guerrillas to Government: Post-Conflict Stability in Liberia, Uganda and Rwanda' (2008) 29 *Third World Q* 357.

McKnight, J, 'Child Soldiers in Africa: A Global Approach to Human Rights Protection, Enforcement and Post-Conflict Reintegration' (2010) 18 *Afr J Int'l L* 113.

Maedl, A, 'Rape as Weapon of War in the Eastern DRC? The Victims' Perspective' (2011) 33 *Hum Rts Q* 128.

Mälksoo, L, 'The Science of International Law and the Concept of Politics: The Arguments and Lives of the International Law Professors at the University of Dorpat/The Iur'ev/Tartu 1855–1985' (2005) 75 *Brit YB Int'l L* 383.

Mares, R, 'Corporate Responsibility and Compliance with the Law: A Case Study of Land, Dispossession, and Aftermath at Newmont's Ahafo Project in Ghana' (2012) 117 *Bus Soc Rev* 233.

Marshall, J, 'Torture Committed by Non-State Actors: The Developing Jurisprudence from the Ad Hoc Tribunals' (2005) 5 *Non-State Actors & Int'l L* 171.

Martin-Ortega, O, 'Human Rights Due Diligence for Corporations: From Voluntary Standards to Hard Law at Last?' (2014) 32 *Neth Q Hum Rts* 44.

Mastorodimos, K, 'The Utility and Limits of International Human Rights Law and International Humanitarian Law's Parallel Applicability' (2009) 5 *Rev Int'l L & Pol* 129.

Mautner, T, 'Grotius and the Sceptics' (2005) 66 *J Hist Ideas* 577.

Mégret, F and Hofmann, F, 'The UN as a Human Rights Violator? Some Reflections on the United Nations Changing Human Rights Responsibilities' (2003) 25 *Hum Rts Q* 314.

Meron, T, 'Is International Law Moving Towards Criminalisation?' (1998) 9 *EJIL* 18.

Miretski, PP and Bachmann, S, 'The UN Norms on the Responsibility of Transnational Corporations and Other Business Enterprises with Regard to Human Rights: A Requiem' (2012) 17 *Deankin L Rev* 5.

Mitnick, LA, 'Multinationals Fight Back with the Doctrine of *Forum Non Conveniens*' (1989) 56 *Defence Counsel J* 391.

Moir, L, 'The Historical Development of the Application of Humanitarian Law in Non-International Armed Conflicts to 1949' (1998) 47 *ICLQ* 337.

Mongelard, E, 'Corporate Civil Liability for Violations of International Humanitarian Law' (2006) 88 *Int'l Rev Red Cross* 665.

Morgenthau, H, 'Positivism, Functionalism and International Law' (1940) 34 *AJIL* 260.

Muchlinski, P, 'Bhopal Case: Controlling Ultrahazardous Industrial Activities Undertaken by Foreign Investors' (1987) 50 *MLR* 545.

Murray, O, Kinley, D and Pitts, C, 'Exaggerated Rumours of the Death of an Alien Tort? Corporations, Human Rights and the Remarkable Case of Kiobel' (2011) 12 *Melb J Int'l L* 57.

Nollkaemper, A and Jacobs, D, 'Shared Responsibility in International Law: A Conceptual Framework' (2013) 34 *Mich J Int'l L* 359.

Nolte, G and Aust, HP, 'Equivocal Helpers – Complicit States, Mixed Messages and International Law' (2009) 58 *ICLQ* 1.

Noyes, J and Smith, B, 'State Responsibility and the Principle of Joint and Several Liability' (1988) 13 *Yale J Int'l L* 225.

O'Connell, ME, 'Enhancing the Status of Non-State Actors through a Global War on Terror?' (2005) 43 *Colum J Transnat'l L* 435.

O'Keefe, R, 'Universal Jurisdiction – Clarifying the Basic Concept' (2004) 2 *JICJ* 745.

Okafor, OC, 'After Martyrdom: International Law, Sub-State Groups, and the Construction of Legitimate Statehood in Africa' (2000) 41 *Harv Int'l LJ* 503.

Okowa, PN, 'Natural Resources in Situations of Armed Conflict: Is There a Coherent Framework for Protection?' (2007) 9 *Int'l CL Rev* 237.

Orogun, PS, 'Resource Control, Revenue Allocation and Petroleum Politics in Nigeria: The Niger Delta Question' (2010) 75 *GeoJournal* 459.

Osiander, A, 'Sovereignty, International Relations and the Westphalian Myth' (2001) 55 *Int'l Organisation* 251.

Oyefusi, A, 'Oil and the Probability of Rebel Participation Among Youths in the Niger Delta of Nigeria' (2008) 45 *J Peace Res* 539.

Paine, J, 'Review Essay: Kelsen, Normativity and Formal Justice in International Relations' (2013) 26 *LJIL* 1037.

Paulson, SL, 'Hans Kelsen's Doctrine of Imputation' (2001) 14 *Ratio Juris* 47.

Paulson, SL, 'The Neo-Kantian Dimension of Kelsen's Pure Theory of Law' (1992) 12 *OJLS* 311.

Paulus, A and Vashakmadze, M, 'Asymmetrical War and the Notion of Armed Conflict – A Tentative Conceptualisation' (2009) 91 *Int'l Rev Red Cross*, 95.

Paust, JJ, 'Human Rights Responsibilities of Private Corporations' (2001) 35 *Vand J Transnat'l L* 801.

Pejic, J, 'The Protective Scope of Common Article 3: More than Meets the Eye' (2011) 93 *Int'l Rev Red Cross* 189.

Pellet, A, 'The Second Death of Euripide Mavrommatis? Notes on the International Law Commission's Draft Articles on Diplomatic Protection' (2008) 7 *Int'l Cts & Tribunals* 33.

Peterson, AG, 'Order out of Chaos, Domestic Enforcement of the Law of Internal Armed Conflict' (2002) 171 *Military L Rev* 1.

Pinzauti, G, 'The European Court of Human Rights Incidental Application of International Criminal and Humanitarian Law: A Critical Discussion of Kononov v. Latvia' (2008) 6 *JICJ* 1043.

Plattner, D, 'The Penal Repression of Violations of International Humanitarian Law Applicable in Non-International Armed Conflicts' (1990) 30 *Int'l Rev Red Cross* 409.

Podgers, J, 'Corporations in the Line Of Fire: International Prosecutor Says Corporate Officials Could Face War Crimes Charges' (2004) 90 *American Bar Association J* 13.

Pufong, MG, 'State Obligation, Sovereignty and Theories of International Law' (2001) 29 *Politics & Policy* 478.

Quigley, J, 'The United States' Withdrawal from International Court of Justice Jurisdiction in Consular Cases: Reasons and Consequences' (2009) 19 *Duke J Comp & Int'l L* 263.

Rakistis, C, 'Child Soldiers in the East of the Democratic Republic of the Congo' (2008) 27 *Refugee Survey Q* 108.

Rama-Montaldo, M, 'International Legal Personality and Implied Powers of International Organisations' (1970) *Brit YB Int'l L* 111.

Ratner, S, 'Corporations and Human Rights: A Theory of Legal Responsibility' (2001) 111 *Yale LJ* 443.

Ratner, S, 'Foreign Occupation and International Territorial Administration: The Challenges of Convergence' (2005) 16 *EJIL* 695.

Richey, KC, 'Several Steps Sideways: International Legal Developments Concerning War Rape and the Human Rights of Women' (2007) 17 *Tex J Women & L* 109.

Rigaux, F, 'Hans Kelsen on International Law' (1998) 9 *EJIL* 325.

Roberts, A and Sivakumaran, S, 'Hybrid Sources of Law: Armed Groups and the Creation of International Humanitarian Law' (2011) 37 *Yale J Int'l L* 125.

Roberts, A and Sivakumaran, S, 'Law Making by Non-State Actors: Engaging Armed Groups in the Creation of International Humanitarian Law' (2012) 37 *Yale J Int'l L* 108.

Roelofsen, CG, 'Some Remarks on the "Sources" of the Grotian System of International Law' (1983) 30 *Neth Int'l L Rev* 73.

Rondeau, S, 'Participation of Armed Groups in the Development of the Law Applicable to Armed Conflicts' (2011) 93 *Int'l Rev Red Cross*, 649.

Ronon, Y, Human Rights Obligations of Territorial Non-State Actors, (2013) 46 *Cornell Int'l LJ* 21.

Roscini, M, 'The United Nations Security Council and the Enforcement of International Humanitarian Law' (2010) 43 *Israel L Rev* 330.

Rose, JN, '*Forum Non Conveniens* and Multinational Corporations: A Government Interest Approach' (1986) 11 *NCJ Int'l L Com Reg* 669.

Ross, ML, 'What do we know about Natural Resources and Civil War?' (2004) 41 *J Peace Res* 337.

Rost, N, 'Human Rights Violations, Weak States and Civil War' (2011) 12 *Hum Rts Rev* 417.

Ryngaert, C and Meulebroucke, A, 'Enhancing and Enforcing Compliance with International Humanitarian Law by Non-State Armed Groups: An Inquiry into Some Mechanisms' (2011) 16 *JCSL* 443.

Ryngaert, C, 'Human Rights Obligations of Armed Groups' (2008) 41 *RBDI* 355.

Samhat, NH, 'International Regimes and the Prospects for Global Democracy' (2005) 6 *Whitehead J Diplomacy & Int'l Relations* 179.

Sassòli, M and Olson, LM, 'The Relationship between International Humanitarian and International Human Rights Law Where it Matters: Admissible Killing and Internment of Fighters in Non-International Armed Conflicts' (2008) 19 *Int'l Rev Red Cross* 599.

Sassóli, M and Shany, Y, 'Should the Obligations of States and Armed Groups Under International Humanitarian Law Really be Equal?' (2011) 93 *Int'l Rev Red Cross* 425.

Schabas, WA, 'State Policy as an Element of International Crimes' (2008) 98 *J Crim L & Criminology* 953.

Schabas, WA, 'United States Hostility to the International Criminal Court: It's All About the Security Council' (2004) 15 *EJIL* 701.

Schaefer, M, 'Al-Skeini and the Elusive Parameters of Extraterritorial Jurisdiction' (2011) 5 *EHRLR* 566.

Scheinin, M, 'International Organisations and Transnational Corporations at a World Court of Human Rights' (2012) 3 *Global Policy* 488.

Scobbie, I, 'Tom Franck's Fairness' (2002) 13 *EJIL* 909.

Seck, SL, 'Home State Responsibility and Local Communities: The Case of Global Mining' (2008) 11 *Yale Hum Rts & Dev LJ* 177.

Seward, AC, 'After Bhopal: Implications for Parent Company Liability' (1987) 21 *Int'l Lawyer* 695.

Seyersted, F, 'Objective International Personality of Intergovernmental Organisations: Do their Capacities Really Depend on the Conventions Establishing them?' (1964) 34 *Nordisk Tidsskrift Int'l Ret* 46.

Sharp, P, 'Prospects for Environmental Liability in the International Criminal Court' (1999) 18 *Victoria LJ* 217.

Sherman, GE, 'Jus Gentium and International Law' (1918) 12 *AJIL* 56.

Simma, B, 'The Contribution of Alfred Verdross to the Theory of International Law' (1995) 6 *EJIL* 33.

Siordet, F, 'The Geneva Conventions and Civil War' (1950) 3 *Int'l Rev Red Cross Supp* 132.

Sivakumaran, S, 'Binding Armed Opposition Groups' (2006) 55 *ICLQ* 369.

Sivakumaran, S, 'Re-envisaging the International Law of Internal Armed Conflict' (2011) 22 *EJIL* 219.

Slack, K, 'Mission Impossible? Adopting a CSR-based Business Model for Extractive Industries in Developing Countries' (2012) 37 *Resources Policy* 179.

Smillie, I, 'Blood Diamonds and Non-State Actors' (2013) 46 *Vand J Transnat'l L* 1003.

Smith, EF, 'Right to Remedies and the Inconvenience of *Forum Non Conveniens*: Opening U.S. Courts to Victims of Corporate Human Rights Abuses' (2010) 44 *Colum JL & Soc Probs* 145.

Smith, GA, 'An Introduction to Corporate Social Responsibility in the Extractive Industries' (2008) 11 *Yale Hum Rts & Dev LJ* 1.

Somek, A, 'Kelsen Lives' (2007) 18 *Eur J Int'l L* 439.

Somek, A, 'Stateless Law: Kelsen's Conception and its Limits' (2006) 26 *OJLS* 753.

Steiger, H, 'From the International Law of Christianity to the International Law of the World Citizen – Reflections on the Formation of the Epochs of the History of International Law' (2001) 3 *J Hist Int'l L* 180.

Steiner, HJ, 'Book Review: Human Rights in the Private Sphere by Andrew Clapham' (1995) 89 *AJIL* 844.

Steinhoff, D, 'Talking to the Enemy: State Legitimacy Concerns with Engaging Non-State Armed Groups' (2010) 45 *Tex Int'l LJ* 297.

Sterio, M, 'A Grotian Moment, Changes in the Legal Theory of Statehood' (2011) 39 *Denv J Intl'l L & Pol'y* 209.

Sterio, M, 'On the Right to External Self-Determination: Selfistans, Secession and the Great Powers Rule' (2010) 19 *Minn J Int'l L* 137.

Stirk, PMR, 'The Westphalian Model and Sovereign Equality' (2012) 38 *Rev Int'l Stud* 641.

Suganami, H, 'Understanding Sovereignty through Kelsen/Schmitt' (2007) 33 *Rev Int'l Stud* 511.

Sylvesta, C, 'Realism and International Law: the Challenge of John H. Herz' (2010) 2 *Int'l Theory* 410.

Tahvanainen, A, 'The Treaty-Making Capacity of Indigenous Peoples' (2005) 12 *Int'l J Minority & Group Rts* 397.

Tams, C, 'All's Well that Ends Well – Comments on the ILC's Articles on State Responsibility' (2002) 62 *ZaöRV* 759.

Tamura, E, 'The Isayeva Cases of the European Court of Human Rights: The Application of International Humanitarian Law and Human Rights Law in Non-International Armed Conflicts' (2011) 10 *Chinese JIL* 129.

Thürer, D, 'The Failed State and International Law' (1999) 81 *Int'l Rev Red Cross* 731.

Van Eikema Hommes, H, 'Grotius on Natural and International Law' (1983) 30 *Neth Int'l L Rev* 61.

Vermeer-Künzli, A, 'As If: The Fiction in Diplomatic Protection' (2007) 18 *EJIL* 37.

Veuthey, M, 'Learning from History: Accession to the Conventions, Special Agreements and Unilateral Declarations' (2003) 27 *Collegium* 139.

Vigny, J and Thompson, C, 'Fundamental Standards of Humanity: What Future?' (2002) 20 *Neth Q Hum Rts* 185.

Vinci, A, 'Anarchy, Failed States and Armed Groups: Reconsidering Conventional Analysis' (2008) 52 *Int'l Stud Q* 295.

Voiculescu, A, 'Human Rights and the New Corporate Accountability: Learning from Recent Developments in Corporate Criminal Responsibility' (2009) 87 *J Bus Ethics* 419.

Wallace-Bruce, NL, 'African and International Law – the Emergence of Statehood' (1985) 23 *JMAS* 575.

Warbrick, C and McGoldrick, D, 'Unrecognised States and Liability for Income Tax' (1996) 45 *ICLQ* 954.

Wehberg, H, 'Pacta Sunt Servanda' (1959) 53 *AJIL* 775.

Weiler, JHH, 'The Geology of International Law – Governance, Democracy and Legitimacy' (2004) 64 *Heidelberg J Int'l L* 547.

Wennmann, A, 'Economic Dimensions of Armed Groups: Profiling the Financing, Costs, and Agendas and their Implications for Mediated Engagements' (2011) 93 *Int'l Rev Red Cross* 333.

Whitmore, A, 'The Emperor's New Clothes: Sustainable Mining?' (2006) 14 *J Cleaner Prod* 309.

Whytock, CA, 'Chevron-Ecuador Case: Three Dimensions of Complexity in Transnational Dispute Resolution' (2012) 106 *ASIL Proc* 425.

Wilson, PH, 'Still a Monstrosity? Some Reflections on Early Modern German Statehood' (2006) 49 *Hist J* 565.

Wirth, S, 'Immunity for Core Crimes? The ICJ's Judgment in the Congo v. Belgium Case' (2002) 13 *EJIL* 877.

Wong, L, 'Revisiting Rights and Responsibility: The Case of Bhopal' (2008) 4 *Soc Resp J* 143.

Worth, JR, 'Globalisation and the Myth of Absolute National Sovereignty: Reconsidering the "Un-signing" of the Rome Statute and the Legacy of Senator Bricker' (2004) 79 *Ind L Rev* 245.

Yusuf, HO, 'Oil on Troubled Waters: Multinational Corporations and Realising Human Rights in the Developing World with Specific Reference to Nigeria' (2008) 8 *AHRLJ* 79.

Zolo, D, 'Hans Kelsen: International Peace Through International Law' (1998) 9 *EJIL* 306.

Research papers/reports

Cronstedt, C and Ronnegard, D, 'International Tribunal on Business & Human Rights – Reshaping the Judiciary' (September 2013) www.l4bb.org/news/tribunal.pdf, accessed 23 April 2016.

Dolidze, A, 'The Arctic Sunrise and NGOs in International Judicial Proceedings' (American Society of International Law Insight, 2014) www.asil.org/insights/volume/18/issue/1/arctic-sunrise-and-ngos-international-judicial-proceedings, accessed 21 April 2016.

European Centre for Constitutional and Human Rights, 'The Danzer Case: German Manager's Liability for Subsidiary in Congo' (15 August 2014) www.ecchr.de/danzer-en.html?file=tl_files/Dokumente/Wirtschaft%20und%20Menschenrechte/Case%20Report%20Danzer%202014–08–15.pdf, accessed 21 April 2016.

Florquin, N and Warner, ED, 'Engaging Non-State Armed Groups or Listing Terrorists? Implications for The Arms Control Community' (Disarmament Forum, 2008) www.genevacall.org/wp-content/uploads/dlm_uploads/2013/12/art-13.pdf, accessed 21 April 2016.

Gagnon, G and Ryle, J, 'Report of an Investigation into Oil Development, Conflict and Displacement in Western Upper Nile, Sudan' (London & Toronto, 15 October 2001) www.globaloilwatch.com/reports/oil-development-sudan-report-gagnon-103001.pdf, accessed 21 April 2016.

Herr, S, 'Binding Non-State Armed Groups to International Humanitarian Law, Geneva Call and the Ban of Anti-Personnel Mines: Lessons from Sudan' (Peace Research Institute Frankfurt, 2010).

International Council on Human Rights Policy, 'Beyond Voluntarism, Human Rights and the Developing International Legal Obligations of Companies' (February 2002) www.ichrp.org/files/reports/7/107_report_en.pdf, accessed 21 April 2016.

Nowak, M and Kozma, J, 'Research Project on a World Human Rights Court' (University of Vienna, June 2009) www.udhr60.ch/report/hrCourt-Nowak0609.pdf, accessed 23 April 2016.

Petrasek, D, 'Ends & Means: Human Rights Approaches to Armed Groups' (International Council on Human Rights Policy, 2000) www.ichrp.org/files/reports/6/105_report_en.pdf, accessed 21 April 2016.

Program on Humanitarian Policy and Conflict Research, 'Empowered Groups, Tested Laws and Policy Options: The Challenges of Transnational Non-State Armed Groups' (Harvard University, 2007) www.hpcrresearch.org/sites/default/files/publications/Report_Empowered_Groups_Nov2007.pdf, accessed 21 April 2016.

Rosemann, N, 'Code of Conduct: Tool for Self-Regulation for Private Military and Security Companies' (Geneva Centre for the Democratic Control of Armed Forces, Occasional Paper No 15, 2008) 35.

Sassóli, M, 'Transnational Armed Groups and International Humanitarian Law' Programme on (Harvard University, Occasional Paper Series, No 6, 2006) www.hpcrresearch.org/sites/default/files/publications/OccasionalPaper6.pdf, accessed 21 April 2016.

Schulze, K, 'The Free Aceh Movement (GAM): Anatomy of a Separatist Organisation' (East–West Centre, Washington, 2004).

Index

accountability: direct accountability:
see direct accountability mechanisms;
home state accountability: *see* home
state accountability, MNE challenges;
host state accountability: *see* host state
accountability, MNE challenges;
state-centric accountability regimes:
see state-centric accountability regimes,
practical failings
ad hoc declarations of compliance: *see
under* non-State armed groups,
voluntary compliance frameworks
Additional Protocol I, non-State armed
groups, binding customary law 156–7
Additional Protocol II: international
humanitarian law, State-centricity in
86–7; non-State armed groups,
binding customary law 135–6, 148,
150, 152, 156–7; non-State armed
groups, binding State law (1977 draft)
135–6; non-state armed groups,
effective power 148, 150
Afghanistan 128
Akpan case 104–8
Albania 49
Algeria 141
Alien Torts Claims Act (1789) (ATCA):
see United States, Alien Torts Claims
Act (1789) (ATCA)
allocating responsibility: *see under*
procedural legitimacy
Allott, P 27–8
alternative theoretical framing:
background 185; conclusions 235–7;
key issues 13–14, 185–6, 241–2;
practical utility: *see* Pure Theory of
Law, practical utility; Pure Theory of

Law: *see* Pure Theory of Law, as
alternative theoretical model
Amco case 218–19
Amerasinghe, CF 62–3
Anaya, SJ 173
Angola 56
Anzilotti, D 33–5, 137
Arena case 217
Aristotle 20, 47
armed conflicts: fragmentation 5–6; *see
also under* international humanitarian
law, State-centricity in
Arrest Warrant case 103–4
Articles on the Responsibility of States
for Internationally Wrongful Acts
(ASRIWA) (ILC) 78, 80
Austin, J 43, 45, 160, 206
Australia, *Barrow and Heys* case
110–11
Arena opinion 137

Barrow and Heys case 110–11
Belgium: *Arrest Warrant* case 103–4;
Barcelona Traction opinion 99–100
belligerency, criteria: *see under*
international humanitarian law, State-
centricity in
belligerent and insurgent communities:
see under Montevideo Convention on
Rights and Duties of States
Bergbohm, C 32
Bernadotte, Count Folke 60
Bhopal gas tragedy 96–7
binding business and human rights treaty
225–37; centralised judicial bodies
234–5; complicity provisions 231–2;
diverse legal issues 227–8; Ecuadorian

initiative (*Ecuador-Chevron* case)
11–12, 225–7, 236; enforcement of
instrument 233–4, 237; joint and
several liability clause 232–3; multiple
duty-bearers, division of responsibility
230–1; practical implementation 235;
public/private obligations 228–9;
scope of duties 229–30
binding customary law: *see* non-State
armed groups, binding customary law
binding quality of international law 14,
239; alternative theoretical framing
188, 198–201, 203, 206, 236; direct
non-State actor regulation, theoretical
scope 182; legal validity, state basis 16,
32, 37–8, 41–2, 66–7, 70; legitimacy,
participation and State-centrism 159,
164, 166, 172; non-state armed
groups, direct humanitarian law
application 132–4, 137–44, 148–9;
see also legal validity, state basis
binding State law: *see* non-State armed
groups, binding State law
Biodiversity Convention 100–1
Bodin, J 37–8
Bogdandy, A von 175
Bosnian Genocide ruling 79
Brownlie, I 51, 63–4, 66
Bull, H 221–2
Burundi state 52
business and human rights treaty: *see*
binding business and human rights
treaty

Cassese, A 136–7, 213; non-State armed
groups, binding State law, domestic/
international obligations 136–7;
Vienna Convention analogy: *see* Vienna
Convention on the Law of Treaties
(VCLT), Cassese's analogy
Chandler v Cape case 108–10
Chappell, Z 179
Chinkin, C 124
Chiomenti, C 117
Cicero 20, 47
Clapham, A 59, 64, 85–6, 116, 154
coercive sanction doctrine 193–4
Colombia 142
command responsibility, international
criminal responsibility of non-State
actors 116–17

command structure and territorial
control, VCLT, Cassese's analogy
144–5
Committee on the Elimination of
Discrimination against Women 177
Common Article 3 86–7, 118, 132–3,
136, 139–42, 144, 148, 153, 155–6
compliance, at international level
159–62; customary law background
159–60; factors inducing 160–1;
fairness and legitimacy 161; positivist
critique 160; procedural/substantive
legitimacy 161–2, 176; State-centric
rationale 160; *see also* procedural
legitimacy, Franck's approach
consent: direct non-State actor
regulation, theoretical scope 183;
discursive democracy scholarship
166–7; Vienna Convention on the
Law of Treaties (VCLT), Cassese's
analogy 146–7
Corfu Channel case 156
corporate social responsibility (CSR)
118–25, 130; content/efficacy
119–20; development/clarification/
interpretation role 124–5; effects-
based models 123–4; Global Compact
96*n*; industry level regimes 121–2;
International Labour Organisation
(ILO) Tripartite Declaration 119;
legal quality 122–3; Marlin Mine
project 121; OECD Guidelines for
Multinational Enterprises 119, 122;
scope of projects 118–19; separation
from hard law sources 125; UN Draft
Norms on Transnational Corporations
119; UN Guiding Principles on
Business and Human Rights 75, 119;
weak governance states
implementation 120–1; *see also* soft law
Craven , M 36, 49, 58
Crawford, J 36, 51, 54
criminal responsibility: *see* international
criminal responsibility of non-State
actors
CSR: *see* corporate social responsibility
(CSR)
customary law: non-State actor
participation, practical feasibility
175–6; *see also* non-State armed
groups, binding customary law

Danzig city 203
Danzig opinion 33, 137, 216
Darfur, International Commission of
    Inquiry 153
D'Aspremont, J 123–5, 213–14
Davarnejad, L 122
de Burca, G 181
defined territory condition: *see under*
    Montevideo Convention on Rights
    and Duties of States
deliberative democracy: *see* discursive
    democracy scholarship
Democratic Republic of the Congo
    (DRC) 8–9, 91–2; *Arrest Warrant*
    case 103–4
direct accountability mechanisms: basic
    issues 114; criminal responsibility: *see*
    international criminal responsibility of
    non-State actors; CSR: *see* corporate
    social responsibility (CSR); non-State
    armed groups: *see* non-State armed
    groups, voluntary compliance
    frameworks
direct non-State actor regulation,
    theoretical scope: consent/multi-
    stakeholder approach 183; key issues/
    conclusions 13, 131–2, 182–4, 240–1;
    legitimacy, participation: *see* legitimacy,
    participation and State-centrism;
    non-State armed groups: *see* non-State
    armed groups, direct humanitarian
    law application
discursive democracy scholarship 166–72;
    consent of parties 166–7; deliberative
    democracy 167–9; Habermas'
    discourse 163, 169–71, 180–1, 183,
    240; international level 170–2; State-
    centric approach/parallels 167, 170
Dryzek, JS 170
Dworkin, R 163, 167–8

Eagle, K 173
Ebernstein, W 189, 211
Ecuadorian initiative (*Ecuador-Chevron*
    case) 11–12, 225–7, 236
effective government criterion: *see under*
    Montevideo Convention on Rights and
    Duties of States
effective power: *see* non-state armed
    groups, effective power
El Salvador 56

Ethiopia 128
extractive industries: *see* resource
    extraction
Extractive Industries Transparency
    Initiative 174
extraterritorial litigation in US: *see* United
    States, Alien Torts Claims Act (1789)
    (ATCA)

fairness and legitimacy 161–6
Finland independence 53
Fitzmaurice, G 55
Fleck, D 141, 152
Forest Stewardship Council (FSC) 174–5
forum non conveniens 106–7, 226
Franck, T 160–1, 175, 240; fairness and
    legitimacy 161–6; *see also* procedural
    legitimacy *passim*
Freud, S 197–8
Frohnen, P. 41

*Gbemre & Others v Shell Petroleum
    Development Company* 97–8
Geiss, R 139, 159
Geneva Call 126–8, 146
Geneva Conventions 81–3, 134; *see also*
    Common Article 3
Gentili 22
Gerber, CF von 31–2, 34
Ghana 93
Gierke, O von 30
Global Compact 96*n*
globalisation effect 5
Goldsmith, J 223
Grant, D 55
Green, F 4
Groation scholarship 19–23; *jus gentium*
    17, 20–2; natural law concepts 19–20,
    209
Grundnorm: and conflict between norms
    207–8; Pure Theory of Law,
    definitions 189, 191–2; and Pure
    Theory of Law, as natural law 208–12;
    sovereignty and law-making capacity
    203–4

Habermas, J: *see under* discursive
    democracy scholarship
Hart, HLA 36, 43–4, 165, 213–14
Hegel, GWF 29–30, 223, 239
Heller judgment 40

Henkin, L 42–3, 45, 165
Herodotus 18
Hobbes, T 38, 43
Hoffman, C 151
home state accountability, MNE
  challenges 99–101; corporate
  structures 99–100; definition of home
  state 99; extraterritorial litigation in
  US: *see* United States, Alien Torts
  Claims Act (1789) (ATCA); human
  rights perspective 100; parent-
  subsidiary relationships: *see* parent-
  subsidiary relationships, challenge of;
  transboundary harm 100–1
home state jurisdiction determination
  101–4; nationality principle 102–3;
  passive personality/protective security
  principles 102; territoriality principle
  101–2; universal jurisdiction doctrine
  103–4
host state accountability, MNE
  challenges 90–9; adverse effects 91;
  civilian courts' procedures 94–5;
  competition between governments
  93–4; corporation assistance 91–2;
  definition of host state 90; domestic
  company laws 95; embedded
  mechanisms 97–8; instances of success
  95–7; justification of presence 90–1;
  summary 98–9
Human Rights Committee (HRC) 74
human rights law: *see* international
  human rights law, state responsibility
humanitarian law: *see* international
  humanitarian law, State-centricity in
Hume, D 188, 197

ILP: *see* international legal personality
  (ILP)
India, Bhopal gas tragedy 96–7
individuals 3; alternative theoretical
  framing 188, 194, 200, 202, 214–17,
  229–30, 233; direct non-State actor
  regulation, theoretical scope 136–40,
  152, 168, 170; legal validity, state basis
  21, 27, 30, 32–6, 47, 58–9; state-
  centric accountability regimes, practical
  failings 72, 74, 82, 87, 93, 100, 102,
  114–18, 130
Indonesia, PT Newmont Minahasa Raya
  (PTNMR) proceedings 95–6

Inter-American Commission on Human
  Rights 76
International Committee on Economic
  and Social Rights 177
International Committee of the Red
  Cross (ICRC) 176–7
International Covenant on Civil and
  Political Rights (ICCPR) 74
International Covenant on Economic,
  Social and Cultural Rights (ICESCR)
  100
international criminal responsibility of
  non-State actors 114–18, 129–30;
  command responsibility 116–17;
  corporate defendants 115; juridicial
  persons 116; non-State armed groups
  117–18; post-WWII 114; restriction
  to natural persons 114–15; State
  practice/policy requirement
  117–18
international human rights law, State
  responsibility 73–80; conduct of
  private entities directly attributed
  78–9; customary status 76–7; direct
  obligations on non-state actors
  76–8; indirect obligation 75; non-
  State armed groups 76; private
  actions imputed to state 78–80;
  private actors, obligations of state
  parties 74–5
international humanitarian law, State-
  centricity in 80–8; Additional Protocol
  II 86–7; armed conflicts, categories
  81–2; armed conflicts, objective
  definition 84–5; belligerency, criteria
  81–2; Common Article 3 86–7;
  compliance enforcement 86–8; human
  rights law, distinction 80–1;
  insurgency/belligerency recognition
  82–3; legitimacy concerns 85–6; non-
  international armed conflict, criteria
  83–4
International Labour Organisation
  (ILO) Tripartite Declaration 119
international law: binding quality: *see*
  binding quality of international law;
  definitions 17–19
international legal personality (ILP):
  background 57–8; presumptive
  approach 63–4; problems in
  international law 65–6; subjects

doctrine 58; subjects/objects
categorisation 58–60, 62–4; summary
of features 68–9; *see also Reparation for
Injuries* opinion
international legal personality (ILP) and
states, redefinition: background in
Pure Theory of Law 195; conclusion
200; generic corporate bodies
199–200; 'is' and 'ought' dichotomy
187–8, 196; juristic concept of State
196; legal sociology 195–6; social
reality 196, 198; spheres of validity
198; tautological definition of ILP
198–9; traditional critiques 197–8
international organisations: alternative
theoretical framing 219; direct non-
State actor regulation, theoretical
scope 154–5, 170, 176–7, 179;
legal validity, state basis 36, 39, 55,
62–9
International Seabed Authority 219
'is' and 'ought' dichotomy 187–8,
196
Israel, establishment fallout 60

Jellinek, G. 30–1, 34
Josselin, D. 3
jus cogens status 64
jus gentium 17, 20–2

Kabila, Laurent 9
Kammerhofer, J 208, 212, 214
Kant, I 188, 194, 210–12
Karavias, M 219
Kaufmann, E 35
Keller, H 175
Kelsen, H 28, 36; Pure Theory of Law:
see Pure Theory of law *passim*
Kennedy, D 23
Kimberly Process 181
Kiobel judgment 113
Klabbers, J. 59–60, 62, 64, 67
Kleffner, K 159
Knight, WSM 22
Koskenniemi, M 22, 27, 45, 196

Laband, P 31–2, 34
LaGrand opinion 137, 216–18
Lauterpacht, H 33–4, 58, 60
law making by non-State actors: *see* direct
non-State actor regulation, theoretical

scope; non-State actor participation,
practical feasibility
law making by states: *see* sovereignty and
law-making capacity
Law of the Sea Convention 1982 219
Lawrence, T.J. 58–9
legal personality: *see* international legal
personality (ILP)
legal validity, state basis: background
15; context for non-state actors 28–9;
empirical basis 28–37, 70; fluidity:
see modern states' fluidity; Hegelian
influence 29–32; ILP: *see* international
legal personality (ILP); *Reparation
for Injuries* opinion; international
obligations/agreements 33–5; key
issues 12, 15–16; social/historical basis
29–32; state-centric effects: *see* state-
centric model; strict positivist method
32; summary 69–71, 238–9; *see also*
binding quality of international law
legitimacy, participation and State-
centrism: compliance: *see* compliance,
at international level; discursive
democracy: *see* discursive democracy
scholarship; key issues 158–9;
procedural legitimacy: *see* procedural
legitimacy
Lesaffer, R 18–19
Locke, John 168
Lotus opinion 35, 102
Lubanga case 118
Lubicon Lake Band v Canada 74

McBeth, A 90
McCorquodale, R 3, 65, 172
Marlin Mine project 121
Mavrommatis case 217
Meron, T 176
Miller, R 171, 178, 181
MNEs: *see* multinational enterprises
modern states' fluidity: capacity to enter
into international relations 54–7; Draft
Declaration on Rights and Duties of
States 48; governmental collapse 53–4;
historical sketch 47–9; key issues 46–7;
Montevideo criteria: *see* Montevideo
Convention on Rights and Duties of
States
monism, and coercion 206–8; *bellum
justum* principle 207; coercive order

206–7; *Grundnorm* and conflict between norms 207–8; and Pure Theory of Law 207–8
monism, and legal validity 205–6; background in Pure Theory of Law 205; choice hypothesis 205–6; primacy of international order 206; problematic issues 206
monograph: research field 2–3, 6–7, 14; structure 12–14; summary 14
Montevideo Convention on Rights and Duties of States 48–9, 198; belligerent and insurgent communities 56; conclusion 57, 71; criteria flexibility 49–57; defined territory condition 49–51; effective government criterion 51–2; interdependence of criteria 52–3; permanent population criterion 51
Morgenthau, H 222
Morocco/Mauritania claims 50
Morrison case 113
Muchlinski, P 90, 218
multinational enterprises (MNEs) 1; resource extraction involvement 9–10; in weak governance states 10–11
multinational enterprises (MNEs), challenge to State-based accountability: background analysis 88; descriptor definitions 89–90; host state: *see* host state accountability, MNE challenges; territorial anxieties 88–9

national liberation movements (NLMs) 55, 141, 172–3
nationality principle: *see under* home state jurisdiction determination
natural law: Groation scholarship 19–20, 209; *Grundnorm* and 208–12; norms and 209
natural persons 77, 114–15, 154, 192, 194, 196
Neff, SC 20
Nicaragua opinion 79, 156
Nietzsche, F 197
Nigeria 74, 93–4; *Akpan* case 104–8; Companies and Allied Matters Act (1968) (CAMA) 95; *Gbemre & Others v Shell Petroleum Development Company* 97–8

NLMs: *see* national liberation movements (NLMs)
Nollkaemper, A 228–9
non-state actors: armed conflict fragmentation 5–6; binary categorisation 1–2; definitions 3; directly enforceable international obligations 11–12; dynamics/ challenges 3–7; empirical state context 28–9, 70; globalisation effect 5; key issues 6–7; meaning 1; plurality/ diversity 4–5; political/economic influence 5
non-State actor direct regulation, theoretical scope: *see* direct non-State actor regulation, theoretical scope
non-State actor participation, practical feasibility 172–82; communicative action process 180–1; continuously open circle of participants 181; customary law 175–6; indigenous peoples 173, 182; international organisations' influence 176–7; law-taker/law-maker entities 173–4; law/non-law distinction 175; manner of participation 179–80; MNE participation 174–5, 182; NLM participation 173; political legitimisation 178–9; procedural-substantive approach 176; sample of participation 172–3; treaty monitoring bodies 177–8
non-State armed groups, binding customary law 151–8; Additional Protocol I 156–7; Additional Protocol II 135–6, 148, 150, 152, 156–7; conclusion 158; developed rule status 155–7; formulation of approach 151–2; humanitarian obligations 155; ILP possession 153–5; indeterminancy of provisions 152; organised military force 154–5
non-State armed groups, binding State law 135–43; Additional Protocol II 1977 draft 135–6; criticisms of view 136–8; domestic/international obligations 136–8; individual citizens/groups or corporate entities, discrepancy 138–9; jurisdictional basis critique 139–43; legislative jurisdiction principle 135–6, 140–1;

non-consenting State nationals
139–40; rejection of humanitarian
values 141–3

non-State armed groups, direct
humanitarian law application: binding
State law: *see* non-State armed groups,
binding State law; disparity in
provisions 132–3; effective power: *see*
non-state armed groups, effective
power; key issues 134–5; theoretical
incompatibility 133–4; Vienna
Convention analogy: *see* Vienna
Convention on the Law of Treaties
(VCLT), Cassese's analogy

non-state armed groups, effective power
147–51; Additional Protocol II 148,
150; present and future status 147;
State succession law 147–8; territorial
control 148–50; variants of view 147

non-State armed groups, voluntary
compliance frameworks 1, 125–9; ad;
ad hoc declarations of compliance 114;
facilitation roles 125–6; Geneva Call
126–8, 146; State reservations 128–9;
targeted initiatives 126

norms: *Grundnorm*, and conflict between
207–8; and natural law 209; stipulation
by 219; system 188–9

North Sea Continental Shelf Opinion
49

Northern Cyprus 55

Nuclear Weapons opinion 101

Nuremberg International Military
Tribunal (IMT) 114

O'Connell, DP 48

OECD Guidelines for Multinational
Enterprises 119, 122

Oppenheim, L. 59

Paine, J 225

Palestine 50

parent-subsidiary relationships, challenge
of 101–4; ancillary jurisdiction
challenges 104–6; direct attribution of
liability 108–9; *forum non conveniens*
reluctance 106–7; procedural rules'
operation 107–8; successful judgments
109–11

participation: *see* legitimacy, participation
and State-centrism

passive personality/protective security
principles 102

Paulson, S 211

permanent population criterion: *see under*
Montevideo Convention on Rights and
Duties of States

Plato 47

political legitimacy 2, 4, 11, 13, 130,
185, 192, 204; direct non-State actor
regulation, theoretical scope 134, 142,
154, 178–9; *see also* procedural
legitimacy

Polybius 47

Portmann, R 36, 66, 167, 214

Posner, E 223

Poverty Strategy Reduction Programme
181

procedural legitimacy 161–6; adherence
164–5; allocating responsibility 162;
background 161–2; coherence 164;
community role 164–5; core ideas 166;
determinacy 163; factors conducive to
legitimacy 162–3; ILPs 165; primary
schools of thought 163; right process
paradigms 166; and substantive
legitimacy 161–2, 176; symbolic
validation 163–4; *see also* compliance,
at international level; political
legitimacy

PT Newmont Minahasa Raya (PTNMR)
proceedings 95–6

Pure Theory of Law, as alternative
theoretical model: key issues 186–7,
241–2; legal personality hybrid
214

Pure Theory of Law, application to
non-State actors: ILP: *see* international
legal personality (ILP) and states,
redefinition; key issues 194; monism:
see monism, and coercion; monism,
and legal validity; natural law: *see* Pure
Theory of Law, as natural law;
sovereignty: *see* sovereignty and law-
making capacity

Pure Theory of Law, definitions 187–94;
coercive sanction doctrine 193–4;
Grundnorm 189, 191–2; 'is' and
'ought' dichotomy 187–8, 196; legal
personality 192; monism 192–3;
norm application/creation 192–3;
norms system 188–9; stipulation by

norms 219; structure of normative
legal order 190–1
Pure Theory of Law, in international
practice: direct rights of corporations
under international teraties 218–19;
LaGrand opinion 137, 216–18; MNEs
and formalistic logic 215–17, 219
Pure Theory of Law, as natural law:
causality presumption/imputation
210–11; and *Grundnorm* 208–12; and
normativity 210–13; norms' distinction
209; value-neutral presumption
209–10
Pure Theory of Law, practical utility:
customary international humanitarian
law 215; formalist approaches 213–14;
international practice: *see* Pure Theory
of Law, in international practice; realist
criticism: *see* Pure Theory of Law, and
realist criticism
Pure Theory of Law, and realist criticism
220–5; centralised adjudication 223;
empirical/normative divisions 220;
enforcement of international law
221–3; primitive nature of
international legal system 222–3;
state-centric model, realist critics 43–5;
States' role 223–5; subjective value
judgments 220–1; war as binary
221–2

Rawls, J 163
Raz, J 44–5
realist criticism: *see* Pure Theory of Law,
and realist criticism
Reparation for Injuries opinion 60–4, 71,
198–9; explanation of approach 62–4;
extrapolation to other non-state actors
64–9; justification 61–2; and
Montevideo criteria 63–4; obligations
of organisations 67–8; opinion 61;
subjective/objective approaches 61–3;
UN background/features 60, 66–7;
will theory approach 62–3; *see also*
international legal personality (ILP)
resource extraction: financing of
rebellions 8–9; MNE involvement
9–10; weak governance zones'
dependence 8
Revere Copper case 218
Ronon, Y 150

Ruggie, John 7, 75, 119, 227–8
Rwanda 52, 118; International Criminal
Tribunal for (ICTR) 83
Ryngaert, C 138, 149–51, 155, 161–2,
166–7, 171, 176, 179, 240

Sadiq Shek Elmi v Australia 150
Sam Hinga Norman case 151
Samhat, N 171
sanction doctrine: *see* coercive sanction
doctrine
SERAC v Nigeria 74
Seyersted, F 63
SHARES project 230
Shell v Enoch 94
Sivakumaran, S 141–2, 147, 152, 155,
175
Al-Skeini case 230
soft law 118–25 *passim*; *see also* corporate
social responsibility (CSR)
Somek, A 223–4
South Africa, *Chandler v Cape* case
108–10
sovereignty: absolute sovereignty 40–1;
concept 37–9
sovereignty and law-making capacity:
background in Pure Law Theory 200;
definitions of sovereignty 200–1;
duality of State, critique 201–2;
Grundnorm 203–4; ILP possession
204–5; self-obligation/auto-limitation
201; State-succession context 202–3
State responsibility: *see* international
human rights law, State responsibility
state-centric accountability regimes,
practical failings: background/
conclusion 12, 72, 129–30; direct
accountability: *see* direct accountability
mechanisms; human rights law: *see*
international human rights law, State
responsibility; humanitarian law: *see*
international humanitarian law, State-
centricity in; key issues/conclusions
72–3, 129–30, 239–40; MNEs:
see MNEs' challenge to State-based
accountability
state-centric model: absolute sovereignty
40–1; breach of international law
42–3; challenges 2; effect on
international law 35–46; historical
critique 19; positivist tradition 42;

privatisation of functions 5; realist
critics 43–5; sovereignty concept 37–9;
validity of international law 41–3
Suarez, F 22–3
substantive legitimacy, and procedural
legitimacy 161–2, 176
Suganami, H 235

Tadić case 84, 152, 156, 176
territorial state and international law:
definitions of international law 17–19;
Grotius: *see* Groation scholarship;
historical emergence of structures
16–17; state criteria 16; Vattel: *see*
Vattelian legal positivism; Westphalia:
see Westphalian Peace Treaties
territoriality principle: *see under* home
state jurisdiction determination
Texaco case 218
theoretical framing: *see* alternative
theoretical framing
transboundary harm: *see under* home
state accountability, MNE challenges
Turkey 128

UN, legal personality: *see Reparation for
Injuries* opinion
UN Draft Norms on Transnational
Corporations 119
UN Guiding Principles on Business and
Human Rights 75, 119
United States, Alien Torts Claims Act
(1789) (ATCA) 9, 111–13; *Kiobel*
judgment 113; MNE human rights
violations in domestic courts 111–12;
presumption against the extraterritorial
application 113; State action element
requirement 112–13; *Unocol* case 112
Universal Declaration on Human Rights
76–7
universal jurisdiction doctrine: *see under*
home state jurisdiction determination
Unocol case 112
US Civil War 147–8

*US (Third) Restatement of Foreign
Relations Law* 99

Van Gend en Loos case 35
Vatican City 51, 203
Vattelian legal positivism 26–8; adoption
of 28; definitions 26–7; voluntary law
27
Vienna Convention on Consular
Relations (VCCR) 137
Vienna Convention on the Law of
Treaties (VCLT), Cassese's analogy
143–7; amnesties to parties 145–6;
consent basis 146–7; intentions of
parties 144; rights and duties for third-
party States, provisions 143–4;
threshold of organisation/command
structure and territorial control 144–5
Vienna School 193
Vietnam 141
Vitoria, F de 22, 25, 47–8

Waldock, H 33
Wallace, W 3
weak governance states: circumstances
7–8; Democratic Republic of the
Congo (DRC) 8–9, 91–2, 103–4;
meaning 7; NMEs in 10–11; resource
extraction in 8–10
Weber, M 163
Westphalian Peace Treaties 23–6;
conclusion of War 23–4; Holy Roman
Empire basis 24–5; 20th cent
significance 25–6
Wheatley, S 170–1
Wolff, C von 27

Yugoslavia, International Criminal
Tribunal for the Former Yugoslavia
(ICTY) 84

Zaire statehood 53
Zegveld, L 134
Zerk, A 123